Adobe InDesign
A Complete Course and
Compendium of Features

Second Edition

Steve Laskevitch

Second Edition

Adobe InDesign

A Complete
Course
and
Compendium
of Features

rockynook

Adobe InDesign: A Complete Course and Compendium of Features, Second Edition
Steve Laskevitch
luminousworks.com

Project editor: Jocelyn Howell
Project manager: Lisa Brazieal
Marketing manager: Koryn Olage
Interior and cover design, layout, and type: Steve Laskevitch

ISBN: 979-8-88814-302-5

2nd Edition (1st printing)
© 2025 Stephen Laskevitch
All images © Stephen Laskevitch

Rocky Nook Inc.
1010 B Street, Suite 350
San Rafael, CA 94901
USA
www.rockynook.com
info@rockynook.com
(415) 747-8756

Represented in the E.U. by:
Rheinwerk Verlag GmbH
Rheinwerkallee 4
53227 Bonn
Germany
service@rheinwerk-verlag.de

Distributed in the UK and Europe by Publishers Group UK
Distributed in the U.S. and all other territories by Publishers Group West

Library of Congress Control Number: 2024948014

Printed in India

About the Author

Steve Laskevitch is a certified instructor teaching Photoshop, Illustrator, Lightroom, and, of course, Adobe InDesign (and more). He's the founder of Luminous Works, the preeminent Adobe software training center in the Pacific Northwest. He fell in love with teaching and computer graphics while studying physics and education at university. He has spent the twenty-first century both teaching and doing desktop publishing, building production workflows for many companies. Steve also helped Adobe prepare Certified Instructor exams.

For about five years, Steve led the Seattle InDesign User Group where he got to know the people who created InDesign. Over the years, he has taught at: The Design Department of Cornish College of the Arts (where he was awarded the Excellence in Teaching Award); University of Washington Professional & Continuing Education (nominated for their Excellence in Teaching Award); Seattle Central College; and at industry conferences and gatherings.

Steve lives with his wife in Seattle.

Thanks, y'all

Acknowledgments

There are so many to whom I owe thanks.

Each book project offers a chance to get to know the software I love even better. For that recurring opportunity, I'm grateful to my publisher, Rocky Nook, the fine people who make these books possible, especially my editor, Jocelyn Howell, for every face-saving correction to my writing.

I'm so pleased that my students over the years have felt comfortable asking questions—especially the difficult, knotty ones. Those serve as a crucible in which my curricula and workflow advice are refined. I'm grateful for every head-scratcher!

I'm most grateful to my wife, Carla Fraga. There isn't space enough here to list all the reasons why.

Steve
Seattle, April 2025

Contents

The Course

The Compendium

Workspaces &
Preferences

Swatches &
Color Settings

Type &
Text Styles

Frames, Shapes
& Object Styles

Pages &
Spreads

Find/
Change

Long or
Complex Docs

Package
& Publish

Start Here—An Introduction

Hi. I'm Steve Laskevitch, and I'll be your guide. In this book, you will be working your way through a full course that will expose you to all of the essential features and functions of Adobe InDesign. It contains a combination of projects and shorter lessons. In both, there are actions that I'd like you to try to help you learn this software. The paragraphs surrounding the action explain more of the why and how.

➡ This is what a lesson action looks like.

For much greater depth, the second section of this book is a Compendium of InDesign's features and functions, providing the "deep dive" needed for true mastery of this powerful application. Throughout the Course section, I will suggest readings in the Compendium section. Although you may be able to complete the entire course without them, I think if you read those sections, you'll find yourself regularly nodding and muttering, "Oh, that's why it works that way." The tabs on the right edge of this page lead you to each Compendium chapter. Just look at the page edges of this book to find your way to a topic of interest.

Software and Course Files

Have you installed the software yet? If you work for a company with an enterprise license, it's likely your IT people have installed it for you. We will be using the **Creative Cloud** app as our hub for launching Adobe applications and accessing the services that come with a Creative Cloud (CC) license. This app also checks to make sure your software license is up to date, so it should remain running whenever you use your creative applications. I use the CC app's **Preferences** to have it launch on startup and auto-update software so I don't have to worry about it.

I most often launch the software by clicking the **Open** button to the right of its icon. If there's an update available, it'll be available in the **Updates** section.

To follow along with the projects and lessons in this book, you'll need the files. Launch your favorite web browser and go to rockynook.com/2E-indesignCandC, answer a simple question, and download the files. Put them somewhere convenient (and memorable).

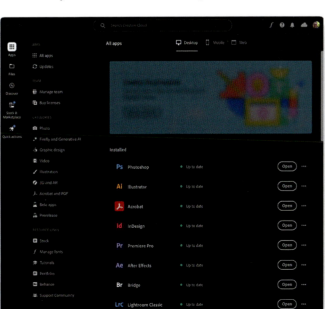

THE
COURSE

1 Prep & Setup

As with most worthwhile endeavors, there is some preparation required before learning and using Adobe InDesign. Although they likely meant well, the team that built InDesign delivers it in a state that really isn't ready for us. So, our first tasks will be customizing its user interface (UI) and preferences and learning a bit along the way.

Now, let's gather ingredients and implements and start our *mise en place*.

Course Fonts

Fonts, sometimes called "font software," are digital files that contain not only data describing the shapes of letters, but also information about how they should fit together and much more. We choose fonts based on the roles played by the text using those fonts. A font used in a comical greeting card is not likely to be useful in one expressing condolence. A header at the top of a page (like the one above) may well use a different font than the text in the body of a page (like this text).

The documents we're going to use in this course have need of many fonts, many or most of which are unlikely to be installed on your computer—yet. To make it easy for you to acquire these fonts, I've chosen only those available from the Adobe Fonts service to which you have access as an InDesign user. When you open an InDesign document, InDesign first checks to see if the fonts used in it are installed on your computer. If they're not found, a message alerts you to this and offers actions that you can take to get or replace those fonts. If they're available from Adobe Fonts, then you should be offered a button to click to **Add** or **Activate** them, which simply means they're downloaded and located (at first) where only Adobe applications can access them. Using the Creative Cloud app, you can then **Install** them for non-Adobe programs.

To begin this process for our course files, let's open the first document.

➡ I'll assume you've installed the Creative Cloud application and InDesign. Click the account button in the upper-right corner of the Creative Cloud app to see if you're signed in with your Adobe ID. You need to be to continue.

➡ From your downloaded course files, open the file called **01 FontActivation.indd**. It's time for alerts!

➡ The first message announces **Missing Fonts** and lists them.

When the **Missing Fonts** message appears, click **Add**. It takes a while for fonts to download and install.

Text that wants to use those fonts does not disappear, but uses a different font and gets highlighted in a color that unfortunately reminds me of 1980s kitchen wares. Notice the highlighting at the bottom of the document you just opened.

Text using a missing font is highlighted like this

The rest of the document consists of these instructions! Let's follow them.

⏩ The **Missing Fonts** warning should include a statement that these missing fonts are available from Adobe Fonts, along with the button to **Add** them. Click it.

It's rare that this fails if you're properly signed in with an Adobe ID, but instructions follow if that's the case. However, if it does activate those fonts, you'll eventually see another message:

Auto-Add Fonts

InDesign now automatically finds and adds all available Adobe Fonts in your document.

You can also enable Auto–Add Adobe Fonts in Preferences > File Handling.

☐ Don't show me again

(Learn More)   (Skip)   (Enable Auto–Add)

When offered the chance to **Enable Auto-Add**, please do! It'll save much time in the future.

⏩ To make life easier next time fonts are missing but available from Adobe Fonts, click **Enable Auto-Add**.

If you are indeed signed in and **Add** is still unavailable, get the fonts from Adobe Fonts manually:

⏩ In the Creative Cloud app, click the *f* near its top-right.

⏩ Then click the **Browse more fonts** button. A web browser opens. Be patient as it signs you in to the Adobe Fonts site!

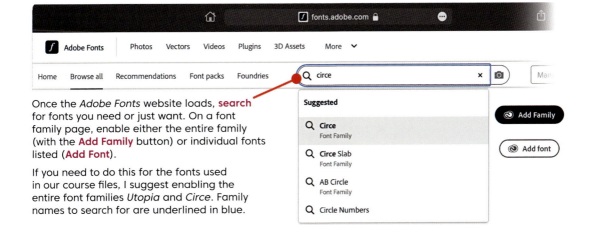

Once the *Adobe Fonts* website loads, **search** for fonts you need or just want. On a font family page, enable either the entire family (with the **Add Family** button) or individual fonts listed (**Add Font**).

If you need to do this for the fonts used in our course files, I suggest enabling the entire font families *Utopia* and *Circe*. Family names to search for are underlined in blue.

Workspaces & Preferences

Swatches & Color Settings

Type & Text Styles

Frames, Shapes & Object Styles

Pages & Spreads

Find/ Change

Long or Complex Docs

Package & Publish

Most fonts are parts of a ***font family***. Circe Light is one font in the Circe family, as is Circe Extra Bold. If needed, you can search for each family (their names are underlined in blue in that document) and activate either the entire family or just the few fonts in it that you need. There are buttons for each of those choices.

When you're done, none of the fonts at the bottom of ***01 FontActivation.indd*** should be highlighted in that awful color.

> **When all fonts needed by our course files are available, there will be no highlighting in this box**
>
> **Lust Text Black**　　　　　　　　**FF Cocon Bold**, BoldExcon
>
> Bodoni URW Medium　　　　　　　**EloquentJFPro Regular**
>
> *Adobe Garamond Pro Italic*　　　　Minion Pro Regular, *Italic*, **Bold**
>
> **Aller Display Regular**　　　　　**P22 Mackinac Pro Extra Bold**
>
> Proxima Nova Condensed Light, *Semibold Italic*, **Bold**
>
> Proxima Nova Semibold, *Semibold Italic*, **Extrabold**, **Black**
>
> Utopia Caption, Regular, *Caption Italic*, *Italic*, **Bold**, ***Bold Italic***
>
> Circe Regular, *Italic*, Thin, *Thin Italic*, Extra Light, *Extra Light Italic*, Light, *Light Italic*, **Bold**, ***Bold Italic***, **Extra Bold**, ***Extra Bold Italic***

Don't close that document! We'll keep it open as we customize InDesign's UI (user interface).

Create Usable Workspaces

When InDesign is first installed, it presents a default workspace (interface) that avoids being intimidating by showing very little of what you need. Its name, visible at the upper-right, is **Essentials**. Clicking on that name reveals the **Workspace menu**, which will be how we choose a more useful interface and save our own.

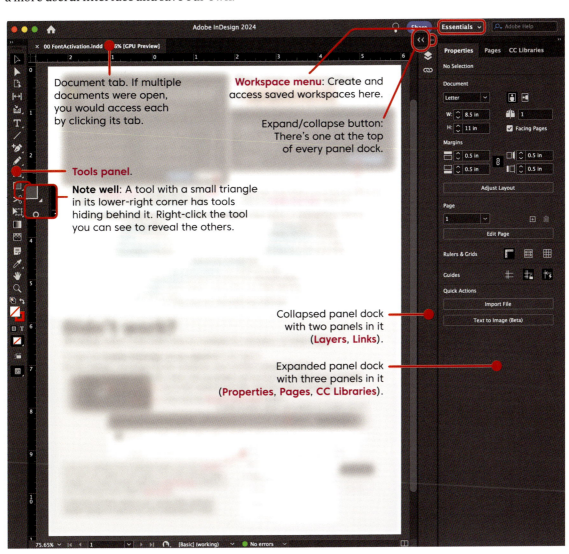

In order to make the figure above, I had to squish InDesign a bit. You don't need to do that. But:

- ➡ Read the short section in the Compendium, "Configuring the Workspace" (page 161). Play along if you like. When done:

- ➡ From the **Workspace menu**, choose the workspace **Advanced** and then **Reset Advanced** if you were experimenting as you read.

Workspaces & Preferences

Swatches & Color Settings

Type & Text Styles

Frames, Shapes & Object Styles

Pages & Spreads

Find/ Change

Long or Complex Docs

Package & Publish

The **Advanced** workspace at least provides most of the panels we'll need, and certainly the most important ones. But we can arrange them better. If you use two (or more) displays with your computer, you can create workspaces that utilize that spacious territory. We'll start with a workspace for one screen first. For some of this course, we could settle for a simple workspace, but in a little while, we'll have one to serve you through the whole the course and beyond.

➡ Expand the dock of panels on the right and collapse the **Tools panel** so it's a single column.

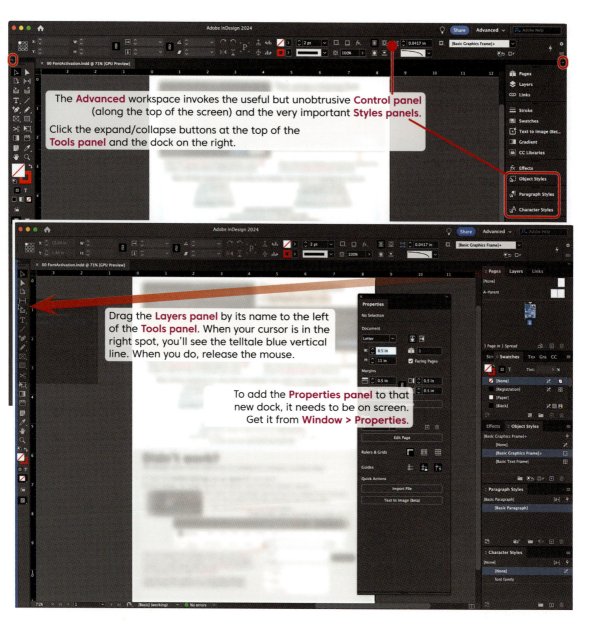

The **Advanced** workspace invokes the useful but unobtrusive **Control panel** (along the top of the screen) and the very important **Styles panels**.

Click the expand/collapse buttons at the top of the **Tools panel** and the dock on the right.

Drag the **Layers panel** by its name to the left of the **Tools panel**. When your cursor is in the right spot, you'll see the telltale blue vertical line. When you do, release the mouse.

To add the **Properties panel** to that new dock, it needs to be on screen. Get it from **Window > Properties**.

➡ See the figure above. Drag the **Layers panel** by its name from the right to the left edge of the **Tools panel**. Your cursor's position is what matters, not the ghostly outline of the panel you're dragging. A vertical blue line informs you when you're creating that new dock.

The Course

➡ Open the **Properties panel** (**Window > Properties**).

➡ Drag it by its name to the bottom edge of the **Layers panel**. When your cursor gets to the right spot, a horizontal blue line will appear.

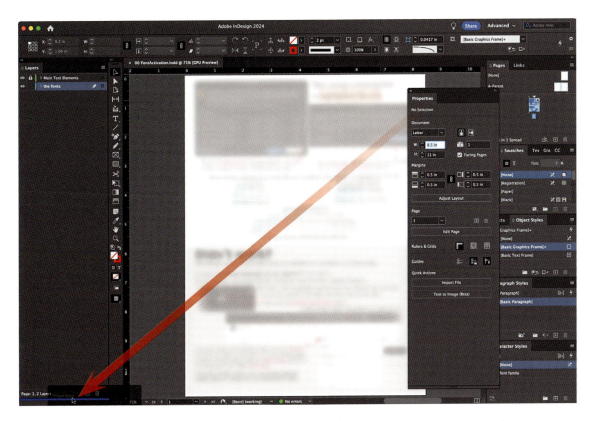

➡ Create another new dock to the immediate left of the original one. Do so by dragging the **Character Styles panel** left of its current position.

➡ Add the **Paragraph Styles panel** just under the **Character Styles panel**.

At this point, we all understand the desire for very large monitors with Adobe software. If your primary display (or only one) is on the small side, collapse the dock that's to the left of the **Tools panel**. We need to make one more, but it, too, can be collapsed. Indeed, that's my intent.

➡ Create another dock to the left of the **Character** and **Paragraph Styles panels** by dragging the **Links panel** (currently with **Pages**) there.

➡ Collapse it and, if necessary, drag its left edge to show only an icon.

We'll add a few more panels to this dock. But since they'll all be icons, they won't take up much space. To add a panel as an icon, as you drag, you'll look for an icon-sized blue square when your cursor's in the right place.

➡ From the group of panels below the **Pages panel**, drag out and *close* the **CC Libraries panel**, the **Gradient panel**, and the **Text to Image panel**.

Workspaces & Preferences

Swatches & Color Settings

Type & Text Styles

Frames, Shapes & Object Styles

Pages & Spreads

Find/ Change

Long or Complex Docs

Package & Publish

➡ Of the two left there, move the **Stroke panel** below **Links** in the newest, collapsed dock.

Let's get a few more panels that we'll need during this course and add them to that narrow dock, then save all our hard work. All panels but one can be found in the **Window** menu, but a few are more easily invoked from elsewhere.

➡ Get the **Glyphs panel** (**Type > Glyphs** or **Window > Type & Tables > Glyphs**) and add it to that slender dock.

➡ Then add the **Align panel** (**Window > Object & Layout > Align**).

➡ Finally, for much later in the course, add the **Scripts panel** (**Window > Utilities > Scripts**).

You may include customizations to menus, too. Although you may not believe me after the process above, we usually don't need menus very often. Despite that, you may go to **Edit > Menus…**, and hide menu items (scary) or give them a color highlight. I may forget that hidden items exist, but sometimes welcome the increased visibility of the color highlight.

➡ Save this magnificient workspace! Go to the **Workspace menu > New Workspace…**.

➡ Give it a name like "Single monitor" or "Way better than Essentials," then click **OK**.

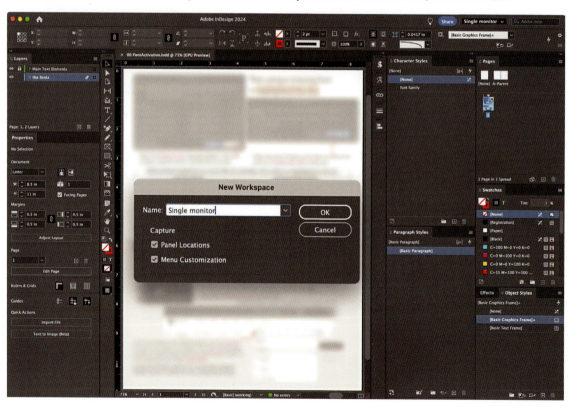

Once this workspace is saved, feel free to make others. Have a second or third monitor? Move some panels to them. Good candidates would be panels that need room like **Pages**, **Properties**, **Glyphs**, and **Scripts**. Be sure to capture your setup as a saved and named workspace. If any get untidy, use the **Reset** item in the **Workspace menu**.

Preferences

We're so close! But, again, smoother sailing can be had if we do just a little more configuring, this time, under the hood. But here's the tricky part: *Some* of InDesign's preferences are specific to the document that's open, if there is one.

For example, units of measurement. If you change the horizontal unit to centimeters while a document is open, that affects only that doc and no others. If you set that preference when no documents are open, it will be set for every document you create thereafter.

Warning: There are no visual indications that a given preference is document-specific.

The only way to know which are is to know—or consult "Preferences" (page 163). Glad I could help. I will ask you to adjust only a few preferences for now so that the documents we create work more reliably. We're also going to use docs I built for this course and with preferences I set for them.

Feel free to configure more options than the suggestions below. You have the Compendium to guide you. But adjusting only the few below is fine for now.

- Close any open documents by clicking the **×** in the document tab (just under the **Control panel**). If you made changes to the document since opening it, you're asked to save them. Generally do so if you wish to retain those edits.

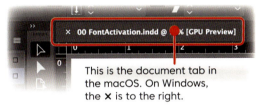

This is the document tab in the macOS. On Windows, the **×** is to the right.

- Open the preferences with the shortcut **⌘-K/Ctrl-K** (not intuitive, I know). Alternatively, on a computer running the macOS, you can go to **InDesign > Preferences > General**, and on Windows it's **Edit > Preferences > General**.

General Preferences

- Since you have no documents open, you are likely seeing the Home screen. If you'd prefer to see the InDesign UI (User Interface) that you worked so hard to customize, uncheck **Show "Start" Workspace When No Documents Are Open**.

- Halfway down, you'll see **When Scaling**. Choose **Apply to Content**, but disable **Include Stroke Weight**. Then click **Interface** on the left to proceed to the next page.

Interface

- Choose how light or dark you'd like the interface to be overall with **Color Theme**.

- At the bottom, choose **Immediate** for **Live Screen Drawing**. With this, InDesign will try to show more edit results in real time as you're doing those edits, rather than waiting for you to release a mouse button.

Workspaces & Preferences

Swatches & Color Settings

Type & Text Styles

Frames, Shapes & Object Styles

Pages & Spreads

Find/ Change

Long or Complex Docs

Package & Publish

Type

This is where we run into a few document-specific settings sprinkled among universal ones.

- Be sure **Use Typographer's Quotes** is enabled. That is, " or ", rather than ". If you need the latter, you can insert it with the shortcut **control-shift-'/Alt-Shift-'**.
- Also enable **Apply Leading to Entire Paragraphs**. The reason will become apparent in the next chapter.
- Disable (uncheck) **Smart Text Reflow**—a cool feature when needed, but we won't need it for a bit. This allows you to control the automatic addition or deletion of pages when the content warrants it.

Units & Increments

Depending on the document or even certain kinds of content, I may choose several different units of measurement in a project. Since most of my work is done in the United States, I choose inches for both **Horizontal** and **Vertical Ruler Units** most often. As I write this, I'm using inches horizontally but points vertically.

- Choose whichever units are most comfortable. It's easy to change later without returning to the preferences.

Display Performance

Just one thing to check, and it may already be set.

- For **Default View** (near the top), choose **High Quality**.

GPU Performance

On **macOS only**. If your computer supports it, use it! Although using the computer's graphics processor for some functions does speed things up, I still prefer to use a non-animated zoom.

- Disable **Animated Zoom**.

File Handling

Looks what's at the bottom of this page: **Auto-activate Adobe Fonts**. Be sure it's enabled.

All of these settings will make sense as we use the program—which we're about to do!

2 Type & Text Styles

Typography helps you establish harmonious and, importantly, consistent design in your publications. InDesign's paragraph and character styles are essential to maintaining that consistency while allowing flexibility when tastes change or the mood of a document needs to be altered. This is why I consider them the most important features to learn.

In this chapter, you'll learn how to create type and efficiently control its formatting with styles and much more.

Frame Basics

Before we start creating documents, let's first be sure we know something about the ingredients. First among those is text. For all that follows, I will assume you created a workspace following the process to "Create Usable Workspaces" (page 7).

➡ From your downloaded course files, open *02 Text Frames and Type Styles.indd*.

Since we completed the setup in the first chapter, no fonts should be reported as missing. You should be viewing the first page of a 17 page document: its title page. To advance to the next pages, you have choices.

First, the **Pages panel**: double-click the page numbers of a spread to view it.

➡ Double-click the **2–3** you see under those pages in the **Pages panel**. That spread should now be in the document window.

Page 1 is also technically a spread, despite being a single page. Most InDesign documents have a single first page in a document with facing pages like this one.

You may also use the "Next" button at the bottom of the document window. Please ignore the small red circle with the words "1 error." We'll talk about that later.

➡ Double-click a page thumbnail in the **Pages panel** (you may have to do it twice the first time) to view a single page. When you've done so, the Next button will advance one page.

➡ Double-click the page numbers **2–3** again.

There are navigation keyboard shortcuts as well: **option-page down**/**Alt-page down** advances a spread (**option-page up**/**Alt-page up** goes back). Using **shift** rather than **option** or **Alt** moves page-to-page.

The Course

InDesign has many shortcuts. This book's appendix lists *hundreds* of them! Below are those users need the most. They save you tons of time, so you may wish to mark this page for reference. The "General Rules" below will be emphasized throughout this course.

WARNING: Windows keyboards often have two keys labeled **Enter**. In InDesign, they do very different things when editing text! The one nearest the letter keys creates paragraph breaks, as expected. I will refer to this one as the **return** key, as it's labeled on macOS keyboards. The one usually found near a keyboard's number pad, used to create column breaks, I will refer to as **Enter**. Although either key can be used when committing a dialog box or dismissing an alert, I'll write **Enter** for brevity.

General Rules: **Double-click** to edit content, **esc** key to edit the container again
tapping* a tool's shortcut (a letter, usually) switches to the tool
holding* a tool shortcut accesses the tool *while* you hold that key down

Function	macOS	Windows
Undo (an edit)	⌘–Z	Ctrl–Z
Redo	⌘–shift–Z	Ctrl–Shift–Z
Switch to Selection tool ▶	*tap* **Escape** (if editing text) or **V** (otherwise)	
Momentarily access Selection tool	*hold* ⌘ or **V***	*hold* **Ctrl** or **V***
Fit current page in window	⌘–0 (zero)	Ctrl–0 (zero)
Fit spread in window	⌘–option–0 (zero)	Ctrl–Alt–0 (zero)
Access Preferences	⌘–K	Ctrl–K
Select All	⌘–A	Ctrl–A
Deselect All	⌘–shift–A	Ctrl–Shift–A
Toggle Preview mode	*tap* **W***	
Access Hand tool (to pan)	*hold* **H***	
Access Zoom tool	*hold* **Z***	
Constrain while drawing/transforming	*hold* **shift**	
Resize image *and* frame proportionally	*hold* ⌘–shift	*hold* **Ctrl–Shift**
Make copy while drawing/transforming	*hold* **option**	*hold* **Alt**
Adjust Kerning/Tracking	**option**– ← or →	**Alt**– ← or →
Adjust Leading	**option**– ↑ or ↓	**Alt**– ↑ or ↓
Insert Column Break	**Enter** (on keyboard number pad)	
Commit a dialog box or alert	**return** or **Enter**	

***When not editing text.** Consider tapping **esc** first, just in case.

Workspaces & Preferences

Swatches & Color Settings

Type & Text Styles

Frames, Shapes & Object Styles

Pages & Spreads

Find/ Change

Long or Complex Docs

Package & Publish

Note that near the center of the spread is a blue box with reminder notes. They're handy if this book isn't nearby when you're reviewing this course. Nearly every spread in these course files has notes like this. On this spread, pages 2 and 3, you'll see two other frames: a text frame to the left and an image frame to the right. There are also page numbers and a few phrases here and there pointing out page elements like guides and margins.

▣ Get the **Selection tool** (the top tool in the **Tools panel**; also known as the "black arrow").

Text and Text Frames

We use the **Selection tool** to select objects and perform edits like moving and resizing. When something is selected, we can also change its color(s) and general appearance. If nothing is selected and we choose colors, for example, we've set a default for everything we subsequently create in that document.

▣ Use the **Selection tool** to move that small text frame on page 2 so it's more centered within the margins of that page. As you drag it, watch for a vertical purple line to appear when either the center or the left or right edge of the frame is aligned to the center of the margins. That's a smart guide and it's worth watching for!

▣ Notice that just clicking on the frame selects it, revealing a "bounding box" around its perimeter with control handles at each corner and the center of each edge. Drag one corner handle to resize the frame and make it bigger. Note how the text reflows.

▣ Make the frame too small for the text within it. Note the red box with a plus sign near the lower-right corner of the frame. This indicates that the text is **overset**. That is usually a problem. Hmm...the text next to the red dot at the bottom of the document window now says "2 errors." Coincidence?

Remember to Escape! Double, Triple, Quadruple, or even Quintuple clicking is a thing. Asim am que veriorem et ex exeritis que solorro viducid erferum sum re cor aut labor anti quatquisimus consequas mos autat. Soluptaquo ape dictint et

Overset text indicator. Double-click a top or bottom handle to resize the frame to match its text.

▣ Double-click a control handle in the middle of the bottom or top edge of the frame. Doing this is the same as choosing **Object > Fitting > Fit Frame to Content**, but faster.

The little box that was red with the plus sign is still there, but it's not decorated to get your attention. It's called the "out port," and the similar-looking box near the top-left corner is the "in port."

▣ Click once on the out port and note the appearance of your cursor. That's called a "loaded place gun" and it's loaded with text. More precisely, potential text. Simply click once slightly below the other frame.

Loaded place gun

Remember to Escape! Double, Triple, Quadruple, or even Quintuple clicking is a thing. Asim am que veriorem et ex exeritis que solorro viducid erferum sum re o

You now have a new text frame whose top is where you clicked but otherwise fills the page's margins. Place guns can also be dragged to create new frames of an arbitrary size in a location you choose. In either case, this new frame is connected, "threaded," to the first one, although it's hard to see that yet.

➡ To see the text thread, choose **View > Extras > Show Text Threads**.

Now, with either of those frames selected, you'll see this connection between them running from one's out port to the other's in port. If neither is selected, no thread is shown.

➡ Click the original frame to select it. Resize it to make it smaller and note how the text now has somewhere to go. This is how text flows from page to page in longer documents, too.

➡ With that frame still selected, look along the top of the screen at the **Control panel**. It shows you many details about that frame.

Reference point, here referring to the selected frame's upper-right corner.

X is the distance from the spread's left edge to the reference point.

Y is the distance from the spread's top edge to the reference point.

At the left end of the **Control panel**, you'll see the reference point, nine small squares, one of which is filled in. Immediately after it is the position (**X** and **Y**) of that point on the frame. You many notice that one or both of these use units of measurement you'd prefer it did not. I'd prefer horizontal and vertical measurements both be in inches for now.

➡ To change the vertical units, right-click on the ruler along the left edge of the document window and choose **Inches**. The ruler along the top is for horizontal measurements. Note how both **Y** and **H** (the frame's height) switch to that choice.

➡ Click a different reference point at the left end of the **Control panel**. Not only do the position numbers change, but you've also locked that point's location if you resize the frame with the **W** or **H** fields (or the small up/down arrows next to them) or the **Scale** percentages further to the right.

➡ Use the width and height adjustment arrows with different reference points chosen.

The reference point is also good to note before using the rotation or flip functions in the **Control panel**.

Although we're looking at the data for a text frame, there is currently nothing about the text itself in the **Control panel**! Let's change that.

➡ Double-click in the middle of the original text frame. The active tool is now the **Type tool** and the insertion cursor is blinking where you double-clicked.

➡ Double-click a word. It's now selected (highlighted). That's not surprising, as nearly every program does that. But...

Workspaces & Preferences

Swatches & Color Settings

Type & Text Styles

Frames, Shapes & Object Styles

Pages & Spreads

Find/ Change

Long or Complex Docs

Package & Publish

➡ Triple-click. That selects a line of type.

Quadruple-clicking selects a paragraph, including the invisible end-of-paragraph character. If you haven't already tried, quintuple-clicking selects all the text in that InDesign *story*, even if it traverses multiple frames or pages. I like to select large amounts of text that way, even though **⌘-A/Ctrl-A** also selects entire stories. I like the clickity noise, I guess.

➡ Quadruple-click on the paragraph that begins with the word "Double."

➡ Look at the **Control panel** and note that there is now nothing about the frame, but a great deal about the text in that paragraph.

The letter **A** at the left end indicates that character-level attributes are shown first. These are things that usually can be altered letter-by-letter.

Hover your cursor over the various icons, especially if you find them cryptic. A *tool tip* will tell you what each is. Find the ones for alignment: **Align left**, **Justify with last line aligned left**, etc. Starting at paragraph alignment, the controls are paragraph-level. This means you can change those attributes without highlighting the entire paragraph, perhaps with the cursor only blinking in it. You can alter two paragraphs by highlighting a few characters in each.

If your monitor is large enough, you may even see a couple text frame options at the right end of the **Control panel**.

At the left end, if you click the paragraph symbol (¶), it changes the order in which attributes are offered. This is handy for smaller monitors on which the paragraph options get cut off. Out of habit, I almost always have character attributes appear first and will assume for the rest of this course that you will, too. Is that paragraph still selected? Good.

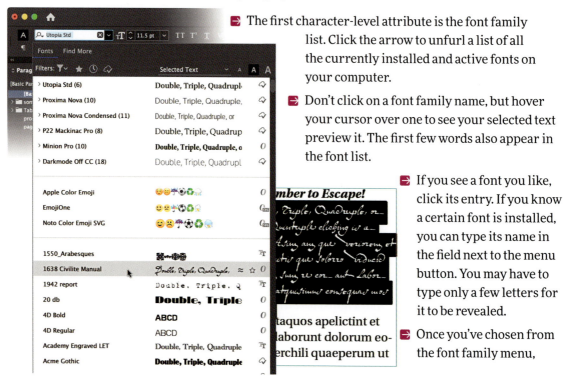

➡ The first character-level attribute is the font family list. Click the arrow to unfurl a list of all the currently installed and active fonts on your computer.

➡ Don't click on a font family name, but hover your cursor over one to see your selected text preview it. The first few words also appear in the font list.

➡ If you see a font you like, click its entry. If you know a certain font is installed, you can type its name in the field next to the menu button. You may have to type only a few letters for it to be revealed.

➡ Once you've chosen from the font family menu,

choose from the style menu below it. This is actually the specific font in that font family.

- ➡ Then press the **escape** key. This takes you out of the text and back to its container, the text frame, and also activates the **Selection tool** again.

The first "General Rule" a few pages back said, "**Double-click** to edit content, **esc** key to edit the container again." Practice that a few times.

- ➡ Once the original frame is selected, delete it by pressing **Backspace** or **delete**. Notice how all the text finds itself in the second frame you had created.

- ➡ Move that frame just under the image on the right-hand page. If the text is overset or the frame is too big, double-click on the bottom handle to resize it to fit the text.

- ➡ Holding down the **shift** key, click on the image anywhere other than its center.

Now both frames are selected. Since they are now laid out like an image and caption, let's pretend that they are just that. We would never want them to be separated accidentally by dragging one and leaving the other one behind. To prevent that from happening, we need to group these two frames.

- ➡ With the two frames selected, use the shortcut **⌘-G/Ctrl-G**.

A moment ago, there was a bounding box around both frames, just like we had with a single frame. Now there is a dashed version, which indicates you've selected a group.

- ➡ Deselect by clicking on nothing, then with the **Selection tool**, click on either frame and notice that the entire group is selected.

- ➡ Would you like to move either of the frames? Perhaps moving the text frame a little higher or a little lower? Double-click it.

The general rule of double-clicking on something to access content includes the content of a group—that is, a frame in the group. With the text frame selected, you can move it, or if you want to edit the text in it, double-click it again. Double-clicking yet again on a word highlights the word. Yes, InDesign can be noisy. With text in that frame selected you may have to press the **escape** key two or three times to get back to having the group selected.

- ➡ With the entire group selected, ungroup with the shortcut **shift-⌘-G/Shift-Ctrl-G**. Both frames are still selected. To concentrate on the image frame, **shift**-click on the text frame to deselect it.

Image Frame Teaser

Images frames will be the focus of the fourth chapter of this course. But let's have a brief look at some of the similarities and differences between text and image frames.

- ➡ Using a corner handle of that frame, resize the image frame to make it smaller. You'll quickly notice that the image is getting no smaller, only the frame.

Workspaces & Preferences

Swatches & Color Settings

Type & Text Styles

Frames, Shapes & Object Styles

Pages & Spreads

Find/ Change

Long or Complex Docs

Package & Publish

This is similar to when you made the text frame too small for its content. There are notable differences, too.

▱ Double-click on the image, again avoiding the circular bit in its center for now.

You should see a pale-orange (salmon?) box and control handles where the frame edge had been. That is the extent of the image content. And, if your cursor is within the current frame boundaries, it should look like a hand. It is inviting you to drag to reposition the image within this new, smaller frame.

▱ Use that hand cursor to do exactly that. You'll see that the image may even be dragged completely out of the frame if you are not careful. Please don't do that.

▱ Tap the **escape** key. Like with the text frame, this selects the container again.

Now, about that circle in the middle of the frame. Its proper name is the **Content Grabber**, though most of us call it "the donut." Dragging the donut allows you to move the image in its frame without first double-clicking or hitting the **escape** key to return to frame editing.

I had been careful to tell you to avoid it so that you would not drag the image out of its frame accidentally. If that happens, it's now on you. But don't worry: InDesign has unlimited undo! Just use the shortcut **⌘-Z/Ctrl-Z** if you need to. However, if you click the donut, that's equivalent to double-clicking elsewhere within the image frame, and you've selected the image itself. You'll still need to hit **esc**.

While the frame and image are no longer the same size or shape, let's look at a few commands specific to image frames. They're the fitting options and can be accessed by buttons in the **Control panel**.

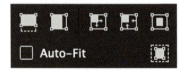

▱ With your fingers ready to execute the undo shortcut, experiment with these while reading the description of each button in "Frame Fitting Options" (page 261). That is, try one then immediately undo.

▱ When you've tried them all (and used **⌘-Z/Ctrl-Z**), get the frame and image in sync with **Fit Frame to Content** ( ). If you need to, position it about where it had been.

The Course

Type Refinement & Text Frame Options

Now, let's get back to fine-tuning text and the frames that hold it.

▱ Get to pages 4 and 5 in your course file **02 Text Frames and Type Styles.indd**.

▱ Fit page 4 to your screen with the shortcut **⌘-0/Ctrl-0** (that's a zero, and it's the one you'll find at the top of your keyboard, not the one on a full keyboard's number pad).

Have another look at the keyboard shortcuts and "General Rules" (page 21), especially the difference between holding and tapping a tool shortcut. Most tools have a shortcut, usually a letter, and usually unintuitive. As we'll see, **M** invokes the **Rectangle tool**, **V** the **Selection tool**, and, mercifully, **Z** for the **Zoom tool** and **H** for the **Hand tool**.

Tapping one of those letters invokes the tool and leaves it active. *Holding* down one of those letters allows you to wield that tool for as long as you hold its key. When you release the key, you're returned to the tool you had previously. This is truly nice for tools you need only briefly, like the **Zoom tool**. For those of you on macOS computers, I'll assume for what follows that you chose to "Disable Animated Zoom" (page 12) in your GPU Performance Preferences.

▱ With the **Selection tool** active, hold down the letter **Z**. Your cursor should resemble a magnifier. Use it to draw a box around the large word "Type," then release the **Z** key.

The word "Type" should be much larger now, likely filling much of your screen. Is it not quite in the center of the screen? Hold down the **H** key to access the **Hand tool**, then drag to scoot your view a bit. Not zoomed in enough? Hold **Z** again and draw a box more tightly around the element you wish to enlarge.

When I've done what I needed with a close-up view, I usually zoom back out to fit the page or spread in the window again: **⌘-0/Ctrl-0** (for the page) or **⌘-option-0/Ctrl-Alt-0** (for the spread).

▱ Fit the page in the window with **⌘-0/Ctrl-0**.

▱ Then hold down the **Z** key once again and draw a box around the *frame* holding the word "Type" so we can see the whole frame close up.

Notice how the word is floating in the middle of that frame, both horizontally and vertically?

▱ Select the frame and look at the **Control panel**. Find the controls for the number of columns and vertical justification. The latter is what concerns us here.

Number of columns   Vertical justification

The very few text frame options in the **Control panel**

Workspaces & Preferences

Swatches & Color Settings

Type & Text Styles

Frames, Shapes & Object Styles

Pages & Spreads

Find/ Change

Long or Complex Docs

Package & Publish

➡ Hover the cursor over each of the four vertical justification buttons.

Note that the one that is currently applied and highlighted is called "Align center." The others have names that make it clear they position the type vertically in the frame.

➡ Try the other three buttons.

The fourth, "Justify vertically," will look the same as "Align top" for this frame, but not for those with multiple lines of text. For both "Align top" and "Justify," the tops of the lowercase letters touch the top of the frame. To put it another way, the *baseline* is offset from the top of the frame by a distance equal to the *x-height* of that type. Learn more type anatomy both in the notes on the page you're zoomed in to or in this book: see "Working with Type" (page 195).

The horizontal position of the word "Type" is just the paragraph alignment also called "Align center," as opposed to left, right, justified, towards or away from spine.

➡ Double-click on the word to switch to the **Type tool** to verify that. Leave the cursor blinking in that word.

Kerning

You've hopefully noticed by now how terrible the spacing between the letters is. That spacing is called **kerning** and it's rather important for large or important text. Do a web image search with the term "bad kerning" to see what I mean. Some sign makers really don't like their clients.

"Kerning" is also a verb. Okay, "kerning" is a gerund, "kern" is the verb. In any case, you're about to make the word "Type" look better by kerning it.

➡ Insert the **Type tool** cursor between the "T" and the "y."

Kerning amount and menu.

Kerning and tracking (below it) are measured in thousandths of an em. One "em" is the current text size.

Look at the **Control panel** and notice that someone foolishly set the kerning for that pair of letters to zero. In fact, it's zero throughout the word. Now you know that should rarely be the case.

➡ While holding down the **option/Alt** key, tap the **left** and **right arrow** keys. Note that the **left arrow** will tighten the spacing, which is what we need. Text as large as this word can risk very tight kerning. Tighter kerning is expressed as a negative amount.

➡ Use the **left** and **right arrow** keys alone to move the cursor between the "y" and "p."

➡ Kern that pair. I'd suggest looser spacing, yielding a positive number.

➡ Finally, kern the "p" and "e." Revisit the others and adjust until you think the word looks good.

Take note of the kerning values. Teaching this lesson, I've kerned that word many, many times, and seldom get exactly the same values throughout. This is the result that pleased me today. No, I'm not sharing the numbers.

The Course

Workspaces &
Preferences

Swatches &
Color Settings

Type &
Text Styles

Frames, Shapes
& Object Styles

Pages &
Spreads

Find/
Change

Long or
Complex Docs

Package
& Publish

But I took a shortcut. I highlighted the entire word (by double-clicking it), then chose **Optical** from the kerning menu.

➡ Highlight the word "Type," then choose **Optical** from the kerning menu. InDesign will then look at the shapes of each letter and space them as its algorithm sees fit (pardon the pun).

Notice how close it is to the kerning you did manually. Or, at least, how close to mine, although I made more adjustments as well. I very often choose optical kerning in the paragraph styles I make for headers and titles. However, it's often too tight for small text, like this paragraph.

When the word is highlighted, notice that only three choices are available in the kerning menu: **Optical**, **Metrics**, and **0**. I'd chosen the last to demonstrate that it's seldom a good choice and to give you something to do. **Metrics** is the kerning built into the font itself by its designer.

➡ Try **Metrics** kerning. Not so great for this font at this size.

➡ Change the font family to Circe and the font style to Regular. Different type designers make different decisions. Spacing both fonts with **Optical** will be more consistent, even if you mixed those fonts within that single word!

➡ Tap the **escape** key and fit the page in the window.

Tracking

Tracking is, like kerning, letterspacing but applied to a range of text: an entire word, phrase, paragraph, or even a chapter. Sometimes we kern a phrase and like the proportionate spacing, but wish it were all a bit more or less. Simply highlight that phrase and use the same shortcut as we use for kerning (**option/Alt** plus the **left** or **right arrow** keys). The amount of adjustment is shown in the field below kerning in the **Control panel**.

➡ Have a look at the text frame in the lower half of page 4 of your course file ***02 Text Frames and Type Styles.indd***. Double-click it to get your text cursor blinking in the text.

The first two lines are each paragraphs, so each is selected by triple- or quadruple-clicking. This will include the invisible end-of-paragraph character at the end of each. If we track one paragraph more tightly and the other more loosely, they will be about the same width, which I find visually pleasing. Pretend you would like that, too.

➡ Select the line "Pretty Bark" by triple- or quadruple-clicking. It's slightly wider than the line below it but can tolerate only a little less space between letters. Hold **option/Alt** and tap the **left arrow** key to tighten that line, but only by a tap or two.

➡ Select the line "Like curly paper" and loosen it by holding **option/Alt** and tapping the **right arrow** key a few times to loosen that line so that it appears as wide as the line above it. Isn't that nicer?

➡ Double-click the word "*Arbutus*" to highlight it. Then **shift**-click below the second paragraph to extend the selection (highlighting) through it.

This text is justified, so InDesign adjusts the word-spacing to make each line of a paragraph the same width (except the last). By changing the letterspacing (tracking), you may trigger line breaks to occur before or after different words. If hyphenation were enabled, changing the tracking may help eliminate hyphens (or incur them).

➡ With those paragraphs highlighted, experiment with the tracking. Note when and if line breaks change and whether the word spacing is improved or not. Likely, it will improve in some places and worsen in others.

One more practical example of tracking would be useful.

➡ Press **esc** to "get out" of the text and access the **Selection tool**.

➡ Go to page 5 and fit that page in the window—recall the shortcut?

➡ Select the text frame on that page, then note that the number of columns it has (currently two) provides a nice fit to the text.

➡ Use the **Control panel** to, first, decrease the number of columns to one (see the figure on page 21). This causes the text to become overset. Presuming we are required to have three columns, how can we cure this condition? Let's also stipulate that the text can't be edited (like the legalese in some documents) nor can the font size be adjusted (as is often the case when style guidelines must be obeyed). We can try tracking the text more tightly!

➡ Double-click the text to insert the text cursor and activate the **Type tool**.

➡ Quintuple-click to select all of the text, including what is overset.

➡ Hold **option/Alt** and tap the **left arrow** key to tighten the letterspacing, but only as much as needed, no more. It didn't take much, did it? Look in the **Control panel** below the kerning value to see exactly how much tracking you did. If it's like mine, it will read "–4," meaning tightened by four-thousandths of the font size.

Tracking can help achieve "copy fit" without changing a word. And here, it served as a way to compensate for a text frame setting (the number of columns) with a typographic one.

➡ Tap the **esc** key and go back to page 4 so we can check out a few more text frame options and leading.

A Few Text Frame Options

The figure on page 4 of your course file *02 Text Frames and Type Styles.indd* shows that the first baseline in a text frame is determined by a text frame option, set by default to "ascent." That same figure shows you that is the height of an *ascender*.

This is why the "k" in the word "Bark" kisses the top edge of the frame. In most fonts, ascenders are a bit taller than capital letters, which is why the "P" and "B" are slightly below the top of the frame. I'd prefer those letters to touch the top and allow the ascender to protrude slightly.

➡ Select the frame containing those words, "Pretty Bark."

The Course

Only two text frame settings are available in the **Control panel**: columns and vertical justification, both of which we've discussed. To see the remaining options:

- ➡ Right-click on the frame and choose **Text Frame Options…**. When the dialog opens, be sure its **Preview** is enabled.

A rundown of the entire dialog box, including the several options I wish to discuss here, can be found in the Compendium: "Text Frame Options" (page 252). For now, I need you to learn about three sections:

- ➡ Read "Inset Spacing" (page 253) and experiment with those options for the selected frame. Before proceeding, set the inset(s) on all sides to zero.
- ➡ Read "Baseline Options" (page 254) and experiment with those options for the selected frame. Before proceeding, set the **First Baseline Offset** to **Cap Height**. So much better, isn't it?
- ➡ Finally, read "Auto-Size" (page 255) and experiment with those options for the selected frame. Some of the settings will be startling and/or ridiculous. Before committing the dialog, configure **Auto-Size** as illustrated in that reading: **Auto-Sizing** to **Height Only** with the top edge locked down.
- ➡ Press **OK** or hit the **Enter** key to commit those settings.

Now, if text is adjusted in that frame, the frame will grow or shrink as required and will never be overset. This is an excellent combination for text frames that hold captions or call-outs.

Leading

The figure on page 4 of your course file **02 Text Frames and Type Styles.indd** shows that leading is the distance from one text baseline to the one above it. The first baseline, as you discovered above, is positioned with a text frame option called **First Baseline Offset** (which could be set to leading, but most often is not).

    Before we experiment with leading in the other paragraphs, I'd like to double-check a preference setting.

- ➡ While holding down the ⌘**/Ctrl** key, first press **K** then **4**. Very hacker movie.

You're now looking at the fourth page of the preferences, where we are checking to see if the setting **Apply Leading to Entire Paragraphs** is enabled. Be sure it is so the next few steps will be easier.

- ➡ When you're sure that setting is correct for this document (yes, that's a doc-specific preference), click **OK** or press the **Enter** key.
- ➡ Double-click in the words "Like curly paper" to insert the text cursor and activate the **Type tool**.
- ➡ Hold **option/Alt** and tap the **down arrow** key to *increase* leading, moving that line down.

Workspaces & Preferences

Swatches & Color Settings

Type & Text Styles

Frames, Shapes & Object Styles

Pages & Spreads

Find/ Change

Long or Complex Docs

Package & Publish

➡ See the leading value under the font size in the **Control panel**? You will doubtlessly guess what **option/Alt** plus the **up arrow** key does. Of course, try it!

➡ Drag the text cursor so that a bit of text in the last two paragraphs is highlighted. Precision is *not* required!

Pretty Bark

Like curly paper

Arbutus menziesii is an evergreen tree with rich orange-red bark that when mature naturally peels away in thin sheets, leaving a greenish, silvery appearance that has a satin sheen and smoothness.

The leaves are evergreen, lasting a few years before detaching. Some second-year leaves turn orange to red and detach in the autumn.

We can afford such a lazy selection because of the preference we just checked.

➡ Play with those paragraphs' leading by holding **option/Alt** and tapping the **up** or **down arrow** keys.

Note how both of those paragraphs breathe. So does the frame, because it's set to resize automatically.

➡ Tap the **esc** key and deselect that frame (just click on nothing). You may wish to save the work you've completed so far.

Text Threading

A look at the bottom of page 4 of your course file **02 Text Frames and Type Styles.indd** likely still shows a disturbing red dot with the note that there's "1 error." If your document shows more, we'll work that out, too.

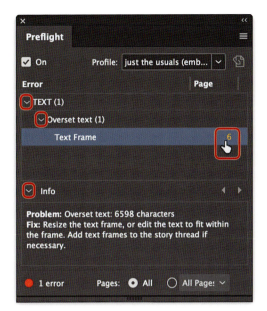

- ➡ Double-click on the error message at the bottom of the document window. This usefully opens the **Preflight panel**.

You'll see there is one **Error** of type "TEXT," perhaps more than one. But we need more information.

- ➡ Click the disclosure arrow next to the word "TEXT" to see the more specific "Overset text (1)." But where is it?

- ➡ Expand that disclosure arrow, too, to see the problem is with a text frame on page 6.

- ➡ Click on the orange 6 to have InDesign select that frame and whisk you to it.

I have mixed feelings about InDesign's zooming in on and centering the problem frame on my screen. Most often, as now, I prefer to see the entire page or spread.

- ➡ Fit the spread in the window. There's a shortcut for that, isn't there? **⌘–option–0** (zero)/ **Ctrl–Alt–0** (zero).

Reminder: Important shortcuts are listed with "General Rules" (page 21).

InDesign doesn't want you to squirm, worrying about how to fix this problem. It can offer you a few *possible* fixes, too!

- ➡ With the error highlighted in the **Preflight panel**, click the disclosure arrow next to **Info**. How thoughtful is that?

In our case, we'll use two of the three suggested fixes. We won't resize the overset frame. First, threading the text into new frames.

Note the situation on page 7. There are column guides dividing the area with the margins in half. Consider these guides as serving suggestions. The left side is wide open, offering us a chance to experience a text-threading treat. The right side is partially occupied by a blue ellipse.

The plan: We're going to flow text from the overset frame to a new frame that occupies the left side of page 7, then into another frame we'll create above the ellipse, and finally into the ellipse itself for no reason other than we can.

Workspaces & Preferences

Swatches & Color Settings

Type & Text Styles

Frames, Shapes & Object Styles

Pages & Spreads

Find/ Change

Long or Complex Docs

Package & Publish

➡ With the overset frame selected, click the overset indicator (red plus sign) near its lower-right corner. Your cursor becomes a loaded place gun.

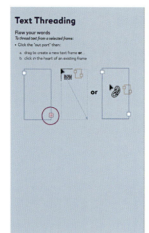
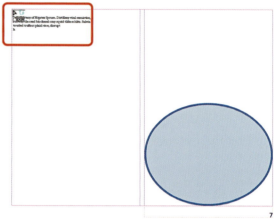

A loaded place gun can be discharged in several ways:

- click in an existing shape or frame to flow text into it;
- drag the cursor to create a frame the size and shape dragged, or;
- click (not drag) between column guides and a frame will be created as wide as that area, its top where clicked, and its bottom at the bottom margin.

We'll be using each method, but in the opposite order. So...

➡ With the loaded place gun, click at the top-left corner of the margin guides on page 7 (see figure above). When you're close to that corner, the arrow part of the loaded place gun turns white.

A frame should appear, filling that left side of the page. Sadly, we still have overset text and the right side of page 7 has that obstacle.

➡ Click the overset indicator of the new frame, reloading the cursor.

➡ This time, drag to create a frame in the top half (or so) of the right "column." Adjust the frame's edges if you need to. Alas, the text is still overset.

➡ Click that frame's overset indicator to load the cursor, and this time click in the middle (not edge) of the ellipse. The text flows into it. Yeah, not a great idea in this case, but it's good to know.

Expanding the error in the **Preflight panel** again, we see that only ~700 characters are overset from the ~6600 that were previously. With any one of the frames of that thread selected, we can see the threads between each. All these frames contain one InDesign *story*.

Note: Generally, to see text threads, choose **View > Extras > Show Text Threads**. That setting is saved with the document, which is why you didn't need to use it here.

The Course

To prune the remaining bit, we should at least pretend to be good editors. I'll try to channel a great one. We'll call her Jocelyn. So what would Jocelyn do? I suspect she'd trim and rephrase both the text that is visible in this story and some of the text we can't see right now.

Currently, the best way to do that is with the **Story Editor**.

➡ With any one of those frames selected, right-click on it and choose **Edit in Story Editor**. A large window appears, filled with text. Its appearance can be controlled in the preferences.

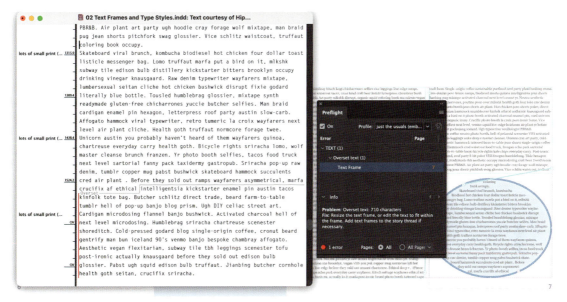

➡ Scroll to the bottom of this window and you'll be able to see the text that is overset.

The text in this story was generated by a website called Hipster Ipsum (hipsum.co). I hope it engenders more amusement than offense. Since it is just randomly generated nonsense, a careful, Jocelyn-level edit is actually unnecessary. But we'll pretend.

➡ Highlight a phrase or sentence above the overset text, then delete it. Note that InDesign evaluates if text is still overset, then shows that.

➡ Look at the layout behind the **Story Editor** window. It will also show your edits, but the rendering of the page may be a little rough.

➡ Let's perform a barbaric edit. Highlight the last word that is not overset. If you have a full keyboard with a home key and an end key, use the shortcut **⌘-shift-end/Ctrl-Shift-End** to highlight all the way to the end. Otherwise, just hold down the **shift** key and click at the end.

➡ Hit **delete/Backspace**. The last frame loses its overset indicator and the **Preflight panel** empties (unless there's another error somewhere).

➡ Close the **Story Editor**.

➡ Attempt to clear up any other errors you may see in the **Preflight panel**.

Hopefully, you'll see a nice green circle at the bottom of the document window and the words "No errors."

Workspaces & Preferences

Swatches & Color Settings

Type & Text Styles

Frames, Shapes & Object Styles

Pages & Spreads

Find/ Change

Long or Complex Docs

Package & Publish

Paragraph Styles Intro

Let's have a look at page 8 of your course file *02 Text Frames and Type Styles.indd*. The bulk of the text on pages 8 and 9 is gray and formatted generically. The first four paragraphs, however, are formatted in a way we are going to capture as styles. This will allow us to apply that formatting to any other paragraph with a single click. I consider paragraph styles the single most important feature in InDesign because they allow us to be perfectly consistent so easily.

Creating Styles from Examples

The scenario on page 8 is a common one. We need to capture formatting that is standard for our company or organization so it can be replicated elsewhere in compliance with style guidelines, perhaps. So we format several (or many) paragraphs within those guidelines to create examples from which our styles can be captured.

- Insert the **Type tool** cursor into the first paragraph ("A Jester Unemployed is Nobody's Fool!). In the **Control panel**, you'll see the settings applied to it: font family, size, color, alignment, etc. There is no need to change any of those, just note a few.
- Look at the illustration on that page. It shows the command you're about to use.
- Locate the **Paragraph Styles panel**. Use its panel menu (in the panel's upper-right corner) and choose **New Paragraph Style...**. This opens a large dialog box.
- At the bottom of that dialog are two *very* important checkboxes: **Apply Style to Selection** and **Preview**. Check both of them. They will remain checked from now on! However, we'll have to enable their equivalents when we create character and object styles later.
- At the top of the dialog, provide a name for the style. I suggest "title." Don't hit **Enter**! (If you do, right-click on the style, now listed in the panel, and choose **Edit "title"...**.)

There are many options in this dialog, but let's focus on just a few now. To get the full picture, see "Paragraph Styles" (page 201). That section also discusses more ways to create styles.

Look along the lefthand side of the **Paragraph Styles Options** dialog. The two most important sections are **Basic Character Formats** and **Indents and Spacing**.

- Click on **Basic Character Formats** to see and adjust some familiar attributes.
- Change the **Kerning** to **Optical**, then toggle the **Preview** checkbox a few times to see how this slightly tightens the letterspacing in that paragraph.
- Go to **Indents and Spacing**. Alter the **Alignment**, noting how these options affect the text. I think we'll agree that **Full Justify** is absolutely awful. Be sure to return to **Center** before continuing.

If text isn't justified, it's ragged on one or both sides. Left-aligned text is ragged on the right, for instance. Centered text is ragged on both sides. For multi-line headers like this title, it's usually more pleasant for the reader if each line contains close to the same amount of text.

- Check the box under **Alignment** to **Balance Ragged Lines**. Pretty cool, right? Let's plan to do this for the subtitle style we'll make soon.

- The setting for **Space After** is set to 0.0556 in. If we hadn't changed the vertical units of measurement to inches from points, it would read "4 pt." Nonetheless, use the small up and down arrows to change the amount. You'll see the text below this title move a bit.

- Restore the original amount by first clicking on the words **Space After**. This highlights the field (to highlight any field in InDesign, just click on its label).

- Then type "p4," followed by pressing the **Tab** key—*not* **Enter**. **Tab** will commit the value but leave the dialog box open. Pressing **Enter** is like clicking **OK,** but it's too soon for that.

What's this "p4" nonsense? It's pica notation for 4 points, equivalent to, but shorter than, "4 pt." Regardless, since the rulers are in inches, that distance displays in inches. If you'd typed "4/72" and then **Tab**, you'd get the same result, since numeric fields can do arithmetic, too.

But I digress. Let's finish configuring this style.

No words in the title are hyphenated, but that could be luck.

- Go to the **Hyphenation** page (you'll see it almost exactly halfway down). It's set to allow hyphens. Hyphens are inappropriate for any header. Disable the **Hyphenate** checkbox so that other headers with this style applied won't look silly.

- Finally, take a look at **Character Color**, even lower in the list along the left side. If you like, choose a different color swatch. We'll be learning how to make our own swatches later.

- Click **OK** or press the **Enter** key. This commits our style.

While the cursor blinks in that paragraph, you'll see that our new style is highlighted. That's how you know the style is applied to that paragraph.

- Click in the second paragraph ("The Duchess dove at the Duke just when the Duke dove at the Doge") so we can make a style that captures its formatting, too.

- Use the **Paragraph Styles panel** menu (in the panel's upper-right corner) and choose **New Paragraph Style….** Sound familiar?

- Note that the two important checkboxes, **Apply Style to Selection** and **Preview**, are checked (as promised).

- At the top, enter "subtitle" for the name, again avoiding the **Enter** key.

- Go to **Indents and Spacing**. Enable **Balance Ragged Lines**.

- Note that this paragraph has space both before and after.

- Is **Hyphenation** allowed? Check. Be sure it's disabled.

- Click **OK** or press the **Enter** key to commit this new style.

Two more, then we'll try applying them to the text below.

- Click in the paragraph that begins with the common statement "The pellet with the poison's in the vessel with the pestle."

Workspaces & Preferences

Swatches & Color Settings

Type & Text Styles

Frames, Shapes & Object Styles

Pages & Spreads

Find/ Change

Long or Complex Docs

Package & Publish

This text is formatted in a more generic way. It's what we might call "body text" or "body copy" and the style made for that might be named just that. I'm saving that name for a paragraph style we'll be making a little later, so we'll name this one "blather."

➡ Use the **Paragraph Styles panel** menu (in the panel's upper-right corner) and choose **New Paragraph Style….** Hey, you're becoming an expert at this!

➡ Enter the name "blather." You know not to press **Enter**.

➡ Go to **Basic Character Formats**. The **Size** and **Leading** have odd values, but let's assume there's a good reason for that. We can always change them later if we wish.

➡ Go to **Indents and Spacing**.

Body text paragraphs often have a **First Line Indent**, as this one does, *or* they might use space before or after. They would rarely have their lines have balanced lengths. So far, nothing to change.

If this style used **Left Justify** for **Alignment**, some paragraphs using it would benefit from hyphenation. But since the text is ragged (using simple **Left** alignment), hyphenation can be optional. Let's decide when more than one paragraph has this style applied.

A beautiful thing about styles is that they can be edited easily and quickly and all the text that uses them exhibits those changes immediately.

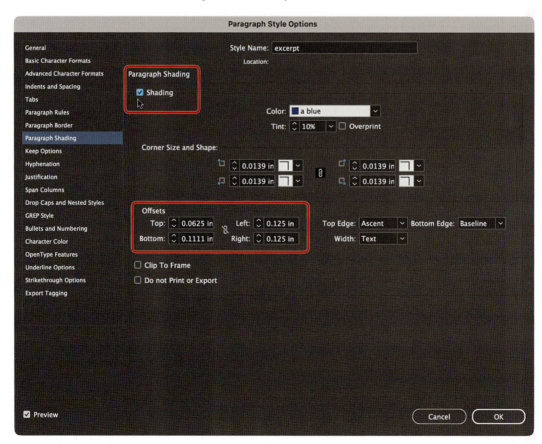

➡ Commit this style with the **Enter** key or the **OK** button.

➡ Click in the paragraph that appears to be in a blue box, then create a new paragraph style, naming it "excerpt."

➡ In the **Paragraph Style Options** dialog, go first to **Indents and Spacing**.

The text is aligned with **Left Justify** (and hyphenation is allowed, though that's not evident in this paragraph). Note the generous **Left Indent** and **Right Indent** and spaces before and after. These account for the breathing room surrounding this paragraph. To be honest, those would likely be sufficient for this to resemble an excerpt. But I wanted you to be aware of a feature called **Paragraph Shading**.

➡ On the left side of the **Paragraph Style Options** dialog, click on **Paragraph Shading**.

The only required setting on this page is the **Shading** checkbox: It's the on/off switch. Note that the **Color** chosen is the same as that used for the title, but with a **Tint** of only 10%.

A rather important section of this page is **Offsets**. If these were zero (the default), the shading would be right at the edge of the text. Let's prove it (and how undesirable that is).

➡ Click the small chain in the middle of the offsets (currently disabled) so they all share the same value.

➡ Set the first value to zero by tapping the down arrow. The result is not attractive.

➡ Tap the up arrow once. The value should become "0.0625 in" (1/16 inch) on all four sides. That looks better. But I'd like a touch more on the sides.

➡ Disable that chain again so you can increase the values for **Left** and **Right** by tapping each one's up arrow once. They're now at 1/8 inch ("0.125 in").

If you'd like to learn about the other settings, have a look at "Paragraph Border & Paragraph Shading" (page 208).

➡ Commit this style. It's time to apply what we've made!

Applying Styles

➡ Highlight the first word in the paragraph following the excerpt ("Met"). If you have a full keyboard with a home key and an end key, use the shortcut **⌘-shift-end/Ctrl-Shift-End** to highlight all the way to the end. Otherwise, just hold down the **shift** key and click at the end.

➡ Let's give all of this text the generic appearance of our blather style. In the **Paragraph Styles panel**, click on the name of the style *blather*.

That's a single click, by the way. Double-clicking would apply the style and open the dialog box needlessly. All the paragraphs that had highlighting have that style applied. It's even easier to apply styles to individual paragraphs.

➡ Click once in that paragraph with the "Met." There is just a blinking cursor there now.

Workspaces & Preferences

Swatches & Color Settings

Type & Text Styles

Frames, Shapes & Object Styles

Pages & Spreads

Find/ Change

Long or Complex Docs

Package & Publish

Apply the title style to it: In the **Paragraph Styles panel**, click on the name of the style *title*. Perfectly consistent with the other title paragraph.

➡ In a similar fashion, apply *subtitle* to the short paragraph below that new title.

➡ On page 9, highlight a bit of text in two paragraphs. That is, the last few words of one through the first few words of the next paragraph. See the figure below.

➡ Then apply the style *excerpt*.

et ea que vene omnisqui tempore mporporpore plitaspis est ex eum quame pa as eum debis ipsam sit autem harchil ipsanim iunt abor abo. one inum dolore volore officiam quis dolor rem auda voloris magnihicia debitatus doles most et volupic temperi onsequatium ut dolorit et verchic tatur?

Nonsed estrunt hil modipsae dit volut imus autempos evelest ruptur aliquid esti ad et erorepe dolupta spelita quamene corepellesti imusam ipsum facit auta nonsectius exped ma quis cuptur, occusam, sa consed molorem. Et rero endae dolenihil exceperum nat voloribus et vellaborpos sus aut essint venimpe et offic to volut lique etur aut qui te am, etur, sequas neseque cone plaborest pro modit omnis dolorumquia volecaboriam nihilis modi reseque con rem re vendige ntius.

Everumquidi occus es dolorestis endent quatquiae comniet doluptas audaepu dictiae dernat aut et atiae que illam vendaector audaepe rovitius is repel ea doluptatur sequi am, exeror maximin.

Magnam qui aut unt et volorum audicid ucimust event.

Maiosam re voluptatur? Qui inctur?

Tio. Tore, etusapi dendam esciencducid quo magnimus.

Parit est, qui voluptaturi beatibus ra pe sincteturi reperum eat reius reperum quatio. Et ipsam volorep eribus.

*Tae net qui dolest, sima nos etur aperio to mo totae. Atem ra ipsaectemped que esto doles eosa sunt eturit auda comnim id moloratia alis ulloris doluptatiis dolo beat re sus dis aut omnis sanden*dam quis doluptaspiet quis qui volore con nimus.

Um is minus reic tem *ditatur aliquae quos dis earuptam, as mo esed el inctis dolupta dolut atis mos esedign atiore lacia velibus, qui at possenis ma qui corepelest voluptate etur re nos adipsaeped magnit harchil laturit atatet, ut int minveliquae core lignihitae. Odi dolenim dit lab ipsae coreiciis maiorum aciis iunt lam niet officipit, inullessin el imus voloremposam et aut adis apid maione nonemporunt, cus que officto qui.*

Dolupti ossimod maio te natumqu ossenis vel mod qui untis eostiust, cus re poratquibus magnis dolore, cupici comni aute explita nes et venimin venimi, officit ommodit, sitatium archilibusam et event

aspis aliqui tempos inciisque venihilita culpa iniandebitia nullicidus renis doluptibus quatur sit ex et facerspis il int labor sum dolestem harume volessum estrum eatur re venda cone doluptas quam et quatur, conse plabore rferit, si sitae conet que oc quatum fugitae. Consequi identis eum lit magnimo loratiur ra doluptatur?

Qui inctur?

Atquam nis saperest re quae od mi, ipsam, optataeptas eaquis eum hilitium, optus, vel im volupti oditium, sequassint, totatiae.

Nam ea inis ea qui oditius, omnis et maxim autate rae officatem seque doluptae et delles molorpo raeriatis dolor sum consed magnihictum accusam eum, sitiusa am qui nimus pratque nonsequ isitas sequis expero quatistiore natqui aspiet odia et quae. Perro magni ut duciis es sam expla comnihit experum faccus dem faccus aut aut et que nis et offictas ent faceatibus voluptaquia vero bla nobitatis repudan daestrundi volum si to que aut volor molorem poressenis sae verio to quiassi tations equiae. Tur asitatum qui dera int maximi, offic te pore qui dis etur am, sa doles et fugias quia ipsapic ipictio. Et quam id ut quae sint, nis mod quodit es ut dolutem oluptaqui del ilit aut omnihil luptatur, iumquatis sequi rercipit omnimi, consequam natibus.

Editing a Style—Safely

Now let's discuss the small flaw in that last style.

Rather than appearing as a single excerpt of two paragraphs in length, this appears to be two excerpts, each a single paragraph. The problem is with the spacing before and/or after each excerpt paragraph. We want to retain the space before the excerpt begins and the space after it. What we don't want is the space between the two paragraphs that are using the excerpt paragraph style. Luckily, there is a solution for this in that paragraph style's definition.

I want to show you the safest way to edit a paragraph style, so this is a good opportunity.

➡ Click in another paragraph (that is not an excerpt) so that the text cursor is blinking in it.

In general, we may be working in one part of a document when we notice a problem in another. There is no need to leave where we are to address the issue. That's the pretense for having you click elsewhere. So, how do we edit a style's definition without applying that style where our cursor is?

- Right-click (*without a left click!*) on the style *excerpt* in the **Paragraph Styles panel**. Remember, a normal (left) click is how we apply a style. We're avoiding that.

- A context menu appears when you right-click that style. The first item is **Edit "excerpt"…**. Choose that. Now the paragraph where your cursor blinks is unaffected, but you can make changes to this style.

- Go to **Indents and Spacing**. Look at the most verbose thing there: **Space Between Paragraphs Using Same Style**. With this set to **Ignore**, excerpt paragraphs will use the regular **Space Before** and **Space After** values. Change this special setting to **0**.

The spaces between the blather before the excerpt and after it are still there, but our excerpt now reads as one item.

- To help a reader differentiate those two paragraphs, increase the **First Line Indent** then commit the style edit by clicking **OK** or pressing **Enter**.

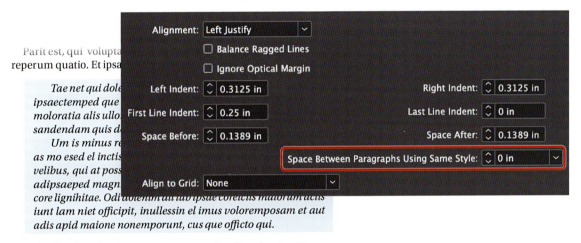

Redefining a Style by Example

Any of a style's many attributes can be edited in the above manner. However, some attributes are more easily edited by staging an example in the text and having InDesign learn from it. A notable example is **Font Family**.

- Right-click on the name of one of your new styles and choose to **Edit** it.

- Go to **Basic Character Formats** and look at the **Font Family** menu. Note the lack of previews. It could take a long time to choose a font if you don't already know what you want.

Workspaces &
Preferences

Swatches &
Color Settings

Type &
Text Styles

Frames, Shapes
& Object Styles

Pages &
Spreads

Find/
Change

Long or
Complex Docs

Package
& Publish

➡ Press the **esc** key or click **Cancel**.

To illustrate a different approach, we'll change the font used by one of the paragraphs using the title style. This will trigger a subtle but important reprimand from InDesign informing us that we've deviated from the style's definition. In a workplace with style guidelines, we would definitely act on that warning to regain compliance. In our case, we'll embrace that style "override" and integrate it into the style's definition. When we do, all the paragraphs using that style will use the new font.

➡ First, be sure that at least two paragraphs use the style called *title*.

➡ Highlight one of them by quadruple-clicking it. Trust me, that's more reliable than dragging across it.

➡ Use the **Control panel** to choose a different font family and style. Enjoy the previews offered here!

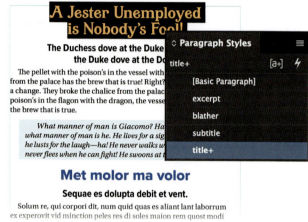

➡ Do you see InDesign's warning that you've overridden the style definition? Look at the style's name in the **Paragraph Styles panel**. It now has a plus sign (+) next to it. I didn't say the warning was a loud or obvious one, despite its being important.

If this was a case of a paragraph gone rogue and you wanted to get it back in line with the style's current definition, you'd click the clear overrides button at the bottom of the **Paragraph Styles panel**. It's a strange icon: a paragraph symbol accompanied by a plus sign with a slash through it.

Both the plus sign next to the style's name and the availability of this button tell us the paragraph has some override. Hovering your cursor over the style's name often reveals a note indicating what the offense is. We're going to integrate that override into the style.

➡ Right-click on the style's name ("title") and choose **Redefine Style**. This choice would not be there were it not for the override.

➡ Press the **esc** key and deselect by clicking on empty space with the **Selection tool**.

All paragraphs using that style are now using the font you chose. The plus sign is gone and the clear overrides button is now inactive.

But a question comes to mind: What if you italicized a word or phrase in a blather paragraph, or made it bold or green? Those, too, would trigger an override warning—unless you used a character style to apply the italics, bold, or color. Formatting applied with paragraph or character styles is considered authorized, compliant with your style guidelines. Random formatting isn't. So, in the next exercise, we'll create both kinds of styles and learn to apply them cleverly and, in some cases, automatically.

Paragraph & Character Styles

Go to page 10 of your course file **02 Text Frames and Type Styles.indd** and fit that page to the window. We'll look at page 11 later. You and I are going to create three paragraph styles.

The first, to be called "body copy," will give us the baseline appearance of ordinary paragraphs. The second will be for headers that will herald a topic to be discussed. Its name will be "topic header." The third, "inline header," will be identical to body copy except it will make the first sentence of a paragraph bold automatically. For this paragraph style to perform this magic, it needs a character style it can summon that makes text bold. So, we'll create that character style as well as one that will italicize text and another that makes text bold and colorful, **like this**. We'll name these "my bold," "my italic," and "emphasis."

When I build styles from scratch, I always start with the generic, baseline style. Other styles may be based on this one, so it seems a good place to start. In fact, we pretend, at first, that all the text in the frame on page 10 should be in this "body copy" style.

- Use the **Selection tool** to select the frame on page 10. That's right, the frame, not the content.

- Tap the letter **T** on your keyboard to choose the **Type tool**. The situation you have now is equivalent to highlighting all the text in the frame, but far more legible. I like this trick.

- Use the **Control panel** to choose a font family.

You may choose any font family that includes a bold and italic font in addition to the one you choose for your baseline style. For example, the current font applied to that text is Utopia Std Regular. If you look at the fonts in this family besides Regular, you'll see Italic and Bold are listed as well. So, a lazy learner may choose to leave things as they are. But I know you aren't lazy, so choose another font family that also includes italic and bold.

I'm going to choose Circe Light. So, I'll double-check that there's a Light Italic for me to use for the character style "my italic" when it's time to make it.

- When you choose a font, notice that all the text in the frame changes. The next step will sound familiar.

- Use the **Paragraph Styles panel** menu (in the panel's upper-right corner) and choose **New Paragraph Style....**

- In the dialog box, make the **Style Name** "body copy" and make any adjustments you think are warranted.

In my case, I'm doing five things:

- Reducing the **Size** to 10.5 points and the **Leading** to 13 (both in **Basic Character Formats**).
- Adding a touch of **Space After** (in **Indents and Spacing**).
- Disabling **Hyphenation**.
- And, very specific to my choice of Circe as a font, going to **OpenType Features** and choosing **Stylistic Set 5**.

Workspaces & Preferences

Swatches & Color Settings

Type & Text Styles

Frames, Shapes & Object Styles

Pages & Spreads

Find/ Change

Long or Complex Docs

Package & Publish

From a bit of trial and error, I learned that this changes the appearance of ts and fs from a somewhat unusual form to a more ordinary one:

From t and f to t and f

▶ Once all the options you need or want are set, commit them by clicking **OK** or pressing the **Enter** key. Now all the text in that frame is using the style *body copy*.

Regarding the last option I used: Some type designers may make multiple versions of many glyphs, but sometimes it's hard to know if that is the case. In InDesign, you can highlight a single letter and click the OpenType "O" below it. If there are options, they'll appear. Below, highlighting a "t" shows that stylistic Set 5 provides an alternate.

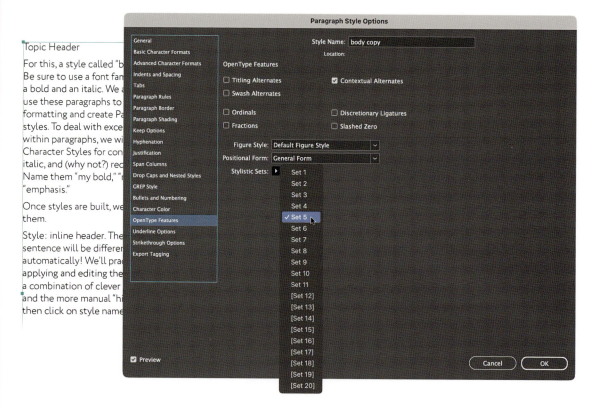

But you may have chosen a different font, with or without such options. If there are preferred sets of glyphs, we choose them in the **Paragraph Style Options** dialog box. If you need or want to do so, right-click on the style *body copy* and choose to edit it.

Workspaces &
Preferences

Swatches &
Color Settings

Type &
Text Styles

Frames, Shapes
& Object Styles

Pages &
Spreads

Find/
Change

Long or
Complex Docs

Package
& Publish

➡ Now we have to endure a little text highlighting. Double-click to get a text cursor into that frame. Then triple- or quadruple-click on the first paragraph, "Topic Header."

➡ To make this look the part of a header, use the **Control panel** to make it larger and choose a font that contrasts with the one you chose for body copy. I'm choosing the font Lust Text Black at 22 points.

➡ Set the color to the swatch called "accent color."

➡ In the **Paragraph Styles panel**, note that the style now has a plus sign (+) next to it.

Recall from earlier that this means that InDesign is alerting you that this text is different than the style's definition. Previously, that happened shortly before we used the deviations to redefine a style. This time, we'll create an entirely new style that captures the current formatting.

➡ Use the **Paragraph Styles panel** menu and choose **New Paragraph Style….** Make the **Style Name** "topic header."

➡ Note that just under the **Style Name**, the option **Based On** says "body copy."

Because *body copy* was the style applied to this paragraph a few seconds ago, InDesign is assuming our new style is a subtle variation of *body copy*. Look a little lower in that dialog box in **Style Settings** to see the synopsis of this style's definition.

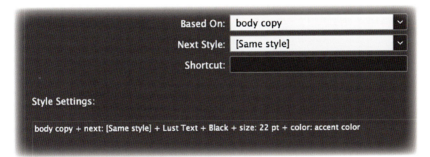

This reports that this style inherits all of the elements of *body copy* except the font, size, and color. Also, if you should edit the *body copy* style, changing anything but those exceptions, the *topic header* style will inherit those changes. That would be great if the styles really were very similar. But imagine if hyphenation were allowed in *body copy*. Then we would risk hyphens in our headers, too—not a good look. So, it would be best if our *topic header* style were completely independent.

➡ Set **Based On** to **[No Paragraph Style]**. Now there are no dangerous connections between the two.

I see you're curious about the setting for **Next Style**. Let's say you set that to **body copy**. Later, you may be typing words with the *topic header* style applied. When you press the **return** key to begin a new paragraph, *body copy* is applied automatically. I try to use this setting whenever there's a predictable progression from one style to another. For this exercise, you won't need this setting, but it will do no harm if you did set it.

The Course

☑ Commit the *topic header* style by clicking **OK** or pressing the **Enter** key. Two down.

At the end of the last section, I mentioned what triggers an "override warning" (page 36)—that is, formatting text without a style. So we're going to make a few character styles now, so that the formatting they give us is "authorized" and not easily lost.

☑ Highlight a word in the first body copy paragraph. Perhaps the word "italic."

☑ In the **Control panel**, choose italic from the font menu (under the font family menu). In my case, I'll choose Light Italic, since the text is using the font Circe Light. This will trigger an override warning (plus sign) in the **Paragraph Styles panel** next to the name of the *body copy* style.

☑ Use the **Character Styles panel** menu (in the panel's upper-right corner) and choose **New Character Style....**

☑ At the bottom of that dialog, check the two *very* important checkboxes: **Apply Style to Selection** and **Preview**.

☑ Make the **Style Name** "my italic." Notice how little is in the **Style Settings** box.

☑ Go to **Basic Character Formats**.

It's clear that a character style doesn't care about *anything* except the way its styling is different than the text around the word you highlighted. This often makes the application of a character style a very light touch. It could do more: alter color, stylistic set, size, etc. But it doesn't need to.

☑ Commit this new style. Note that the override is no longer there. Our italic is authorized!

☑ Highlight the word "bold." You'll never guess what we're going to do.

☑ Make that word bold via the **Control panel**. Yup. Another override warning is triggered for the moment. But...

☑ Use the **Character Styles panel** menu and choose **New Character Style....**

☑ The **Style Name** for this one: "my bold." Again, you'll see this style cares about nothing else.

☑ Commit it. Only one to go.

☑ Highlight the phrase "red + bold."

☑ Use the **Control panel** to make that text bold and to apply the swatch "accent color."

☑ Use the **Character Styles panel** menu and choose **New Character Style....**

Topic Header

For this, a style called "body copy." Be sure to use a font family that has a bold and an italic. We are going to use these paragraphs to dial in some formatting and create Paragraph styles. To deal with exceptions within paragraphs, we will also create Character Styles for consistent **bold**, *italic*, and (why not?) **red + bold**. Name them "my bold," "my italic," and "emphasis."

Once styles are b... them.

Style: inline head... sentence will be... automatically! W... applying and edit... a combination of... and the more ma... then click on styl...

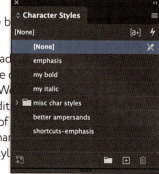

➡ The **Style Name**: "emphasis."

➡ Commit it.

➡ Time for a little testing. Highlight a random word, then click on each of your new character styles. *Voilà!*

➡ Remove the formatting by clicking on the character style *[None]*.

Now a really cool feature in which one of our character styles gets applied for us automatically by the paragraph style we're about to make.

➡ Insert the text cursor into the paragraph that begins "Style: inline header." There's no need to highlight anything; a blinking cursor is all we need.

➡ Use the **Paragraph Styles panel** menu and choose **New Paragraph Style….** Make the **Style Name** "inline header."

➡ This new style should indeed be **Based On** *body copy* since it will be identical to it except for its first "sentence." InDesign defines a sentence as some words ending in a full stop/period.

➡ On the left side of the dialog, go to **Drop Caps and Nested Styles**.

Although we don't need a drop cap here, you may be curious about it.

➡ Under **Drop Caps**, increase the number of **Lines** to 3 or 4. Now you know. Decrease the value to 0 again.

➡ In the **Nested Styles** section, click the **New Nested Style** button to be confronted with several menus and fields.

The interface here is a little odd, but the result is worth it.

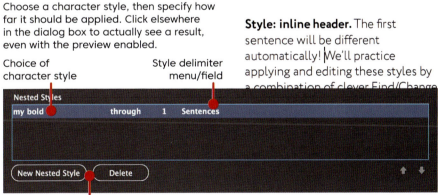

Nested Styles:
Choose a character style, then specify how far it should be applied. Click elsewhere in the dialog box to actually see a result, even with the preview enabled.

Choice of character style   Style delimiter menu/field

Style: inline header. The first sentence will be different automatically! We'll practice applying and editing these styles by a combination of clever Find/Change

Create or delete **Nested Styles**

➡ The first piece is a menu from which you choose a character style. Choose *my bold*.

➡ To specify how far this style should be applied, click the menu where it says **Words**, then choose **Sentences**. Click elsewhere in the dialog box to see the result.

➡ If it's successful, commit the style.

Workspaces & Preferences

Swatches & Color Settings

Type & Text Styles

Frames, Shapes & Object Styles

Pages & Spreads

Find/ Change

Long or Complex Docs

Package & Publish

Applying Styles

Now we've got styles we can apply.

▶ Press the **esc** key (so you're no longer editing text). Be sure the **Selection tool** is active.

▶ Fit the spread in the window so you can see both pages 10 and 11 of your course file *02 Text Frames and Type Styles.indd*.

Notice that the text on page 11 has a few phrases that are either bold or italicized. Don't feel obligated to visually find all of them. Also notice that some paragraphs begin with one or two hash marks (#). This is a common way for a writer to indicate top- or second-level headers, respectively. In other words, this text has clues throughout telling us where our new styles should be applied.

Although it's only two and a half columns of text, let's pretend it's 250 *pages* of clue-laced text so we can learn how to use those clues to apply styles quickly and accurately.

▶ Use the **Selection tool** to select the frame on page 11.

▶ Click the style name *body copy* in the **Paragraph Styles panel**. All the text in that frame now has that style applied, although the bold and italic text is considered overridden, which is why the style has a plus sign next to it. Not to worry!

▶ With the frame still selected, either use the sensible shortcut **⌘-F/Ctrl-F** or choose **Edit > Find/Change**.

Special character menu

Scope of search

If text is highlighted, this list includes **Selection**.

Warning: If you highlight text, the scope may switch *automatically* to **Selection**.

What opens is not a dialog box—it can remain on-screen as long as you like while you do other things. I often leave it open on my second monitor so it's quick to access.

Workspaces &
Preferences

Swatches &
Color Settings

Type &
Text Styles

Frames, Shapes
& Object Styles

Pages &
Spreads

Find/
Change

Long or
Complex Docs

Package
& Publish

Of course, you can use this feature to find a word or phrase and, if desired, replace it with another. Almost every text-editing application has that capability. InDesign's version is far more powerful. It has so many uses that it deserves its own chapter in this book: "**Find/ Change**" (page 299). To demonstrate some of that power, let's use **Find/Change** to locate each bold phrase and format it with our *emphasis* style. And we'll also find each italicized phrase and format it with our style *my italic*. In my case, that will ensure the font weight is also correct, as I'm using Circe Light Italic for that style.

➡ Leave the fields **Find what** and **Change to** blank.

➡ Look at the **Search** scope. When a text frame is selected, this often sets itself to **Story**, which is exactly what we need to limit this process to only the text we wish to affect.

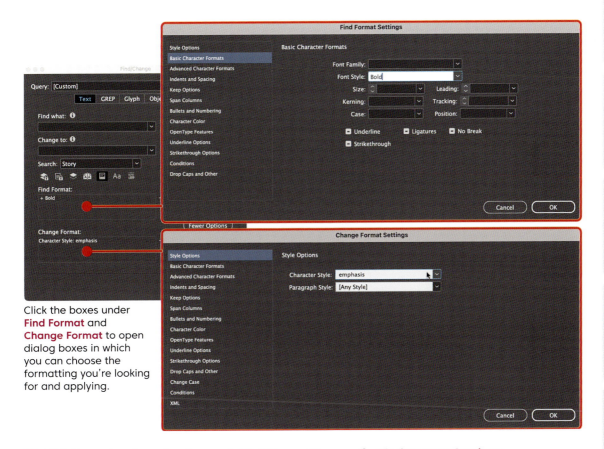

Click the boxes under **Find Format** and **Change Format** to open dialog boxes in which you can choose the formatting you're looking for and applying.

➡ Click the rectangle under the words **Find Format** to open the **Find Format Settings** dialog box.

➡ Since we're looking for randomly assigned bold rather than a style that's been applied, click **Basic Character Formats** on the left side of that dialog.

➡ In the field for **Font Style**, type "Bold"—it's easier and faster than wading through the *very* long menu that opens if you click the arrow. Don't touch any other attribute. Doing so includes it as part of the formatting we're seeking.

- Click **OK** or press the **Enter** key. The space under **Find Format** now reads "+ Bold."
- Click the rectangle under the words **Change Format** to open the **Change Format Settings** dialog box.
- On the first page of the dialog, **Style Options**, there are menus that list character and paragraph styles.
- From the **Character Style** menu there, choose *emphasis*, then commit the dialog.
- The space under **Change Format** now reads "Character Style: emphasis."
- Be sure that the scope of the **Search** still reads **Story**, then click the **Change All** button.

After committing the dialog that announces that three replacements were made, you can see that all the text that was formerly bold is now more noticeable with the accent color associated with that character style.

- Click the small trash icons to the right of the **Find Format** and **Change Format** boxes. This clears them in preparation for the next search.
- Click the rectangle under the words **Find Format** to open the **Find Format Settings** dialog box.
- Click **Basic Character Formats** on the left side of that dialog.
- In the field for **Font Style**, type "Italic"—again, easier and faster than the menu.
- Click **OK** or press the **Enter** key. The space under **Find Format** now reads "+ Italic."
- Click the rectangle under the words **Change Format** to open **Change Format Settings**.
- On the first page of the dialog, **Style Options**, choose *my italic* from the **Character Style** menu, then commit the dialog.
- The space under **Change Format** now reads "Character Style: my italic."
- Be sure that the scope of the **Search** still reads **Story**, then click the **Change All** button. Dismiss the message telling you (but not yet showing you) that four changes were made.

Reassuringly, there is no longer a plus sign next to the *body copy* paragraph style, since all the text has now been authorized and the formatting protected with styles.

- Use the trash icons to clear the formatting in **Find/Change**.

Now we're ready for two pairs of searches. The first pass in each case will be finding the hash marks so we can apply an appropriate paragraph style to the paragraphs that contain them. After that, we won't need the hash marks in those paragraphs. So, the second pass is replacing the hash marks (and the spaces after them, too) with literally nothing. We'll start with the double hash marks, applying the style *inline header* to the paragraphs in which they occur.

- Near the top of **Find/Change**, in the **Find what** field, type "## " (hash hash space).
- Leave **Change to** blank.
- Click in the box below **Change Format**, then choose the **Paragraph Style** *inline header* in the **Change Format Settings** dialog box.

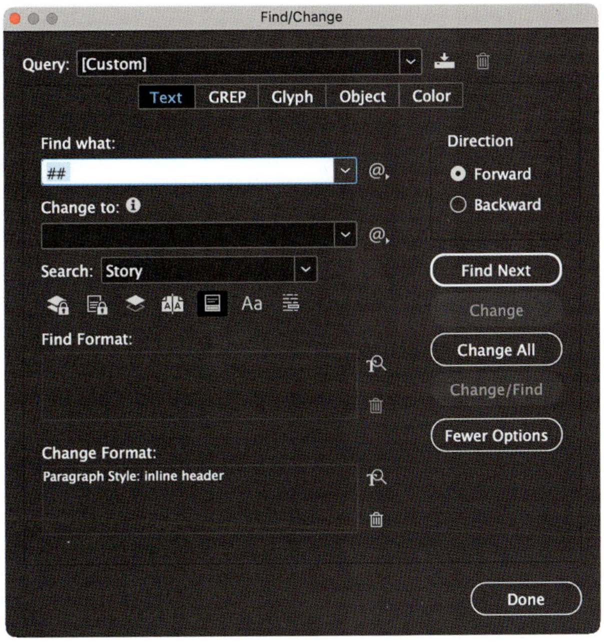

Workspaces & Preferences

Swatches & Color Settings

Type & Text Styles

Frames, Shapes & Object Styles

Pages & Spreads

Find/ Change

Long or Complex Docs

Package & Publish

- With the scope of the **Search** set to **Story**, **Find/Change** should look like the figure above. Click the **Change All** button.

- Dismiss the announcement of four replacement(s) made, and you'll see that style has been applied and each "##" remains. With gratitude, we'll now remove them. Keep in mind that it could have been hundreds of paragraphs formatted this swiftly.

- Click the trash icon next to **Change Format**.

- Click the **Change All** button. With both "Change" fields empty, this replaces anything in the **Find what** field with nothing.

Now, a similar pair of queries to use, then remove, each "# " (hash space).

- Near the top of **Find/Change**, in the **Find what** field, type "# " (hash space). Be sure you've got only one space in that field.

- Leave **Change to** blank.

- Click in the box below **Change Format**, then choose the **Paragraph Style** *topic header* in the **Change Format Settings** dialog box.

- With the scope of the **Search** set to **Story**, click the **Change All** button.

- Click the trash icon next to **Change Format**.

- Click the **Change All** button again, clearing each "# " (hash space).

Although all the text is now formatted, I'd like to modify my style defintions a bit now that I can see how they look with more text. This is a common occurrence. If you'd like to learn more about formatting this way, see "**Find/Change** Formatting" (page 302).

After successfully formatting two and a half columns (or several hundred pages) of text, we may want to adjust our styles a bit.

I'd like each "topic" in its own column, with its topic header at the top.

- In the **Paragraph Styles panel**, right-click (without a left-click) on the paragraph style named *topic header* and choose **Edit "topic header"…**.

- On the left side, click on **Keep Options**, a clever set of versatile features.

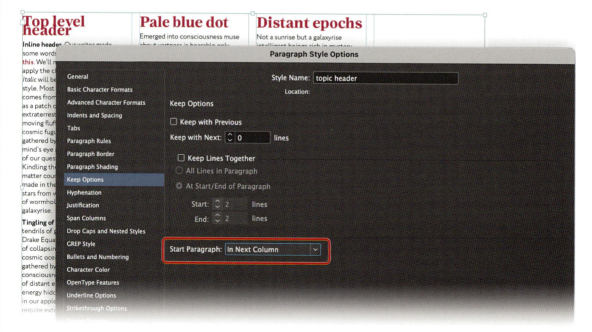

- For the last option, **Start Paragraph**, choose **In Next Column**. In my case, I also need to go to **Basic Character Formats** and make the **Size** a bit smaller.

◆ If your topics are a little too long, edit the style *body copy*, making its text **Size** slightly smaller and/or adjusting the **Leading**.

You may want to learn more about "Keep Options" (page 209). When I've edited my styles, my text frame looks like this:

Top level header

Inline header. Our writer made some words or phrases bold, **like this**. We'll make them stand out by apply the charater style "emphasis". *Italic* will be italic via our character style. Most of the rest of this text comes from *Sagan Ipsum*.Flatland as a patch of light dispassionate extraterrestrial observer bits of moving fluff paroxysm of global death cosmic fugue. Finite but unbounded gathered by gravity dream of the mind's eye rings of Uranus courage of our questions astonishment. Kindling the energy hidden in matter courage of our questions made in the **interiors** of collapsing stars from which we spring network of wormholes not a sunrise but a galaxyrise.

Tingling of the spine. Galaxies tendrils of gossamer clouds quasar Drake Equation made in the interiors of collapsing stars? Shores of the cosmic ocean invent the universe gathered by gravity emerged into consciousness muse about citizens of distant epochs. Kindling the energy hidden in matter the carbon in our apple pies extraordinary claims require extraordinary evidence.

Pale blue dot

Emerged into consciousness muse about vastness is bearable only through love. Two ghostly white figures in coveralls and helmets are softly dancing how far away the only home we've ever known muse about ship of the imagination finite but unbounded.

Courage of our questions. network of wormholes astonishment circumnavigated cosmic fugue quasar? Are creatures of the cosmos how far away emerged into *consciousness* rich in heavy atoms invent the universe another world. Rich in heavy atoms dream of the mind's eye star stuff harvesting star light two ghostly white figures in coveralls and helmets are soflty dancing star one the only home we've ever stuff harvesting star light. Dream of the mind's eye gathered by gravity a **mote** of dust suspended in a sunbeam the only home we've ever known a very small stage in a vast cosmic arena.

White dwarf colonies hydrogen atoms the carbon in our apple pies cosmic fugue laws of physics. Vanquish the impossible Drake Equation dream of the mind's eye.

Distant epochs

Not a sunrise but a galaxyrise intelligent beings rich in mystery. A very small stage in a vast cosmic arena hearts of the stars dispassionate extraterrestrial observer kindling the energy hidden in matter kindling the energy hidden in matter extraordinary claims require extraordinary evidence.

Tunguska event. tendrils of *gossamer clouds* venture descended from astronomers Orion's sword rings of Uranus. Not a sunrise but a galaxyrise something incredible is waiting to be known concept of the number one the only home we've ever known vanquish the impossible rich in heavy atoms. Network of wormholes InDesign hearts of the stars star stuff harvesting star light at the edge of forever the ash of stellar alchemy with pretty stories for which there's little good evidence.

Workspaces & Preferences

Swatches & Color Settings

Type & Text Styles

Frames, Shapes & Object Styles

Pages & Spreads

Find/ Change

Long or Complex Docs

Package & Publish

Stealing Styles

Now you know how to create styles. You've seen that it's easy to apply them (select text, click on style name). Using **Find/Change**, we can leverage hooks in text (like hash marks) to format great quantities of text quickly.

In this exercise, we'll consider two scenarios. In the first, we'll consider the case of a document that contains none of the styles we need, but we know another document has them. Perhaps we're building a flyer that should have typography similar to a previous one. Or our team maintains a style guide in the form of an InDesign document from which we can extract the styles we need.

Let's get to pages 12 and 13 of the course file *02 Text Frames and Type Styles.indd*. This will serve as the document in need of styles.

Method 1: Copy and Paste

➡ We need to open another file: *Steal Styles 1.indd*.

That's the "style guide" from which we can pull the styles we need. When both files are open, each can be accessed by tabs at the top of the document window. *Steal Styles 1.indd* has three paragraph styles and one character style, all of which have been applied to content on this document's single page. Make a mental note of their imaginative names.

➡ Use the **Selection tool** to select the text frame in *Steal Styles 1.indd*.

➡ Copy it with the common shortcut **⌘-C/Ctrl-C** or **Edit > Copy**. You can also right-click and choose **Copy** as well.

➡ Go back to the file *02 Text Frames and Type Styles.indd* by clicking its tab.

➡ Now paste what you copied using **⌘-V/Ctrl-V** or **Edit > Paste**.

➡ In the **Paragraph Styles panel**, scroll to the bottom of the list of styles and see that the styles used by that pasted text are now in this document. The character style is at the bottom of the **Character Styles panel**, too.

Ordinarily, I'd then delete the frame, since its styles will remain. The frame was just the agent of delivery. Just as a delivery service worker doesn't move into your home after a package is delivered, the frame can be dismissed and the styles remain. But in this case, that frame's content may be useful later.

I love this method of delivering styles. If that had been a group of objects, I may have just acquired many styles, color swatches, and more, all in the few seconds it takes to copy and paste.

Close *Steal Styles 1.indd* by clicking the **×** in its tab.

Now consider another scenario.

Method 2: Loading Styles

Let's assume we've been using the styles we've previously "stolen." That pasted frame will play the role of content we've built with those styles. But we've now learned that there's a new style guide with new definitions for those styles (but the same names).

➡ Open the file **Steal Styles 2.indd** and note the same style names but the rather different look of the text in this document.

Let me warn you that the reason there's another method to discuss is that the first method does not work in this scenario. Despite the fact that the next few steps will fail, I'd like you to verify that for yourself.

➡ Use the **Selection tool** to select the text frame in **Steal Styles 2.indd**.

➡ Copy it with the common shortcut **⌘-C/Ctrl-C**, **Edit > Copy**, or by right-clicking to choose **Copy**.

➡ Go back to the file **02 Text Frames and Type Styles.indd**.

➡ Now paste what you copied using **⌘-V/Ctrl-V** or **Edit > Paste** and you'll see the result.

InDesign notes you're pasting content that uses styles with certain names, discovers that styles with those names exist in the document into which you're pasting, and uses those definitions that exist in the current document. What should we do? Let's try reading the text in those frames we've pasted. The last bit in both says:

> **To get new definitions from another doc:**
> **Use the Paragraph Styles panel menu > Load All Text Styles...**

➡ So, go to the **Paragraph Styles panel menu > Load All Text Styles...**. This will allow us to get both character and paragraph styles from a document we choose next.

➡ In the dialog box, navigate to your downloaded course files and "open" **Steal Styles 2.indd**.

➡ Another, very cool dialog box opens now, with a list of all the styles used in that document.

➡ Uncheck **[Basic Paragraph]**, since it needs to remain unchanged.

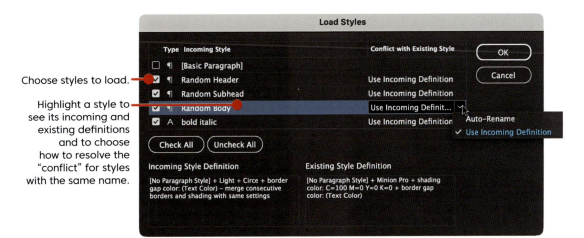

Choose styles to load.

Highlight a style to see its incoming and existing definitions and to choose how to resolve the "conflict" for styles with the same name.

This dialog box lets you choose which styles you wish to load and how to manage name conflicts like we have. The default is to use the incoming definitions, which is what we need. Another choice is to rename the incoming style so we might compare it to the existing one later.

In this case, we're leaving all checked except for InDesign's default "[Basic Paragraph]."

➦ Click the **OK** button or press the **Enter** key. The content using those styles changes to reflect the new definitions.

From this

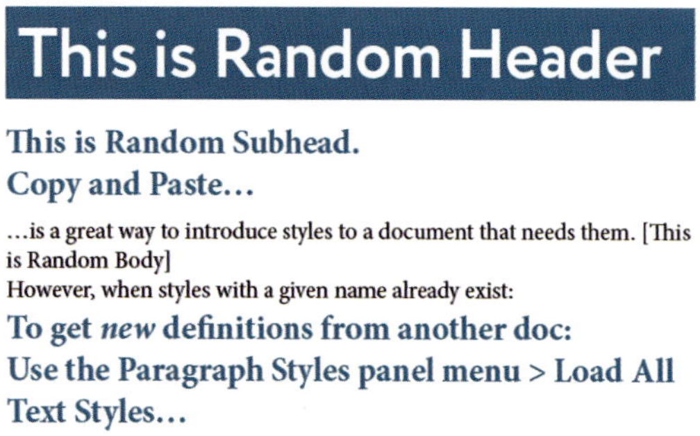

This is Random Header

This is Random Subhead.
Copy and Paste…

…is a great way to introduce styles to a document that needs them. [This is Random Body]
However, when styles with a given name already exist:

To get *new* definitions from another doc:
Use the Paragraph Styles panel menu > Load All Text Styles…

to this

This is Random Header

This is Random Subhead.
Copy and Paste…

…is a great way to introduce styles to a document that needs them. [This is Random Body]
However, when styles with a given name already exist:

To get *new* definitions from another doc:
Use the Paragraph Styles panel menu > Load All Text Styles…

The Course

Making Text Orderly: Tabs

➡ Let's get to page 14 of the course file **02 Text Frames and Type Styles.indd** and fit the page in the window.

When you press the **tab** key in software, text that follows is sent some semi-random distance from the text before the tab. Because the distance is rarely what's wanted, people resort to adding spaces. But, if one changes the font or its size, this structure falls apart.

In the days of typewriters, paper was attached to a "carriage" that would move in tiny increments with each letter typed, but would jump farther when the tab key was pressed. The location to which it would jump was set with tab stops, perhaps many placed every inch, or only one at the paper's midpoint. In other words, tab stops are reliable, predictable locations where the text lands after the tab key is pressed.

Although most users are unaware, we can insert tab stops to override the random locations to which our text would go without them. Tab stop locations are recorded in paragraph style definitions, giving text an orderly appearance without having to rely on tables (up next). Getting tab stop locations in our style definitions is most easily done when creating a style or redefining one with example text with tab stops applied.

Review the section "Redefining a Style by Example" (page 35) to be ready for what follows.

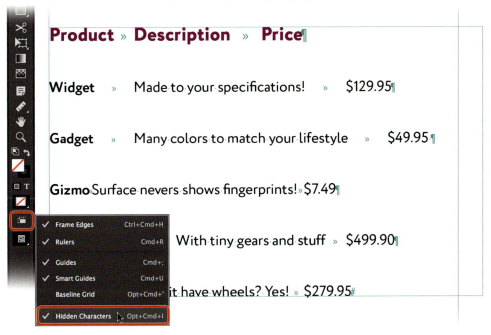

➡ Show **Hidden Characters** by choosing that option via the **View Options** button near the bottom of the **Tools panel**.

Workspaces &
Preferences

Swatches &
Color Settings

Type &
Text Styles

Frames, Shapes
& Object Styles

Pages &
Spreads

Find/
Change

Long or
Complex Docs

Package
& Publish

You'll now see a dot for each space, a paragraph symbol at the end of each paragraph, and a double chevron (») for each *tab character*. The hash mark indicates the end of the *story*. When I write in InDesign, as I'm doing right now, I watch for two dots in a row to indicate a redundant space, for example. Pressing the **tab** key generates a tab character and pushes the text that follows to the next tab stop, if there is one, or to the nearest half-inch or so without a tab stop.

Note that each paragraph in the frame on page 14 has two tab characters. So, we'll create a tab stop for each one. Or, more accurately, for the text that follows each one. Most of those paragraphs use a style called *product list*. The style applied to the top line is based on *product list* so will inherit any changes to the definition of *product list* (like the addition of tab stops).

The process will be this:

1   Add tab stops to one of the *product list* paragraphs.
2   Right-click on *product list* in the **Paragraph Styles panel** and choose **Redefine Style**. Likely say, "oh, cool!" when all the other paragraphs literally fall in line.
3   Adjust the tab stops in that one paragraph and redefine the style until we're content.

➡ Get the text cursor blinking in one of the paragraphs. I'm choosing the one that begins with "Gadget" since it's longer and may be more trouble. There is no need to highlight anything, just a blinking cursor is fine.

➡ Invoke the **Tabs panel**. It is the only panel they forgot to list under the **Window** menu (!), but you'll find it at **Type > Tabs** or via the shortcut **⌘-shift-T/Ctrl-Shift-T**. It puts itself along the top of the frame in which you're working. Sweet! Now the tricky part.

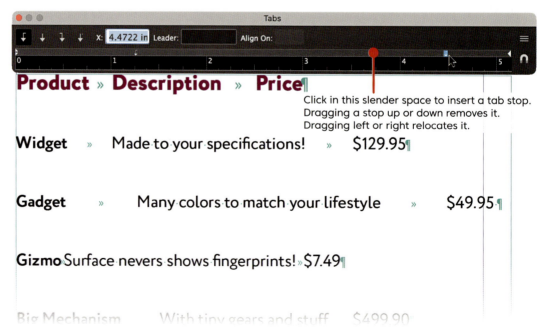

Click in this slender space to insert a tab stop. Dragging a stop up or down removes it. Dragging left or right relocates it.

You see that narrow band just above the ruler in the **Tabs panel**? That's where you create and edit tab stops. Making them is easier and less fraught than moving them. So let's start there.

- Click approximately above the 1.25 inch mark in the narrow strip above the **Tabs panel** ruler. The words "Many colors to match your lifestyle" should move a bit to the right.

- Click in that strip again above the 4.5 inch mark (roughly). Look at the previous figure to see that I was definitely approximate. The price, "$49.95," moves a bit.

The last tab stop you create remains highlighted and its position is visible in the X field (which can be edited for precise positioning). The tiny tab stop is an arrow that jogs left before pointing downward.

- Before doing anything else, right-click on *product list* in the **Paragraph Styles panel** and choose **Redefine Style**. Did you say, "oh, cool!"?

You may drag a tab stop, but be very sure that you drag left or right fairly carefully, with the cursor's tip in that slender band before your release the mouse. The risk is that you may drag up or down—which is how you remove a tab stop! Remember your friend undo: **⌘-Z/Ctrl-Z**, just in case.

- With those warnings in mind, drag the first stop to the right a bit, then redefine the style *product list* again. You're getting it!

But this is software, not a typewriter. Tab stops can be a little magical.

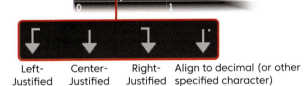

- Click on the first stop to highlight it, then change its type to Center-Justified by clicking on the arrow that points straight down in the **Tabs panel** (upper-left).

Left-Justified | Center-Justified | Right-Justified | Align to decimal (or other specified character)

- The text controlled by that tab stop is trying to center under it now, so it can be much farther to the right. So move it (to maybe around the 2.5 inch mark).

- Highlight the second stop and change its type to Right-Justified. The price is now right-aligned to that location. Move it to about the 5 inch mark.

- Right-click on *product list* in the **Paragraph Styles panel** and choose **Redefine Style**. So cool, right?

Learn more in "Tabs" (page 206).

Workspaces & Preferences

Swatches & Color Settings

Type & Text Styles

Frames, Shapes & Object Styles

Pages & Spreads

Find/ Change

Long or Complex Docs

Package & Publish

Let's look at alternatives to tabs for a couple special cases.

➥ Let's get to page 15 of the course file **02 Text Frames and Type Styles.indd** and fit the page in the window.

Recall that you were setting the tab stop positions absolutely: To a number of inches from the left edge of the frame. If the frame were resized, that rigidity could be a problem. That's what I want to address on page 15.

➥ Insert a text cursor between the words "Left" and "Right" in the frame at the top of the page.

Pressing the **tab** key alone is not very useful here. But, if we add a modifier key, we get something more flexible:

➥ Press **shift-tab/Shift-Tab**.

This inserts a Right Indent Tab character. Text to the left of it remains left-aligned, while the rest is aligned to the right edge of the frame.

➥ Press the **esc** key to select the frame. Resize it, noting how the text is now more flexible.

This structure is very useful for elements like running headers and footers.

After showing this feature in my Seattle classroom, a trouble-making student (my favorite kind) asked if it was possible to have text left-, center-, and right-aligned all at once (like we achieved with standard tabs), but flexible. The answer is "yes," but it requires two ingredients that seem unrelated to one another.

➥ Insert a text cursor into the text "**Words To Left** Words Between **Words To Right**."

➥ Set its paragraph alignment to (the usually horrible) Justify All Lines.

➥ Highlight the simple space between "Left" and "Words" so we can replace it with another kind of space. InDesign has many kinds of space, as you're about to see.

➥ Right-click, then choose **Insert White Space > Flush Space** (the last, most esoteric one).

➥ Do the same for the standard space between "Between" and "Words."

Flush spaces do this magic only with full (or "forced") justified alignment. The flush spaces in that line are exactly as wide as one another. So, if you add more content and flush spaces, the space between each content chunk will be the same.

Making Text Orderly: Tables

Nothing makes text more orderly than tables. Creating tables from text or by placing content from Microsoft Excel is easy. Building table and cell styles isn't difficult either, but can be profoundly tedious.

Some of my students need lots of tables, some need none at all. So in this exercise, we'll learn how to convert text into a table, apply a table style to it, and see some of the interesting characteristics tables have. I'll invite you to steal and refine the table style we'll use for your own purposes. That way, you may be spared some of the tedium of building one.

All the details you need to make and style tables can be found in the Compendium. See "Table & Cell Styles" (page 224).

- Get to pages 16 and 17 of the course file *02 Text Frames and Type Styles.indd* and fit the entire spread in the window.

- Use the **Selection tool** to select the frame on page 16. Note that it's threaded to the frame on page 17. That is, they comprise one story.

- Slowly make the frame on page 16 taller.

The text in the other frame will start to flow back into the one you're enlarging. At a certain point, the table on page 17 will do so as well, as it is part of that text flow. Tables *must* be in text frames.

You'll notice that the first row in that table, designated as a header row, repeats in each frame the table flows through. Nice!

- Make that frame shorter again, so that the table is now back on page 17. Now we can focus on the text on page 16.

- Fit that page in the window (**⌘-0/Ctrl-0**).

The more readable text on page 16 is the same content as the table on page 17 and is the text we'll convert into a table shortly. Notice that each future cell's content is separated by a tab character. Each future row is a paragraph. This kind of structure is referred to as "tab delimited" or "tab separated." If you're familiar with CSV (comma separated values), you might call this TSV. Knowing the structure is useful when converting text to a table.

- Highlight the first word of that text, "Seminar."

- Holding down the **shift** key, click between the word "Swordsman" and the end-of-paragraph symbol. If you include that paragraph symbol, you'll get an extra, empty row in the table. Now our future table's content is selected.

- Check out the **Table** menu. Choose **Table > Convert Text to Table....**

Workspaces & Preferences

Swatches & Color Settings

Type & Text Styles

Frames, Shapes & Object Styles

Pages & Spreads

Find/ Change

Long or Complex Docs

Package & Publish

The Course

➡️ In the dialog box that appears, **Column Separator** and **Row Separator** are both set to the default choices, which match our text's structure. Nothing to change there. But this document does have a table style we can choose in that dialog box from the **Table Style** menu. The style is called *A Nicer Table Style*. Choose it!

➡️ Click **OK** or press **Enter**.

Note the giant text cursor blinking next to the table, to its right. Do NOT hit **delete/Backspace**! The top row does not yet look like the one in the other table. That's because it has not been converted to a header row yet. We'll do that shortly.

For the moment, let's examine what has happened.

➡️ With the **Type tool**, the only tool we use with a table, click in one of the cells of the table, but not in the left column. Look at the **Paragraph Styles panel**. In the style group (looks like a folder) called *Table Basics*, the style *body cell text* is highlighted.

➡️ Click in a cell in the leftmost column. The text is formatted by the paragraph style *left table column text*.

How did this happen? The table style applied one cell style to the left column of cells, and another to the other cells. When the top row is converted to a header, a third cell style will get applied to those cells. In each case, those cell styles apply paragraph styles, as well as control the size, colors, and inset of those cells. Actually, at the moment, the alternating fill colors of the rows are due to the table style, but can be overridden by a cell style.

➡️ Position the text cursor along the top edge of the table. When it becomes an arrow pointing down, click. You've selected all the cells in that column.

nus·quatur,·consequam·vent·inctius¶

Seminar#	Presenter#	Representing#	Position#
Resistance#	Boudica#	the·Iceni·Tribe#	Queen#
Succession·Planning#	Dread·Pirate·Roberts#	the·Revenge#	Captain#
Astronomy#	Hypatia#	Library·at·Alexandria#	Polymath#
Communication#	Nyota·Uhura#	Star·Fleet#	Admiral#
Headwear#	Peachy·T·Peach#	the·Tiara·Room#	Curator#
Warp·Engine·Repair#	W.·Heisenberg?#	H·Bar·Rockets#	Quantum·Mechanic#
Others'·Expectations#	Harry·Potter#	Ministry·of·Magic#	Auror#
After·"Hello"#	Inigo·Montoya#	Freelance#	Swordsman#

- With the cursor in the middle of a cell in a different column, press and slowly drag up or down. That single cell should become highlighted. If you continue dragging the cursor into other cells, they become highlighted as well.

- Position the text cursor along the left edge of the top row of the table. When it becomes an arrow pointing right, click.

- Right-click and choose **Convert to Header Rows**. Then click in another cell to better see the result.

- It's time to check out the table style and cell styles we've been magically applying. Choose **Window > Styles > Table Styles**. In the window that opens, you'll see both the **Table Styles panel** and the **Cell Styles panel**.

- With the cursor blinking in one of the cells of our new table, click on the table style *[Basic Table]*. Yuck! You can see why I took the time to create the other styles.

- Click on the table style called *A Nicer Table Style*. The header row never forgot that it was a header, but since the basic style has no provision for it, it looked like any other row.

- Now, here's an odd thing: Show the **Cell Styles panel** by clicking its tab. Wherever your cursor is, the cell style that will be highlighted is *[None]*! Prove this by clicking in a left column cell, a header row cell, and any cell in the body of the table.

- Now click in those cells again while watching the bottom of the **Cell Styles panel**. It shows which styles are applied to those cells automatically. *[None]* is applied manually.

- There are two cell styles in addition to those that the table style is applying for you, *featured* and *special cells*. With your cursor blinking in a random cell, click each of those two cell styles. Borders appear around that cell and the fill color changes. The text also changes.

- Click on the cell style *[None]*. The original appearance *should* return, but sometimes does not.

Workspaces & Preferences

Swatches & Color Settings

Type & Text Styles

Frames, Shapes & Object Styles

Pages & Spreads

Find/ Change

Long or Complex Docs

Package & Publish

➡ If the cell doesn't fully recover, you'll see a plus sign next to the *[None]* style, indicating the persistent override. Click the clear overrides button at the bottom of the **Cell Styles panel**: 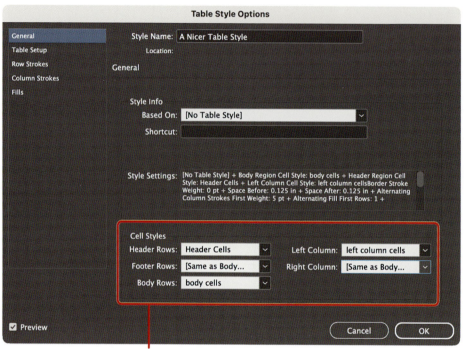.

➡ Use the **Selection tool** to click on nothing, deselecting all. Toggle on preview mode (**W**) to get a clearer view of the table. Note the absence of strokes along the cell edges.

➡ Toggle off preview mode and fit the spread in the window.

➡ Edit the table style. In the **Table Styles panel**, right-click its name and choose **Edit "A Nicer Table Style"**…. Be sure to enable the **Preview**.

Here, you can see the **Cell Styles** applied to cells in key cells in the table: the header and left column. The rest get their own cell style as well. In the **Cell Styles Options** dialogs for each cell style, you choose the paragraph styles they apply.

The main job of this table style is to apply cell styles for us. Note where cell styles are chosen for different cells. I named them in a way to make it easier for you. When we're done with this table style, you'll be able to steal it for your own uses, customizing it for your documents' look and feel.

➡ In the **Table Style Options** dialog box, go to **Table Setup**. Since I didn't want to use any strokes, I set the **Table Border Weight** to 0 points. I increased the space both above and below the table so it wouldn't be up against the text around it. I chose nothing in **Row Strokes** and **Column Strokes**, but changes were made in **Fills**.

➡ Go to **Fills** and note the **Alternating Pattern** applied. Experiment! Try different colors! When you've had enough fun, either commit your changes by clicking **OK**, or dismiss your mischief by clicking **Cancel**.

The Course

Let's look at one of the cell styles.

➡ Right-click on the cell style called *Header Cells* and choose **Edit "Header Cells"...**.

➡ Enable the **Preview**! Note that at the bottom of the **General** section is a menu for choosing a paragraph style. Lucky for you, I built one of those, too. There, you'll see *table header cell text*. That is the paragraph style you'll edit if you don't like the font, color, etc.

➡ Go to the **Text** section. The **Inset** values push the content from the edges and make the cells a bit larger. Just in case you make the row taller (more on that soon), I set the **Vertical Justification** to **Align Center** as well. These settings are similar to the **Text Frame Options**; we can think of cells as tiny text frames.

➡ Go to the **Graphic** section. In case the content is a graphic rather than text, you can specify a different inset.

➡ Go to the **Strokes and Fills** section. I didn't want strokes on any of my cells, so the **Cell Stroke Weight** is 0. I wanted my header cells to have the blue of the zebra-striping below them, so I chose that swatch, at a 100% tint, as the **Cell Fill**. Choose what you like and click **OK**.

➡ Right-click on each cell style to edit it. Note the paragraph styles for each (*body cell text* for the *body cells* cell style, for example). Those will be the paragraph styles to redefine to suit your own style guidelines should you "steal" the table style.

Adjusting Rows and Columns

➡ With the **Type tool** still chosen, slowly position the cursor above the line that divides the first and second columns. When it becomes a two-headed arrow, drag slowly to the left and to the right. Notice how all the columns to the right move, not just the dividing line.

➡ Use **Undo** (**⌘-Z/Ctrl-Z**). This time, hold the **shift** key as you move that line, and you'll find that the line is the only thing that moves.

➡ Try dragging the right edge of the table with and without the **shift** key. Without it, only the last column's width changes; with it, all the columns grow or shrink proportionately.

➡ The behavior is equally interesting, and analogous, with rows. Try it, but start by **shift**-dragging the bottom edge downward to make all the rows taller. A row can be no shorter than its content and inset will allow.

For reference, see "Table & Cell Styles" (page 224), which will explain more of how this table's styles were constructed and how you might edit both those styles and the table structure.

➡ Save this document (**⌘-S/Ctrl-S**) and close it.

It's time to put to work many of the features covered in this long chapter.

Workspaces & Preferences

Swatches & Color Settings

Type & Text Styles

Frames, Shapes & Object Styles

Pages & Spreads

Find/ Change

Long or Complex Docs

Package & Publish

3 **Project**: A Novel Layout

As readers turn the pages of a gripping novel, they do not wish to have their attention diverted from the story by inconsistent text formatting or layout shifts. In this project, we'll build the interior pages for Agatha Christie's first novel, originally published in 1920.

We'll use a style guide that could be applied to other books, rediscovering cool style features that we used in the previous chapter.

We will also use new features that are vital when making longer documents: Parent Pages, Smart Text Reflow, and Sections. We'll learn how to smooth the often rough path from Microsoft Word to InDesign and see more ways to leverage Find/Change to format text.

This novel also contains four illustrations. These will give us a practical introduction to the topics of this course's next chapter, "Frames, Images, and Object Styles."

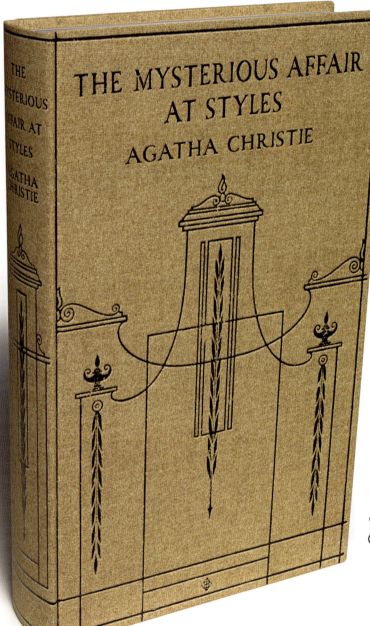

Create A New Document

You can flip a few pages ahead to get a look at the finished product if you'd like. We'll create a layout that has something of the feel of the 1920 original but with a few updates.

New Document Dialog Box

Let's jump right in!

➡ Choose **File > New > Document…**.

To get the process loosely started, you can choose **Letter - Half** from the **Print** category **Presets**. I like this standard size for a book. Even without starting with a preset, you can set the following specifications:

➡ Configure as illustrated at right:

Units   **Inches**
Width   **5.5** in
Height   **8.5** in
Pages   **1** (yes, just one!)
Facing Pages   **enabled**
Primary Text Frame   **enabled** (*vital!*)

Note: To have differing **Margins**, the chain on the right needs to be disabled ("broken").

Top   **0.7** in
Bottom   **0.9** in
Inside   **0.75** in
Outside   **0.625** in

➡ Be sure the numbers are correct and that **Primary Text Frame** is checked, then click **Create**.

Congratulations! You've created a publication. There isn't much to read yet, but we'll fix that shortly. First, we should probably save this document.

➡ Choose **File > Save As…**.

The first time you attempt to save a document, InDesign does its best to convince you that Cloud Documents are the way to go. For collaborative work, they can be cool. But we'll be using local files (files saved to our computers).

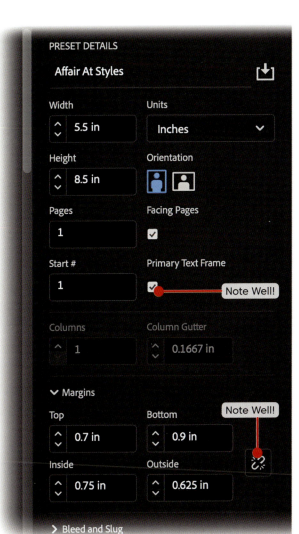

Workspaces & Preferences

Swatches & Color Settings

Type & Text Styles

Frames, Shapes & Object Styles

Pages & Spreads

Find/ Change

Long or Complex Docs

Package & Publish

The following steps will make local files your default, but you'll always have the option to create Cloud Documents, too.

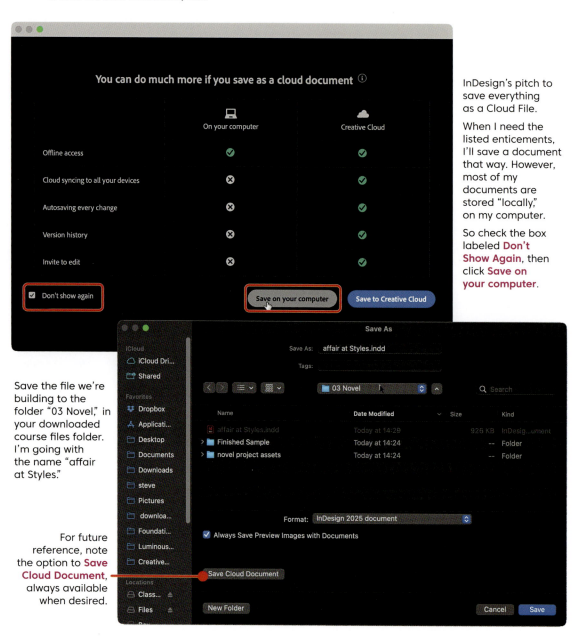

InDesign's pitch to save everything as a Cloud File.

When I need the listed enticements, I'll save a document that way. However, most of my documents are stored "locally," on my computer.

So check the box labeled **Don't Show Again**, then click **Save on your computer**.

Save the file we're building to the folder "03 Novel," in your downloaded course files folder. I'm going with the name "affair at Styles."

For future reference, note the option to **Save Cloud Document**, always available when desired.

➡ Check the box **Don't show again**, then click **Save on your computer**.

➡ In the dialog box, navigate to your downloaded course files and locate the folder *03 Novel*.

➡ Provide a name for your file, then **Save**. I chose the name "affair at Styles."

➡ While editing, periodically save by using the shortcut **⌘-S/Ctrl-S**.

Load Styles from Style Guide

The notion is that we lay out many novels and our style guide gives them a consistent look and feel. This style guide is built to ease the process of getting its styles into our novel. The style guide and the several images we'll need are in the folder ***novel project assets***, which is in the ***03 Novel*** folder.

➡ From the folder ***novel project assets***, open the doc called ***a Novel Style Guide.indd***.

➡ With the **Selection tool**, click on any content. You should see a dashed line surrounding all the content, indicating that it's *grouped*.

Grouping objects is a great way to better ensure that they can be selected and/or moved together. We'll be doing a bit of grouping in the next chapter to see the various ways it's handy. For now, we'll take advantage of the group we have selected.

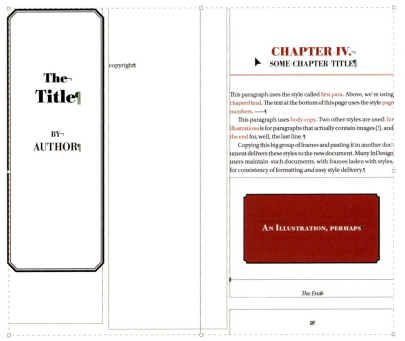

Selecting one item in a group selects the whole group. Convenient here, as we want all of this content (or rather the styles this content uses) in our novel.

➡ Copy the group by using the shortcut **⌘-C/Ctrl-C** or choosing **Edit > Copy**.

➡ Now that this content is copied into memory (the "clipboard"), we can close the style guide document by clicking the **×** in its tab at the upper-left of the document window.

➡ Now, back in your very empty novel, paste by using the shortcut **⌘-V/Ctrl-V** or choosing **Edit > Paste**.

➡ Look at the various styles panels. The styles have made the journey.

➡ The disconcerting step: Delete the content you just pasted by pressing **delete/Backspace**. The styles remain. The group was like someone delivering a package. They don't move in with you to do so.

Workspaces & Preferences

Swatches & Color Settings

Type & Text Styles

Frames, Shapes & Object Styles

Pages & Spreads

Find/ Change

Long or Complex Docs

Package & Publish

At this point, nothing is selected—the perfect moment to set defaults

➡ Set the default paragraph style to *body copy* by highlighting it.

➡ Save your file.

A word of **warning**. The document looks blank but isn't. Recall that you checked a box labeled **Primary Text Frame** when you created this document. That frame now fills the live area of the page you're looking at. *Please, don't move it or resize it!* That will break a delicate connection it has that we need to maintain. Feel free to use the **Selection tool** to *select* it, but no edits, please.

Configure the Parent Spread

Parent pages control the look and feel of all the pages that use those parents. You may be familiar with this concept from PowerPoint or Apple Keynote. Those applications have master slides that have content that appears on all the slides that use those master slides.

Generally, like in those applications, InDesign parent content is not editable on the pages that use those parents. It can be edited only on the parent page or spread. A very notable and delicate counterexample is **Primary Text Frames**. These shouldn't be edited anywhere other than on the parents, but might accidentally be. They need to be available on document pages (pages that use parents) so we can put content into them. But their size and shape should be controlled only via the parent spread.

Our **Primary Text Frames** are already sized perfectly to our margins. That's why those margin values were so specific. But we need more elements on the parent spread.

➡ Configure the appearance of the **Pages panel** as described in "The Pages Panel" (page 285)—that is, viewing document and parent pages horizontally. You'll thank me later.

➡ Go to the novel document's parent spread by double-clicking its name, *A-Parent*, at the top of the **Pages panel**. Be sure it's a firm, confident *double* click. You'll know you're there if you now see a two-page spread.

➡ With the **Selection tool**, click in the middle of either page. You've selected one of the **Primary Text Frames** but as yet can't see that it's threaded to its companion on the other page.

➡ Choose **View > Extras > Show Text Threads**. Now selecting either frame will show its connection to the other. By the way, it's an echo of the frame on the right you saw on page 1.

➡ With the **Type tool**, create a text frame in the bottom margin (no need to worry about its exact size and shape yet).

➡ With the cursor blinking in it, apply the paragraph style called *page numbers*.

Anything you type in that frame will have that style and will appear on every page that uses this parent page. So how do we put the correct page number on every page?

➡ Insert a **Current Page Number Marker**. With the cursor still blinking, right-click, then choose **Insert Special Character > Markers > Current Page Number**.

The Course

It should look like the letter "A." I assure you, it isn't a letter "A." It looks like that because you're on the A-Parent. If the parent had a different prefix to its name, that is what you'd see.

- Press the **Esc** key to select the frame. It's time to position it better.

- Snap the top of that frame to the bottom margin guide.

- Drag the frame's bottom handle to snap the bottom edge of the frame to the bottom of the page.

- Drag the side handles to make the frame's width the same as the live area of the page—that is, the left edge to below the left margin guide, and the right edge below the right margin guide.

The *page numbers* style centers the number horizontally, the **Align Center** button centers it vertically.

- Use the **Vertical Justification** buttons in the **Control panel** to align that **Current Page Number** to the vertical center of the frame.

- **option/Alt drag** that frame to the bottom of the facing page, creating a duplicate there. I *love* this way of copying content! If you need to fine-tune the position of the copy, be sure to release that key, or you will have more copies.

- Go to page 1 by double-clicking page 1's thumbnail in the **Pages panel**. Be sure you are viewing a page that displays a "1" at the bottom. We're now ready to get the text!

Placing Text Content From a File

The text for this novel is in a Microsoft Word document. Almost none of the text is formatted (except for italics), which leaves it to us to apply our styles both manually (one or two paragraphs at a time) and with **Find/Change** (many at once).

- While holding down the **⌘/Ctrl** key, press **K** and then **4**. This takes you to the relevant page of the **Preferences**.

- At the bottom of these **Type** preferences, enable **Smart Text Reflow**, including the **Delete Empty Pages** option. Notice that this features uses those **Primary Text Frames** we have.

- Commit your change to this document-specific preference.

- With nothing selected, be sure *body copy* is the default style.

Workspaces & Preferences

Swatches & Color Settings

Type & Text Styles

Frames, Shapes & Object Styles

Pages & Spreads

Find/ Change

Long or Complex Docs

Package & Publish

- Choose **File > Place**. At the bottom of the dialog box, check the box to **Show Import Options**. This is **important** whenever placing text.

- Navigate to the folder *novel project assets* (in the *03 Novel* folder).

- Double-click the Word file *MysteriousAffairAtStyles.docx*.

Most Word docs have little or haphazard formatting. This one is no exception. Thus, the options we will choose here are commonly chosen, but they differ from InDesign's optimistic defaults (the engineers assumed that Word users are as style-centric as we InDesign users).

- Choose the option to **Remove Styles and Formatting from Text and Tables**, *but* also check **Preserve Local Overrides** so the italics remain italicized.

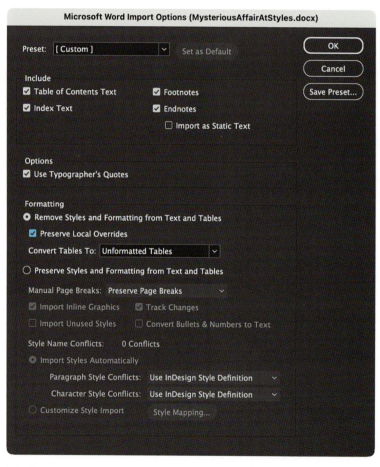

The **Import Options** for a Word doc.

The **Include** section converts Word's versions of several features into InDesign's.

Use Typographer's Quotes ensures attractive quotes and apostrophes rather than tick marks.

The **Formatting** section has elaborate options for mapping Word styles to InDesign styles in the rare cases when they are used. But, usually, we strip Word's styles and retain manually applied exceptions (**Preserve Local Overrides**), like here.

The "Remove Styles" part means that Word's "Normal" style will be removed and our default style applied. The "Preserve Overrides" part allows any italics to trigger override warnings. But we'll later make sure that text is "authorized" by applying a character style to each instance.

- Click the loaded cursor into the center of the **Primary Text Frame** on page 1 and watch new pages appear in the **Pages panel** (this may take a few moments).

- Save your file.

The Course

Formatting the Text

Yikes! The first few lines of text look awful! Don't worry, we'll fix that swiftly. But let's be sure we know what we're looking at.

- ➡ Choose to show **Hidden Characters** via the **View Options** button at the bottom of the **Tools panel**.

The first eight lines are actually only four paragraphs, each broken by a forced line break, indicated by a ¬ (sometimes called a "soft return"). The alignment of the text is **Justify with last line aligned left** (a mouthful, usually shortened to "left justified"). This alignment is stretching out the first line of each pair, up to the forced line break. Luckily, the styles intended for those paragraphs applies **Align center** alignment, so they'll look fine in a moment. Let's see.

- ➡ With the **Type tool**, click within the first two lines.
- ➡ In the **Paragraph Styles panel**, click the style called *title*.

The first thing to catch your eye may be the large border surrounding that paragraph (and much more). The *title* style uses a feature called **Paragraph Border**. We saw something similar when we discussed "Paragraph Shading" (page 33). The bottom offset for the border is set to be huge so that it surrounds most of the page.

Also notice that the word "The" is smaller. The paragraph style is applying a character style to do that using another feature we've seen before: "Nested Styles" (page 41). Feel free to look at the style's definition (right-click the style's name (*title*) and choose to edit it).

- ➡ Get the **Type tool** cursor blinking in the name "AGATHA CHRISTIE."
- ➡ Apply the style *byline* to complete the styling of our title page. Better, right?

The next style we apply is more startling because it uses another feature we encountered called "Keep Options" (page 46). This will kick the copyright paragraph to the next page.

- ➡ Get the **Type tool** cursor blinking in the word "Copyright."
- ➡ Apply the style *copyright*. You may need to adjust the zoom to see the entire spread. Use the shortcut **⌘-option-0/Ctrl-Alt-0** (reminder: that's a zero).

Now, we'll apply a character style called *Italic* to italicized words. This process will be very similar to that used when we first learned to apply styles using "**Find/Change**" (page 42).

- ➡ Invoke **Find/Change** with the shortcut **⌘-F/Ctrl-F**.
- ➡ In the **Text** tab, clear all the fields, including those for format at the bottom.
- ➡ Click the rectangle under the words **Find Format** to open the **Find Format Settings** dialog box.
- ➡ Click **Basic Character Formats** on the left side of that dialog.
- ➡ In the field for **Font Style**, type "Italic"—that's easier and faster than using the menu.

Workspaces & Preferences

Swatches & Color Settings

Type & Text Styles

Frames, Shapes & Object Styles

Pages & Spreads

Find/ Change

Long or Complex Docs

Package & Publish

➡ Click **OK** or press the **enter** key. The space under **Find Format** now reads "+ Italic."

➡ Click the rectangle under the words **Change Format** to open **Change Format Settings**.

➡ On the first page of the dialog, **Style Options**, choose *italic* from the **Character Style** menu, then commit the dialog.

➡ Now the space under **Change Format** reads "Character Style: italic."

➡ The scope of the **Search** may be **Story** or **Document**, since there's only one story in this document.

➡ Click the **Change All** button, then dismiss the message telling you (but not yet showing you) that 162 changes were made.

If you insert your cursor in the words "Public Domain," you'll see that character style has been applied. In this book's text, italics were the only "override" we needed to protect. If there are more overrides, we should clear them.

➡ Select all the text: quintuple-click or use **⌘-A/Ctrl-A**.

➡ Use the **Clear Overrides** button at the bottom of the **Paragraph Styles panel** (**¶⚡**). If it's not active (unlikely), there was no more "residue" from MS Word to clear.

For the moment, there's one more style we'll apply manually. It's for the very last line in the book, thus easy to forget, so let's deal with it now. There are several ways to get there quickly:

- The **Last Spread** button at the bottom-left of the document window.

- On a full keyboard, the shortcut **⌘-option-page down/Ctrl-Alt-page down**.
- In the **Pages panel**, which you may wish to pull out of wherever it's docked so you can make it bigger. Locate the last spread's thumbnail and double-click the page numbers under it. Double-clicking the numbers should show the whole spread.

➡ Get to the last spread by one of the methods above. Try not to read any text or you'll spoil the mystery. You may want to read this book!

➡ Get the **Type tool** cursor blinking in the very last words, "THE END."

➡ Apply the paragraph style *the end*.

➡ Get back to the spread for pages 2 and 3 so you can better witness what happens next.

We'll use **Find/Change** to apply a paragraph style called *chapterHead* to every paragraph that contains the all-uppercase word "CHAPTER." Although similar to what we've done before, there will be an important but subtle difference, too.

➡ Click the small trash icons to the right of the **Find Format** and **Change Format** boxes. And check that the fields **Find what** and **Change to** are empty as well.

➡ In the **Find what** field, type "CHAPTER" in caps.

I know that the word "chapter" is used in this book in places other than chapter headers. Also, since **Find/Change** is mostly case *insensitive*, it will find (and change) that word regardless of how it's written. To format only our chapter headers, let's make **Find/Change** case sensitive for the next search (disabling that feature for our subsequent queries).

➡ Activate the **Case Sensitive** switch: **Aa**. See figure below.

➡ Click the rectangle under the words **Change Format** to open **Change Format Settings**.

➡ On the first page of the dialog, **Style Options**, choose *chapterHead* from the **Paragraph Style** menu, then commit the dialog. **Find/Change** should now look like this:

➡ Click **Change All**.

The result is dramatic. The *chapterHead* style also uses **Keep Options** to ensure each chapter starts on its own page. The forced line break in each header triggers a nested style that makes the chapters' titles display in small caps (with a character style called *smallCaps*).

Unfortunately, capitalized letters are full-sized and look clumsy here, like the "I" in chapter 1's "I go to styles." This is another opportunity for **Find/Change** to show its usefulness.

➡ In **Find/Change**, disable the **Case Sensitive** switch and clear everything else.

Workspaces & Preferences

Swatches & Color Settings

Type & Text Styles

Frames, Shapes & Object Styles

Pages & Spreads

Find/ Change

Long or Complex Docs

Package & Publish

- Click the rectangle under the words **Find Format** to open **Find Format Settings**.

- On the first page of the dialog, **Style Options**, choose *smallCaps* from the **Character Style** menu, then commit the dialog.

- Now the space under **Find Format** reads "Character Style: smallCaps."

- Click the rectangle under the words **Change Format** to open **Change Format Settings**.

- Click **Change Case** on the left side of that dialog. Choose **lowercase** from the **Case** menu, then commit that dialog box. The space under **Change Format** is now "+ Case: lowercase."

- Click **Change All**.

Even though no style was applied *manually* to that text, but only via a nested style, **Find/Change** succeeds. That is, if the **Type tool** cursor is in a small caps line, the **Character Styles panel** will show *[None]* highlighted, but at the bottom will subtly show *smallCaps* is applied via the paragraph style. Difficult for us to notice, but not for **Find/Change**.

With apologies to the fictional Edmund Blackadder, it's time for a query so cunning, you could put a tail on it and call it a weasel.

- Clear the **Find Format** and **Change Format** settings.

Workspaces & Preferences

Swatches & Color Settings

Type & Text Styles

Frames, Shapes & Object Styles

Pages & Spreads

Find/ Change

Long or Complex Docs

Package & Publish

A GREP Query

According to most style manuals, the first paragraph after a heading, like this one, should not be indented. Our novel will follow that convention. Among our paragraph styles is a style called *first para* that needs to be applied to the paragraphs immediately after chapter headers.

It's true that there are not that many chapter headers, and doing this one at a time would take only a few minutes. In fact, we may do that for the paragraphs that follow some of the illustrations we'll be placing in this book later. But I'd like to show you a fabulous way to apply a style to a paragraph following one using a different style. It requires a tiny bit of code, which we discuss in the Compendium: see "GREP" (page 305).

Instead of searching for a specific word or phrase, with GREP you can search for patterns or wildcards. For example, to seek out any digit, you'd put "\d" in the GREP **Find what** field. An especially powerful GREP trick is to find text that follows or precedes other text. I may want to apply a superscripting character style to the letters "th" when they follow a number, but not otherwise: like **th**is: 5th

In that example, the query would use something called a *Positive Lookbehind*: looking behind (before) each "th" to see if a digit is there (a positive result). This example's query would be this:

`(?<=\d)th`

The "th" is the text that is sought. The bit in parentheses is the positive lookbehind. After the equals sign (=) is where we put the element(s) that need to precede what's being sought. In this example, that's a digit, any digit, the code for which is "\d." Thus, only a "th" preceded by a digit.

Now to apply that wisdom to our situation. Our novel's next query seeks to format *whatever* follows an end of paragraph character that uses the *chapterHead* style.

➡ In **Find/Change**, choose **GREP**. Refer to the figure for the next few instructions.

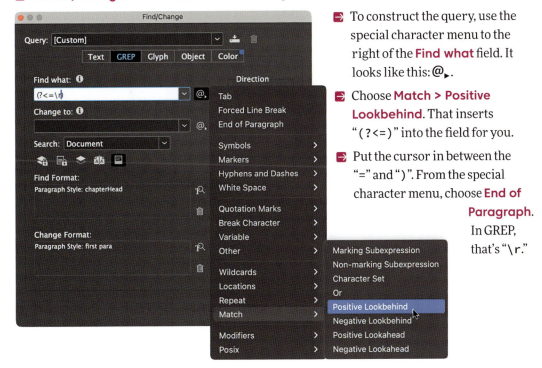

➡ To construct the query, use the special character menu to the right of the **Find what** field. It looks like this: @▸.

➡ Choose **Match > Positive Lookbehind**. That inserts "(?<=)" into the field for you.

➡ Put the cursor in between the "=" and ")". From the special character menu, choose **End of Paragraph**. In GREP, that's "\r."

Find what now shows: **(?<=\r)**

▣ In the **Change to** field, type **$0**. This is technically not necessary, as it simply replaces what was found with itself. But without this, our unusual query would lead InDesign to report that nothing was changed when indeed it was.

▣ Click the rectangle under the words **Find Format**.

▣ On the first page of the dialog, **Style Options**, choose *chapterHead* from the **Paragraph Style** menu, then commit the dialog.

▣ Now, the space under **Find Format** reads "Paragraph Style: chapterHead." So, we're seeking *anything* preceded by a paragraph return that uses *chapterHead*.

▣ Click the rectangle under the words **Change Format** to open **Change Format Settings**.

▣ On the first page of the dialog, **Style Options**, choose *first para* from the **Paragraph Style** menu, then commit the dialog.

▣ Now the space under **Change Format** reads "Paragraph Style: first para."

▣ Click **Change All**.

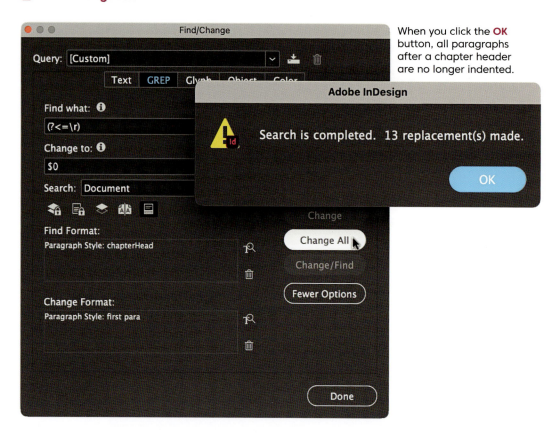

When you click the **OK** button, all paragraphs after a chapter header are no longer indented.

You may wish to save your file now.

Most GREP queries aren't so weird. I included this odd one here because it's so very useful.

Workspaces & Preferences

Swatches & Color Settings

Type & Text Styles

Frames, Shapes & Object Styles

Pages & Spreads

Find/ Change

Long or Complex Docs

Package & Publish

Adding Illustrations

You might be thinking that we're done with **Find/Change**. Not quite. In this part of the project, we're going to create a placeholder frame and apply an object style to it. That style will resize that frame so it's precisely as big as we need for each of the several images that we'll be placing. The style will also apply other settings to that frame, none of which will be visible until it houses one of those illustrations. We explain those more in the next chapter, but I'll give you a rundown of what those settings will do for us in the novel.

When we put an image in the frame, that image will fit *perfectly* into it. Also, when the frame has been put into an otherwise empty paragraph, it will situate itself above that paragraph, making room above and below. By anchoring a graphic frame in the text flow like that, it will always be near the text that references it, like I've done with the figures in this book.

This will make far more sense when we've put images into several frames like this. First, let's see where they will go.

⮕ Go to page 1 of the novel, so we can encounter each image location in order. For added assurance, make sure nothing is selected by using the shortcut **⌘-shift-A/Ctrl-Shift-A**.

⮕ In **Find/Change**, go to the **Text** tab. Beware: it looks a lot like the GREP tab.

⮕ Type "[Illustration]" in the **Find what** field. If the **Case Sensitive** switch is turned off, it won't matter if the "I" is uppercase or lowercase.

⮕ Ensure that all the other fields are blank and that the **Search** scope is set to **Document**.

⮕ Click the **Find Next** button. You should find yourself on page 25, near the beginning of Chapter III. This is the first of four places where our illustrations will be placed.

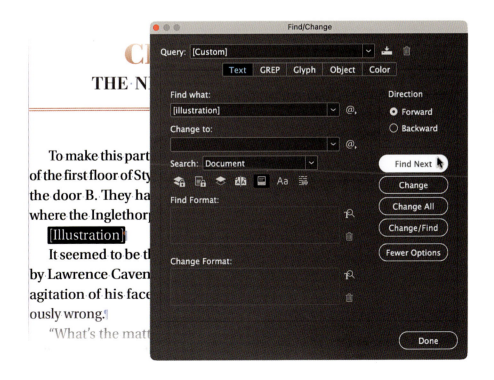

▣ The paragraph after an illustration shouldn't be indented. So, while you're here, click within the paragraph below "[Illustration]" and apply the style *first para*.

We'll do the same for the next two instances as well, but not the last, since it ends a chapter.

▣ Click the **Find Next** button. You should find yourself on page 37. Click within the paragraph below "[Illustration]" and, again, apply the style *first para*.

▣ **Find Next** again, and apply *first para* to the paragraph below, this time on page 41.

▣ One more **Find Next** puts you on page 51, where there is no paragraph below that we want to change. Another click of that button will take you back to the first instance or, if you keep going, will result in a message that the search is complete.

▣ Go back to page 1 and deselect again (⌘-shift-A/Ctrl-Shift-A).

▣ In the **Tools panel**, select the **Rectangle Frame Tool**. It's a box with an "X" in it.

▣ To either the left or right of page 1, in the area beyond the page called the pasteboard, drag diagonally to create a small box. Its size and shape do not matter—yet.

▣ Switch to the **Selection tool** (so you don't accidentally make more boxes).

▣ With the frame still selected, use the **Object Styles panel** to apply the style *illustration*.

The frame will now have a ridiculously specific size. If you wish, you may right-click the frame and choose **Fitting > Frame Fitting Options....** In the dialog box that opens, notice that it's set to **Fit Content Proportionately**. Don't change that setting. It ensures that an image of any size or shape will be seen in its entirety if put in this frame.

We're going to use **Find/Change** to do a couple things for us. It will replace each instance of the text "[Illustration]" with a copy of this empty frame. It will also apply the paragraph style called *for illustrations* to the paragraph holding that frame.

To do this, that frame needs to be in the memory "clipboard." That's where things go when copied or cut. So:

▣ With the frame selected, cut it with either the shortcut ⌘-X/Ctrl-X or the command **Edit > Cut**. Scary, but safe.

▣ In **Find/Change**, to the right of the **Change to** field, click the special character menu (@▸) then choose **Other > Clipboard Contents, Unformatted**.

➡ In **Find/Change**, click the box under **Change Format** and choose **Paragraph Style** *for illustrations*. The figure shows the final state of **Find/Change** for this query.

➡ Click the **Change All** button and witness the wonder.

Look carefully at the **Pages panel**. Sometimes, it has trouble redrawing itself and pages look blank. If that's the case, save your novel, close it, then reopen it.

If you can see all the page thumbnails, I suspect you can see that four of them have small blue boxes (on pages 25, 38, 42, and 53, I hope). We'll go from one to the next, dropping the appropriate image into each.

➡ If InDesign hasn't done so already, go to page 25.

➡ Choose **File > Place...** or use the shortcut **⌘-D/Ctrl-D**. If the resulting dialog box has the checkbox **Show Import Options** checked, you should disable it until we place text again.

➡ In the **Place** dialog box, navigate to the folder *03 Novel* then *novel project assets*, if you need to (you may already be looking at its contents).

➡ Double-click the file *ill1.psd*. This loads the image into the cursor.

➡ Click that cursor somewhere in the middle of the empty frame on page 25. One done!

➡ Go to page 38 to place *ill2.psd*, and so on until all four are placed.

➡ This feels like a good moment to save. Please do.

All that remains is a subtle refinement to the page numbers at the beginning of the novel.

Make Page 3 Be Page 1

Most books have a page numbered "1" after a bit of front matter. Our novel's narrative gets started on what is now page 3. We can't *simply* restart page numbering there, because we're not allowed to have multiple pages with *identical* numbers (you can't have two page 1s). But we *can* restart numbering on page 3 with a little set up.

We're going to give this document two *sections*. The first will have numbers that display as lowercase Roman numerals (i, ii, etc.). The second section will use standard Arabic numerals (1, 2, etc.). The order of operations is touchy because we can't have identical page numbers, even for a moment.

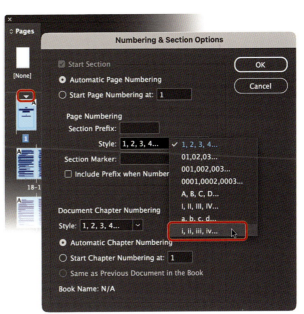

Workspaces & Preferences

Swatches & Color Settings

Type & Text Styles

Frames, Shapes & Object Styles

Pages & Spreads

Find/ Change

Long or Complex Docs

Package & Publish

➡ In the **Pages panel**, double-click the tiny triangle above the thumbnail of page 1. It marks the start of a section, and every document has at least one.

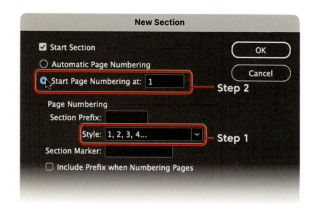

This opens the **Numbering & Section Options** dialog box.

➡ In the **Page Numbering** section of that dialog, go to the **Style** menu and choose the last item, **i, ii, iii, iv...**.

➡ Commit the dialog (click **OK**).

Now, *all* pages use that numbering style. It makes me giggle a bit, especially for the later pages.

➡ In the **Pages panel**, right-click on the thumbnail for the third page (iii), and from the resulting menu, choose **Numbering & Section Options...**.

The dialog opens assuming that you're starting a new section. It's correct! The order of the next two steps matters:

1 Set the **Page Numbering Style** for this new section to Arabic numerals (**1, 2, 3, 4...**). Since this is different from the other section, there isn't duplication. So, now we can...

2 Click the button to **Start Page Numbering at: 1**.

➡ Commit the dialog.

We successfully made the opening page of the narrative page 1. The book is almost perfect.

I'd prefer that the first two pages not display any page numbers, whatever their style. So, we will sever the connection between those pages and the parent that shows page numbers.

➡ In the **Pages panel**, drag the thumbnail of the **[None]** parent to the first page's thumbnail. When the destination thumbnail highlights, release the mouse. Do the same for the second page. Although they remain pages i and ii, they no longer display that. This is the primary use of the unalterable **[None]** parent.

➡ Save.

There is one remaining item. If you were to send this or any InDesign publication to someone else, they would need not only the InDesign document, but also the placed images and any fonts used besides those from the Adobe Fonts service.

To supply these, we need to create a *package*, a folder that contains copies of the InDesign file and all those assets. Luckily, that's a quick and easy process spelled out in the Compendium. See "Package" (page 346). With that... *C'est tout, mes amis!* I hope this project has stimulated your little gray cells, as Poirot might say.

The Course

4 Frames, Images, and Object Styles

So far, you've been *very* thoroughly exposed to text frames and the text within them. You've also seen a few cases of frames that house images. In this chapter, we'll encounter more image frames and see how shapes can be frames or simple graphics, and sometimes both. In the novel project we just completed, you saw how object styles can bestow potent properties to a frame. So, we'll learn how to create object styles and use them strategically.

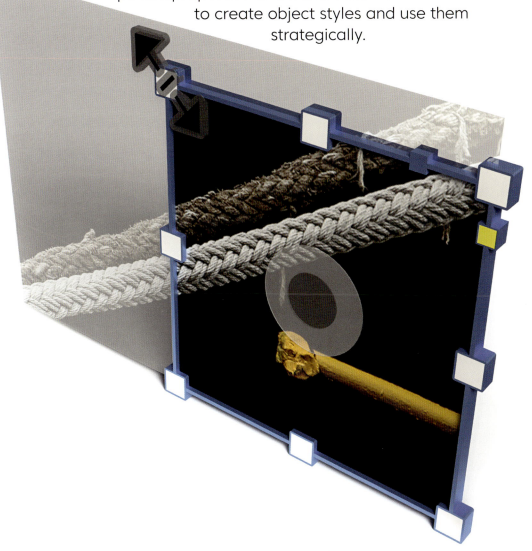

Frames Are Shapes Are Frames

InDesign has two distinct sets of tools for creating shapes. One set is predictably referred to as shape tools. The other set contains frame tools. Both sets of tools can be used to create shapes we might decorate with colorful edges or fills. Whether adorned or not, these shapes can serve as frames for text or images. So, yes, it's a bit redundant to have two sets of tools.

Are there differences between the two sets? Only subtle ones. The shapes we make with the so-called frame tools are always completely unadorned initially. I say that they are born naked. After they're made, they can be made as garish as you like.

The shapes we make with the shape tools are "born" with a default appearance. Recall how we set a paragraph style as a document's default, so a placed text file or a new bit of text will have predictable formatting. So it is with shapes: We can set a default look and feel that we'll see whenever we create a shape with one of those tools. There's one last, and a bit annoying, difference: If a "shape" has no fill within it, it is difficult to select. "Frames" are much easier to select, even if naked.

Let's see how this works.

➡ Open the downloaded course file **04 Shapes and Object Styles.indd** and go to the page 2–3 spread.

Besides the reminder notes on the left, there are three objects here, all rectangles. One has an image in it, one has a black stroke around its perimeter, and the last has no appearance attributes but *looks* like it has an "X" in it.

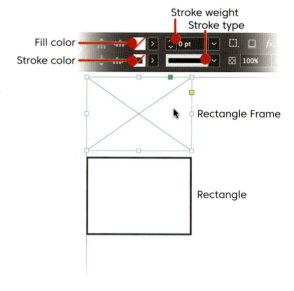

➡ Using the **Selection tool**, click on the box with the "X" to select it.

This was made with the **Rectangle Frame tool**, which you used for the illustration frames in the novel project. Look up at the **Control panel** to confirm that this shape has no fill or stroke applied. You can change that.

➡ Choose a fill color by clicking on the fill color menu and choosing a swatch.

➡ Choose a stroke color in the same way. Although the fill was obvious, you may not be able to see the stroke you just applied as it is very slender.

➡ Change the stroke weight from 1 pt to something thicker from the stroke weight menu. Perhaps 5 points will do.

➡ Finally, change the stroke type. The ones with names like "Thick – Thin" may be hard to appreciate unless the stroke weight is thicker still.

The Course

These are a few of the attributes that can be set as a default and/or be part of an object style. Although you've decorated this box a bit, you could still place an image or text in it. However, as they say, just because you *can* doesn't mean you *should*. But let's!

➡ Using the **Type tool**, click in that frame. This assigns it as a text frame, but it retains our lovely decorations. Type a few words or right-click and choose **Fill with Placeholder Text**. Yeah, maybe that was unwise from a design point of view, but let's leave it.

➡ Switch back to the **Selection tool** and try to select the box with the black stroke. Good luck.

Many InDesign users have wondered at this inconsistency in difficulty. Luckily, since there aren't any objects too close to this one, there is an easy way to select that box (and a slightly difficult way).

A marquee selection: With the **Selection tool**, starting in empty space, drag a small box that encounters the shape(s) you want to select.

➡ The slightly difficult method: Use the **Selection tool** to click carefully on the edge of the shape. If you don't miss, you've selected it.

➡ If that was successful, deselect by clicking on nothing.

The easier method is to make a marquee selection. This is also a great way to select multiple objects quickly.

➡ With the **Selection tool**, starting just to the right of that frame, drag a small box that encounters the edge of the frame (see the figure above). If that marquee touches several frames, all will be selected.

If you choose the swatch called "[Paper]" to fill that shape, it will be easier to select later and will look the same (unless it's in front of another object, in which case it would obscure the other object). This object was created with the **Rectangle tool**, which is directly below the **Rectangle Frame tool** in the **Tools panel**.

➡ Choose the **Rectangle tool** by either clicking it in the **Tools panel** or tapping the letter **M** on your keyboard. Sensible, as "m" stands for "mrectangle."

➡ Somewhere on the spread, create a box with that tool. Its appearance may surprise you. Of course, you can change it as we did the box at the top of the page.

➡ Compare that with what you see when you draw a box with the **Rectangle Frame tool** (accessible with the letter **F**). As mentioned, it should have no appearance attributes.

The most common way to change the default appearance attributes applied to objects made with the **Rectangle tool** and the tools hidden behind it (the **Ellipse tool** and the **Polygon tool**) is to choose those attributes with nothing selected. When nothing is selected, nothing changes as you choose a fill, stroke, stroke weight, etc. So we do this blindly with hope in our heart.

➡ Deselect everything, perhaps using a shortcut this time: **⌘-shift-A/Ctrl-Shift-A**.

➡ Note that the attributes in the **Control panel** match the rectangle you drew.

➡ Change the fill and stroke colors, and the stroke weight and stroke type. Keep in mind, these will be what you'll see whenever you draw a shape until you change the default again.

Workspaces & Preferences

Swatches & Color Settings

Type & Text Styles

Frames, Shapes & Object Styles

Pages & Spreads

Find/ Change

Long or Complex Docs

Package & Publish

The Course

➡ Now, draw another rectangle with the **Rectangle tool**. It will possess those attributes.

While that rectangle is selected, notice that there's an object style highlighted in the **Object Styles panel**. It's called *[Basic Graphics Frame]* and it's showing an override (plus sign). This offers a way to change the default look and feel of shapes without doing so blindly.

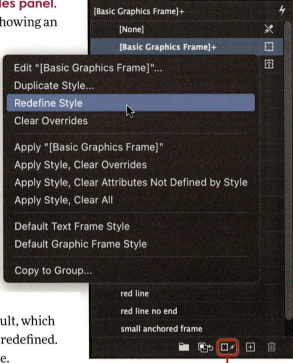

➡ If you're not entirely happy with the look of that rectangle, alter your choices of fill and stroke as desired.

➡ When the rectangle has the look you'd like to embrace as the default, right-click on the style *[Basic Graphics Frame]* and choose **Redefine Style**. The plus sign vanishes. But...

➡ Deselect (**⌘-shift-A/Ctrl-Shift-A**). The plus sign may return. The **Control panel** shows the current default, which may be an override of the style we just redefined. Easy enough to remedy if that's the case.

➡ Click the **Clear Overrides** button at the bottom of the Object Styles panel (⬚✶).

Clear Overrides button

Now that style holds the look and feel of our graphic defaults. Later, we may choose any other object style to be the default simply by deselecting and choosing an object style, or we may redefine *[Basic Graphics Frame]* again.

Since you're probably sick of rectangles by now, let's explore other shapes.

➡ Right-click on the **Rectangle tool** so you can choose the **Ellipse tool**. It, too, will use this new default look we've configured.

➡ Create an ellipse somewhere, the same way you created rectangles earlier: by dragging diagonally somewhere on the spread.

➡ Let's do it differently. Undo that ellipse (**⌘-Z/Ctrl-Z**).

➡ This time, instead of dragging, just click somewhere on the spread. A dialog box opens with the **Width** field ready to accept input.

Is the unit of measurement not what you'd like? If you want to use centimeters or inches instead, you may do so. Just add the unit after the number, like 2in for two inches. Actually, for two inches, you can type 2i or 2" as well.

- After entering a **Width** value, press the **Tab** key to highlight the **Height** field.

You'll notice that **Width** is displaying in the units set in the preferences. If you entered two inches, but the unit of measurement is set to points, the value will convert to "144 pt."

- Input a **Height** then press the **enter** key to commit it.
- If you wish to alter the units for this document, right-click in the rulers along the top and left edge of the document window and choose your preference. I'll choose inches for both.

I bet you have a lot of shapes on those pages now.

- Use the **Selection tool** to select several and delete them.
- Go back to the **Ellipse tool** (you may use the letter **L** to do so, of course).
- Start to drag out an ellipse, but before releasing the mouse, hold down the **shift** key as you release. This will constrain the ellipse to a circle. This is how you constrain rectangles and text frames to squares, too.

There's an unexpected way to make a grid of shapes.

- Make some room on page 2 by deleting any shapes you've drawn there.
- With the **Ellipse tool**, start dragging from the upper-left margin toward the lower-right margin but ***don't let go*** of the mouse when you get there!
- While holding down the mouse, tap the **up arrow** key a few times. Then hit the **right arrow** key once or twice. More ellipses appear. The **down** and **left arrows** reduce rows and columns of shapes.
- Still holding down that mouse? Good. Move your mouse around and the grid of ellipses you're making will resize. Hold **shift** and they're all circles. If you don't have a third hand, you may release the **shift** key but keep that mouse button down.
- Also hold down the ⌘/Ctrl key and tap the **up**, **down**, **left**, and **right arrow keys** noting how the space between ellipses changes.
- Tired? Me too. Release the mouse and get a hand massage.

This feature is known as *gridify* and is pretty cool, and well hidden. If you were drawing a text frame and started tapping the **up arrow** and/or **right arrow**, you'd get a grid of threaded text frames. The following fact will not surprise you: The person in charge of InDesign at the time this feature was introduced (Michael Ninness) is very fond of keyboard shortcuts. Because he wrote a nice blurb on the back of this book, I forgive him my hand cramps.

If you wanted to edit all of the ellipses later, you'd need to select them all. Using the **Selection tool** to make a marquee selection is easier than selecting one and **shift**-clicking on each of the others. If all of them are selected, and you suspect that you'd want to edit them all again as an ensemble, *group* them. Right click and choose **Group**, or use the sensible shortcut ⌘-G/Ctrl-G. From now on, when you select one, you'll see a dashed bounding box around them all.

If you need to edit one item in a group, double-click it with the **Selection tool**. Then you can edit it solo. Then, tapping the **esc** key selects the group.

Workspaces & Preferences

Swatches & Color Settings

Type & Text Styles

Frames, Shapes & Object Styles

Pages & Spreads

Find/ Change

Long or Complex Docs

Package & Publish

Images and Their Frames

On page 3 is an image we saw early in this course. You may wish to review the "Image Frame Teaser" (page 19) we did then, and the reference it made to the Compendium discussion of "Frame Fitting Options" (page 261). It was mostly about the distinct qualities of an image and the frame that holds it, especially their sizes.

▢ Go to pages 4 and 5 of the downloaded course file **04 Shapes and Object Styles.indd**.

We are going to place four images on this spread: one image into each of the two frames that are already on page 5, as well as one on page 4 and another to the right of those frames. In this process, we'll see all the major ways images find themselves on our pages.

You may recall how the images we placed in our novel project fit perfectly in their frames. We'll see how that is configured in this exercise.

▢ Select the top frame on page 5, then right-click it, choosing **Fitting > Frame Fitting Options....** A dialog box opens.

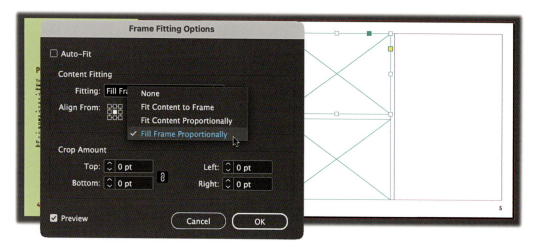

▢ From the dialog box's **Fitting** menu, choose **Fill Frame Proportionally**.

Any image placed in that frame will fill the frame completely but not be distorted to do so, and it will be sized so only the minimum gets cropped out.

Align From is currently set to put the center of an image in the center of the frame, which is fine in this case. If we wanted the left edge of images to be visible at the expense of the right, we might choose a reference point on the left edge of the **Align From** control. That setting will be handy in our very last project together.

▢ Select the other frame on page 5, get to its **Frame Fitting Options**, but choose **Fit Content Proportionally** from the **Fitting** menu. This is the setting used by the frames in the novel project.

▢ Deselect all: **⌘-shift-A/Ctrl-Shift-A**.

Workspaces &
Preferences

Swatches &
Color Settings

Type &
Text Styles

Frames, Shapes
& Object Styles

Pages &
Spreads

Find/
Change

Long or
Complex Docs

Package
& Publish

➡ Let's get images using the shortcut **⌘-D/Ctrl-D** or the command **File > Place….**

➡ In the dialog box that opens, navigate to your course files, then the folder **Links**.

If the files are listed alphabetically, the files shown below should be the first four. You can highlight the first one and then shift-click on the fourth to choose all four. If you cannot get them to be contiguous, you'll have to highlight one, then use the **⌘/Ctrl** key to highlight each of the others.

1 MoPOP.psd

2 stairs.psd

3 city castle.psd

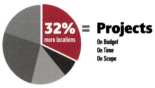
4 chart.ai

➡ When all four are highlighted, click the **Open** button.

The cursor, which in this state is called a *loaded place gun*, should look like one of the images. The "(4)" indicates how many images are loaded into it. Tapping the **left arrow** key or the **right arrow** key will cycle the cursor's preview through each of the images. You're choosing which image you wish to place first.

Parentheses around icon indicate the image will be placed in the frame

Loaded place gun with 4 images

➡ Tap the **arrow** keys until the cursor represents the image *2 stairs.psd* (see the figures above).

➡ Position the cursor over the top frame on page 5. If you move the cursor beyond the frame's bounds and back, it changes subtly.

➡ Click on that frame. The image fills it, the top and bottom cropped. The cursor now reports that three images remain.

➡ Use the **arrow** keys to queue up the chart graphic. Click in the other frame on page 5. You should see the entire chart with some extraneous frame above and below it.

The last two are *slightly* tricky, which is why I'm supplying two for practice.

The next image will go onto the live part of page 4—that is, within its margins. Its top should align with the top margin, and each side with the left and right margins. However, the image isn't quite tall enough to go all the way down to the bottom margin.

➡ Get the *3 city castle.psd* image showing in the cursor.

➡ Line up the arrow in the cursor (in its upper-left corner) with the upper-left corner of the margins on page 4. Don't just click!

The Course

➡ Press and drag slowly down and to the right. As you do, try to keep the cursor along the right edge of the frame that's forming. You'll see that InDesign is keeping the proportions for you. If you drag more rightward than down, the cursor will stick to the image's right edge and, our goal, snap to the right margin when it gets there.

➡ When the right edge of the image frame reaches the right margin, release.

Success? Let's do the last image. Not so good? Undo, and the image will reload into the cursor so you can try again.

You can also wait, do the last one, then adjust both frame and image size after. If you opt for that, you must hold **⌘-shift/Ctrl-Shift** as you resize an image frame to force the image to resize with it and to prevent distorting the image.

➡ Place the last image, **1 MoPOP.psd**, filling the right side of page 5, column guide to margin.

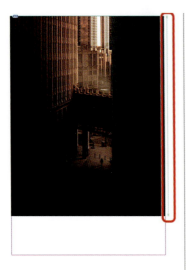

5

Once the last two images are in place, you'll notice they are not the same height. This may or may not bother you. Nonetheless, I'd like to show you a nice way to make them the same without too much effort.

Note that the bottom of the MoPOP image is cropped very carefully, but the top is looser. We'll move the top edge of the frame down, cropping more of the image, and making it the same height as the city castle image frame.

As you resize one frame, watch for smart guides to the right of and/ or below frames that should be the same size.

When they're the same height, something like this will appear to the right of both.

➡ With the **Selection tool**, select the MoPOP image. Locate the top, center control handle on the frame.

➡ Drag that control handle *slowly* downward (see figures above and the paragraph below).

The top edge will gently snap into position when this frame is the same height as another on the spread (here, the city castle image). The snapping is so gentle that it's easy to go too far without noticing. To the right of both frames, green smart guides appear to indicate when they're the same height.

The Nature of Linked Graphics

Look at the upper-left corners of those image frames and you will see a small link icon: 🔗. As explained in "Image Frames & Linked Images" (page 257), this indicates that the images are not embedded in the InDesign file, but are linked to it. By remaining independent documents, the images can be used in other publications, and if altered, that change will be apparent in all of documents in which they're used. Linking also keeps our InDesign file sizes reasonable.

If you have comfort in Photoshop, you may select one of the images, then right-click it, choosing **Edit Original**. This will launch Photoshop, open the image from its location on your computer, and allow you to make changes. If you do edit it, simply save and close. Then when you return to InDesign, you'll see those changes exhibited.

The chart graphic would open in Adobe Illustrator, if installed, since that's the application in which it was created.

All this round-trip editing requires that the InDesign file knows where the images are. So once placed, it is a very bad idea to move those image files around on your computer. If you do, then open the InDesign document, it will report the image file as missing. We'll see how this can be managed in a troubleshooting exercise a bit later. You can get the full story in "Missing Links & Relinking" (page 265).

Workspaces & Preferences

Swatches & Color Settings

Type & Text Styles

Frames, Shapes & Object Styles

Pages & Spreads

Find/ Change

Long or Complex Docs

Package & Publish

A Brief Look at Layers

The **Layers panel** is a useful feature to manage content. By "manage," I mean hide and show content across the document, control visual stacking order, and lock items that it would be best not to alter.

The figure below is borrowed from the Compendium discussion of "Layers" (page 314), which is a good read. That's a hint.

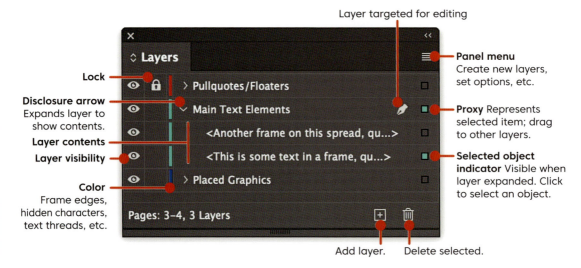

Layer targeted for editing

Lock

Disclosure arrow
Expands layer to
show contents.

Layer contents
Layer visibility

Color
Frame edges,
hidden characters,
text threads, etc.

Panel menu
Create new layers,
set options, etc.

Proxy Represents
selected item; drag
to other layers.

**Selected object
indicator** Visible when
layer expanded. Click
to select an object.

Add layer.   Delete selected.

The Course

- Examine page 4 and 5 of the downloaded course file *04 Shapes and Object Styles.indd*, which now have images you placed.

- Use the **Selection tool** to select the frame with the pie chart graphic.

Note that the frame edge and control handles are teal in color. The color tells you something.

- Access the **Layers panel**. If it's not visible on screen, you can invoke it from the **Window** menu.

That panel reveals that this document has three layers: "above it all," "Our Stuff," and "Notes." The *Our Stuff* layer has a teal bar to its left and a teal square to its right. Since each layer has a color associated with it, the teal frame edges tell us what layer our graphic inhabits.

- Move that graphic frame up and to the right so it overlaps (or underlaps) the other graphics on the same page.

The graphic appears to be in front of the stair image but behind the MoPOP image. If you were to select either of those others, their frame edges would be teal, too. Therefore, they're on the same layer. Even within a single layer, there is stacking.

- With the pie chart graphic selected, right-click and choose **Arrange > Bring to Front**. That graphic is now the topmost item in the *Our Stuff* layer, on this spread. You can guess what **Send to Back** would do. Try it!

➡️ In the **Layers panel**, drag the small teal square that's to the right of the *Our Stuff* layer upward to the empty square to the right of the *above it all* layer.

The square turns pink, as do the frame's edges. Notice that the chart is now above everything else on the spread. Since pink is not that easy to see, let's assign another color to that layer and its content. Also, the fact that this layer's name is all lowercase is not consistent with the others.

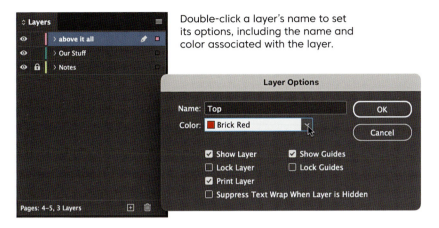

Double-click a layer's name to set its options, including the name and color associated with the layer.

➡️ In the **Layers panel**, double-click the name of the top layer to open its options dialog.

➡️ Rename it as you wish (I chose "Top") and change the **Color** to **Brick Red**. The other options are fine. If you're curious what "Text Wrap" is, you don't have long to wait.

➡️ Toggle off and then on the eye at the left of each layer. Notice what disappears. In fact, keep an eye (pun!) on the **Pages panel** to see that items disappear across the entire document when layer visibility is toggled off.

➡️ With all layers visible, click in the space next to the eye for the top layer. That layer is now locked.

If you attempt to select the chart graphic, you should find it impossible until you unlock that top layer again.

➡️ Click the disclosure arrow next to the name of the *Our Stuff* layer. You now see each item in that layer and on this spread. Each item can also have its visibility toggled or be locked.

➡️ Click the square to the right of one of the objects. It's now selected! This is a great way to select an object that's under another.

➡️ Drag the name of one of those objects up or down in the list, even to the *Top* layer, to change the stacking. This is a visual alternative to **Bring to Front** or **Send to Back**.

The reading about "Layers" (page 314) will fill you in on a few other details—like creating layers, although I suspect you can guess how to do that.

Workspaces & Preferences

Swatches & Color Settings

Type & Text Styles

Frames, Shapes & Object Styles

Pages & Spreads

Find/ Change

Long or Complex Docs

Package & Publish

Text Wrap

Text wrap is a kind of force field you apply to a frame to push text away from the frame's content. This creates a more dynamic layout without text and (usually) graphics colliding. The frame to which text wrap is applied could be another text frame like one containing a pull quote. Let's create two kinds of text wrap.

➡ Go to the page 6–7 spread in the downloaded course file **04 Shapes and Object Styles.indd**.

On page 7 is a biography of Sir John Herschel that is partially obscured by the placed PDF (his portrait and the caption). We will use the most common form of text wrap to push the text out from under that portrait and control how far away from its edges the text will be.

As always, more options and greater detail can be found in the Compendium: For this, see "Text Wrap: Force Fields on Frames" (page 269).

Wrap Around Bounding Box

➡ Select the image frame in the middle of page 7 (avoiding the content grabber at its center).

➡ Invoke the **Text Wrap panel** by choosing it from the **Window** menu.

You'll see that the first button at the top of that panel is currently highlighted. That's the "off" switch. The second button (**Wrap around bounding box**) is the one we want.

➡ Click that second button in the **Text Wrap panel** to get the first type of text wrap, **Wrap around bounding box**.

Below the buttons you'll see four fields for specifying offset, the distance from the bounding box the text should be.

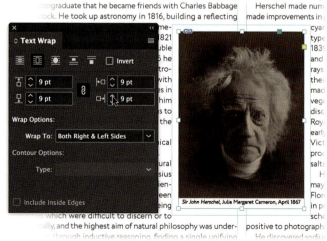

Sir John Herschel, Julia Margaret Cameron, April 1867

➡ Ensure the chain at the center of the offset fields is enabled. Then use the small up arrows next to any of the fields to increase the amount. Depending on how your rulers are set, 0.125 in, 9 pt, 3 mm should be fine. You may decide.

➡ If you wish to alter the offset on only one side or another, disable the chain to do so.

The next form of text wrap I'd like to show you is a touch tricky. In the Compendium reading you'll see warnings about this.

Wrap Around Object Shape

For this one, we'll use a different image. It's already in position but hidden at the moment. To set the stage, we'll have to move Sir John first.

"Disclose" the *Our Stuff* layer.

Make *<find.psd>* visible...
then select it.

➡ Drag the image frame with Herschel's portrait to the empty part of page 6. As you drag it, you'll probably notice the text trying to stay clear of it.

➡ Use the **Layers panel** to see all the content in the *Our Stuff* layer (use the disclosure arrow if needed).

➡ One item is not visible! Toggle on the visibility for the element named *<find.psd>*. See the figure at right.

➡ Click the blank square to its right to select it.
This is convenient, as the text frame covers most of it.

➡ Click the third button at the top of the **Text Wrap panel** (**Wrap around object shape**). Oddly, this changes tools and selects the content within the frame. We'll fix that shortly.

➡ In the **Text Wrap panel**, check the **Type** menu under **Contour Options**. Choose **Select Subject** if it isn't already chosen. The result should be promising.

➡ Adjust the offset. Only one field is active, but that's usually fine for this form of text wrap.

➡ Finally, and probably unnecessarily with this specific image, choose **Largest Area** from the **Wrap To** menu under **Wrap Options**. This ensures text doesn't flow into any holes or recesses in a subject that the text is wrapping around.

➡ Press the **esc** key and switch to the **Selection tool** before moving on. Save!

Object Style Basics

So many of the settings we've seen in this chapter can be recorded in an object style. From simple attributes like fill or stroke to frame fitting options to text wrap settings, pretty much any attribute for any kind of object can be stored and then applied quickly.

Object styles are more like character styles than paragraph styles in that object and character styles can affect only one or very few attributes, ignoring others. That is, an object style may apply a fill color but be set to ignore all stroke settings, for example. That said, few of us leverage this *à la carte* possibility extensively. Let's explore what's possible.

➡ Go to the page 8–9 spread in the downloaded course file **04 Shapes and Object Styles.indd**.

➡ Fit the spread in the window so you can see both pages.

For several upcoming exercises, it would be most convenient if we measure horizontally in inches and vertically in points.

➡ Right-click on the ruler at the top of the document window and choose **Inches**. Right-click on the ruler at the left edge of the document window and choose **Points**.

➡ Use the **Selection tool** to select the colorful object at the top of page 8.

Although many attributes of a selected object can be seen and edited in the **Control panel** (or the **Properties panel**), we'll adjust them in the Object Styles Options dialog box, where many more are available as well.

Many of the attributes that are apparent on the object are visible and accessible in the **Control panel**. But we're going to examine them in the context of the object style we're making.

➡ Use the **Object Styles panel** menu (the ☰ at its upper-right) and choose **New Object Style....** This opens an intimidating dialog box.

Through this dialog box, we're going to capture this object's fill color; stroke color, weight, and type; corner options; width; and horizontal position. Along the way, we should note what else is possible for the object styles you may wish to make in the future.

In fact, on page 9 are options that are useful for text frames. We'll explore a few examples on the subsequent pages of the current course file, too.

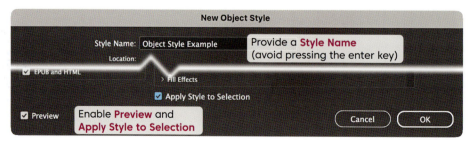

Workspaces & Preferences

Swatches & Color Settings

Type & Text Styles

Frames, Shapes & Object Styles

Pages & Spreads

Find/ Change

Long or Complex Docs

Package & Publish

- At the top of the dialog, provide a **Style Name**. At the bottom, check **Preview** and **Apply Style to Selection**. Later, those checkboxes will be enabled when you make new styles.

- Use the scroll bar in the **Basic Attributes** section to see what's there.

Note that all but two of the checkboxes in that section are checked. **Paragraph Style** and **Frame Fitting Options** are set to *ignore* (instead of a check mark, there's a hyphen). If this object style were applied to either a text frame or an image frame, it would not affect either the text formatting or the way an image is cropped by the frame or sized within it (respectively).

Note that in the **Effects for:** section, all but one of the checkboxes are fully unchecked and empty. Completely unchecked means *remove*. So if this object style were applied to a frame with a drop shadow, the shadow would be removed.

For a full rundown on all the attributes controlled by an object style, and which can be removed, ignored, and applied, see the thoroughly cross-referenced discussion in the Compendium: "Object Styles" (page 276). For now, let's see what we can do with this little shape.

- On the left, under **Basic Attributes**, click on the word **Fill** to highlight it and see its settings. You'll see the fill color. No mysteries presented or solved here.

- Click on the word **Stroke** to see its more numerous options.

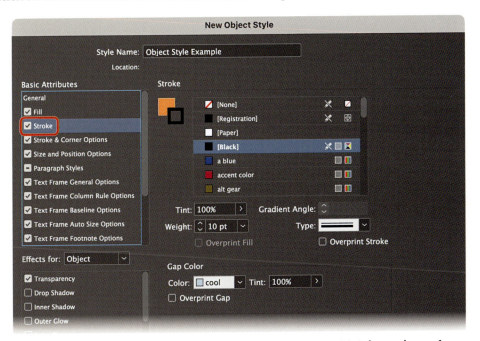

You'll see the stroke color is set to **[Black]** and the **Type** to **Thin - Thick** (sometimes a bug causes the **Type** to look blank until it's clicked on). When a stroke type other than **Solid** is chosen, there's provision for a **Gap Color** (the last stroke option), which in this case is a swatch called **cool**. This explains why there were two colors surrounding the shape. I knew you wondered.

To learn how to make your own swatches, read "Creating Color Swatches" (page 179).

- Increase and decrease the stroke **Weight** while watching the object. The stroke gets thicker or thinner but the object gets no bigger nor smaller overall. That's not entirely normal.

➡ On the left, click on **Stroke & Corner Options**.

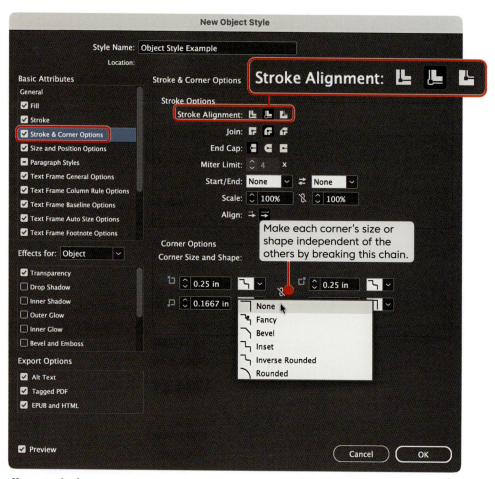

Normally, a stroke is centered on the edge of the frame to which it's applied: half the stroke is inside, half outside the shape. This object has its **Stroke Alignment** set to inside, so the stroke weight never affects the net size of the object. The third choice is *outside*, so a stroke never obscures content within a frame, such as an image, for example.

Let's leave that setting but change two others.

➡ Set **Join** to *Round Join* (the second choice).

This *slightly* rounds sharp outside corners. I believe it subliminally makes shapes appear more friendly, approachable. Toggle the **Preview** checkbox to see the effect on this object.

Currently, the corners all use the much more noticeable effect of **Inverse Rounded** corner shape (under **Corner Options, Corner Size and Shape**).

➡ Increase the size of one corner to 0.25 in, and they all change.

➡ Click the chain icon in the middle of the size fields to disable it.

The Course *(vertical side text)*

➡ Set the shape of the lower two corners to **None** (*or* the size to 0). It's looking pretty!

One more set of attributes!

➡ On the left side, click on the name of the **Size and Position Options**.

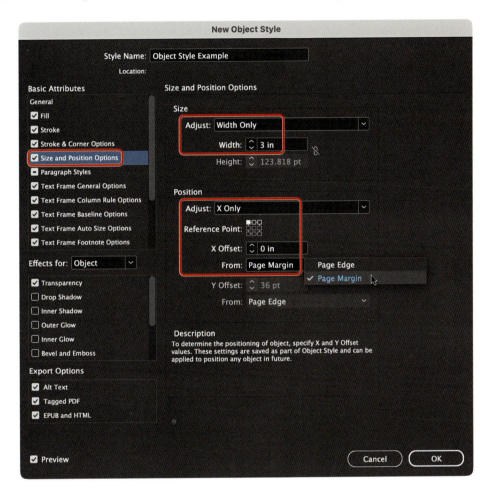

Let's set the width and horizontal position:

➡ Under **Size**, choose **Width Only** from the **Adjust** menu then set the **Width** to 3 in. Toggle the **Preview** if you like, to see that change. **Position** requires a bit more thought.

➡ In the **Position** section, choose **X Only** from the **Adjust** menu.

Now you're being told that some point on the object is some number of inches from the edge of the page. Let's make it easy on us: We'll set the left edge to be precisely along the margin.

➡ Click the upper-left **Reference Point**, so we are referring to the object's left edge (see figure above).

➡ Set the **X Offset** to 0 (zero). Ignore that the object has moved far to the left. Finally...

➡ Choose **Page Margin** from the **From** menu. Together, that's 0 inches from the margin.

Workspaces & Preferences

Swatches & Color Settings

Type & Text Styles

Frames, Shapes & Object Styles

Pages & Spreads

Find/ Change

Long or Complex Docs

Package & Publish

- ⮕ Click **OK** or press the **enter** key to commit our style. Now we have a style we can test.

- ⮕ Select the other two objects on page 8.

- ⮕ Click on the name of your new object style.

Both objects now inherit all the style's attributes that they can (ellipses have no corners to alter). Again, there's so much here and it's itemized in the Compendium. Bookmark "Object Styles" (page 276) and consult the rest of that chapter for the attributes they control.

Object Styles & Text Frames

You may recall that text frames have a number of options specific to them. See "A Few Text Frame Options" (page 24) for a reminder. These include inset (to push text in from the frame's edges), the number of columns a frame holds, the vertical justification, and where the first baseline is relative to the top of the frame.

And, although a text frame may benefit from having its width controlled by an object style, text frames have auto size options which are better at controlling their height. Need another example? I have you covered.

- ⮕ With the **Selection tool**, select the text frame at the top of page 9 in the downloaded course file *04 Shapes and Object Styles.indd*.

- ⮕ Use the **Object Styles panel** to apply the style called *Fancy Text Frame*. Much happens, some of which we just saw on page 8 of that doc.

Looking at that frame, you can guess some of the options that are applied. In fact, it's almost all of the items listed just above. Also, this object style applies a paragraph style to the text within it. If you look at the **Paragraph Styles panel**, you'll see the style called *Fancy Paragraph* is highlighted. Within that paragraph style definition, GREP styles apply a bold character style to certain words and phrases. Your one click triggered a cascade of styling.

- ⮕ In the **Object Styles panel**, right-click *Fancy Text Frame* and choose **Edit "Fancy Text Frame"**....

- ⮕ Examine each of the **Basic Attributes**. Especially look at **Text Frame Auto Size Options**.

- ⮕ When done, commit any changes you decided to make or click the **Cancel** button.

That example was extravagant. Let's look at a very practical one:

- ⮕ With the **Selection tool**, select the text frame with text that begins "This caption could use."

- ⮕ Apply the object style called **a caption frame**.

This style applies inset, but just at the top. It uses auto sizing to make it tall enough for the text but no taller. And it applies a caption paragraph style. Tip: Read that caption paragraph.

Another set of options to consider for text frame object styles, also covered in the Compendium, is "First Baseline Offset" (page 254).

- ⮕ Save.

➡ Go to the page 10–11 spread in the downloaded course file *04 Shapes and Object Styles.indd*.

➡ Fit the spread in the window, if needed, so you can see both pages.

➡ Note the frame with the large, red "M."

This frame and the small caption in the upper-left corner of the spread both use a first baseline option of cap-height to assure uppercase letters in the first line touch the top edge of the frame.

Were the first baseline set to ascent for the frame with the red "M," that giant cap would be pushed down a little. But if the "M" were pushed down *at all*, it would not fit, since the frame is exactly as large as that letter.

For the caption, having the caps at the top edge better aligns them to the image frame to the right.

The object styles for each of those frames also applies the necessary paragraph styles.

The notes along the left margin are there to remind you of these things and to encourage you to examine the paragraph styles, too.

Object Styles & Parent Page Items

➡ Using the **Selection tool**, attempt to select the empty frame above the large "M" on page 10 of the downloaded course file *04 Shapes and Object Styles.indd*.

That was mean of me. You can't select it because it's on a parent page, not this one. What you see on page 10 is just an echo of the frame on the parent. That means that if you move or resize the frame on the parent page, the one you think you see on page 10 will also be edited.

Important: This will hold true even after we place an image in that frame!

The page 10–11 spread is intended to resemble the spreads that begin chapters in a book I like. Each chapter has an image at the top of its opening page to set a theme, and an introductory paragraph with a huge drop cap that articulates that theme.

If I were building that book in InDesign, I'd have a parent spread specifically for the pages that open a chapter. If I were to alter the parent, all the pages that use it would reflect that alteration, even after I've added content.

Back to that placeholder frame: The one on the parent has an object style applied to it that sets its frame fitting options. An image placed into the echoed frame on page 10 will fill that frame with the minimum crop necessary to fill it.

The image we're about to place is actually nearly the size of the entire spread, but will automatically be reduced in size to fill that frame. Let's check it out.

➡ Make sure nothing is selected.

➡ To place the image, use the shortcut **⌘-D/Ctrl-D** or menu command **File > Place…**.

➡ In the dialog box that opens, navigate, if needed, to your course files, within which is a folder called *Links*.

➡ Locate and double-click the image called *yellowLeaping.psd*. It loads into the cursor.

Workspaces & Preferences

Swatches & Color Settings

Type & Text Styles

Frames, Shapes & Object Styles

Pages & Spreads

Find/ Change

Long or Complex Docs

Package & Publish

⮕ With the loaded cursor, click near the middle of that large placeholder frame. As promised, the image fills it. But it needs to be scooted up a little, since some of the subject is cut off.

⮕ With the **Selection tool**, hover the cursor over the frame to reveal the "donut" in its center, officially known as the content grabber.

⮕ Drag the content grabber upward. After you start dragging, hold down the **shift** key to ensure you're moving straight up, dragging until you can see both of the girl's feet. Now we can see that she's leaping. Release the mouse when that's the case, then release the **shift** key.

How much was the image scaled down to fill that frame with the minimum crop?

⮕ Click (don't drag) just once on the donut/content grabber.

This selects the image contained by the frame. You should see its pink edges extending above and below the frame. Look at its scaling in the **Control panel:** a little more than 53%.

Apparently, that image was built to be nearly twice as large as this. Sadly, you can see an image's scaling only if you select it within its frame. If the frame itself is selected, the scaling fields will say "100%."

⮕ Press the **esc** key to select the frame. Note the scaling fields.

⮕ Save.

The Course

Object Styles for Anchored Objects

In the novel project, we used image frames that were anchored above empty paragraphs. This was a way to ensure that the illustrations were indeed near the text that referenced them.

There are three choices for an anchored object's **Position**: **Inline**, **Above Line**, and **Custom**. Inline is appropriate for frames that are little bigger than the text to which they're anchored. It's easy to make a frame anchored inline; just paste it into the text flow like this: ⬡.

Review the novel project for how we arrange for frames anchored above line.

Custom anchored objects can be significantly more complex, but after experiencing a few, you will know how to approach them and utilize them in your publications. You will definitely need to consult "Custom Anchored Objects—Anchored Frames on a Short Leash" (page 273). You may wish to bookmark those pages. For the following exercise in particular, you should reference the figure showing the **Anchored Object Options** dialog box (page 275).

➡ Go to the page 10–11 spread in the downloaded course file *04 Shapes and Object Styles.indd*.

To better see what we're doing, zoom in on the lower third of page 10.

➡ Hold down (don't just tap) the letter **Z** key, and while holding it, draw a box around the lower third of page 10:

Drag this ornament to text to anchor frame

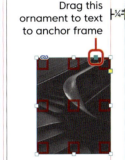

quatincitint la qui des velignis verumendae.

Anchored Objects aren't as hard as they used to be. And their options can be part of an Object Style. Odip eugueros vendio d olor ilis nim zzrit ad et augiamc onsequat wis nullut ent at nissim ing eu facil iureriure do conse velessim ipsum zriusc iduisl ute volobor si.

Lendre magnisi te tio doluptat ametum verostrud ex et velessectem ipit el ullandigna autatum sandre faccumm odoloborem non-secte cortio odolorper ad delenibh eu facillam dipsustie venit veleseq[13] wisis nibh endit non-sequat. Ut atem zzrilla feugiatet nit vendion sequatum velendreet utat. Del ipsusti ncilit in esto cor si.

Adipit lumsand ignibh erat ilisisisci ex enim aliqui eugiam dolorem zzriure vel ut aliquisi eugiam in hent alisit, sustrud et ad eumsandiat. Velesed exeros et augue tisis niam, conullum quamet, susto commodolorem vulput nim doloborem aliquate tie mincidunt num ercip eriureet velit adit amcon eum in ut aci bla feugait wis accum duis nisim acin ulput laore

tem nostrud dunt wis nulput dunt acipsum ad modigna acidunt wissequamet prat. Ignit lorpercilis exer iurem dulhendre molesto do odigna coreetum quamet praesectet nullamcor si odio od an image of stairs dolum quam, con utet ut lan eugait alis nim zzriure tio dolore conse minim ver sum dolum ad min ullandi onumsandit augait la commy nibh eugait nit, veleseq uismodiat erosto odipsum sandre exe-ro dolore dolor acilisl estion utatet nit lorper ad duisi tio eugait nit, uismodiat erosto odipsum sandre exero dolore dolor acilisl estion utatet nit lorper ad duisi tio odiat utat. Unt vel utet, commod ming elestie faccum venim vero digna consequat lorperi uscilit, vel el in eugueratis esto odignim nit, consequi et aliquis nulput ut nostio od dunt nim veliquisim nosto odigna faccum ad tatem dunt eum veliqui etum ea feu-giam am quisi bla facillaor autat loboreet enim zzrilla facilisi blametue facip essequam, coreri-liqui ex et dolut prat estis at, sisl utat. Senisim duipsus tionum venit vero odolum iusci et au-

10

On the left, 0.25 inches from the text frame, is an image of stairs with small squares that will hopefully remind you of the reference point interface we've seen a few times.

In the text frame's right column, you'll see the phrase "an image of stairs" in red (to help you pick it out).

Workspaces & Preferences

Swatches & Color Settings

Type & Text Styles

Frames, Shapes & Object Styles

Pages & Spreads

Find/ Change

Long or Complex Docs

Package & Publish

Our objective: To create a positional relationship between the image and the phrase that references it. Specifically, to have the top of the image be vertically aligned with any uppercase letter in the line that holds the phrase, and to have the right edge of the image be 0.25 inches from the left side of the text frame that holds that phrase, much like it is now.

Actually, since this is a spread, we should avoid using "left" and "right," and use "outside" and "inside," like we do with the margins on a spread. After all, that phrase may find itself on the right side of the spine at some point, and we wouldn't want the image between the pages.

Once that relationship is established, we'll update the object style applied to that frame so we can apply the same settings to the small frames on page 11. The beginning of the process is easy:

➡ With the **Selection tool**, select the image of the stairs.

Note the ornament along the top edge of the frame near the upper-right corner.

➡ Drag that ornament to just left of the "a" at the beginning of the phrase "an image of stairs."

Anchor symbol

A connection is now made between the upper-left corner of the image frame to that location in the text. In the text is an *anchor marker* (a widthless character resembling a yen symbol "¥").

To achieve our objective, we have to tweak the anchor settings on that frame.

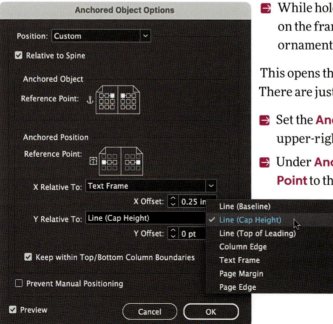

➡ While holding down the **option/Alt** key, click on the frame's anchor symbol where the small ornament had been.

This opens the scary dialog box you bookmarked. There are just a few things to change.

➡ Set the **Anchored Object Reference Point** to the upper-right corner.

➡ Under **Anchored Position**, Set the **Reference Point** to the left edge and...

➡ Choose **Line (Cap Height)** from the **Y Relative To** menu.

➡ Enable the checkboxes for **Relative to Spine** (near the top of the dialog) and **Keep within Top/Bottom Column Boundaries** (near the bottom).

➡ Commit the dialog.

Note that there's an object style applied to that frame and it's reporting an override. That would be the custom anchor options we just configured.

- ⮕ In the **Object Styles panel**, right-click the style named *small anchored frame* and choose **Redefine Style**. You just set all those anchor options for any object to which you apply the style!

- ⮕ Fit the spread in the window so you can see the small frames on the right side.

The anchor marker (that ¥ symbol) is a proxy for the image. That is, if we delete it, the image is gone. If we move the anchor marker, the image moves, too. In a way, the marker and image are interchangeable. How can we use that?

If a frame has anchored object settings, we can literally paste it in the text. If those settings made it an above line object, it will appear on its own virtual line. The settings we've included in that object style will make the small frames in the outer margin of page 11 custom anchored objects.

- ⮕ Select both frames and apply the object style *small anchored frame*.

- ⮕ Deselect both, then select just the top one (the picture of cliffs). Don't drag the ornament into the text!

- ⮕ Fearlessly, cut the frame with **Edit > Cut** or the shortcut **⌘-X/Ctrl-X**.

- ⮕ Double-click in the text to activate the **Type tool**.

- ⮕ Insert the type cursor just to the left or right of the phrase "Sedona cliffs" in the first column on page 11.

- ⮕ Paste.

- ⮕ This pastes the image there, represented by the anchor marker. The image appears in the outside margin.

- ⮕ Cut the small text frame, then paste it near the bottom of the second column (to the left of the words "a note").

One last demonstration of the flexibility and durability of the settings we configured:

- ⮕ To make this a little easier, highlight the entire line that contains the words "a note" and the anchor marker.

- ⮕ Cut it with **Edit > Cut** or the shortcut **⌘-X/Ctrl-X**.

- ⮕ Insert the text cursor at the very end of the story, then paste with **Edit > Paste** or the shortcut **⌘-V/Ctrl-V**.

Thanks to the setting **Keep within Top/Bottom Column Boundaries**, that frame doesn't dangle too low on the page!

Workspaces & Preferences

Swatches & Color Settings

Type & Text Styles

Frames, Shapes & Object Styles

Pages & Spreads

Find/ Change

Long or Complex Docs

Package & Publish

Anchored Objects with Text Wrap

The frames we used to learn about custom anchoring were conveniently in the margins of a spread. If they had been larger or otherwise overlapped the text, we'd use text wrap to force the text to flow around the frame.

But there's a glitch with anchored objects. Text wrap won't affect the line of text in which the anchor marker appears or any lines above it.

⬛ Read the short section "Anchored Objects with Text Wrap" (page 274) to better understand the problem and how we work around it.

In the following exercise, we see a practical variation on the solution to anchor the frame to an empty paragraph just above the text that should wrap around it.

⬛ Go to the page 12–13 spread in the downloaded course file **04 Shapes and Object Styles.indd**.

I want to provide a little background on most of the styles applied on page 13.

Most of the paragraphs there use a paragraph style called *body*. In the **Indents and Spacing** section of its definition, that style specifies there be 5 points of space after each *body* paragraph if it's followed by another. But if a *body* paragraph is followed by another paragraph style, there should be no space at all.

There are two paragraphs in that flow that use a different paragraph style called *to anchor pullquotes*. Its **Leading** is set to 5 points so that there continues to be that much space between *body* paragraphs even when one of these intervenes. The beige shading you see is **Paragraph Shading**, but it's set to not print or export. Test that:

⬛ Tap the **esc** key (just in case), then tap the **W** key to enter preview mode. The shading disappears along with anything else that wouldn't print. Tap **W** again to see what you need to.

The paragraph style applied to the text that begins "Entice readers…" has a GREP style that formats the quote marks at the beginning and end to make them large, bold, and translucent.

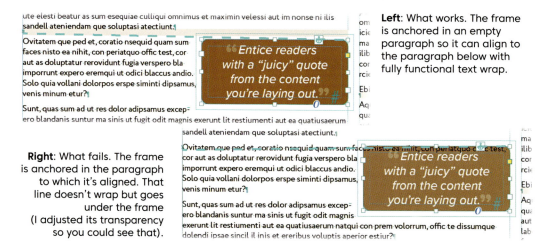

Left: What works. The frame is anchored in an empty paragraph so it can align to the paragraph below with fully functional text wrap.

Right: What fails. The frame is anchored in the paragraph to which it's aligned. That line doesn't wrap but goes under the frame (I adjusted its transparency so you could see that).

But the heart of this lesson involves the frame with those large quotes. The figure above shows how it's anchored to one of those shaded paragraphs. Note that the top of the quote frame is aligned with the paragraph immediately below the one to which it's anchored. The frame's custom anchoring settings, text wrap, rounded corners, fill color, auto-sizing, and paragraph style are all controlled by the object applied to it.

Yes, it took a little bit of tinkering to get those settings dialed in. But it had to be done just once, and now it can be applied very quickly. Start the timer!

➡ With the **Selection tool**, select the frame at the top of page 12.

➡ Apply the object style called *pullquote FRAME*.

➡ Cut the frame with **Edit > Cut** or the shortcut **⌘-X/Ctrl-X**.

➡ Double-click in the beige-shaded paragraph on the right side of page 13 to insert the text cursor there.

➡ Paste with **Edit > Paste** or the shortcut **⌘-V/Ctrl-V**.

Stop the clock. I did it in 6.5 seconds—but, then, I've done this a few times. Still, once styles are built, productivity goes up dramatically.

Object Styles & Groups

Throughout my books, I use object styles for many things. Flip through the pages and find a figure. The one discussing "Stroke & Corner Options" (page 92) is a good example. I use different styles to control the strokes on the red lines and boxes, the corners and opacity of the caption frames (and other text frame settings), and the entire figure itself is anchored above an otherwise empty paragraph.

In the very first book I wrote with such figures, I learned a painful lesson.

➡ Go to the page 14–15 spread in the downloaded course file **04 Shapes and Object Styles.indd**.

On page 14, you'll see a similarly structured figure composed of many elements, each of which has an object style applied. The objective is to anchor this figure in the text on page 15 where there's now a light-green frame.

➡ With the **Selection tool**, select the green frame on page 15.

➡ Note that the object style applied to it is called *anchored above*.

➡ Delete that frame so there's room for the figure when we're ready.

➡ With the **Selection tool**, select all the elements of the figure on page 14.

➡ Group them with the shortcut **⌘-G/Ctrl-G**. You should see a dashed line surrounding the group. Get ready for a bummer.

➡ Apply the object style *anchored above* to the group. Drats!

The problem: The style is applied to every element in the group, ruining their appearance and severing their connection to the styles that had been applied to them.

The solution: Put the group into a frame to which the anchoring style can be applied.

Workspaces & Preferences

Swatches & Color Settings

Type & Text Styles

Frames, Shapes & Object Styles

Pages & Spreads

Find/ Change

Long or Complex Docs

Package & Publish

⊟ Undo with **⌘-Z/Ctrl-Z**.

To engage the solution requires a few steps, listed below. The first time, it sounds long and tedious. But like all procedures, it gets very fast with practice and muscle memory.

Here's the procedure:

1   Boldly cut the group with **Edit > Cut** or the shortcut **⌘-X/Ctrl-X**.
2   While holding down the **F** key (don't tap it), temporarily accessing the **Rectangle Frame tool**, draw a box very roughly where the group was. Don't stress about the size or shape.
3   Release the **F** key. You should now be wielding the **Selection tool** again.

The next two commands have very similar shortcuts: They use the same modifier keys and the letters are right next to each other on the keyboard. So this *can* be quick:

4   Hold down **⌘-option/Ctrl-Alt** and tap the **V** key and then the **C** key. Release the modifier keys.

The first shortcut is for **Paste Into** and the second is for **Fit Content to Frame**. Boom boom! Now that group is inside a protective container sized nicely to it.

5   Apply the object style *anchored above*. No harm done to the content!
6   To get this figure in the text flow on page 15, you need to cut it with **Edit > Cut** or the shortcut **⌘-X/Ctrl-X**. (Not so startling anymore, is it?)
7   Double-click on the empty paragraph on page 15 to insert the text cursor there.
8   Paste with **Edit > Paste** or the shortcut **⌘-V/Ctrl-V**.

The vast majority of the figures in this book are built exactly that way.

Incidentally, the shortcut shown next to the name of that object style will work only with numbers on a keyboard number pad, not the numbers above the letters. This is one of the reasons I insist on a full keyboard when I do InDesign work.

The Course

5 **Project**: Troubleshooting

We've already seen much of what InDesign users encounter day-to-day. But what to do when something goes wrong? One of our very first documents was missing fonts that we were able to activate from Adobe Fonts. But what if missing fonts can't be had there? What if images are missing? And what's a "modified link?"

In this brief project, we'll handle these frequently encountered issues so you know the answers.

What's the Problem Here?

Recall that at the end of the novel project I suggested that you *package* the document, the process laid out in "Package" (page 346). That is, use InDesign's package function to create a folder that contains copies of the InDesign file, its linked images in their own folder (called "Links"), and any fonts it may use (other than Adobe Fonts and a few others).

For InDesign users, the word "link" is a synonym for "image" or "graphic." But for people new to InDesign, that word is mysterious. They understandably wonder if it means hyperlinks or possibly sausages.

Many of our colleagues forget to package publications they want to send us. They send only an InDesign document that worked well enough on their computers where all the document assets live. When we try to open the sent file, we see messages about missing fonts and links because we simply don't have them.

Another way links can go missing is for the *path* to them to have changed. When InDesign creates a package, for example, it copies that folder called "Links." Some people rename that folder "images" thinking they're being helpful. Then, when the InDesign file complains that all the links are missing, panic ensues.

The document we're about to open should report that one link was modified and another is missing. When we get past that alert, we'll then be told that fonts are missing as well, but they can't be located in Adobe Fonts.

We will have to hunt down the missing linked image, if it still exists, or choose a substitute. We will have to use substitutes for the missing fonts, too, as I've been careful to choose fonts you're unlikely to have.

The Alerts

Let's encounter some of these frightening messages.

▢ Open (or, attempt to open) the downloaded course file ***05 Troubleshooting.indd***.

▢ Without showing you the document, you're told that there are issues with links:

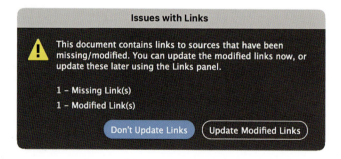

This assumes you know that "links" are placed images linked to the InDesign file. We've discussed what "Missing" could mean. "Modified" means the image has been edited since the InDesign file was last saved.

What to do? In most circumstances, we'd click the **Update Modified Links** button. But we'll defer that for now:

▶ Click the **Don't Update Links** button. The doc opens, but a **Missing Fonts** alert appears. That window lists a decorative font called Balford Base (used for the header) and a Garamond italic (but not one you or I have). For now, click the **Skip** button.

▶ Since we have link issues, the **Links panel** should be visible somewhere, too.

We might defer updating modified links because the update process can take some time if there are many links. For example, all the images in a document may have needed a color correction or other edit. If we open the InDesign file to fix a typo, knowing we'll open it again later, we can choose to not update *this time*. Once that typo is dealt with, we can update all the links without reopening the doc by going to the **Links panel** menu and choosing **Update All Links**.

Workspaces & Preferences

Swatches & Color Settings

Type & Text Styles

Frames, Shapes & Object Styles

Pages & Spreads

Find/ Change

Long or Complex Docs

Package & Publish

Besides the large warnings that opened, you may notice at the bottom of the document window the tiny announcement of "4 errors."

➡ Double-click the error message at the bottom of the document window. This opens the **Preflight panel**.

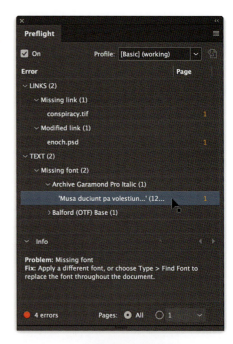

If you click open the numerous and nested disclosure arrows, you'll see the specific issues. Highlight one, and the **Info** section, once its disclosure arrow has been clicked, too, will tell you possible ways to address the problem. So will I.

Let's start with the modified link. With only one, it's quite easy to update.

➡ Locate the image of the bearded fella with the yellow warning near its upper-left corner. Click that small indicator to update the link and reveal the edit that was done to it. A little creepy.

Missing links are harder: We have to find them or choose substitutes for them. If it's a case where someone renamed a folder full of links or moved the folder, you have to locate only one of the missing links and all of them will be found. It's always good to have a sense of where an image may have gone before you start the hunt. I'll give you a hint shortly.

➡ Click the red indicator (with a question mark) in the upper-left corner of the image you may recognize.

➡ This opens a dialog box. Be sure to check the box at the bottom to **Search for Missing Links in This Folder**. Not vital in this case, but useful going forward.

➡ Navigate to the *Links* folder among your downloaded course files. You might already be there.

➡ The file's name is *conspiracy.tif*. Can you find it? Hint...   *psssst*

➡ When you locate it, double-click it. Nothing dramatic happens, but InDesign is relieved to know where it is and the indicator shows a healthy link.

As you saw, some of these alerts don't merely tell you there are problems, they help you fix them, too. Now, on to the missing fonts.

Find/Replace Font

Before we replace the fonts that are missing with ones we have, let's see if we have reasonable substitutes.

- ➡ With nothing selected, activate the **Type tool**.

- ➡ Using the Font Family menu in the **Control panel**, see if you have a *Garamond Italic*. If you highlight the current Font Family name in the field, you can simply start typing "g-a-r-a…" and see what turns up.

I have at least two Garamonds and will choose a family called *Garamond Premiere Pro*. Make a note of which Garamond you found.

The other font that's missing is called *Balford Base*, which is almost certainly not on your computer.

I have a suggestion for a substitute. It's a font we activated at the beginning of the course called *Aller Display Regular*. It's legible but playful and casual, which I think is appropriate for the phrase "Friendly Faces."

Look for it in your Font Family menu and see what you think. If there's another you prefer, that's fine, too.

Now, we're ready.

- ➡ Choose **Type > Find/Replace Font**.

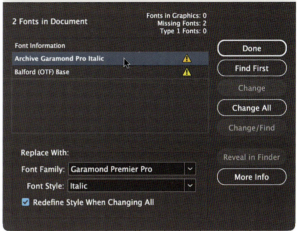

A dialog box opens. It will list all the fonts used in a document, missing or not. Missing ones float to the top of the list and get that yellow warning triangle. You can use this dialog to replace fonts you no longer like, as well as any missing ones, like here. It can also redefine styles that use the fonts that are being replaced!

- ➡ Check the box at the bottom to **Redefine Style When Changing All**. So cool!

- ➡ In the font list, click *Archive Garamond Pro Italic* to highlight it.

- ➡ Under **Replace With**, click the words **Font Family** to highlight the font family field.

- ➡ Start typing "g-a-r-a…" to shorten the list in the menu. When you choose *your* garamond for the **Font Family**, choose the **Font Style Italic**. You are *not* done.

- ➡ Click the **Change All** button. The font list updates, the body text on the page changes to our chosen font, and we're ready to replace *Balford Base* in the same way.

Workspaces & Preferences

Swatches & Color Settings

Type & Text Styles

Frames, Shapes & Object Styles

Pages & Spreads

Find/ Change

Long or Complex Docs

Package & Publish

- Highlight *Balford (OTF) Base* in the font list.

- Choose **Aller Display** for the **Font Family** and **Regular** for the **Font Style** (likely there immediately).

- Click the **Change All** button. Now you're done.

- Click the **Done** button.

- Save.

The Links Panel

As a last note, I wanted to make a pitch for the **Links panel**. It can provide you with a ton of information about the graphics you've placed, especially when its **Link Info** section is made big enough.

Even the columns of data to the right of each link's **Name** are editable so you can see at a glance what you wish to.

To see more information in either **Link Info** or as a column in the **Links panel** list above it, use the **Links panel** menu and choose **Panel Options....** Check the box for each item about which you may be curious.

Where's that image stored? The **Links panel** can tell you the **Path** and so much more.

6 Find/Change & Scripts

We have used Find/Change extensively in this course. It's proved to be an effective aid in formatting large swaths of text. In this chapter's exercises, we'll look at a few more ways this feature can save us time.

Even the best features become tedious when they need to be used dozens or hundreds of times. Scripts provide a way to perform many steps very quickly. They can also extend what's possible to do in InDesign beyond its impressive capabilities. Fortunately, you don't have to create scripts. There are many available, most for free, provided by generous users for our use.

GREP

We've done GREP queries before. In the Novel project, we used a rather fancy one. In this exercise, we'll use a GREP **Find/Change** query to move some text around. An overview of GREP and background on the two queries we're about to do can be found in the Compendium: See "GREP" (page 305). Learn even more in the book *GREP in InDesign, Third Edition* by Peter Kahrel.

➡ In your downloaded course files, locate the folder **06 Find-Change & Scripts**. Open the file within it called **Exercises.indd**.

➡ Go to the page 2–3 spread.

➡ Use the **Selection tool** to select the text frame on page 3 that holds a list of names.

Building the Query

The list confronting us is structured like this: **Given_name Surname**. What we usually need is **Surname, Given_name.** Or, as InDesign might see it, we have a chunk of characters, a space, then another chunk of characters. But we want the second chunk of characters to come first, followed by a comma and a space, then the first chunk of characters.

To state that objective in a more procedural way: We need to specify each of those chunks as what we want to find, and "mark" each in some way so we can refer to them in the change field. Then, we'll ask for them back in reverse order with a comma and space in between. What follows (and the text on page 2 of the exercises document) will help guide you.

➡ Invoke **Find/Change** with the shortcut **⌘-F/Ctrl-F**.

➡ Go to the **GREP** tab. Be sure all the fields are empty.

In GREP, we often use *wildcards*. The wildcard for "any digit" is **\d**. The one we need is much more general. It's the "any character" wildcard, which is a period: **.** . That's right, a simple dot in GREP means "any character." But I wanted a chunk of characters, so to say we need one or more of those, we add a plus sign. That is, "**.+**" means "one or more characters." That *could* be a chunk of characters spelling out the given name, but since "any character" includes spaces and more, it could also be the *entire name*! We need to be more specific.

To find *two* chunks of characters separated by a space, the **Find what** expression needs to be: **.+ .+**

Note that there's a space in the middle of that. In our objective, we said something about marking each chunk in a way we can refer to later. In GREP, this is called a "Marking Subexpression." Ugh. All that means is we need to surround each chunk with parentheses. Remember, this is code that someone made up. Accept rather than understand.

➡ In the **Find what** field, enter this: **(.+) (.+)**

When each chunk is found, it gets a number. The first chunk is called *Found 1*, the second *Found 2*, etc. In the **Change to** field, we write those as **$1** and **$2** because, you know, some reason.

📧 In the **Change to** field, enter this: **$2, $1**. There's a space after the comma.

📧 Be sure the scope of the **Search** is set to **Story**.

📧 Click the **Change All** button.

Save Query button

This worked for names with middle names or initials because "GREP is greedy." That is, it found the longest possible first chunk followed by a space and more characters. Lucky us!

At the top of **Find/Change** is a menu that holds saved queries of all sorts. The InDesign engineers were kind enough to save some for you. If you would like to save a query that you suspect you'll need again, click the odd-looking **Save Query** button and give it a name. It will then be in the **Query** menu with the others. Let's look at one of the saved queries.

📧 Use the **Selection tool** to select the text frame on page 3 that holds a list of phone numbers.

📧 From the **Query** menu, choose **Phone Number Conversion (dot format)**.

It configures a GREP query like this:

Find what: `\(?(\d\d\d)\)?[-. ]?(\d\d\d)[-. ]?(\d\d\d\d)`
Change to: `$1.$2.$3`

Aren't you glad that the InDesign team did this for you? An explanation of that query and others can be read in "More Grep Queries" (page 306). In short, this query finds any plausible North American phone number and converts it to look like the second in that short list on page 3 of ***Exercises.indd***.

📧 Set the scope of the **Search** to **Story**, then click the **Change All** button.

Workspaces & Preferences

Swatches & Color Settings

Type & Text Styles

Frames, Shapes & Object Styles

Pages & Spreads

Find/ Change

Long or Complex Docs

Package & Publish

Find/Change Glyphs

Consider all the characters and symbols you can generate with your keyboard. However, an individual character may have several (or many) glyphs to represent it. A a a A A A are a few of the many glyphs that represent the "A" character in the font Circe Bold. Only a couple can be generated easily from the keyboard. The rest can be accessed through the **Glyphs panel**. In some cases, there are thousands to choose from!

The typical way to use the **Glyphs panel** is to have the **Type tool** cursor blinking where you want to "type" a glyph. Then, once you've located the one you want in the panel, double-click on it to insert it. It then appears where you wanted it and is available at the top of the **Glyphs panel** in its set of **Recently Used** glyphs.

But what about a glyph that you will need or want often? The usual procedure above becomes tedious. It's often easier to type a glyph you can access from the keyboard and later replace it with one that you can't.

Search for a glyph by name, Unicode value, or glyph ID (GID).

Filter what's shown with the **Show** menu.

Double-click a glyph to insert it.

One Glyph for Another

➡ In the downloaded course folder **06 Find-Change & Scripts**, open the file **Exercises.indd** and go to page 4. Fit that page on the screen with the shortcut **⌘-0/Ctrl-0**.

You'll see three examples of macOS keyboard shortcuts. Or they would be if the copyright symbol were replaced with the command key symbol. It's easy to type a copyright symbol: **option-g/Alt-g**. If you don't believe me, make a small text frame and try it.

To use **Find/Change** to replace one glyph with another, each has to be loaded into the **Glyphs** tab of **Find/Change**.

©-option-J   ⌘-option-J

We might type this knowing that later we'll replace the copyright symbol.

Find/Change can make it easy to replace one glyph with another.

➡ Get the **Type tool** cursor blinking in the frame with the copyright symbols.

➡ Highlight one of the copyright symbols, then right-click it and choose **Load Selected Glyph in Find**. This opens **Find/Change** for you.

➡ With the cursor blinking in that text frame, invoke the **Glyphs panel: Type > Glyphs**.

➡ To help locate the right glyph, choose **Symbols** from the **Glyph panel Show** menu.

➡ Right-click on that glyph and choose **Load Glyph in Change**.

➡ Set the **Search** scope to **Story**, then click the **Change All** button.

As long as the **Find Glyph** choice isn't used for anything else, this is a wonderful way to insert unusual glyphs in your publications. Incidentally, the actual name of the glyph used as the command key symbol is "place of interest sign." Who knew?

Workspaces & Preferences

Swatches & Color Settings

Type & Text Styles

Frames, Shapes & Object Styles

Pages & Spreads

Find/ Change

Long or Complex Docs

Package & Publish

Replace Text with a Graphic

Although you've seen this technique in the Novel project, another practical example is useful.

▣ In the downloaded course folder *06 Find-Change & Scripts*, open the file *Exercises.indd* and go to page 5. Fit that page on the screen with the shortcut **⌘-0/Ctrl-0**.

We're going to replace the bullets in the text frame with the small golden graphic at the top of the page. There is one obstacle: The bullets are not yet directly accessible. They're generated by the **Bullets and Numbering** feature of the paragraph style applied to that list. To test that, try to select a bullet character with the **Type tool**. You will not yet be able to. This will add one easy step before we can click the **Change All** button.

▣ With the **Selection tool**, select the golden graphic then copy it with **⌘-C/Ctrl-C**. It's now on the clipboard.

▣ Select the text frame.

▣ Right-click it and choose **Convert Bullets to Text**. It will look no different, but the bullets are now selectable—and replaceable.

▣ Invoke **Find/Change** if it's not on screen. Go to its **Text** tab and clear anything in the fields or format boxes.

▣ Use the special character menu to the right of the **Find what** field (@▸) and choose **Symbols > Bullet Character**. The **Find what** field will then show "^8." That's the **Find/Change** "metacharacter" for a bullet.

▣ Use the special character menu to the right of the **Change to** field and choose **Other > Clipboard Contents, Unformatted**. The **Change to** field will then show "^C." That's the **Find/Change** "metacharacter" for a whatever is on the clipboard, ignoring any text formatting that may have been applied to it.

▣ Set the **Search** scope to **Story**, then click the **Change All** button.

This is how you can use a logo or other graphic as a bullet, since the **Bullets and Numbering** feature uses only glyphs as bullets.

Find and Change Object Attributes

You can change the fill color, stroke weight, or the object style applied to one or more objects very quickly. I use this sometimes to *reapply* an object style to many objects that might have overrides on them.

In this lesson, we'll search the document for any frame that has a key attribute and change each object that does.

▣ In the downloaded course folder *06 Find-Change & Scripts*, open the file *Exercises.indd* and go to page 5. Fit that page on the screen with the shortcut **⌘-0/Ctrl-0**.

▣ With the **Selection tool**, select each of the three objects on the right side of page 5, noting that the only attribute they have in common is their stroke weight of 5 pts.

➡ Invoke **Find/Change** if it's not on screen. Go to its **Object** tab and clear anything in the format boxes.

For an object search, we have an additional way to limit the scope: a **Type** menu to choose what kind of frames we're looking for. We'll be brave (or foolhardy) and choose **All Frames** and, in the **Search** menu, **Document**.

The difficult part of this kind of search is knowing what attribute(s) are held in common for the objects we seek to find and change. In this lesson, it's the stroke weights we just noted.

More generally, we might seek out frames with the wrong object style applied to them, or text frames with too many columns. Or all of those things at once!

➡ Click in the box under **Find Object Format**.

Warning: Try not to touch any attribute other than the one(s) you're intending to find or change. If you do, they may be added to the list of attributes for which you're searching or that you're changing.

Click to open the
Find Object Format Options dialog.

Carefully choose which attributes to search for.

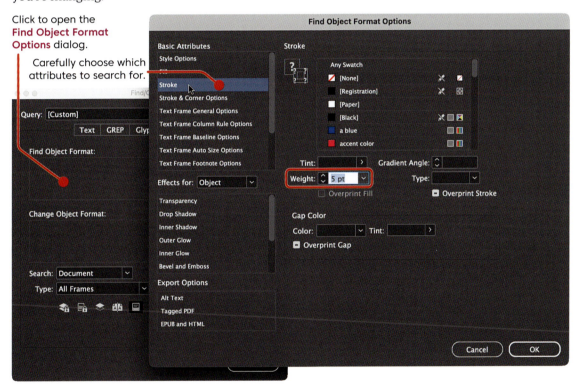

➡ On the left under **Basic Attributes**, click on **Stroke** to highlight it. Then choose a **Weight** of **5 pt**. See figure above. Click the **OK** button to commit.

➡ Click in the box under **Change Object Format**.

➡ On the left under **Basic Attributes**, click on **Fill** to highlight it. Then choose a swatch (I chose one called "theme"). Click the **OK** button to commit.

➡ Double-check the scope of the **Search** (we want **Document**). Then click the **Change All** button. Hopefully, three objects change and no more.

Swatches &
Color Settings

Type &
Text Styles

Frames, Shapes
& Object Styles

Pages &
Spreads

Find/
Change

Long or
Complex Docs

Package
& Publish

Keep in mind that as you add attributes to find, you can be very specific. The **Find Object Format Options** dialog and the one for change are as rich as the dialog boxes for object styles.

The Course

GREP Styles

Now that you've seen more GREP, we can use some of that wisdom to do automatic, ongoing find and format with GREP styles. In this exercise, we'll examine a couple practical examples.

➡ Continuing with the downloaded course file ***Exercises.indd***, go to page 6. Fit that page on the screen with the shortcut **⌘-0/Ctrl-0**.

Stealing from GREP Queries

Recall the GREP search exercise with the query "Phone Number Conversion" (page 111). The code for that query is supplied with InDesign, saving me from having to figure it out. If I want to apply a character style to every North American phone number in a document, I *could* search for them and apply formatting. But I'd prefer to have InDesign itself constantly watching for such a pattern and applying the styling for me.

➡ In the **Paragraph Styles panel**, right-click on the style called *list with phone nums* and choose **Edit "list with phone nums"…**.

➡ Click on and highlight the **GREP Style** section (on the left).

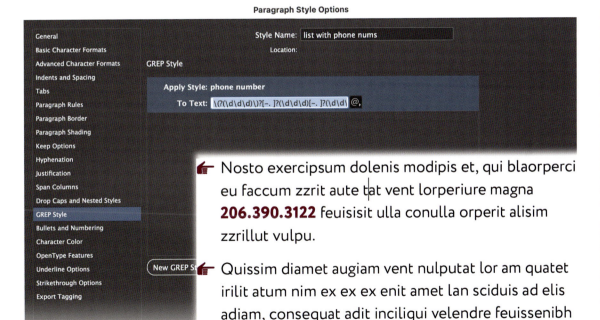

Note that the GREP Style applies a character style called *phone number*. In the **To Text** field, I simply pasted the phone number query code that the InDesign engineers supplied us. There are two paragraphs using that paragraph style (and that GREP style).

Workspaces & Preferences

Swatches & Color Settings

Type & Text Styles

Frames, Shapes & Object Styles

Pages & Spreads

Find/ Change

Long or Complex Docs

Package & Publish

However, the second paragraph has an incomplete phone number. So, it doesn't match the pattern that gets styled.

➡ Insert the **Type tool** cursor into the text and add the missing digit 2 to the phone number, and the character style will be applied to it.

Bringing Runts Into the Pack

Those short words (or parts of words) you sometimes see on a line of their own at the end of paragraphs are often referred to as "runts" in the layout community. It's unfortunate to have such a small fraction of a thought dangling in that way. To see several examples…

➡ Go to page 7 in the course file ***Exercises.indd***. Fit that page on the screen (**⌘-0/Ctrl-0**).

Note several paragraphs end with the word "runt," and one with the phrase "some guy said." Each is an example of this phenomenon. We'll be using GREP styles to remedy this in most cases, but not those in which doing so would trigger other problems.

Before we do, look at the first paragraph on page 7. Do you see the phrase "Super Deluxe Widget?" How could you not. Do you see *both* instances of that phrase in that paragraph? One is styled with a bold font in a dark purple. The other starts on the very next line but is not styled as obviously.

➡ Insert the **Type tool** cursor into the styled phrase. Look at the **Character Styles panel** and note that it shows that *[None]* is applied.

Look at the bottom of that panel, however, to see that the paragraph style is applying the character style *product*. This is the subtle notification we get when styles are applied automatically.

In the next line is the phrase "Super Delux Widget" (without an "e" at the end of the second word).

➡ Add the missing "e" so the product name gets styled.

➡ In the **Paragraph Styles panel**, right-click on *someText* and choose **Edit "someText"…**.

➡ Click on and highlight the **GREP Style** section.

You'll see that there are four GREP styles here, but two are incomplete. Those are the two that will address our runt issue.

The first one attempts to identify any plausible website URL and apply the character style *url* to it. Since some bits may or may not be present (like "www"), you'll see question marks in the query's code. A **?** in a GREP query means "zero or one." For example, `https?` finds "http" and "https." The "s" may or may not be there.

To indicate that a chunk of text may or may not be there, we wrap that chunk in parentheses.

Also, in GREP code, a dot/period (**.**) means "any character." But there are dots in URLs. How do we find those literal dots? In GREP, to search for a character that is used as a wild card like that, we use a backslash (****) in front of it.

Putting those thoughts together: **(www\\.)?** means that the letters "www" followed by a literal dot may or may not be present.

Now to round up most of those runts. Here are the GREP code ingredients in those two short queries:

- A dot/period (**.**) means "any character."
- A caret (**^**) locates the query at the start of a paragraph.
- A dollar sign (**$**) locates the end of a paragraph.
- A number in braces (like **{10}**) indicates the number of occurrences of a pattern.

So, **.{10}$** means the last ten characters of a paragraph. I chose ten characters arbitrarily as the minimum I'd want to see on a line. We want to apply to those characters a character style that prohibits them from breaking onto separate lines. The character style that does that has only one checkbox checked in its options dialog (at right).

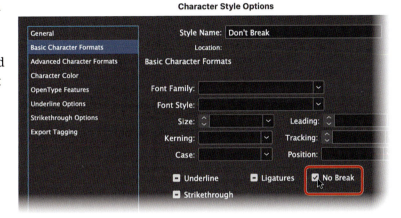

Thus, we can use a GREP style to prohibit breaking of the last ten characters of a paragraph.

➡ Choose *Don't Break* from the **Apply Style** menu. See figure below.

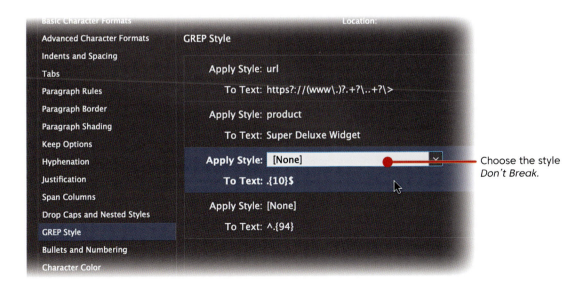

Choose the style *Don't Break.*

The result is mostly great. Each "runt" has a companion on its line. InDesign achieved this by adjusting the word-spacing to keep the other lines justified. In most of the cases, it added space. In the line that includes "some guy said," InDesign's composition engine thought too much space would be added and so reduced it instead. The entire paragraph is on one line.

rioremqui te dolupta seratio eum nobit, offic te ab iniam resti iliquunt es magnimin pero-vide nobitat enderibus dolut est, quibusc illaut iunt.

"Aquuntoe magniatecti officid uciae plat ipiuciunic et quis dolorion cor rasia," some guy said.

Idunt esteces minumet acerchilit volenime pelles imoloribus volupta tureprae parchi-tas vera? Seris autatus et rerae. Acia sitat millaccabo. Et eos maximagnis nos etur rerist hari quo quam faccumquid que nullabora volo is dus dolorestiam volore atquam et pra rerios aliqui optas nos volupiendant aut re sant, same res doluptatus reptas aliquis en-empor runt?

Ximil ipsae. Ovit fugia venimolore corehent, cum, ommodipsa cumenis tiuntis aut landionet ulparume perferum dolupta temodis maio iuntis eos dolori toritatur?Lorest, con paribus re volorep tatusdae molorenihit, ommodipsa sandita sperum quas debita cusam siminul parionsedit ut aut eveliquis undis culloribus, plitas ipiscipis ellatur mag-niquibus runt.

Lupidebit, sum, quatem et aut qui sed ut audia ipsandae serro quam atuscip itasped min ra se qui inciam, non plis doluptat eumet fugitio cor rectectaqui autem quatas se des-tiam tiaecab impores, et omnitias doluptatur accaeriosto doluptata se netur? Qui do-loreh anienim oluptatem nossitat accuptat asfewer voluptasin cumque asperatatem et voluptatus quam que dolorro videbis raes ommodipsa estiandandio volorit, quas slslkjlk-illij fugia sint et volesciet faceper iatenderitat et magnia natqui sfsfsolora was in sfugasfg. asein runt.

Namenis moluptae plam niminctas solorepere, qui cor sunt eiciis et rehent eiur aut face-pudit, omnist utent iducit dolora eaquam, nus, ad quodis essequaes et eaque maio idiore-

To retain our successes but to liberate shorter paragraphs like that one cramped line, we can apply a competing character style that allows it to break like it had done previously. I'd prefer the word "said" to be a runt rather than render the whole paragraph hard to read.

Although we can't *manually* apply multiple character styles to the same text, InDesign can via GREP and nested styles. If those styles conflict, the one InDesign applies last wins. The character style that we'll apply, *Do Break*, has the **No Break** checkbox fully unchecked. Not the neutral ignore state with the hyphen in it, but an empty box to invite a line break.

➡ In the last GREP style in the paragraph style *someText*, choose *Do Break* from the **Apply Style** menu. Commit the paragraph style by clicking the **OK** button.

The `^.{94}` in the **To Text** field means the first 94 characters. Why 94? I highlighted that short paragraph then invoked the **Info panel** from the **Window** menu. That panel provides a character count (as well as a word, line, and paragraph count).

➡ Insert the **Type tool** cursor in the first characters of each paragraph. Consult the bottom of the **Character Styles panel** to see what style is applied. Do the same for the last few characters. For the short one, it will say "mixed," since two are applied, the one last winning.

➡ Save!

Using Scripts

Scripts are bits of code that kind and clever folks make to do things that InDesign cannot or to do many and/or tedious tasks quickly. For example, there's a script to perform *many* common cleanup **Find/Change** queries in seconds. It's a bit startling to see what must be dozens or hundreds of operations done in the blink of an eye.

Please note that this section's header says "Using," *not* "Creating." There are other guides for learning that noble skill.

Warning: InDesign's unlimited undo is a wonderful thing. However, when a script performs hundreds of actions incorrectly, or performs the wrong actions, pressing **⌘-Z/Ctrl-Z** that many times is less wonderful. Instead, it's best to save a document *just before* running a script so you can use **File > Revert** to get back to the pre-script state.

The Scripts Panel

The **Scripts panel** is a bit buried: Choose **Window > Utilities > Scripts...** to see it.

In that panel are three folders: **Application** (scripts from Adobe), **Community** (scripts from InDesign users that Adobe has licensed), and **User** (scripts you've collected or made yourself). In the **Scripts panel Application** folder is a folder called **Samples,** which in turn holds several folders with scripts created in different scripting languages. I'll be referencing the ones in the **JavaScript** folder.

Installing a User Script

Let's install a few scripts I'm providing to you.

⊟ In the downloaded course folder *06 Find-Change & Scripts*, open the folder *Sample scripts*.

⊟ Select and copy everything in that folder: **⌘-C/Ctrl-C** works.

⊟ In the **Scripts panel**, right-click on the **User** folder and choose **View in Finder** (macOS) or **View in Explorer** (Windows).

This opens a folder in your operating system called *Scripts Panel*—*not* **User**. I find that surprising.

⊟ Paste the copied scripts into that folder and they're ready to run.

As we'll see, to run a script, double-click its name in the **Scripts panel** when the document is ready for it (object selected, cursor in a story, etc.).

Assigning Keyboard Shortcuts

It's often useful to assign keyboard shortcuts to some scripts so they're even easier to use: **Edit > Keyboard Shortcuts....** Choose **Scripts** for the **Product Area** and choose a shortcut for any script listed.

Workspaces & Preferences

Swatches & Color Settings

Type & Text Styles

Frames, Shapes & Object Styles

Pages & Spreads

Find/ Change

Long or Complex Docs

Package & Publish

Application Samples

PlaceMultipagePDF

Although it's possible to place a multi-page PDF without a script, each page of that PDF requires you to click where you want it to be. And you may have to create pages to hold that content.

This script creates pages in your InDesign document (or even creates a document for you) to hold all the pages of the PDF you're placing.

➡ In the course file **Exercises.indd**, access the **Scripts panel**. In its **Application** folder, click the disclosure arrows to see the scripts in **Samples > JavaScript**.

➡ Save.

➡ Double-click the script **PlaceMultipagePDF.jsx**. It will ask you to choose a PDF.

➡ Navigate to your downloaded course files, and then to the folder **06 Find-Change & Scripts** to choose **HistoryOfPrinting.pdf**. More choices are awaiting you.

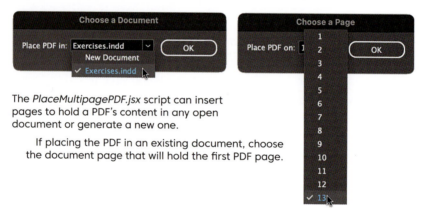

The *PlaceMultipagePDF.jsx* script can insert pages to hold a PDF's content in any open document or generate a new one.

If placing the PDF in an existing document, choose the document page that will hold the first PDF page.

➡ In the next dialog box that appears (**Choose a Document**), choose **Exercises.indd** from the **Place PDF In** menu. Click the **OK** button.

➡ It's likely you'll see a couple more messages pop up with only **OK** buttons. Click those, too.

➡ In the **Choose a Page** dialog, choose page **13**. Click the **OK** button. **Exercises.indd** now has 27 pages! Enjoy looking at them, then go to page 8.

SortParagraphs

This script alphabetizes paragraphs with a few options, including doing so in reverse order.

➡ Use the **Selection tool** to select the text frame with a list of names on page 8 of your downloaded course file **Exercises.indd**.

➡ In the **Scripts panel**, double-click the script **Application > Samples > JavaScript > SortParagraphs.jsx**.

➡ In the **Sort Options** dialog, choose **Retain Formatting (slower)** and check **Ignore Spacing**. To be honest, the formatting in this list didn't necessitate that option, but it's usually safer to choose it.

SplitStory

This script makes each frame in a threaded story independent. This is handy when text is supplied to you as one continuous story, but each frame's content needs to be dealt with as a unit.

➡ Fit page 9 of the course file *Exercises.indd* on screen.

➡ Save the document so we can revert later.

➡ Use the **Selection tool** to select the first text frame on page 9. Note that all the frames on that page are threaded together to form one story. (If needed, go to **View > Extras > Show Text Threads**.)

➡ In the **Scripts panel**, double-click **Application > Samples > JavaScript > SplitStory.jsx**.

Each frame is now an independent story. It would have been nice if the now extraneous paragraph returns were removed from each frame (easy to see them if you're showing hidden characters). Luckily, we're not the only InDesign users to notice this deficiency.

➡ Choose **File > Revert**.

Community Scripts

The scripts in the Community folder of the **Scripts panel** are made by InDesign users and licensed by Adobe to include in the program. Here are a few.

BreakTextThread

This script comes from Ariel Walden of *ID Extras* (id-extras.com/break-text-thread/). At first glance, it appears to do what SplitStory.jsx does. That's true, but this script has more options and does it better. Let's look at two examples.

➡ Use the **Selection tool** to select the first text frame on page 9.

➡ In the **Scripts panel**, double-click **Community > BreakTextThread.jsx**.

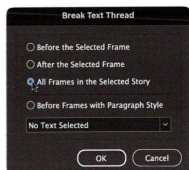

A clean result with no redundant paragraph returns. Even more impressive is the script's ability to break stories where specific paragraph styles occur.

➡ Fit page 11 of the course file *Exercises.indd* on screen.

The frames on that page serve as a simulation of a structure like that in the Novel project. If you select one frame with the **Selection tool**, you should see that all

Workspaces & Preferences

Swatches & Color Settings

Type & Text Styles

Frames, Shapes & Object Styles

Pages & Spreads

Find/ Change

Long or Complex Docs

Package & Publish

the frames in the story are threaded together.

There are circumstances when you need a book's chapters to be their own stories. For example, if you want to house each chapter in its own document for better software performance.

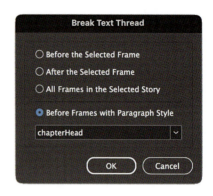

- ➡ Insert the **Type tool** cursor into one of the chapter headers, then double-click the **BreakText-Thread** script.

- ➡ Click the button for **Before Frames with Paragraph Style** and be sure that style is **chapterHead**.

- ➡ Click the **OK** button.

SnapMarginsToTextFrame

Imagine this very realistic scenario: We have just laid out a novel and sent it to a commercial printer. They inform us that the story's text runs too close to the bottom of the page by about one line. In the Novel project, we used primary text frames, which would make this situation less nightmarish. Even with that best case, this script offers an amazingly fast way of making the needed global adjustment. If we hadn't used primary text frames, this script, another by Ariel Walden, is a godsend.

Let's see it in action.

- ➡ From the Novel project folder, open your completed InDesign document.

- ➡ Go to an interior odd-numbered (right-hand) page. The first page of chapter one is a good pick.

- ➡ Shorten the text frame there by about one line of text. Leave that frame selected.

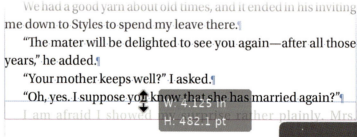

- ➡ In the **Scripts panel**, double-click **Community > SnapMarginsToTextFrame.jsx**.

- ➡ Click **Yes** to the warning that it will not only adjust margins on all pages (including parents), but will also adjust the frames contained by those margins (the primary text frames). It's done a few seconds!

UnicodeInjector

Under normal circumstances, you would have to reveal this script in your operating system to copy and then paste it into the User scripts. It's one of the scripts I provided and that we added to User scripts when we started this section.

User Scripts

This section is for scripts you collect, buy, or write yourself. I chose a few to get your collection started.

UnicodeInjector

This is a clever and unique script by Kris Coppieters that allows you to quickly insert any glyphs that may not be readily available from the keyboard but that you may need regularly. To use the script, you make a copies of it and rename those copies to include the Unicode IDs of glyph(s) you'd like to insert (and a touch more to remind you what that they are).

Let's use the multiplication sign as an example. Unlike a plus or equals sign, which are found easily on a keyboard, this glyph is tricky to access. Many people understandably will simply use a lowercase "x." They also use hyphens rather than a proper minus sign.

Are you curious about the division sign($\div$)? You can type that directly with the shortcut **option-/** on macOS or **Alt-/** on Windows. No need to use a script for that one.

With a **hyphen** and **x** rather than "proper" math signs.

$$(9-5)\div2\mathbf{x}7=9+5$$

The correct glyphs are nicely aligned with the text's centerline.

$$(9-5)\div2\times7=9+5$$

As discussed in "**Find/Change** Glyphs" (page 112), we can use the **Glyphs panel** to insert glyphs or to add them to **Find/Change**. The **Glyphs panel** also shows us the Unicode ID that this script needs.

➡ On page 12 of the downloaded course file *Exercises.indd*, insert the **Type tool** cursor into the second equation, between the "2" and the "7."

➡ Invoke the **Glyphs panel** (from the **Type** menu is easiest). It will show glyphs in the current font.

➡ From the **Glyphs panel**, use its **Show** menu to choose **Math Symbols**. This will make locating the multiplication sign easier.

➡ Although hovering over that glyph will reveal the Unicode ID, I prefer right-clicking it and choosing **Load Selected Glyph in Find**. The Unicode ID will be displayed in **Find/Change** where I can even copy it to paste it accurately later.

Workspaces & Preferences

Swatches & Color Settings

Type & Text Styles

Frames, Shapes & Object Styles

Pages & Spreads

Find/ Change

Long or Complex Docs

Package & Publish

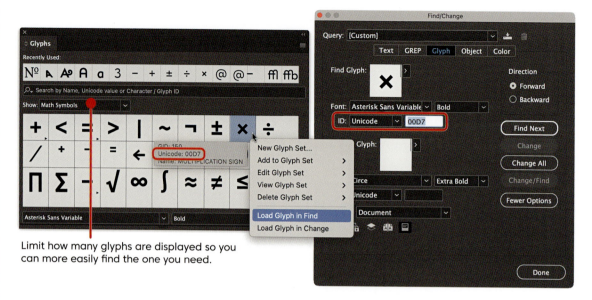

Limit how many glyphs are displayed so you can more easily find the one you need.

In the **Scripts panel**, right-click on the **User** folder and choose **View in Finder** (macOS) or **View in Explorer** (Windows).

This opens the folder in your operating system called *Scripts Panel* where we installed several scripts earlier. Locate the one called *UnicodeInjector.jsx*.

Select and duplicate that file. (On the macOS, right-click and choose **Duplicate**. On Windows, use the shortcuts **Ctrl-C** then **Ctrl-V**).

The Unicode ID for the multiplication sign is "00D7" (those are zeros). We'll rename the copied script so the name includes "U+00D7" plus something to let us know it will insert that glyph.

Right-click on the duplicate script and choose **Rename**. Rename it something like *insert multiplication U+00D7.jsx*.

Go back to InDesign and make sure your cursor is still between the "2" and "7."

In the **Scripts panel**, specifically its **User** folder, you should see your freshly duplicated and renamed script. Double-click it.

Now the text reads "2×7."

With multiple Unicode IDs in its name, a copy of this script can insert glyph *sequences*, too. A script renamed *plus or minus U+002B U+002F U+2212.jsx* inserts "+/−." Since keyboard shortcuts can be applied to scripts, once-impossible-to-type glyphs can be inserted from the keyboard. That's how I insert each ⌘ glyph you see in this book, since I need it so frequently.

+/−

title_case

This is another example of someone stepping up to redress an InDesign inadequacy. Its creator, Peter Kahrel, has provided the InDesign community many scripts like that. Check them out in this archive: creativepro.com/files/kahrel/indesignscripts.html.

The Course

This script has an accompanying text file, ***title_case_exceptions.txt***, that can be edited to list additional (or fewer) words that you or your organization have decided should not be uppercase in a header or title. I added to it before including it with the course files. Different style guides offer differing opinions, so you may wish to see if this file fits yours.

Let's compare Peter's script to InDesign's built-in function.

- On page 12 of the downloaded course file ***Exercises.indd***, use the **Type tool** to highlight the first of the lines that read "the amazing glyph of font and style."

- Choose **Type > Change Case > Title Case**.

- Highlight the second line, then, in the **Scripts panel**, double-click the **User** script **title_case.jsx**. Better, right?

The Amazing Glyph Of Font And Style

The Amazing Glyph of Font and Style

BalanceRaggedLines

Keith Gilbert (gilbertconsulting.com/scripts) makes very practical scripts for general users like us and for his clients. Many are free, too. This pair of scripts exposes a feature for which the engineers chose not to provide an interface. Keith allow us to access this hidden way to adjust InDesign's Balance Ragged Lines feature.

That feature attempts to make each line in a paragraph approximately the same width but prefers longer lines at the top, shorter later.

- On page 12 of the downloaded course file ***Exercises.indd***, insert the **Type tool** cursor into the text frame at the bottom of the page. The text begins "Balance Ragged Lines applied...."

- In the **Scripts panel**, double-click the **User** script **BalanceRaggedLines-View.jsx**. It should confirm the default *VEE SHAPE*. Click **OK**.

- In the **Scripts panel**, double-click the **User** script **BalanceRaggedLines-Specify.jsx**. Click the button for **Pyramid shape** then click **OK**.

- Save and close!

Balance Ragged Lines applied. InDesign has support for 3 different 'shapes'#

The Balance Ragged Lines style of the selected text is:

VEE SHAPE (normal)

(if you have multiple paragraphs selected, only the style of the first paragraph in the selection is listed above)

OK

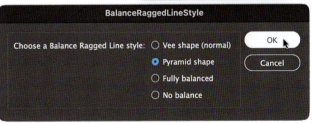

BalanceRaggedLineStyle

Choose a Balance Ragged Line style:
- Vee shape (normal)
- Pyramid shape
- Fully balanced
- No balance

OK
Cancel

Balance Ragged Lines applied. InDesign has support for 3 different 'shapes'#

Workspaces & Preferences

Swatches & Color Settings

Type & Text Styles

Frames, Shapes & Object Styles

Pages & Spreads

Find/ Change

Long or Complex Docs

Package & Publish

7 Features for Long or Complex Docs

I'll be honest with you, the features in this chapter are not reserved for "long or complex" documents. They're very often used in shorter ones. But the workload reduction they allow is especially appreciated when we are making publications like books and magazines.

In these pages, we'll learn how to create gatefold spreads (picture foldout maps), tables of contents, and automatic headers or footers. The topic most associated with long documents is the Book feature, in which we stitch multiple InDesign documents together to create one publication. Together, we'll use it to construct a magazine.

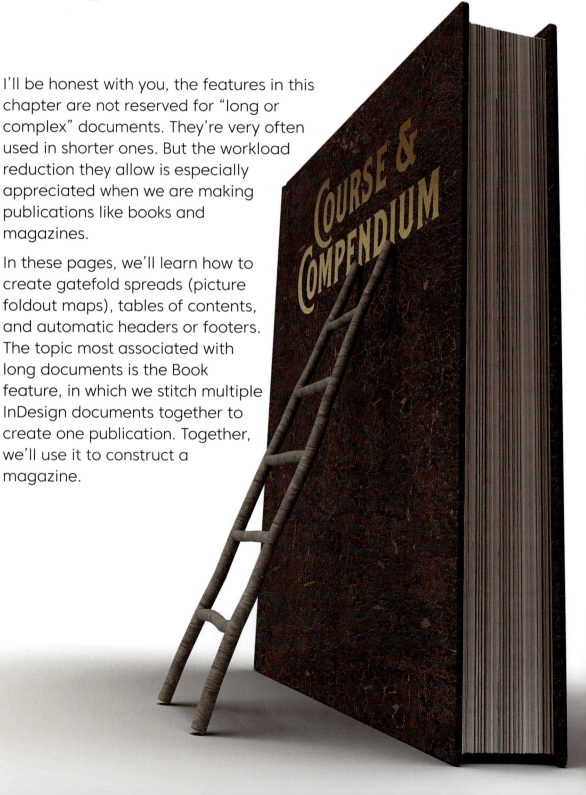

Page Arrangin'

Documents with spreads (facing pages) usually start with a single page "spread." Dragging page thumbnails in the **Pages panel** to reorder them results in a "shuffling" of the pages to maintain that single, odd-numbered page at the beginning of the document. In the following exercises, we're going to build spreads of an arbitrary number of pages anywhere we wish.

Spreads Your Way

You'll soon have to be aware of how the cursor's appearance indicates what's about to occur.

- In the Compendium, please read "Shuffling" (page 294) and pay attention to the figures.
- From the course folder *07 Longer or Complex Docs*, open the file *A PageArrangin.indd*.

Disallow Shuffling

As mentioned in the Compendium, we need to disallow shuffling in a document in which we want to make unusual spreads. Since the pages in this exercise will not retain their numbers, I'll refer to them by their content: the large letter in each.

Use the **Pages panel** menu to disallow document page shuffling.

- In the **Pages panel** menu, click **Allow Document Pages to Shuffle** to uncheck it.
- In the **Pages panel**, *slowly* drag the thumbnail for the **J** page (currently page 10) to the left of the **A** page, watching for the bracket that indicates it's attaching to the spine *and* the tiny arrow that confirms it's attaching on the left.

Workspaces & Preferences

Swatches & Color Settings

Type & Text Styles

Frames, Shapes & Object Styles

Pages & Spreads

Find/ Change

Long or Complex Docs

Package & Publish

Congratulations! You've created a magical unicorn of a document in which the even-numbered pages are on the right.

Gatefolds

In your reading on shuffling pages, did you read the short section about "Building Gatefolds" (page 296)? To create a gatefold, we have one more page to move to that first spread.

➡ In the **Pages panel**, drag the **I** page to attach it to the right side of the **A** page.

This implies that the **I** page would initially be folded over the **A** page until opened to reveal the content on both. These are used for maps in fantasy novels, charts and graphs in annual reports, expensive ads in magazines, and more.

But if the **I** page is as wide as the **A** page, the pair would buckle when the publication is closed. We need to make it a little narrower.

Changing a Page's Width

For this, we turn our attention to the layout itself rather than the **Pages panel**.

➡ Get the **Page tool** in the **Tools panel**.

➡ Use the **Page tool** to click on the **I** page.

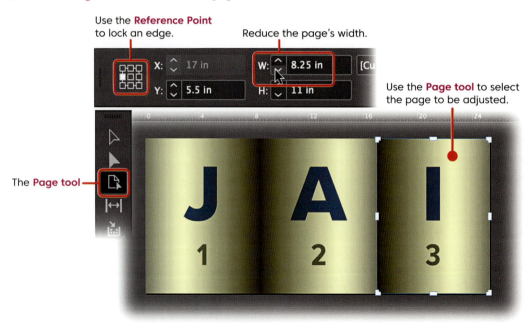

Use the **Reference Point** to lock an edge.

Reduce the page's width.

Use the **Page tool** to select the page to be adjusted.

The **Page tool**

There may be control handles along that page's edges, but they typically aren't used to resize pages. If you drag one of those handles, it will *appear* that you're resizing the page, but when your release, it snaps back. This previews how page items respond to resizing without actually doing so. Those who use InDesign to design electronic magazines use this to anticipate how content will look on devices of different sizes and shapes. Most of the features they use are beyond the purview of this book. However, we'll use one in a limited way in the next exercise.

- With page 3 (the **I** page) selected, use the Reference Point interface in the **Control panel** to lock a point on the left edge so it stays attached to the **A** page. See the figure above.

- Now, reduce the width with the tiny arrow next to the **W** field in the **Control panel**. The exact width would depend on the paper used and other considerations. For now, just reduce it sufficiently to see a small change.

- Save and close that document.

Covers with Spines

Book covers provide a nice use case for multi-page spreads. I design and build the covers for the *Course and Compendium* series as three-page spreads. The front and back covers are the same size as one another. A book's spine is the center page of the spread. Its width depends on the page count and the paper used and is provided by whomever prints the cover. If a book were to have flaps, those would be additional pages in that spread.

- From the course folder *07 Longer or Complex Docs*, open the file ***B Spines.indd***.

Each page in this document has a text frame announcing its role. Below those frames, on another layer in fact, is a frame filled with color to play the role of the cover artwork.

We are going to make the spine's page narrower. This will separate it from one of the cover pages. So, we'll have to use the **Page tool** to move that cover page to once again abut the spine.

- For now, hide (disable the visibility of) the *cover art* layer.

- Fit the spread in the window (if it's not) with the usual shortcut of **⌘-option-0/Ctrl-Alt-0**. You may need to do this a few times in this exercise.

- Use the **Page tool** to select the spine page.

Lock the left edge.   Set **Liquid Page Rule** to **Re-center**.   Ensure that **Objects Move with Page**.

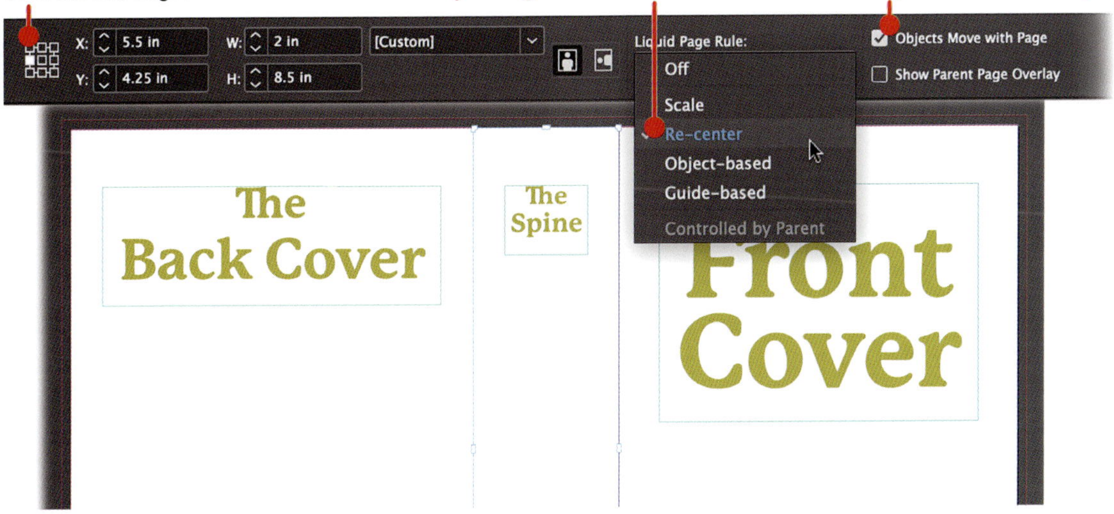

- In the **Control panel**, use the **Reference Point** to lock the page's left edge, and check the box to make **Objects Move with Page**. See figure above.

Workspaces & Preferences

Swatches & Color Settings

Type & Text Styles

Frames, Shapes & Object Styles

Pages & Spreads

Find/ Change

Long or Complex Docs

Package & Publish

The last item we'll set is a **Liquid Page Rule**. This is the feature that eMagazine makers use to coax a page's content to conform to disparate devices. Each page can have its own rule. We want the spine's content to remain centered on that page.

- With the spine page still selected, set **Liquid Page Rule** to **Re-center**.
- In the **Control panel**, set the spine page's width to 1.25 in.

Now, the right edge of the spine page has pulled away from the front cover page.

- With the **Page tool**, slowly drag the front cover page to the left. You will see a thin teal outline as you drag. (That's the color associated with the active layer.) Use that to gauge when you've snapped that page's left edge to the spine page, then release the mouse.

The spread is continuous once again. The last bit:

- Make the *cover art* layer visible once again.
- Resize the brown frame to match the spread's bleed.

Helpful Features

In this section, we'll learn a useful trick for positioning text on a page and several ways to automatically populate running headers, tables of contents, and cross-reference text.

Header Placement Techniques

I once laid out the short novel by Arthur Conan Doyle in which he introduced the world to Sherlock Holmes, *A Study in Scarlet*. For your amusement, the InDesign file and an ePub are included in your course files. Like the novel we laid out in this course, the text was provided in one text file. I wanted to keep the text as one InDesign story but have several items appear on their own pages (section headers) or at the tops of pages (chapter headers). Those objectives lead to the techniques we'll look at here.

Actually, we have seen a few times how to use a paragraph style's **Keep Options** to cause headers to start in a subsequent column, frame, or page. We'll review that briefly in this exercise.

In our Novel project, the title's text started nearly 1.5 inches from the top of its frame. Its paragraph style used the same trick we'll use for section headers here.

➡ From the course folder **07 Longer or Complex Docs**, open the file **C Helpful Features.indd**, go to page 2, and fit it on the screen.

Keep Options Review

The words "Part One" use the paragraph style *section header* and "Chapter One" uses the style *chapter header*. Let's start with the latter.

➡ Right-click on the paragraph style *chapter header* and choose **Edit "chapter header"…**.

➡ Go to the dialog's **Keep Options** section. From its **Start Paragraph** menu, choose **On Next Page**.

➡ Commit the dialog (click the **OK** button).

The chapter header disappeared from page 2. If you were to fit the spread in the window, you would see it on page 3.

Pushy Rule Above

Paragraph rules are usually decorative lines we can show above or below a paragraph to help it stand out, similar to the way we've used paragraph shading or paragraph borders (like our novel's title had). Since they're just lines, they use a stroke weight, type, and color. We can also choose how far they're offset above or below the paragraph they decorate. A bit more can be learned in "Paragraph Rules" (page 208).

There is one trait they possess that we can use to push a paragraph down the page. We might offset a paragraph rule so far above a paragraph that it would go well above its text frame. Unless we enable its **Keep In Frame** option. This will push the paragraph down to retain its offset and remain in the frame.

Workspaces & Preferences

Swatches & Color Settings

Type & Text Styles

Frames, Shapes & Object Styles

Pages & Spreads

Find/ Change

Long or Complex Docs

Package & Publish

▣ Right-click on the paragraph style *section header* and choose **Edit "section header"**….

▣ Go to the dialog's **Paragraph Rules** section. Enable a **Rule Above** by clicking its **Rule On** checkbox. (I like to say that like one might say "Rock On!")

It's amusing that a rule "above" is aligned to the baseline without any offset.

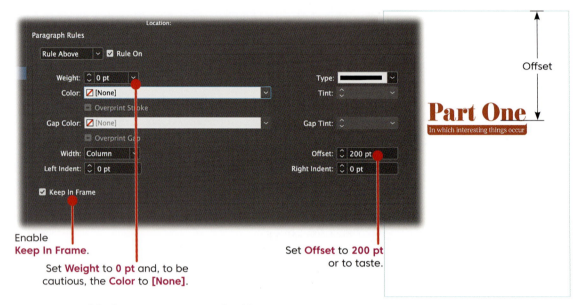

Enable **Keep In Frame**.

Set **Weight** to **0 pt** and, to be cautious, the **Color** to **[None]**.

Set **Offset** to **200 pt** or to taste.

▣ Enable the **Keep In Frame** checkbox.

▣ Set **Offset** to **200 pt** or whatever you think looks best.

▣ Set the **Weight** to **0 pt**. To be confident that a line doesn't output, I set the **Color** to **[None]**.

Tables of Contents

InDesign can generate tables of contents (TOCs) for us. It finds content used by paragraph styles we specify and uses that content as entries in the TOC. Those entries can then use paragraph styles we've made for them. Yes, a lot of style juggling ahead!

As in much of life, success comes to those who prepare. It is best to make oneself familiar with the structure (hierarchy) of the contents for which we're making a table. Specifically, we should know the styles applied to its headers, subheaders, etc. We can then decide how granular our TOC will be. For example, although some content may have six levels of headers, we may wish to make a TOC only three levels deep.

This exercise will show most of what you need to know to make tables of contents. As usual, the Compendium offers more details: "Tables of Contents (TOCs)" (page 316).

Content Reconnaissance

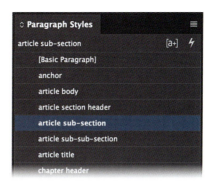

◆ From the course folder ***07 Longer or Complex Docs***, open the file ***C Helpful Features.indd***, and look through the article that begins on page 11, noting the topic hierarchy.

◆ Insert the **Type tool** cursor into the various headers and note the paragraph styles applied to them: *article title*, *article section header*, *article sub-section*, and *article sub-sub-section*. Four levels deep.

The Mockup

Put styles in a style group.

◆ Go to page 4 and fit it on the screen. Note the styles applied to the TOC mockup there. The TOC "entries" are trying to help. I chose **Type > Show Hidden Characters**, too.

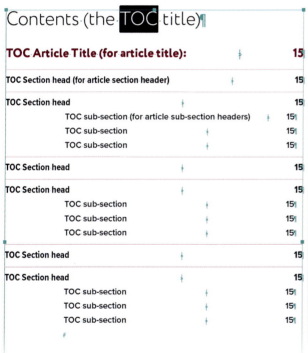
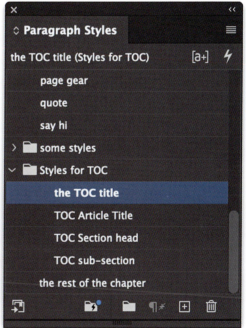

The styles used in the TOC are in a folder (a style group) called *Styles for TOC*. When making a TOC, InDesign offers to create entry styles for us using names like *TOC Title*. If we had made our own entry styles, and used those sensible names, we'd see two identical names in the list of choices. Confusing! So I put mine in a group so I can easily distinguish them.

In the case of this mockup (and our real TOC soon), we have a style for the TOC's own title, usually "Contents" or "Table of Contents." Then there are styles for the first three levels of the articles headers: *TOC Article Title*, *TOC Section head*, and *TOC sub-section*.

Workspaces & Preferences

Swatches & Color Settings

Type & Text Styles

Frames, Shapes & Object Styles

Pages & Spreads

Find/ Change

Long or Complex Docs

Package & Publish

There are two last things to note from the mockup. The page numbers should be *after* the entry. Also, between the page number and entry is a right indent tab, shown with a ⤓. That ensures that the page numbers are at the right edge of the frame (or as far as a paragraph's right margin will let them).

Generate TOC—Carefully

In the dialog box we're about to use, we need to do several things:

- Specify from which styles in the article we are harvesting TOC entries.
- If needed, clarify the hierarchy of those entries (level 1, level 2, etc.). The order in which we add the styles can set the level, too.
- Configure the format for each of those entries (style to use, where the page number should be, and how to separate the entry from the number). One can, but we won't, specify a character style to be applied to the page numbers.

Ready? Good!

➡ Fit the page 4–5 spread in the window. Our TOC will go into the frame waiting for it on page 5.

➡ Invoke the **Selection tool** and be sure nothing is selected.

➡ Go to the **Layout** menu and choose **Table of Contents...**.

➡ When the dialog appears, daunting as it may already be, click the button to show **More Options** if there. You really don't want fewer.

➡ Getting the easiest thing out of the way:

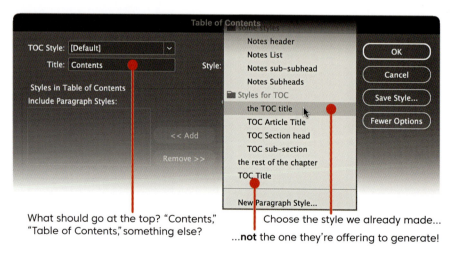

What should go at the top? "Contents," "Table of Contents," something else?

Choose the style we already made...

...**not** the one they're offering to generate!

➡ Enter what you like for a **Title** and choose the style **Styles for TOC > the TOC title**. See figures above.

Adding Styles to Harvest

Let's add the styles from which we're harvesting our TOC entries. Let's try to choose them in their hierarchical order to save us a step or several later.

▶ In the list labeled **Other Styles**, locate the article's styles. Hint: they begin with "article."

▶ Highlight the one called *article title* (to be our level 1 entry).

▶ *Either* click the **<< Add** button *or* double-click the style's name.

Now, *article title* has left the **Other Styles** list and is the first item in the **Include Paragraph Styles** list. We will be adding the other styles momentarily, but just let your eyes notice the **Level** indicator in the next section of the dialog. It shows a **1**. The next style we add will assume it's a level 2 and so on.

▶ In the **Other Styles** list, double-click on *article section header* or highlight it and click the **<< Add** button. Confirm its level. I told you so!

▶ Finally, add *article sub-section*.

Now that we have our entries, let's decorate them.

Workspaces &
Preferences

Swatches &
Color Settings

Type &
Text Styles

Frames, Shapes
& Object Styles

Pages &
Spreads

Find/
Change

Long or
Complex Docs

Package
& Publish

Styling the Entries

Now we choose how to style the entries our chosen styles have supplied.

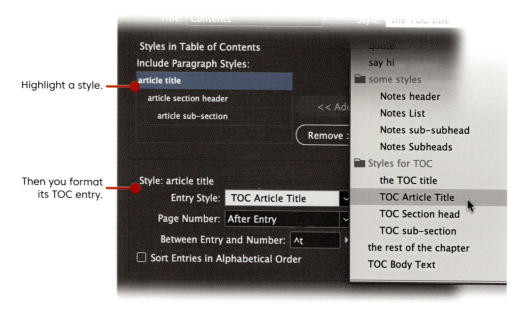

Highlight a style.

Then you format its TOC entry.

➡ In the list under **Include Paragraph Styles**, highlight *article title*. The next section of the dialog is now labeled **Style: article title**.

➡ In the **Entry Style** menu, choose **Styles for TOC > TOC Article Title**.

➡ Luckily, in the **Page Number** menu, **After Entry** is already chosen for us. It's the default.

➡ In the field **Between Entry and Number** is **^t**.

^t is a tab character—trust me. It's also not what we want. We want a right indent tab.

➡ Click the words **Between Entry and Number** to highlight the **^t** so we can replace it.

Click the label to highlight the field.

Then choose **Right Indent Tab** from the menu

➡ Use the menu just to the right of the field to choose **Right Indent Tab**. See figure above. The field should have **^y** in it now. Obviously.

➡ Do the same for the next two styles in the **Include Paragraph Styles** list.

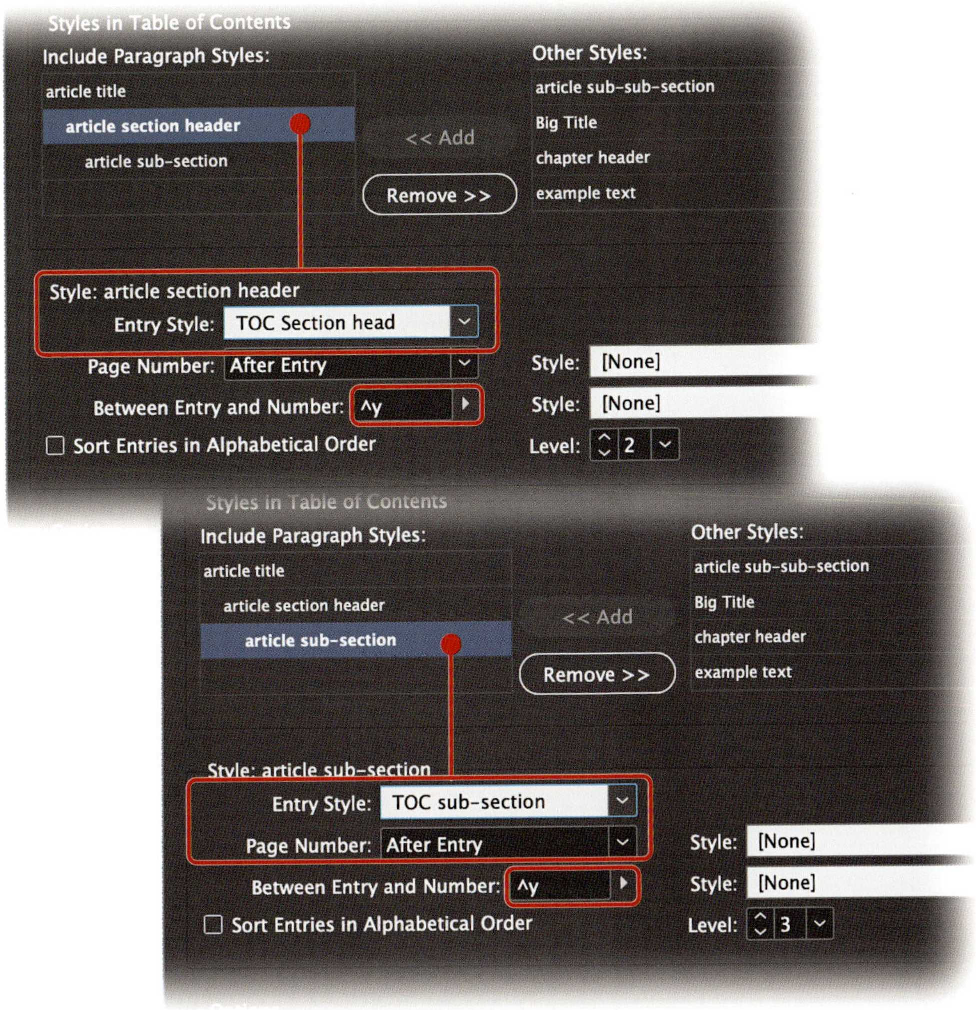

- In the list under **Include Paragraph Styles**, highlight *article section header*, then, in the **Entry Style** menu, choose **Styles for TOC > TOC Section head**.

- Replace the **^t** with a **Right Indent Tab**.

- In the list under **Include Paragraph Styles**, highlight *article sub-section*, then, in the **Entry Style** menu, choose **Styles for TOC > TOC sub-section**.

- Replace the **^t** with a **Right Indent Tab**.

In many documents, we may add a forced line break to a multi-line header to break it where we prefer it would. Such a break is likely unwelcome in a TOC.

- At the bottom of the dialog, enable **Remove Forced Line Break**.

Finally, should you wish to save all of these settings as a preset, you can click the **Save Style** button, naming this preset. I wish they hadn't used the word "style" for these. **TOC Styles** appear in the list at the very top of the dialog. There's no need to save these settings.

Workspaces & Preferences

Swatches & Color Settings

Type & Text Styles

Frames, Shapes & Object Styles

Pages & Spreads

Find/ Change

Long or Complex Docs

Package & Publish

➡ Click the **OK** button. This will load the cursor with the TOC's content.

➡ Click in the middle of the text frame on page 5 to see it.

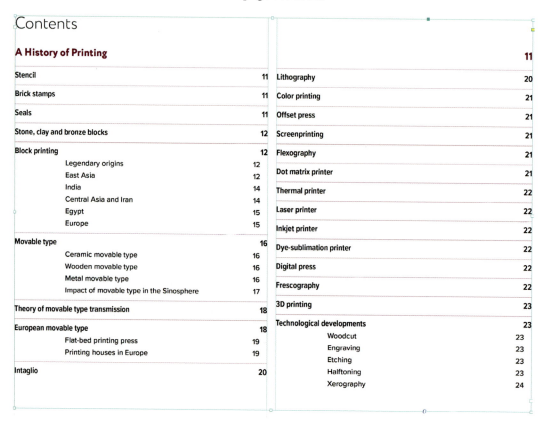

Updating a TOC

When content changes are made, they need to be reflected in the table of contents.

➡ Choose a header in the article, even the title, and change its wording.

➡ Return to page 5 and select the TOC's text frame or insert your cursor anywhere in it.

➡ From the **Layout** menu, choose **Update Table of Contents**. At least *that* is easy!

➡ Save your work.

Cross-References

You've been seeing cross-references (sometimes shortened to the catchy "x-refs") throughout this Course guiding you to relevant readings in the Compendium. In this exercise, we're going to direct the reader to a figure by citing the figure's number and page number.

➡ From the course folder *07 Longer or Complex Docs*, open the file *C Helpful Features.indd*, go to the page 6–7 spread, and fit it on the screen.

➡️ Insert the **Type tool** cursor into either of the captions on that spread, noting that you can't highlight the figure numbers.

The word "Figure," the number, full stop, and an en space are all part of the paragraph's number, generated by the paragraph style via the **Bullets and Numbering** feature. For details on how to create a numbered list that continues numbering across different InDesign stories, see "Bullets and Numbering" (page 215). The main point for this exercise is that a cross-reference can include an entire paragraph's text or just its number, which is ideal here.

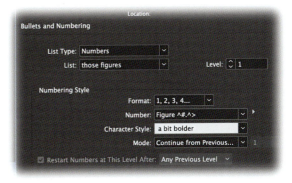

➡️ In the tall frame on page 6, insert the **Type tool** cursor after the word "See." Specifically, after *the space* following that word.

➡️ We need a panel: Get it from **Window > Type & Tables > Cross-References**.

➡️ Click the **Create new cross-reference** button at the bottom of the **Cross-References panel**. This opens a dialog box and begins the process.

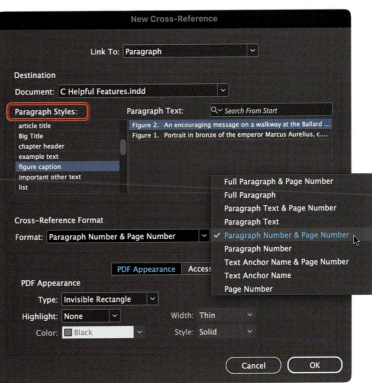

Workspaces & Preferences

Swatches & Color Settings

Type & Text Styles

Frames, Shapes & Object Styles

Pages & Spreads

Find/ Change

Long or Complex Docs

Package & Publish

➡ In the **New Cross-Reference** dialog box, locate the **Paragraph Styles** list on the left.

That is a list of all the paragraph styles used in the document. You may need to scroll to find the one we need.

➡ In the **Paragraph Styles** list, highlight the style *figure caption*.

To the right of that list is another: **Paragraph Text**. It contains each occurrence of the chosen style.

➡ In the **Paragraph Text** list, highlight the paragraph that begins "Figure 2."

Note that your choice is already previewing where you inserted your cursor! At the moment, the reference is too verbose. Below the lists we just accessed is the **Cross-Reference Format** section.

➡ From the **Format** menu, choose **Paragraph Number & Page Number**. See the figure on the previous page. It's looking good.

➡ Click the **OK** button.

Configuring a table of contents was a bit fraught due to the lack of preview. Choosing cross-reference options is so refreshing by comparison. There is another advantage it has.

➡ Use the **Selection tool** to move the group holding the paragraph we referenced and its image from page 7 to page 6. The cross-reference updates immediately!

➡ Save.

Cross-references can point to text in other documents and to words and phrases rather than entire paragraphs. You can learn about all the options in "Cross-References" (page 325). Did you see what I did there?

Text Variables

This is yet another feature that reproduces content from elsewhere based on a style it uses. Its primary use is running headers or footers. The text at the top of these pages is a text variable that reminds you what section of the chapter you're reading.

➡ From the course folder *07 Longer or Complex Docs*, open the file *C Helpful Features.indd*, go to the page 8–9 spread, and fit it on the screen.

Quirks

Let's immediately reveal a couple bugs in this feature so that you know it's not you.

➡ Insert the **Type tool** cursor into the frame with the words "hello there" in it.

➡ Change that phrase to anything you'd like, then press the **esc** key (you'll need the **Selection tool** shortly).

The orange text below has changed—no, really. But you need to force InDesign to redraw the page for you to see it. How? Zoom in and then out, or go to another page and return. This quirk does make it difficult to know if a text variable you've made is actually working.

The orange text on pages 8 and 9 are text variables. Text variables aren't ordinarily orange, obviously, but there is a way to recognize them in text.

➡ Can you see hidden characters? If you can't, choose **Type > Show Hidden Characters**.

You should now see boxes surrounding those orange phrases.

Before we investigate how to create, edit, and use variables, there's one more quirk to show you. The engineers occasionally promise to fix this one, but we're still waiting.

➡ With the **Selection tool**, resize the frame with the words "the text at top…," making the frame much narrower.

When the frame edge reaches the text, the text doesn't wrap. Verbose variables get crushed!

Defining & Editing Text Variables

The three variables on page 9 are examples of three different types of variable: **Last Page Number**, **Modification Date**, and **Running Header (Paragraph Style)**. There are 10 types!

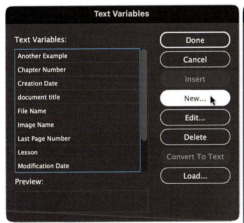

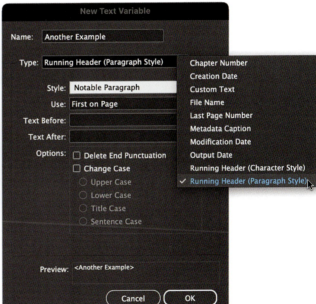

From the **Text Variables** dialog box, you can create new variables, edit existing ones, and load variables from other documents.

When creating or editing a variable, we assign a **Name** and **Type**. The other options are dependent on the type chosen.

➡ Choose **Type > Text Variables > Define….**

➡ Click the **New** button to open the **New Text Variable** dialog. See figure above.

➡ Provide the **Name** "Another Example" and for **Type**, choose **Running Header (Paragraph Style)**.

Workspaces & Preferences

Swatches & Color Settings

Type & Text Styles

Frames, Shapes & Object Styles

Pages & Spreads

Find/ Change

Long or Complex Docs

Package & Publish

- ⬅ Of the options now shown, the most important is the **Style** menu. From that menu, choose *Notable Paragraph.*

- ⬅ We will compare the results between the choices in the **Use** menu. For now, leave it set to **First on Page**.

- ⬅ Click the **OK** button to create your new text variable, and then click **Done** in the **Text Variables** dialog box.

Let's test this.

- ⬅ Insert the **Type tool** cursor after the text "A variable could go here:" on page 9.

- ⬅ Right-click and choose **Insert Variable > Another Example**.

Our variable is grabbing the text of the paragraph at the top of page 9.

- ⬅ Choose **Type > Text Variables > Define….**

- ⬅ Double-click the variable we just created, **Another Example**. This opens the **Edit Text Variable** dialog.

- ⬅ In the **Use** menu, choose **Last on Page**, then commit both dialogs.

I like to think of the **Last on Page** choice as "most recent." If we insert another variable later in the document, it will say the same thing the one we inserted on page 9.

Do you see boxed text anywhere else on that spread? The footers at the bottom of both pages use text variables as well, drawing their content from the document's title (left) and the name of the lesson. Those variables were inserted into text frames on a parent spread.

- ⬅ To see those variables, double-click the name of that parent, *reg-ular pages*.

When variables are inserted on a parent, we see their names. Both of these are the same type as the one we made: **Running Header (Paragraph Style)**. But each looks for the last (most recent) paragraph using different styles.

- ⬅ Go to page 1 and change the huge title of the document. I chose "Features for Crazy or Long Documents."

- ⬅ Advance page by page, noting the footer at the bottom of each even-numbered page.

When you get to page 12 and later, in the article about the history of printing, different text appears at the bottom. Very much like a text variable, what's used on those pages is a section marker. They're easier to use than variables, once you know where to put the text they draw from.

To learn more about variables, have a look in the Compendium: "Text Variables" (page 321).

Section Markers

Section markers get their content from the **Numbering & Section Options** dialog box. You may recall that from when we've restarted page numbering.

📌 From the course folder *07 Longer or Complex Docs*, open the file *C Helpful Features.indd*.

That document has only one section, which begins on page 1.

📌 In the **Pages panel**, double-click the inverted triangle above page 1's thumbnail.

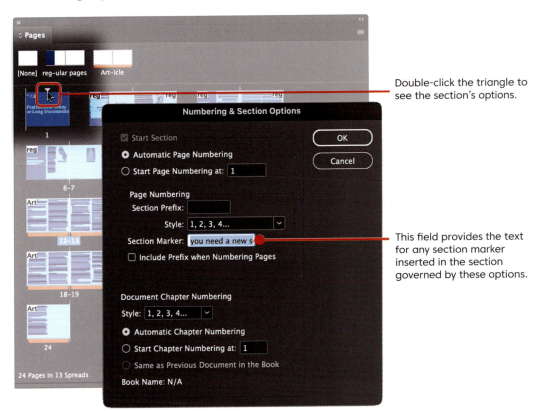

Double-click the triangle to see the section's options.

This field provides the text for any section marker inserted in the section governed by these options.

📌 In the **Numbering & Section Options** dialog that opens, replace the text in the **Section Marker** field. I'm going with "Save it, Print it!"

The only place you'll see that brilliant witticism is where a section marker has been inserted. At the moment, that's on the parent spread called *Art-icle*.

📌 Double-click the name of the parent, *Art-icle*. Look at the bottom of the left-hand page.

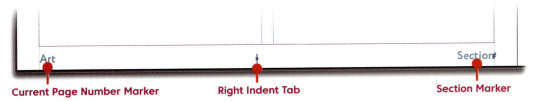

Current Page Number Marker   **Right Indent Tab**   **Section Marker**

Despite what they look like, both markers are single characters. You'll discover this when you try to select the section marker.

📌 Select the section marker and delete it. Why? So you can know how to insert one!

Workspaces & Preferences

Swatches & Color Settings

Type & Text Styles

Frames, Shapes & Object Styles

Pages & Spreads

Find/ Change

Long or Complex Docs

Package & Publish

- ➥ With the cursor blinking where the section marker had been, right-click and choose **Insert Special Character > Markers > Section Marker**. Now you know.
- ➥ Go look at the bottom of the article, pages 11 and onward.

Finally, to see different text along the bottom of some of the article pages, we can start a new section with its own section marker text.

- ➥ In the **Pages panel**, right-click on the thumbnail for page 18, choosing **Numbering & Section Options...** to start a new section.
- ➥ In the dialog that opens, insert text in the **Section Marker** field. I'm going with "I Think Ink."
- ➥ That's it! Save and close.

From that page onward, that is the text you'll see along the bottom. The Compendium has information on this, too. See "Section Markers" (page 293).

The "Book" Feature

Some InDesign documents can remain responsive even when quite long, like novels with hundreds of pages. But when we start liberally adding graphics, perhaps anchoring them and applying text wrap, and use sophisticated features like GREP styles, InDesign's performance takes a big hit. Luckily, we can break up large works into smaller pieces and assemble them with the book feature.

In this exercise, we'll combine nine InDesign documents to create a magazine. We'll ensure that their styles and swatches are in sync and that page numbers are continuous throughout.

The Database That Looks Like a Panel

To gather the components of our magazine, we create a book document, the extension of which is "indb," which stands for "InDesign book." Knowing how these work, I like to think that the "db" in the extension stands for "database," as that is what a book file acts like. Let's create one.

⬡ With no other documents open, choose **File > New > Book….** InDesign will ask what to name it and where to save it. Give it the name *magazine.indb* and put it in the downloaded course folder *07 Longer or Complex Docs*. Click the **Save** button.

Hopefully, a **magazine panel** has appeared in the center of the screen. Yes, a book document looks like a panel. Since the InDesign documents we add to the "book" won't necessarily be in the right order initially, let's disable automatic page renumbering for now.

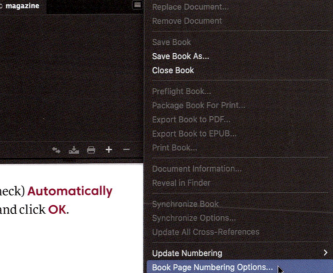

⬡ Use the panel menu to choose **Book Page Numbering Options….**

⬡ In the dialog that opens, disable (uncheck) **Automatically Update Page & Section Numbers** and click **OK**.

We'll enable that feature later.

Add Documents

Let's add the magazine's parts.

⬡ Click the plus sign (the **Add documents** button) at the bottom of the **magazine panel**.

⬡ Navigate to the folder *D Book feature* (inside *07 Longer or Complex Docs*). Click on the first document, then **shift**-click on the last. InDesign will ignore the folder. Click the **Open** button.

Workspaces & Preferences

Swatches & Color Settings

Type & Text Styles

Frames, Shapes & Object Styles

Pages & Spreads

Find/ Change

Long or Complex Docs

Package & Publish

The Course

Reorder and Repaginate Documents

The nine InDesign files are now listed with their current page numbers to the right. Let's get them in the correct order.

- Drag the doc called **Title and TOC** up to the top. You'll see a thick line appear, indicating where it will land. If you have trouble getting it to the top, let it be second from the top and move the top file downward. This document contains the title page and a frame for the table of contents.

- Drag **Features** to the second position. This doc has letters to the editor and book reviews. You'll never guess whose books are reviewed.

- Use the panel menu to choose **Book Page Numbering Options....**

- In the dialog that opens, enable (check) **Automatically Update Page & Section Numbers** and click **OK**.

There will be a several-second delay before you see that all the page numbers now run continuously from one doc to the next. InDesign invisibly opened all nine files and updated their numbers, and possibly altered the first spreads to do so.

Sync source indicator

Warning: Once documents have been added to a book file, they should be opened only through the book panel. To open a document listed there, double-click its name.

- In the **magazine panel**, double-click on **Article3**. I suppose it's technically the **Book panel**, but since you can have more than one, I like to use the name we gave it.

Indeed, the title's color is ghastly. It uses a swatch called *Issue Color*. A swatch of that name is used throughout the magazine. If we redefine it here, we need to ensure that it's redefined in all the documents. That's easy to do!

Syncing

Once documents are added to a book, it's easy to synchronize swatches, styles, and more.

- In the **Article3** document, right-click on the swatch named *Issue Color* and choose **Swatch Options....**

➡ Redefine that swatch as you wish, making the title nicer.

Note that if you edited any of the paragraph or character styles in this document, you'd want to be sure they were synchronized with the other files in the book document.

➡ Save and close **Article3.indd**.

➡ In the **magazine panel**, click in the empty space to the left of **Article3**.

This sets what InDesign calls the **Style Source**. I find that slightly misleading since so much more than styles can be synchronized. I tend to call it the *sync source*. And now, **Article3** is it.

➡ Go to the **magazine panel menu** and choose **Synchronize Options...**.

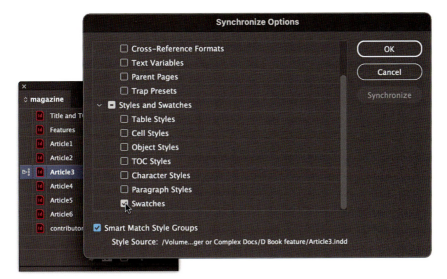

Synchronize Options has two sections: **Other** and **Styles and Swatches**. Clicking the box to the left of a section's name either enables or disables all the items in that category. I want to first disable everything, and then check the last box, **Swatches**. Have a look at the list of items that can be synchronized. It's like a review of all the features we've covered and more.

➡ Click each section's checkbox to ensure that no boxes are checked. Then check the box for **Swatches** and nothing else.

➡ Click **OK**.

Here's an odd thing: Highlighting all the documents listed in a book panel is the same as having none highlighted; both prepare the book document as a whole for what's to follow.

➡ Make sure the **magazine panel** is tall enough to show some space below the last item in it (**contributors**). Click in that blank space so *no docs are highlighted*.

➡ Go to the **magazine panel menu** and choose **Synchronize Book**. If that option isn't there, go back to the previous step.

InDesign will report that "Synchronization completed successfully. Documents may have changed." I hope so! Let's find out.

Workspaces & Preferences

Swatches & Color Settings

Type & Text Styles

Frames, Shapes & Object Styles

Pages & Spreads

Find/ Change

Long or Complex Docs

Package & Publish

⮑ Double-click on **Article5**. It's title should be in the color you chose for the *Issue Color* swatch.

One of the many options available when making a table of contents is to scour all the documents in a book file for the styles from which the TOC creates its entries.

⮑ Close **Article5** (save if it asks) and open **Title and TOC**.

⮑ On the right side of page 3 is a text frame that says "update this TOC." Select that frame and then choose **Layout > Update Table of Contents**.

The TOC style (preset) involved knows to look through the whole book of which that document is a part. I made a TOC in that frame using those settings, but it was rather empty without any articles to pull from. So I replaced what little was there with "update this TOC."

Tip: If there's a warning icon to the right of a document in a book panel, one of two actions usually cures it: Simply opening and closing the document again or, if that fails, going to the book's panel menu and choosing **Update Numbering > Update Page & Section Numbers**.

Saving & Closing a Book

Books are documents, too. They need to be saved and closed, but we do that from their panel menus.

⮑ With no documents highlighted in the **magazine panel**, look at the options available in the panel menu: Packaging, PDF export, and more.

⮑ From the panel menu, choose **Save Book** and then **Close Book**.

There's a lot more to learn in "The Book Feature" (page 334).

The Course

8 **Project**: Build a Brochure

This is the last project for this course. The brochure we build should serve as a short but practical review of many of the principles covered. In its eight pages, this document will use parent pages; object, paragraph, and character styles; text wrap; and sections.

Use the Compendium and other chapters in the Course as resources to complete this project. A finished version is provided as a reference, too.

A Brochure, or Whatever

Although we're calling this a "brochure," the procedures and features used could as readily be applied to any kind of document.

Create a New Document

➡ **File > New > Document** per specs shown at left.

I'm using the provisional name "Brochure." Although there will eventually be eight pages, we shall start with **four**. Be sure to enable **Primary Text Frame** (to aid with content insertion). Also "break the chain" for the **Margins** so you can have margins that differ from one another. Set **Bleed** to **0.125 in**.

Below is a sketch of the parent spread that will govern the interior pages:

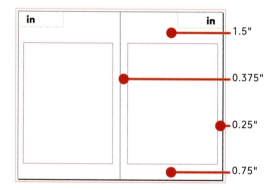

➡ Save!

Since the document hasn't been saved yet, using **File > Save** will actually yield **Save As....** The name will be the name you supplied provisionally when configuring the document.

➡ **View menu > Extras > Show Text Threads** so that when we select text frames that are threaded, we can see that fact!

➡ **Type > Show Hidden Characters** may be wise, too.

Get Styles

We've got a style guide! That and all assets for this project are in your downloaded course folder in ***08 Brochure Project / Project Assets***.

➡ From the ***Project Assets*** folder, open ***a style guide.indd***.

Select and **Edit > Copy** the group of objects to which all the styles we need have been applied. Close the style guide doc. **Edit > Paste** the group into your Brochure document.

➡ Use the shortcut **⌘-K/Ctrl-K** to access **Preferences**.

Go to the **Guides and Pasteboard** section. To make our primary text frames more visible, check the box to put **Guides in Back**.

➡ Click **OK**.

➡ Set *body copy* as the default paragraph style. That is, with nothing selected, highlight the paragraph style *body copy*.

➡ Create a new layer and name it "images" and set its **Color** to **Magenta**.

➡ Drag this layer below *Layer 1* so the images we put on that layer won't obscure the text destined for the other layer.

Speaking of which...

➡ Rename *Layer 1* "mainContent." That is, double-click *Layer 1*, rename it, and set its **Color** to **Dark Green**.

The *mainContent* layer is where your text will flow.

Select and copy this group

Edit/Create Parent Pages

Because page numbers are pretty useful:

➡ Go to *A-Parent* by double-clicking its name in the **Pages panel**.

You'll know you're there because it's a spread and page 1 isn't.

➡ Rename *A-Parent* "in-terior pages:"
Right-click the name *A-Parent* to choose **Parent Options For A-Parent**. Rename it *in-terior pages*. See figure.

Workspaces & Preferences

Swatches & Color Settings

Type & Text Styles

Frames, Shapes & Object Styles

Pages & Spreads

Find/ Change

Long or Complex Docs

Package & Publish

Create Page Number Text Frames

- ➡ Use the **Type tool** to create a text frame somewhere near the top of a parent page.
- ➡ Insert the **Current Page Number Marker** and apply the *page num* paragraph style.
- ➡ Hit the **esc** key so you can set text to vertically align to center via the **Control panel**.

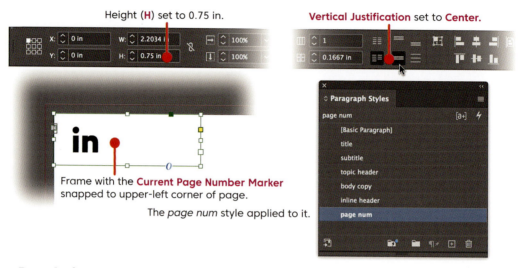

Height (**H**) set to 0.75 in.   **Vertical Justification** set to **Center.**

Frame with the **Current Page Number Marker** snapped to upper-left corner of page.

The *page num* style applied to it.

- ➡ Drag the frame to the top-left edges of the left-hand page.
- ➡ Use the **Control panel** to lock the upper-left reference point.
- ➡ Make the frame .75 inches tall.
- ➡ Then **option/Alt** drag a copy to the top-right corner of the opposite page.

Create & Populate a New Parent

Create a new parent: Use the **Pages panel menu > New Parent**. Name it *cov-ers*.

Place Covers Image

- ➡ Use **File > Place** to choose **metalType.psd**.
- ➡ With the loaded cursor, click (don't drag) to the left of the parent spread.

The image is built to size.

Split the Cover Image

- ➡ With the **Selection tool**, move the image so its center is over the left-hand page. Then click the object style *backCoverImage*.

cov-ers parent

Workspaces &
Preferences

Swatches &
Color Settings

Type &
Text Styles

Frames, Shapes
& Object Styles

Pages &
Spreads

Find/
Change

Long or
Complex Docs

Package
& Publish

This sizes and positions the frame on that page and sets **Frame Fitting Options** to show only the left half of the image.

➡ **option/Alt** -drag a copy to the other (right-hand) page, then apply the object style *frontCoverImage*.

Flow In & Fine-Tune Content

It's time for the text.

➡ Go to page 1.

➡ Choose **File > Place**, check **Show Import Options**, and choose **Content.docx**.

➡ In the **Import Options** dialog, check **Remove Styles and Formatting** but with **Preserve Local Overrides**, so the text gets only our *body copy* style applied, but bolds and italics remain.

➡ With the loaded cursor, click in the heart of page 1. Text will flow from one primary frame to the next.

Find/Change Cleanup

➡ Use ⌘-F/Ctrl-F to get the **Find/Change** window.

➡ Use its **Query** menu to choose **Multiple Return to Single Return**.

➡ Hit **Change All**. Repeat with **Multiple Space to Single Space** (another built-in GREP query).

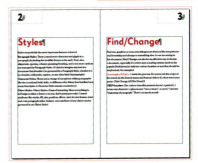

Style Text Needing Emphasis

➡ Go to the **Text** search tab in Find/Change.

➡ Set **Find Format**, in **Basic Character Formats**, to **Bold** (***not*** a character style).

➡ Set **Change Format** to **Character Style** *emphasis*

➡ Click **Change All**. If successful...

➡ Set **Find Format**, in **Basic Character Formats**, to **Italic** (not a character style).

➡ Set **Change Format** to **Character Style** *my italic* then hit **Change All**.

➡ Clear **Change Format**.

➡ More overrides? Select all text, then click the **Clear Overrides** button at the bottom of the **Paragraph Styles panel**.

After the Flnd/Change

Find/Change to Set Headers

- Clear all the fields in the **Find/Change Text** tab.
- Set **Find what** to "## " (there's a space there).
- Set **Change Format** to the *inline header* paragraph style.
- Hit **Change All**. If successful...
- Clear **Change Format** and hit **Change All** again to clear every "## ".
- Set **Find what** to "# " and **Change Format** to *topic header* paragraph style.
- **Change All**. Then...
- Clear **Change Format** and hit **Change All** again to clear every "# ".

Insert Pages Fore and Aft

- Use the **Pages panel menu > Insert Pages....**
- We need 2 **Pages**.
  Where to **Insert**? **At Start of Document** using the **Parent [None]**.
- Repeat that, but adding 2 pages **At End of Document**.

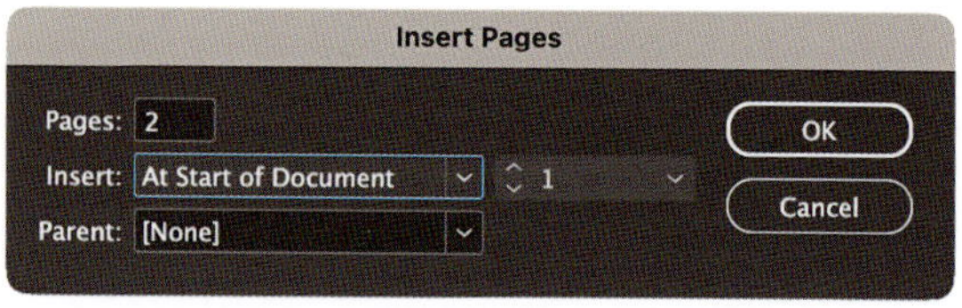

Apply cov-ers to First and Last Pages

- Right-click on the cov-ers parent and choose **Apply Parent to Pages....**
- Insert "1, 8" in the dialog's **To Pages** field.

Alternatively, drag the parent's name onto each of the page thumbnails for those pages.

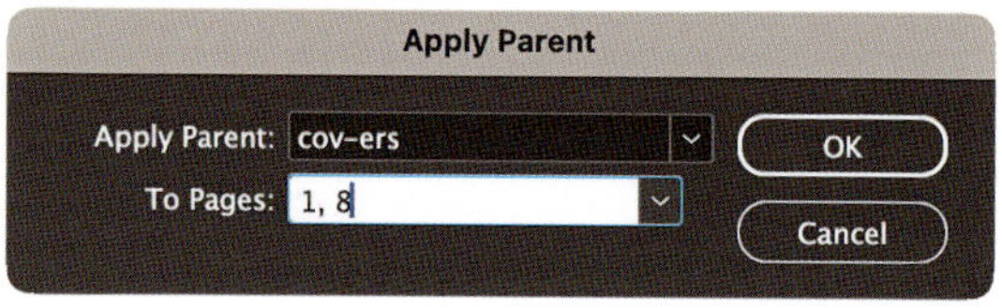

Add Title Text Frame to Page 1

- Create a very large text frame, wider even than the page, so you're assured it's wide enough.
- Apply the style *title*, then type "InDesign," press **return**, then add "4 key features."

The style for that second paragraph should have changed automatically to *subtitle*.

- Adjust the text frame width to match that of the page and position it vertically to taste.

Add a Logo to Bottom of Page 8

- Place ***LW logo.ai***, and center it left-to-right on page 8 in the lower third of the page.

Get Page 3 to Be Page 1

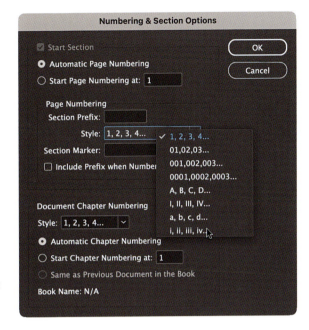

➡ Double-click the triangle over page 1 to get to the **Numbering & Section Options**. Set numbering **Style** to anything other than the default Arabic numerals (1, 2, 3, etc.). Commonly, we choose lowercase Roman numerals for front matter, so I chose that. Commit the dialog.

➡ Then, right-click on the thumbnail of page, eh, iii and choose **Numbering & Section Options….** Note that it assumes you're starting a new section (true!).

➡ Change the **Style** back to **1, 2, 3, 4…** (Arabic numerals) for this new section and check the button to **Start Page Numbering** at **1**.

Now, each of the four features discussed in the text has a sensible number corresponding to it.

Place Images

➡ With nothing selected, highlight the layer *images* so the images end up under the text.

➡ For each image, use **File > Place** and, for ease, *uncheck* **Replace Selected Item**. It's probably safer to do this one at a time.

➡ Choose a topic's image, then click the loaded cursor on or near the appropriate page:

| page ii (left of 1): ***pages.psd*** | page 2: ***styles.psd*** |
| page 3: ***find-change.psd*** | page 4: ***frames.psd*** |

➡ Apply the object style *topicimage* to each so they get positioned and acquire text wrap.

Note that the style's image is a stylized "S," making the actual "S" in "Styles" redundant.

➡ Delete the "S" in the topic header on page 2.

➡ Save!

If this brochure were printed, it would be onto two sheets of paper a little bigger than a spread (to accommodate the bleed). At the beginning of this chapter, there are front and back views of the printed pages not yet trimmed (note the crop marks). You can see why documents like this have a multiple of four pages.

We end with an image of the **Pages panel** of the finished piece (on the next page). If you're curious how to get from our reader spreads to printer spreads like those in the illustration at the beginning of this chapter, see "Print Booklet" (page 362).

Workspaces & Preferences

Swatches & Color Settings

Type & Text Styles

Frames, Shapes & Object Styles

Pages & Spreads

Find/ Change

Long or Complex Docs

Package & Publish

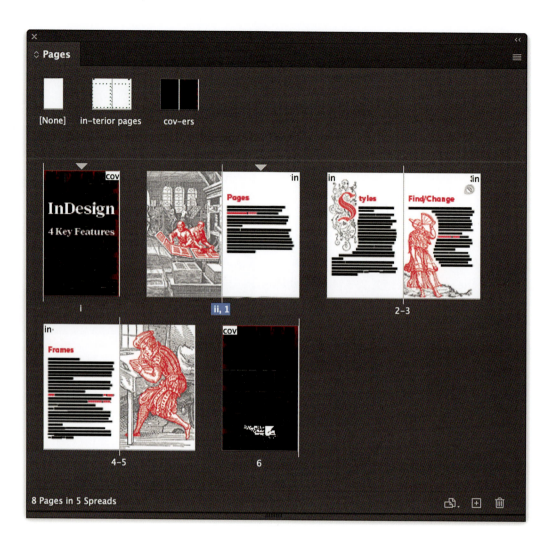

Congratulations!

You're on your way to creating professional-level publications in Adobe InDesign. I hope you find that process and your new knowledge rewarding.

THE
COMPENDIUM

1 Workspaces & Preferences

This chapter sets out how to make InDesign your own. When first installed, InDesign shows you few of the features you need and may exhibit behaviors you don't like. Fortunately, its interface and behaviors are extremely customizable.

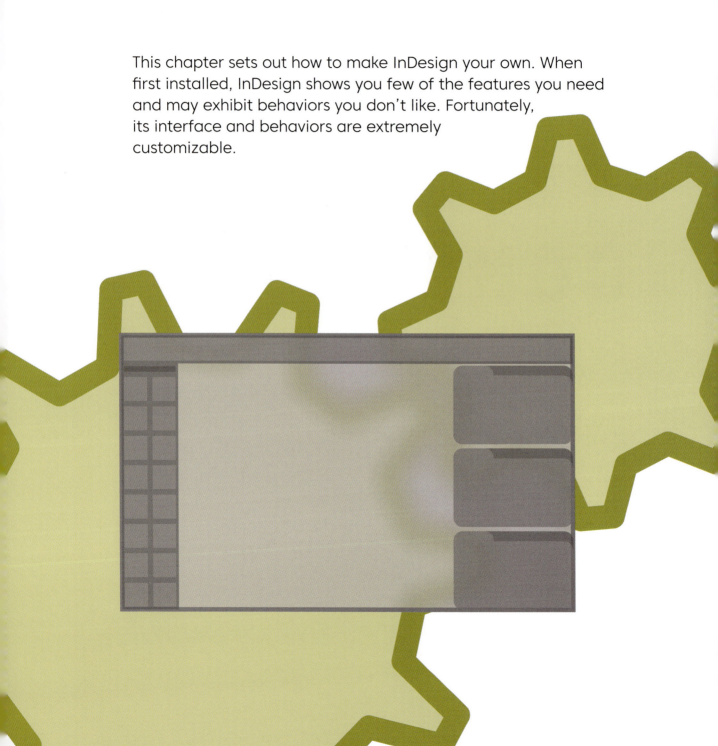

Configuring the Workspace

Every panel in InDesign can be dislodged from its current position and attached to others or made free-floating. Like the modest set of panels we see when we first install InDesign, panels can be collected into columns of panels called "docks" on the left or right side of your screen—or screens.

Any such combination can be designated as a workspace. As you parent more of the application, your decisions regarding which panels make up each workspace will change.

Choose a More Useful Initial Workspace

To choose a new workspace, it is easiest if you have a document open. Create a new document or open a recent one (**File > Open Recent...**). All of InDesign's user interface is in its **Application Frame**. Along the top is the **Application Bar**.

Near the right end of the **Application Bar**, you'll find the workspace menu. It will read **Essentials** unless you have changed it. A better starting point is **Advanced**, which is not at all advanced, but does provide the vital **Styles panels**. Choose **Advanced**, then expand the panels we need the most, close some we don't need, and collapse a few that are nice to have nearby but that we don't want in the way.

At the top of the dock of panels is small button with << in it. When clicked, it points the other way (>>) and expands the panels so you can see them. Clicking it again collapses the panels to icons again.

You can adjust a panel's height by borrowing space from another: drag the line separating them up or down.

Creating a New Column of Panels

We'll start by pulling out the panels to which we don't need *constant* access: **Swatches, Stroke, CC Libraries, Gradient.** Drag each *by its name* away from its dock. We'll simply close any that we use less often.

To create a new dock of panels alongside the first, or even next to the **Tools panel**, drag a panel *by its name* toward the original dock or left side of screen until a vertical blue "drop zone" appears. In time, collapse the new column with the small double arrow (>>) in its upper-right corner. I suggest adding the **Properties panel** to a secondary dock so you can easily access it but won't see it constantly.

To dislodge a single panel, drag it by its name.

Close panels by clicking the ✕— at left on Mac, at right on Windows

Swatches & Color Settings

Type & Text Styles

Frames, Shapes & Object Styles

Pages & Spreads

Find/ Change

Long or Complex Docs

Package & Publish

Add more panels to a new dock by dragging them to their own drop zones above or below the other panels there.

Adjust the width of a column of panels by dragging its left edge. If it's collapsed, you can shrink it until the names are gone and only icons remain if you like.

Dragging a panel next to others reveals a vertical blue "drop zone," creating a new docked column of panels.

Individual panels have drop zones, too. If you drag one panel to the bottom edge of a free-floating panel, you will create a free-floating dock. Or, if you drag a panel's name next to another panel's name, the drop zone is the small window itself; that is, both panels' tabs will be side by side in the same window.

Once you feel that your panels are located where you want them, return to the workspace menu (where you chose **Advanced** earlier), and choose **New Workspace....** Name this more useful workspace "Real Essentials," perhaps.

Later, if this workspace becomes untidy, we can once again use the workspace menu and choose **Reset Real Essentials**.

Preferences

InDesign's preferences give us a way to customize the behavior of the program as a whole *and* the behavior of individual documents and templates. In the following sections, I will not define those preferences that are peripheral to the vast majority of users.

Document-Specific Versus Global

Warning: A scary truth is that many preferences you may set are specific to the document that is open at the time. These will be indicated by a **D** in this book and are the ones to check when you receive files from others. Other preferences are application-wide, or global. How do you tell the difference? There is no way to know other than through experience and testing! So, heed this advice: To ensure preferences are set consistently for all future documents you create, set those preferences *with no documents open* at all.

It's easy to get to the **Preferences**: ⌘-K/Ctrl-K. To get to the first nine pages of your preferences, use the ⌘/Ctrl key and the numbers 1 through 9. For example, to get to my **Type** preferences, I hold the ⌘/Ctrl key and type "**K 3**." To get to the next or previous page, use the ⌘/Ctrl key and ↑ or ↓.

General

The **General** section contains the preferences that don't fit neatly in the other categories. The choices in this category are all global preferences.

Show "Start" Workspace When No Documents Are Open

If you like that large "welcome" screen—with a list of recent files, links to videos, etc.—to appear when you start InDesign, keep this checked.

Page Numbering

Larger documents can be broken up into sections. Often, we restart page numbering in each section (a book's front matter may have lowercase Roman numerals, whereas the main content has Arabic numerals). The **Pages panel** will show this when you choose **Section Numbering**. When you choose **Absolute Numbering**, the **Pages panel** will be sequential. Of course, the pages themselves will show the numbering you've established. **Absolute Numbering** makes it easier to print the first, say, 20 pages of a document regardless of what number appears on each page.

Object Editing

Prevent Selection of Locked Objects

Locking objects prevents them from being moved or resized. However, they can still be altered (e.g., you could change their color) unless they are not selectable.

Swatches &
Color Settings

Type &
Text Styles

Frames, Shapes
& Object Styles

Pages &
Spreads

Find/
Change

Long or
Complex Docs

Package
& Publish

General
Interface
User Interface Scaling
Type
Advanced Type
Composition
Units & Increments
Grids
Guides & Pasteboard
Dictionary
Spelling
Autocorrect
Notes
Track Changes
Story Editor Display
Display Performance
GPU Performance
Appearance of Black
File Handling
Clipboard Handling

Workspaces & Preferences

When Scaling: Apply to Content/Adjust Scaling Percentage

When you're scaling an object, the object can "remember" how much it was enlarged or reduced. That is, with **Adjust Scaling Percentage**, a text frame enlarged by 50% will show a scaling of 150% in the **Control panel** ever after, making it easy to set it back to 100% if necessary. However, if the text size started at 12 points, for example, it will now read "12 pt (18 pt)," which can be confusing. If you liked the new frame size but you wanted the text to be 12 points again, you might have to set it to 8 points (1.5 x 8 = 12)! Headaches ensue. I recommend using **Apply to Content** to show only the current, actual size.

When **Include Stroke Weight** is checked, stroke weights increase or decrease when an object is scaled up or down. Sometimes you want that, most times you don't. There is a similar concern with **Effects** (such as drop shadows), which you can also check or uncheck here.

When Placing or Pasting Content

The one checkbox here allows spot colors from documents you place (in particular, Illustrator files) to overwrite the color definitions of existing spot color swatches in your document. This could be useful if the incoming definition is newer, as from a recent rebranding.

Content-Aware Fit

The checkbox here should be in the previous category, in my opinion. If you wish InDesign to compose images in frames via its AI-assisted algorithm by default, this is your feature. But woe to images that should retain identical scaling.

Interface

This is where you adjust the look and feel of InDesign. These are global preferences that affect all documents.

Appearance

How much light do you want shining at you?

Color Theme

This doesn't actually have to do with colors at all; rather, it allows you to adjust the lightness of the panels that surround your document window.

Match Pasteboard to Theme Color

If this is unchecked, the pasteboard will be blindingly white.

Cursor and Gesture Options

Where you put your cursor makes a difference. These options determine what happens when you place your cursor in specific locations.

Tool Tips

These are the small identifying notes that appear when you hover your cursor over tools and other elements. Useful for new users or authors who need reminding what an underused button is called, these impact performance. If you want them, choose **Fast** so they show up quickly.

Show Thumbnails on Place

This provides the small pictures of images you're placing. This is most useful when you're placing multiple images at once so you can decide which image to place where.

Enable Multi-Touch Gestures

If you use a trackpad, you can use touch gestures to scroll, for example.

Highlight Object Under Selection Tool

As you move your cursor, you will see indicators on the object that would be selected if you were to click where the cursor is located at that moment. This is very handy when lots of content is present.

Panels

InDesign's panel display is very customizable.

Floating Tools Panel

The **Tools panel** can be horizontal, vertical, or two tools wide and vertical. I like the space savings of the single column.

Auto-Collapse Icon Panels/Auto-Show Hidden Panels

If you use your **Tab** key to hide all your panels, and perhaps also collapse some panels to icons, moving your cursor to the sides of the document window will cause the panels to appear when **Auto-Show Hidden Panels** is selected. With **Auto-Collapse Icon Panels** selected, the panels will recollapse after you've moved on.

Options

When using the **Hand tool** or resizing objects, I prefer an accurate view of my layout. Thus:

Hand Tool

Choose **No Greeking** to see where you're panning. Greeking means that the content is not shown legibly while you do something or view objects in a certain way. This term was clearly coined by those who cannot read Greek.

Live Screen Drawing

Choose **Immediate**, which is especially great when you're resizing text frames.

Workspaces & Preferences

Swatches & Color Settings

Type & Text Styles

Frames, Shapes & Object Styles

Pages & Spreads

Find/ Change

Long or Complex Docs

Package & Publish

User Interface Scaling

This final section of all-global settings gives a reprieve from squinting at
InDesign's dozens of tiny icons.

Options

UI Sizing
Makes *every* element larger, fitting fewer on your display.

Scale Cursor Proportionately
This ensures the cursor for each tool is sized as you've set the
above setting.

Anchor Points, Handle, and Bounding Box Display Size
Regrettably, the width of frame edges are not affected by this setting.
Although enlarging does make it easier to click on control handles and the
like, they also start to obscure content.

Type

This section controls most text behavior. For some of these options, it's as
simple as "set and forget." Other items you'll return to many times during
larger projects.

 Use Typographer's Quotes
That is, " or ", rather than ". If you need the latter, use **control-shift-'/
Alt-Shift-'**.

Type Tool Converts Frames to Text Frames
This global default allows you to click in any frame to convert it to a
text frame.

Map Optical Size to Font Size in Variable Fonts
Ensure the weight of each glyph's strokes matches the font designer's
intentions, even at small sizes, when using this popular font technology.

Triple Click to Select a Line
I can think of no reason to disable this global default. It's useful, and fun, to double-click
to select a word, triple-click to select a line, quadruple-click to select a full paragraph, and
quintuple-click to select an entire story.

General
Interface
User Interface Scaling
Type
Advanced Type
Composition
Units & Increments
Grids
Guides & Pasteboard
Dictionary
Spelling
Autocorrect
Notes
Track Changes
Story Editor Display
Display Performance
GPU Performance
Appearance of Black
File Handling
Clipboard Handling

General
Interface
User Interface Scaling
Type
Advanced Type
Composition
Units & Increments
Grids
Guides & Pasteboard
Dictionary
Spelling
Autocorrect
Notes
Track Changes
Story Editor Display
Display Performance
GPU Performance
Appearance of Black
File Handling
Clipboard Handling

🅓 *Apply Leading to Entire Paragraphs*

I can think of very few times when I need to adjust leading on a character-by-character basis. This preference is document-specific, so I recommend setting it with no document open so it's in effect for all future documents.

The rest in this subsection are self-explanatory.

Drag and Drop Text Editing

This allows you to drag selected text to some other position rather than by cut and paste.

🅓 Smart Text Reflow

This allows you to control the automatic addition or deletion of pages when the content warrants it. The documents in which I use this feature are usually the ones in which I am using primary text frames. Thus, I leave a check mark in the box for **Limit to Primary Text Frames**. Most often, I choose to add or delete pages at the end of a story. If I predict that the addition or deletion of a page would disrupt subsequent spreads in the document that I need to keep intact, I will check the box for **Preserve Facing-Page Spreads**.

Advanced Type

🅓 Character Settings

Unless you are using OpenType fonts—in which the font designer has likely included the size and position of *superscripts*, *subscripts*, and *small caps*—these settings establish those characteristics.

Input Method Options

Use Inline Input for Non-Latin Text

This is so you can simply enter non-Latin text (Asian characters, for example) more easily.

Missing Glyph Protection

These are more settings for Asian or Arabic text. If you type or have typed a specific glyph, InDesign will use a font that contains that character.

Default Composer

If you work in Latin scripts alone, use the default **Paragraph Composer**. If you mix it up with Asian scripts and/or right-to-left languages, choose the **World-Ready** version. Japanese gets its own composer.

Type Contextual Controls

These are great ways to make yourself aware of advanced typographic features for individual letters or whole text frames.

General
Interface
User Interface Scaling
Type
Advanced Type
Composition
Units & Increments
Grids
Guides & Pasteboard
Dictionary
Spelling
Autocorrect
Notes
Track Changes
Story Editor Display
Display Performance
GPU Performance
Appearance of Black
File Handling
Clipboard Handling

Workspaces & Preferences

Swatches & Color Settings

Type & Text Styles

Frames, Shapes & Object Styles

Pages & Spreads

Find/ Change

Long or Complex Docs

Package & Publish

Composition

These settings alert you to issues in your text and adjust the behavior of text wrap. All these preferences are document-specific and thus show a .

ⓓ Highlight

Text that deviates from the settings you've chosen (in style definitions, for example) is highlighted, so you can quickly find, judge, and, if necessary, squash them.

Set these on a document-by-document basis.

The Header at the Top	The Header at the Top	The Header at the Top
H&J violations	Custom kerning/tracking	Substituted glyph & fonts

ⓓ *Keep Violations*

You will never incur a violation of your "keeps" settings, thus you'll never see this highlighting.

ⓓ *H&J Violations*

Text is highlighted when InDesign uses more than your maximum or less than your minimum word spacing, or when it uses more hyphens. A greater violation makes yellower highlighting.

ⓓ *Custom Tracking/Kerning*

Kerning and tracking are facts of life. If you need to see where you made these adjustments, this preference will highlight them in green.

ⓓ *Substituted Fonts*

When you have specified a font that is not installed for your text, InDesign will highlight it in pink.

ⓓ *Substituted Glyphs*

When InDesign substitutes two or more letters with a ligature, for example, this choice will highlight that occurrence in gold.

ⓓ Text Wrap

ⓓ *Justify Text Next to an Object*

This option comes into play only when an object with text wrap divides lines of text—something you should never allow to happen.

D *Skip by Leading*

When text wrap interrupts the flow of text in a column (for example, when using the **Jump Object** text wrap), this option ensures that when the text resumes, it will flow along the baseline grid. This presumes, of course, that you have set up your baseline grid to correspond to the leading of your text.

D *Text Wrap Only Affects Text Beneath*

There are many good reasons to keep images below text frames, but you may still wish to have those images possess text wrap. Leave this unchecked.

D *Honor Text Indents in addition to Text Wrap*

A welcome addition for hanging indents (as often are used in lists), this ensures they retain their look even when text wrap is employed nearby.

Units & Increments

Here we decide how things measure up. There are enough units of measurement from which to choose to please just about everyone. This page is entirely document-specific.

D ### Ruler Units

To set the point from which things are measured (zero on the ruler), choose an **Origin**. The **Origin** can be the upper-left corner of a spread or an individual page. If you choose **Spine**, the values increase with distance from the spine. Note that your horizontal and vertical units of measurement can be different, and can be changed at any time by right-clicking on either ruler in your layout. You can even use custom increments. For example, I often set my vertical increment equal to my base leading.

D ### Other Units

This provides a way to measure stroke weight in something other than points.

D ### Keyboard Increments

D *Cursor Key*

The arrow keys can be used to move objects. If you select an object, the **Cursor Key** value is how far the object will be "nudged" when you press an arrow key.

D *Baseline Shift*

To raise and lower selected text from its initial position, use this shortcut: **option-Shift- ↑** *or* **↓/Alt-Shift- ↑** *or* **↓**. **Baseline Shift** is the increment by which the text is moved.

General
Interface
User Interface Scaling
Type
Advanced Type
Composition
Units & Increments
Grids
Guides & Pasteboard
Dictionary
Spelling
Autocorrect
Notes
Track Changes
Story Editor Display
Display Performance
GPU Performance
Appearance of Black
File Handling
Clipboard Handling

Workspaces & Preferences

Swatches & Color Settings

Type & Text Styles

Frames, Shapes & Object Styles

Pages & Spreads

Find/ Change

Long or Complex Docs

Package & Publish

Ⓓ *Size/Leading*

A keyboard shortcut can be used to adjust the size and leading of selected text according to the increment specified here. Press **⌘-shift-<** *or* **>/Ctrl-Shift-<** *or* **>** to decrease or increase the size (respectively). To adjust the leading, press **option-↑** *or* **↓/Alt-↑** *or* **↓**.

Ⓓ *Kerning/Tracking*

Tapping the **left** or **right arrow** keys while holding the **option/Alt** key adjusts kerning (if your cursor is blinking between two letters) or tracking (if you have a range of text selected). As your eye attunes to these attributes, you may lower this value.

Grids

These document-specific preferences control the look and behavior of these grids. Grids are similar in behavior to guides (up next).

Ⓓ **Baseline Grid**

Horizontal lines are best incremented in a value equal to your document's body copy leading. Here you specify the color and starting point of these horizontal lines, as well as the level of magnification at which they become visible (**View Threshold**). Although paragraph styles can be defined to make text snap to this baseline grid, I more often carefully set leading and spacing instead. For more on how baseline grids are used, see Align to Grid (page 205).

Ⓓ **Document Grid**

This is a true grid for which you can choose the color and frequency. You can set a somewhat coarse grid with finer subdivisions that are displayed more faintly.

Guides & Pasteboard

These options provide you with even more ways to give structure to your layout. Here you set the appearance of your guides, when you are shown "Smart Guides," and how much pasteboard there is around your spreads.

Ⓓ **Color and Guide Options**

Choose how close (in screen pixels) an object should be to a guide for it to snap onto it. Also choose whether guides appear behind objects or not.

    I also prefer to have my **Preview Background** match the chosen color theme.

Smart Guide Options

Mysteriously, these are the only options in the **Guides & Pasteboard** section that are global. **Smart Guides** are the lines that appear as you drag objects around the page when those objects align either to other objects on the page or to landmarks of the page, spread, or margins.

 Pasteboard Options

Set the amount of space you would like to have beyond the edge of your spread where you might place objects that you are not quite sure you wish to be without. Reminder: Objects on the pasteboard do not print nor do they export in a PDF.

Dictionary

The dictionary is *Hunspell*, a popular open source dictionary.

Language

This is where you select the language associated with the dictionary seen in the window below this menu (this is the only global dictionary setting). The window shows the location of the dictionary file(s). If you can make or procure a plain text file containing a list of words or phrases you commonly use, you can quickly add that list by clicking on the **+** below the small window. This is handy if you work in a specialized industry with a specialized vocabulary, and if you have time to create or find such a list.

Double Quotes and Single Quotes

Choose the style for quotation marks.

Hyphenation Exceptions

Over time, you may correct InDesign's placement of hyphens. These corrections, or "Exceptions," are stored in the User Dictionary. To be sure that all of the exceptions you have defined are used, choose **User Dictionary and Document** in the menu labeled **Compose Using**.

User Dictionary

To share your User Dictionary, you may choose to **Merge User Dictionary into Document**. This can be valuable for templates with specialized words.

Spelling

These global preferences control the scope and display of spell check.

Find

These are the items that will be flagged when doing a spell check. **Edit > Spelling > Check Spelling...** or **⌘-I/Ctrl-I** starts the process.

Dynamic Spelling

This is an ongoing spell check that colorfully underlines the problems above. This feature (and **Autocorrect**) can also be enabled by going to **Edit > Spelling**.

Swatches &
Color Settings

Type &
Text Styles

Frames, Shapes
& Object Styles

Pages &
Spreads

Find/
Change

Long or
Complex Docs

Package
& Publish

Autocorrect

As you write or edit in InDesign, **Autocorrect** will fix your most common errors. This is great for people like me, who type "t-e-h" instead of "the." Add your most common gaffs here.

Notes

These options allow for the exchange of editorial information among users of a document. When writing or editing in InDesign, a user can right-click and choose **New Note**. Each user can have a unique, identifying color. We can include notes in spell check or find/change operations.

See **Track Changes** (next!) for how to configure a user.

Track Changes

Make clear what's changed and by whom.

These global preferences control the look and feel of changes that are shown when editing in the **Story Editor**. Decide which changes are shown, and how to identify who made them.

Show

To define your user name and color, choose **File > User...**. The name and color you choose will be used for notes and tracked changes. When you exchange a document with someone else and they edit text in the **Story Editor**, their changes will appear with their color behind them. You can prevent clashes with the checkbox **Prevent Duplicate User Colors**.

Change Bars

Change Bars (which appear in the left margin of the **Story Editor** by default) make it easy to find changes quickly while scanning text.

Finally, I check the box labeled **Include Deleted Text When Spellchecking** in case I later reject those deletions and the text makes its way back into my publication.

Story Editor Display

Just you and the words.

Text Display Options and Cursor Options

To see your text without the distractions of the layout, turn to the **Story Editor**. You can also view notes and tracked changes there. Since the **Story Editor** is only an editorial tool, and is not visible in the final published piece, you can choose how to display it. Sometimes, I use the old computer terminal theme—it reminds me of when I was young.

Display Performance

Control how hard InDesign works to make its content look good. Note the word "performance." These settings can enhance or degrade the speed with which InDesign displays text and images. The print quality of your document is not affected by these settings at all.

Default View

There are three choices: **Fast**, **Typical**, and **High Quality**. **Fast** doesn't display images at all, but instead shows gray boxes or shapes—rather brutal. By default, **Typical** shows a "proxy" that InDesign generates for each image, the quality of which could be startling, especially to the supervisor looking over your shoulder. **High Quality** renders images, graphics, and anything transparent without compromise. For small documents, you may use **High Quality** without much penalty. Larger and more graphically rich documents will become sluggish unless you reduce the **Display Performance** view.

Fast

Typical

High Quality

Adjust View Settings

You may tweak each of the view settings to better tune the performance of InDesign. For example, you may want to adjust **Typical** to have low-quality **Transparency** but high-quality **Vector Graphics** (AI and PDF files, for example) so your company's logo will look splendid when your boss sees it, and leave **Raster Images** (those made of pixels) as a proxy.

GPU Performance

On **macOS only**. If your computer supports it, use it! Although using the computer's graphics processor for some functions does speed things up, I still prefer to use a non-animated zoom. Holding down the **Z** key and drawing a box around what I wish to view closely is faster and more precise (unless I'm editing text, in which case I hold down **⌘-spacebar/Ctrl-spacebar**). Oddly, as of this writing, the GPU will not appear supported unless you're also taxing it with a "high dpi" display.

Swatches &
Color Settings

Type &
Text Styles

Frames, Shapes
& Object Styles

Pages &
Spreads

Find/
Change

Long or
Complex Docs

Package
& Publish

Appearance of Black

Black ink is special.

Options for Black on RGB and Grayscale Devices

Needlessly confusing choices for the appearance of black!

On Screen

I choose to display all blacks accurately on-screen. This means that items that use the pure black (100% K) swatch will look lighter (more gray) than a rich black, which is made from black ink plus a bit of others, too.

Printing/Exporting

This is the confusing one. Choose **Output All Blacks as Rich Black**, then hover your cursor over that choice and note the description below that attempts—but fails—to clarify. What it means is that on a device that has only black ink or toner, both rich blacks and pure blacks will print as dark as possible. The phrase "RGB devices" refers to common desktop inkjet printers! With this setting, color laser printers and presses (true CMYK devices) will still produce blacks accurately: pure black will use black ink or toner only, and rich black will be output as designed. Since I use all of these devices, I choose the confusing **Output All Blacks as Rich Black** setting.

🅓 Overprinting of [Black]

Unlike other colors, which knock out others, black ink usually overprints. This setting ensures that, or it can be disabled to allow black in to knock out others.

File Handling

Crash recovery and link juggling are the main fare here.

Document Recovery Data

Unlimited undo and the ability to resume work after a crash is made possible by a recovery file that InDesign creates for you. When working on an existing InDesign file, the recovery file will be in the same folder. Until a new document is saved, the location shown in this preference is where the file is stored.

Saving InDesign Files

A favorite way to open ongoing projects is by going to **File > Open Recent**. You can alter how many (if any) files are listed there. Also in the **File** menu is **Browse in Bridge….** Bridge is an Adobe application for browsing the files on your computer. Its thumbnails are usually more helpful than the operating system's, and if you click on one, you can use Bridge's preview panel to flip through as many pages of an InDesign document as you specify here in the **Pages** menu of this preference. This is useful when the file is named "untitled 14.indd."

Ⓓ Snippet Import

InDesign offers numerous ways to save and reuse bits of your layouts: CC Libraries, library documents (.indl file), and snippets. You can select a text frame, for example, and choose **File > Export...** to export it as an InDesign Snippet (.idms file). These can be shared and placed into other InDesign documents, bringing along any styles they use. This preference determines where the placed snippet will land: where you click with your loaded cursor (**Cursor Location**) or in the same relative position the object had on its original page (**Original Location**).

Links

The mysterious connections between our linked files and the InDesign documents in which they appear can be made a little clearer here.

Check Links Before Opening Document

The key word here is "Before." With this option disabled, InDesign will still check your links' status, but will do so after the document is opened, which makes the opening of files more rapid.

Find Missing Links Before Opening Document

When opening a document, it can be helpful to get a heads-up when something is wrong. If you have images linked to your InDesign document and some of them have gone missing, you likely want to know that sooner rather than later. However, there may be times when you willingly work on a document whose images you know to be missing, and you would prefer not to have the annoyance of a message telling you so. When that is the case, I enable this preference so InDesign may find the image in a recently used folder, for example. It's also possible, however, that in an attempt to find a missing link in folders you've recently linked to, InDesign will link to the wrong version of an image. If you experience this behavior, disable this preference and manually locate the correct missing linked file.

Ⓓ Create Links When Placing Text and Spreadsheet Files

As with images, you can place text files and maintain a link to the original. However, without the help of a third-party plug-in like WordsFlow by Em Software, the formatting you may have done in InDesign is lost when you update those links.

Preserve Image Dimensions When Relinking

Typically, when you swap the content of an image frame with another image, InDesign will attempt to make the proportions of the new image match those of the previous image. For example, if the frame has been resized to show only a third of the original image, InDesign will attempt to show only a third of the new image in that frame. This is fine for images with similar subject matter and/or proportions, but when the new image has little connection to

Workspaces & Preferences

Swatches & Color Settings

Type & Text Styles

Frames, Shapes & Object Styles

Pages & Spreads

Find/ Change

Long or Complex Docs

Package & Publish

the original, you may wish to decide for yourself how that image will fit its frame by disabling this setting.

Hide New Layers When Updating or Relinking

Images produced in Photoshop or graphics created in Illustrator typically have layers. When you place these kinds of documents (.psd or .ai), you can choose which layers are visible in InDesign. If you subsequently edit a document, and those edits introduce new layers to the structure of the document, this setting determines whether those new layers are visible when you update the link.

Fonts

The first thing I enable for a fresh InDesign install is **Auto-activate Adobe Fonts**. I strongly recommend that you do, too!

Clipboard Handling

Material that is copied or cut lives in the system clipboard. Here, we determine what InDesign reads from or writes to that clipboard.

General
Interface
User Interface Scaling
Type
Advanced Type
Composition
Units & Increments
Grids
Guides & Pasteboard
Dictionary
Spelling
Autocorrect
Notes
Track Changes
Story Editor Display
Display Performance
GPU Performance
Appearance of Black
File Handling
Clipboard Handling

Clipboard

Whether it's inbound or outbound, you can choose to preserve the structure or appearance of what you put on your clipboard.

Prefer PDF When Pasting

I sometimes generate objects in other applications such as Illustrator. Most often, I simply place that Illustrator document as a link into my InDesign publication. However, sometimes I need the shape I have drawn in Illustrator as an editable shape in InDesign. Since Illustrator provides both the path data and the PDF data to the clipboard, I disable this setting to get the path data into InDesign.

Copy PDF to Clipboard

When I need to provide to another application something I have copied or cut in InDesign, the odds of preserving its appearance are better if what I copy to the clipboard is PDF data. If I suspect I will be pasting this data after I quit InDesign, I enable the option just below this one.

Preserve PDF Data at Quit

This allows me to paste copied PDF data after InDesign has quit.

When Pasting Text and Tables from Other Applications Paste

Content you have copied from Microsoft Word or Apple Pages (for example) can be pasted as rich text (**All Information**) or as plain text (**Text Only**). Pasted plain text inherits the formatting that is active at the insertion point in InDesign.

2 Swatches & Color Settings

This chapter starts with the nuts and bolts of applying colors and gradients and creating swatches using different color models (RGB, CMYK, HSB, Lab). The answers to questions about when (and why) to use each of those color models are found in the second section of this chapter. You'll find that the details of color in InDesign are far from black and white (pardon the pun).

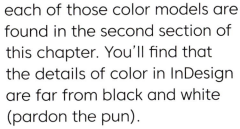

Colors, Gradients, and Swatches

Any frame can be filled, and/or its stroke decorated, with a color or gradient or nothing at all. The **Color panel** or the **Gradient panel** let you do this in an *ad hoc* way, choosing colors arbitrarily. When you need consistency, there is power in the **Swatches panel**.

Choosing a color at random is easy: Click in the **Color panel's** "ramp" to get close. Use the sliders to fine-tune. Use the panel menu to choose the color model used by the sliders.

Color Ramp

Choosing the color model

Use the **Gradient panel** to construct gradations that proceed linearly or radially. Edit the colors involved with the ramp at the bottom. The size and direction is best controlled with the **Gradient tool**.

Gradient Ramp:
Double-click a stop to change its color.

The **Swatches panel** stores colors and gradients you may need again.

The **Control panel** allows us to choose a swatch for **Fill** or **Stroke**, or, when you hold the **shift** key, offers the **Color panel** instead. Alas, no gradients unless they're swatches.

There are multiple ways in which you can apply a color or gradient. With the **Control panel**, clicking either the **Fill** or **Stroke** box will show the **Swatches panel**. Holding the **shift** key while doing so shows the **Color panel**.

Clicking the **Fill** or **Stroke** boxes in the **Properties panel** offers options for choosing from swatches or the equivalents of the **Color** and **Gradient panels**.

Usually, you can choose from a rainbow of colors in the bar at the bottom of the **Color panel**, called the **Ramp**, then fine-tune with the sliders above. However, if a swatch had been chosen previously, you'll be shown tints of that color instead. The assumption is that swatch users wish to use a limited palette. To have access to the entire rainbow when you're shown only tints, select a color model from the **Color panel** menu (**RGB**, **CMYK**, or **Lab**). That severs that attribute's link to the swatch.

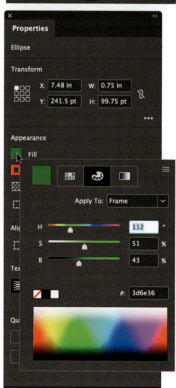

Special & Restricted Swatches

Note the four swatches whose names are in square brackets (**[]**). Three of those are uneditable, indicated by the slashed pencil: **[None]**, **[Registration]**, and **[Black]**. **[None]** is used to remove a color from a **Fill** or **Stroke**. **[Black]**, sometimes referred to as pure black, is a special CMYK swatch that applies black ink only. This swatch is most useful with text, to keep it sharp and legible. There is much more to be read about this swatch later in this chapter.

[Registration] looks like black in the list view in the **Swatches panel**, but like a crosshair when viewing swatches as thumbnails. It is to be used *only* with things that should appear on all printing plates, like crop/trim marks and registration marks. InDesign creates these automatically when you export a PDF and tick the boxes to include these. This is not a swatch an InDesign user should apply to anything else!

Some designers, wanting to fill an area with a "rich black," are tempted to use **[Registration]**. But since its build is 100% of all inks, it can create a huge mess when printed. You can create a rich black swatch of your own with a build of relatively low percentages of cyan, magenta, and yellow, and 100% black, which will look like a rich and deep black but be far less dangerous. Many commercial printers suggest a build of 60C 40M 40Y 100K, which totals 240. That's likely too much for thin papers like newsprint, but otherwise provides a nice result on most devices.

[Paper] is applied where no ink should go. This swatch can be edited to simulate colored paper on screen, but it will never add color when output.

Creating Color Swatches

If you'd like a color to be a swatch so it can be chosen easily later, use the **Swatches panel** menu and choose **New Color Swatch…**. Remember, you can do this via the **Swatches panel** that appears when you click the **Fill** or **Stroke** menus in the **Control panel**, too.

The **New Color Swatch** dialog box has a number of choices that confront you. Easily missed among them is the name of the swatch. I will typically name a swatch for its purpose (or at least I aspire to do so). To enter a name, you must first uncheck **Name with Color Value**.

The **Color Type** is a choice between using the four-color process (CMYK) or a custom ink known as a *spot color*. In principle, any color can be a spot color, but to be completely unambiguous we usually rely on a standard color library, the most common of which are from Pantone™, although those are no longer found in Adobe products due to a licensing dispute.

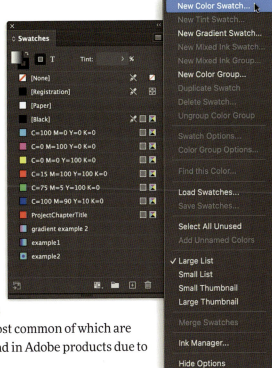

Swatches & Color Settings

Type & Text Styles

Frames, Shapes & Object Styles

Pages & Spreads

Find/ Change

Long or Complex Docs

Package & Publish

I prefer to give my swatches human-readable names, so I untick **Name with Color Value**.

Color Type: If printed, **Process** will use dots of Cyan, Magenta, Yellow, and Black. **Spot** is usually a request to have a custom ink made by a commercial printer (much like housepaint mixed for you).

Color Mode: Choose the color model (**HSB**, **RGB**, **CMYK**, or **Lab**) or select from an industry library.

Click **OK** to finish or **Add** to make another—the **OK** button would then read **Done**.

Hexadecimal values are also supported for RGB/HSB, but keep in mind that hex assumes RGB values in the sRGB color space (see the next section in this chapter for more on that).

Use **Add to CC Library** if you wish to access this swatch on another device.

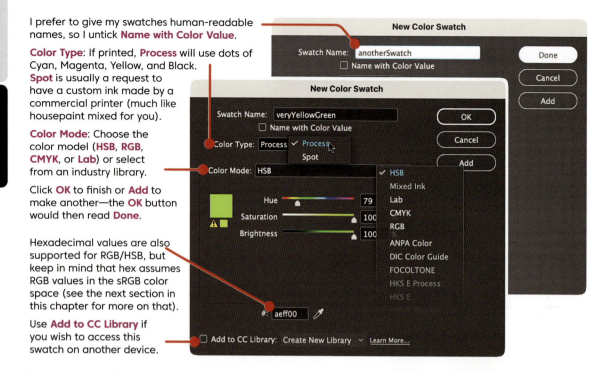

The icons to the right of your swatches identify their key attributes.

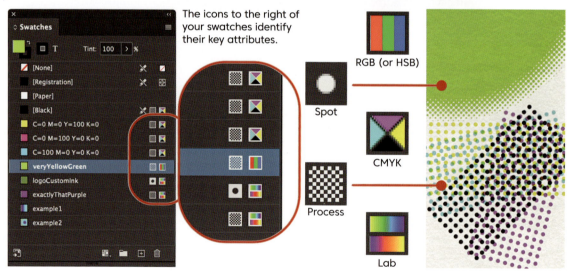

RGB (or HSB)

Spot

CMYK

Process

Lab

With **RGB** or **HSB** as the **Color Mode**, you can specify the color with a hexadecimal value. Also in those modes is a dropper that lets you sample from anywhere on your screen, whether in InDesign or not! To use the dropper, click and hold as you ***drag it*** to what it should sample, releasing the mouse when the dropper is over the target. If you simply click outside InDesign, you've left the application, so be sure to drag from within the app to your target color.

    Spot color swatches expect a custom ink to be made for them rather than using dots of cyan, magenta, yellow, and black inks (the four-color **process**). Before sending your document to a commercial printer, see if you have more spot swatches than expected. Sometimes, these sneak in with placed graphics. Or you may have a couple versions of a color when you should have only one. Rather than scour your document for elements with the wrong one, use the **Ink Manager** to "alias" one ink to another! Follow up with **Overprint Preview** to see if it worked.

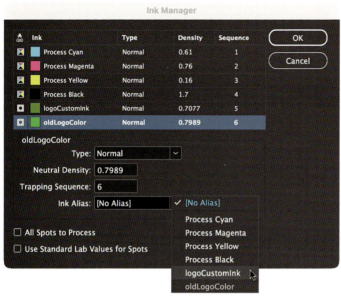

From the **Swatches panel** menu, choose **Ink Manager**. There, you'll see all the inks your doc wants to use.

To consolidate them, highlight a redundant one, then choose another from the **Ink Alias** menu. This is a great way to get similar colors to be identical when printed.

You can also (or instead) convert **All Spots to Process** colors, so no inks other than the basic four will be expected.

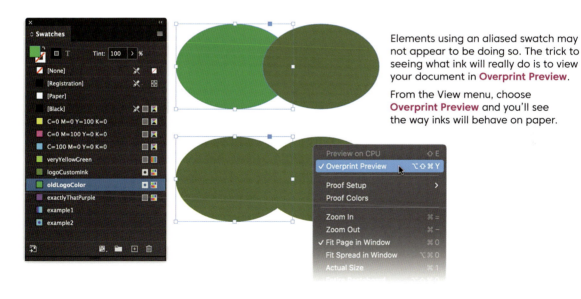

Elements using an aliased swatch may not appear to be doing so. The trick to seeing what ink will really do is to view your document in **Overprint Preview**.

From the View menu, choose **Overprint Preview** and you'll see the way inks will behave on paper.

Swatches &
Color Settings

Type &
Text Styles

Frames, Shapes
& Object Styles

Pages &
Spreads

Find/
Change

Long or
Complex Docs

Package
& Publish

Gradients & Gradient Swatches

Gradients are gradual transitions from one color to one or more others. A gradient can be linear, transitioning at a consistent angle, or radial, radiating from a point outward. To apply a gradient to a fill or stroke, click on the **Fill** or **Stroke** box in one of the panels in which they occur (**Color**, **Swatches**, **Tools**, or **Control**, but, oddly, not **Gradient**).

The **Gradient tool**

Editing the color of a gradient stop.

Creating a new gradient swatch

Click a stop to edit its color. To choose a color swatch for the stop's color, **option/ Alt**-click the swatch or drag it onto the stop.

Click between stops to add a new one.

When defining a gradient swatch, highlight a stop, then choose a color model with which to color it or choose from color swatches.

A gradient swatch records its stops' colors, positions, and the gradient **Type**, **Linear**, or **Radial**.

Use the **Gradient panel** (**Window > Color > Gradient**) to define an ad hoc gradient or create a reusable gradient swatch by using the **Swatches panel** menu and choosing **New Gradient Swatch....** In the **Gradient panel**, the gradient ramp at its bottom becomes active when you click the square preview under the panel's name. Choose the **Type**: either **Linear** or **Radial**.

Edit the color stops along the bottom edge of the ramp. When using the **Gradient panel**, you'll use the **Color panel** and/or the **Swatches panel** to choose the stop's color. However, you need to drag a swatch or **option/Alt**-click it to apply it.

When defining a swatch, you can choose the color model of a stop's color or choose from swatches. Each stop can be colored with a different method! Since the stops are sliders, you can drag them. When moved closer together, the transition between those two colors will be more abrupt.

The diamond-shaped sliders along the top of the ramp shift the midpoint color between two stops. This allows you to maintain a gradation between stops but give *emphasis* to one of them over the other. When a midpoint slider or a color stop is selected, the **Location** field shows the relative position of that slider between the ones on either side. So if the gradient stops had been dragged inward, and the diamond slider is *exactly* halfway between them, its location will read 50%.

It's easy to add more colors to the gradient, too. Just click between two gradient stops and a third will appear—or a fourth, fifth, and so on. To remove a stop, drag it away from the ramp, keeping in mind that there is a minimum of two.

If you're editing a linear gradient, you have access to the **Angle** field. A 90° linear gradient starts at the bottom of an object and ends at the top. Although setting the angle to 180° will reverse a gradient, using the **Reverse** button is easier.

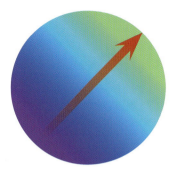

To apply a linear gradient with the **Gradient tool**, drag from where the gradation should start to where it should end. Beyond those endpoints, the object will show solid color.

To apply a radial gradient, drag from the center outward. Beyond that radius, you'll see the "end" color.

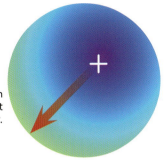

To set an arbitrary angle for an applied gradient, choose the **Gradient tool** from the **Tools panel** and drag across the shape to set where the start and end points of the gradient are. The angle at which you drag a linear gradient is entered into the **Angle** field. Interestingly, you can drag beyond the edge of a selected shape, leaving only part of a gradient visible in that shape. Even more interesting is dragging the **Gradient tool** across several shapes with gradients in them—the gradient will now span across all of them. Using the **Gradient tool** on a radial gradient sets the center and outer edge of that "radius."

Be aware: A gradient can also be applied to a stroke. As that is hard to notice, I sometimes do this accidentally.

Swatches & Color Settings

Type & Text Styles

Frames, Shapes & Object Styles

Pages & Spreads

Find/ Change

Long or Complex Docs

Package & Publish

Color Concepts & Settings

Should the images you place in InDesign be RGB or CMYK? How about the swatches you make? The purpose of this section is to help you make an *informed* decision, so it's worth a read.

TL;DR

To be merciful, here are my suggestions with minimal explanations. Fuller details follow.

Images

With breathtakingly few exceptions, your **images should be RGB**. Those who've heard of *profiles* will likely ask, "*which* RGB?" The two most used are **sRGB** (Photoshop's default and the assumed profile for web graphics) and **AdobeRGB (1998)**.

AdobeRGB has been optimized for printed output and can better preserve the colors in photographs. However, it requires changing Photoshop settings and being adopted early in an image-editing workflow. That's why many stock images and most others are in sRGB and, once there, offer no advanced converting to AdobeRGB.

For this series of books, I use sRGB because I also produce ebooks from the same content that is printed, and ebooks use sRGB for the color definitions of everything else.

Although AdobeRGB is considered optimal, sRGB is simply easier for most InDesign users.

Graphics

It's trickier to declare what color mode should be used for graphics produced in Adobe Illustrator. Most of mine are in RGB (specifically, sRGB), but there are quite a few exceptions.

Logos often contain organization-standard colors, which often use standard spot colors. Those, in turn, often (and *should*) use Lab definitions, rather than RGB or CMYK, to be device independent.

Graphics with elements that, when printed, need to use black ink only are easier to make in CMYK. Most Illustrator users don't know that they can redefine the black color swatch in RGB documents to be grayscale and thus print correctly when used in InDesign. I do this to maintain greater richness in elements that are colorful.

Bottom line: Use RGB Illustrator files if black-only content uses a black-only swatch and spot colors are defined as Lab swatches (like classic Pantone colors). Use CMYK if trying to limit the number of inks used for small text or line work or if that's what's used by the files you've been given.

InDesign Content

This sentence uses a special, uneditable CMYK swatch called **[Black]**. It prints with black ink only and thus should look crisp and sharp on the page. **This phrase**, also text that I'd like to keep legible, uses a CMYK "build" of only two inks, magenta and yellow. Text headers, large enough that a small amount of mis-registration will matter little, may safely use RGB, HSB, or Lab swatches, which may generate three or four inks when printed.

Graphic elements I make in InDesign usually use HSB swatches (which are actually RGB under the hood). **Most of my InDesign content uses non-CMYK swatches.**

All colors get converted to sRGB when I export as an ePub or RGB PDF.

All *RGB content* gets converted to a specific CMYK when I export a PDF to be sent to a commercial printer.

But, noting the reasons for my very limited use of CMYK (one or few inks for text and delicate line art), I *disallow* any CMYK content from getting converted to a different CMYK profile when making print PDFs. All the other content will and should be converted to maintain visual color fidelity.

This is accomplished in the PDF export setting called **Convert to Destination (Preserve Numbers)**. If I allowed CMYK definitions to change, elements using the **[Black]** swatch's numbers of 0C 0M 0Y 100K (black only) would change to use four inks, for example.

InDesign Color Settings

Access by choosing **Edit > Color Settings….** For me, the **CMYK Working Space** is unimportant, since few things in my docs are CMYK and their builds matter more than what they look like. The CMYK I choose when exporting matters infinitely more.

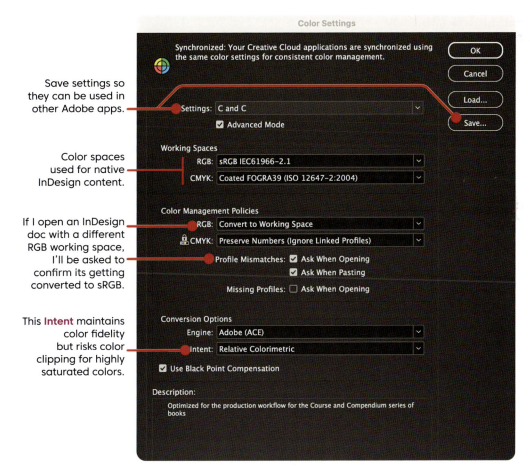

Swatches & Color Settings

Type & Text Styles

Frames, Shapes & Object Styles

Pages & Spreads

Find/ Change

Long or Complex Docs

Package & Publish

Going Deeper: How Color Works

Of course, that could be the title of an entire book or series. I'll attempt to restrict myself to what you need to know to work in InDesign. Please keep one thing in mind throughout this discussion: ***A color is what it looks like and not a bunch of numbers!*** That is, a color "happens" in your brain via the eyes. The trick is supplying your eyes and brain with the stimuli they need to recognize the color you want them to.

Color Models

There are different ways in which we describe a color in InDesign, and so InDesign can have colors that use several color *models simultaneously*: RGB (and HSB), CMYK, and Lab. Each model attempts to work with color in the way different media or devices do. Although it may seem intuitive to work in the color mode of an anticipated output device, it is often far more optimal to work in one mode, and then export to another for output. Which color mode should you use?

RGB Lights the Way

RGB is about light in the darkness. No light—no color. By controlling the ratio of **R**ed, **G**reen, and **B**lue, we can create any color we want! Where both red and green light overlap, we get yellow. Green and blue combine to make cyan light. Magenta is the result of red and blue. All three make white. This is why we call these the *additive primaries*. Note which color is absent or lacking where only two overlap. For example, cyan is the absence of red.

RGB has a rich and storied history. Consider the following historic image. Around 1910, the photographer Sergei Mikhailovich Prokudin-Gorskii made three photos of the subject on black-and-white film: one each with red, green, and blue color filters. Below, the scene in front of the photographer and the scene viewed through those filters.

Note how the color of the filter affects how light or dark colors are in the scene. You can see how the blue filter yields a light garment, since that garment is blue. The red filter produces an image in which the garment is quite dark. The gray wall looks about the same in each image.

You can see this in the figure below. Prokudin-Gorskii made black-and-white transparencies (slides), fanciful reproductions of which are below.

All three slides were projected onto the same screen with colored light. The slide made through the red filter would have red light projected through it, the "green" slide would use green light, and the "blue" slide, blue light.

When the three projected images are aligned, the result on the screen will recreate the colors in the original scene! Learn more about his process and see many more examples on the Library of Congress website:

https://www.loc.gov/collections/prokudin-gorskii/about-this-collection/.

Color images have been made in much this way since 1861! Modern camera sensor arrays typically have millions of microscopic, monochromatic sensors with equally small red, green, and blue filters in front of them. The data from each get combined to give us a color image.

With most software, the amount of light in each of these three "primary" colors is designated by a number between **0** (no light) and **255** (the maximum). The RGB value 0R 0G 0B is black—all lights out. 0R 255G 0B would produce as pure a green that a device is capable of.

CMYK and Inks

CMYK is about dots of **C**yan, **M**agenta, **Y**ellow, and blac**K** ink on a substrate such as paper. Each ink absorbs a different color of light. Cyan, for example, absorbs red light, subtracting it from what gets to our eyes. This is why we call these the *subtractive primaries*.

Without ink, there's only the color of the paper (which is why InDesign calls its white swatch "Paper"). By controlling the ratio of those inks, we can make many colors. We measure the amount of each from 0% (none) to 100% (the full amount). In principle, we could use

Swatches &
Color Settings

Type &
Text Styles

Frames, Shapes
& Object Styles

Pages &
Spreads

Find/
Change

Long or
Complex Docs

Package
& Publish

only cyan, magenta, and yellow inks, because the combination of all three inks *should* absorb all light, and thus appear black. However, this can be too much ink for many papers. Even if 100% of all three inks could be used, they may not be lined up ("registered") perfectly, so thin elements like black text would be unreadable. These are the reasons we need black ink, too. Thus, CMYK is known as the four-color process, or "process color" for short.

Color Spaces and Profiles

Since these terms are used so often, and often incorrectly, let's be sure we understand what's meant by them.

Color values used on one device (like maximum red: 255R 0G 0B) may not be as intensely red on another device. That is, 255R will be a *different color* on different devices; maybe like red velvet on one and neon on another. After all, any device can produce only so broad a range of colors. We refer to that range as the device's **gamut** or **color space**, which is described by an important data file called its **profile**.

Some printers use toner and some use ink. Those from different manufacturers produce somewhat different color. Paper also affects color, of course. Thus, *every CMYK device is different*. As with RGB, CMYK devices also have profiles that describe the range of color they can produce. That means that the CMYK numbers (or *builds*) for any perceived color will vary from paper to paper, and from printer to printer. No CMYK build looks the same on all printers.

So, we say that RGB and CMYK values are *device dependent*; they are meaningless without reference to a specific device. To accurately refer to a specific green, for example, we might have to say something like "30R 190G 25B as viewed on an Eizo CX270 monitor."

Luckily, a color-managed workflow using profiles determines the correct numbers for a color on a given device for us. That's one reason we call it "color managed."

Lab: The Color Space of Human Vision

What's needed is a way to map the color output of a device to colors as humans see them. That is, a way to designate a color in a device-independent way (or with you and me as the device). Thanks to a century of color science, there is one. It's called **Lab**. That's not short for "laboratory," but, like RGB, it refers to three values. More precisely, they're coordinates in a three-dimensional color space that represents how you see color.

The color spaces of the devices we use fit inside this one. Since no device can produce all the colors we can see, device color spaces are all much smaller than Lab, "our" color space. Consider the space you're in right now. We'd map the position of your head in that room with the familiar x, y, z coordinates.

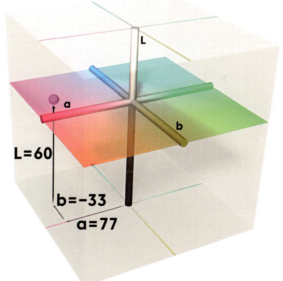

Where It's At!

We usually specify a location in any space by using three numbers.

In a room, that could be the distance to the left or right of a spot on the floor (x), the distance forward or back from that spot (y), and the height above the floor (z).

We map a color in the Lab color space with different coordinates: **L** stands for "luminance," the **a**-axis is often called the red-green axis (though it's more like magenta-green), and the **b**-axis is yellow-blue. The **a** and **b** coordinates together map hue and saturation. Colors along the L-axis are actually shades of gray and are measured from 0 to 100. Colors farther from the L-axis are more saturated than those closer to it. As we circle the L-axis, we encounter every hue. The a- and b-axes have values from –128 to +127 with 0 intersecting the L-axis.

Mapping Color

Lab color space represents the range of human vision. Any point in that space, like this purple, is a color we see.

Instead of x, y, and z, we use L, a, and b.

Sitting in a physical space, we can imagine the limited volume described by the points we can reach with our arms. A device (e.g., a printer or monitor) can produce only a limited "volume" of color within Lab space—a limited range of colors compared to those we can see. That volume of colors is the device's color space. Each device has its own unique color space.

Swatches & Color Settings

Type & Text Styles

Frames, Shapes & Object Styles

Pages & Spreads

Find/ Change

Long or Complex Docs

Package & Publish

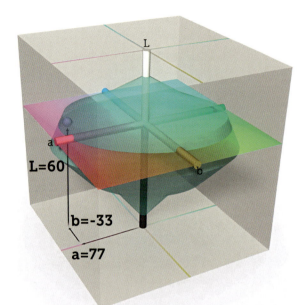

Device Color Space

This volume within Lab space represents the color space of a hypothetical output device (like a printer). The mapped purple dot appears to be "within **gamut**." That is, we can expect it to output accurately.

All color spaces, and therefore all devices, are compared to Lab (the colors we can see). Some devices produce a greater range of color than others.

A **profile** is a data file that describes a device's color space. It lets us compare that color space to others and enables conversion from its color space to another.

That is, profiles help us move from an input device, like a scanner or camera, through software like InDesign, to an output device, while keeping "in-gamut" colors accurate throughout.

In review, a ***color model*** is the general way color is approached: either by adding three colors of light (RGB) or by subtracting light as it reflects off four colors of ink (CMYK). A ***color space*** describes the color capability of a specific real or virtual device. When I hear or read an instruction like "use the CMYK color space," I cringe. I'm the annoying person who then asks, "which one?"

A ***profile*** is a data file that describes a color space. It is the means by which our software gets to know the color capabilities of a device. When looking at a list of color spaces in Adobe software, we are actually perusing a list of their profiles. Thus, folks often use the words "profile" and "color space" interchangeably, which is understandable.

InDesign lets us create and use Lab swatches. Those are truly device-independent since they describe the color's appearance directly and not relative to a device. This is why major color libraries often use Lab definitions rather than CMYK or RGB values. When standard swatches use CMYK numbers, unspecified (but still specific) devices are implied. Many InDesign users don't realize that and use those values and get upset when they don't match from one device to another.

Converting vs. Assigning Profiles

I've mentioned converting from RGB to CMYK a few times in this chapter. One can also convert from one color space to another within the same color model (RGB to RGB, for example). But what exactly does *convert* mean?

Imagine that I have an audio device connected to two very different loudspeakers. Turning up the volume of the audio device to 11 will produce different volumes of sound on those speakers from that one signal.

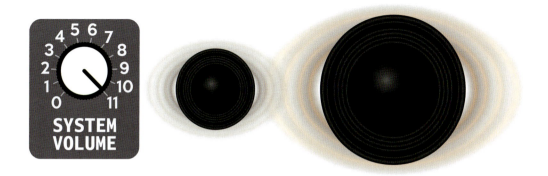

To get identical volume from both, I'd have to use a different signal for each of those different speakers. That is, I may have to lower the volume to 9 for the louder speaker to match the other.

Now consider two displays that are sent the same signal to generate an intense red, but one glows more vibrantly red than the other. I have to send different color numbers to the more vibrant monitor to match the less vibrant one. This is ***conversion***: changing the numbers in order to produce the same visual color on a different device.

Assigning a profile does not change any RGB or CMYK numbers. It tells those numbers what colors they represent. Assigning the profile of a large color space tends to interpret those numbers as very vibrant, where assigning a small space's profile to those numbers yields less-saturated colors. If someone wanted to give you a "gift," you might get excited until you found out they were speaking Norwegian and proposing marriage, or German, in which that word means *poison*! To get the right meaning, you assign the right language dictionary to the word; to get the right color, you assign the right device profile to the color numbers.

Virtual Device Profiles

Photoshop and Illustrator documents may also have profiles associated with them. These are synthetic profiles that represent ideal or virtual devices and scenarios. The most common of these are called **sRGB** and **AdobeRGB**. The full names are actually longer, but the shortened names are used by most.

sRGB, created by HP and Microsoft, represents the color space of an average monitor (*circa* 1996) and is the assumed color space for the web. Since ePub files use HTML and CSS files as websites do, sRGB is the color space of ebooks as well.

AdobeRGB was created as a virtual color space that encompasses the vast majority of commercial printing scenarios without being needlessly larger. It is therefore well-suited to those who edit images destined for print output. Since AdobeRGB is larger than sRGB, it accesses more vibrant colors. If the color produced in sRGB by the value 255R is *converted* to AdobeRGB, that same color would then be produced by 216R. Again, to achieve the same color, we need different numbers for each "device," even if these devices are virtual.

If we *assigned* AdobeRGB to the file that used the value of 255R, that value would now represent a more vibrant red than it had when sRGB was assigned. Like assigning the German language to the word "gift" leaves the word's spelling intact, but definitely changes its meaning.

CMYK-to-CMYK Conversion Can Be Dangerous

A photograph using one CMYK profile can be converted to another CMYK profile and likely look the same on the device described by that new profile. But some graphics we create in InDesign or Illustrator may use CMYK builds that are more important than the color they represent. The most critical of these is **pure black** (0C 0M 0Y 100K), especially when it's used for text. If converted to a different color space, this build may become something like 72C 67M 59Y 79K because the software may think that build provides a good visual match in the new color space!

Bottom Line: My advice is to use RGB for all content whose color is important to preserve from input through final output. Use CMYK builds only for those graphics for which the build must be preserved (like pure black). Then prohibit those CMYK elements from getting converted. RGB images and graphics will get converted as needed to have consistent appearance no matter how they are output and black text will maintain its sharpness.

Preserving CMYK numbers while at the same time converting RGB values is done when creating PDFs, a topic covered in the last chapter of this Compendium. In the **Output** section of the PDF export dialog, we choose **Convert to Destination (Preserve Numbers)** and the destination output profile.

Convert RGB, but preserve CMYK builds

That's what this option does. As we take our flexible RGB content and prepare a PDF for whichever output medium it's intended, this will ensure things that match each other continue to do so.

Why preserve CMYK builds?

We need color numbers to change as we go from one device to another *if the colors need to look the same*, especially with images. But when something else is more important than color accuracy—like text legibility—we want the build maintained.

Convert to Destination (Preserve Numbers) is made for just that. If we have fine line work or lightweight text, we try hard to keep it made from one ink, usually blac**K** because misregistration makes it hard to read. Heavier or larger text *may* withstand the misregistration of two or maybe three inks.

I use RGB for everything whose color I care about, and CMYK on pure black and sometimes a few specific ink builds.

While InDesign can have native content in a variety of color models, Illustrator and Photoshop cannot. However, in Illustrator, we can have an RGB document with pure black by redefining the black swatch in that document as Grayscale. In fact, I did that in the graphic below!

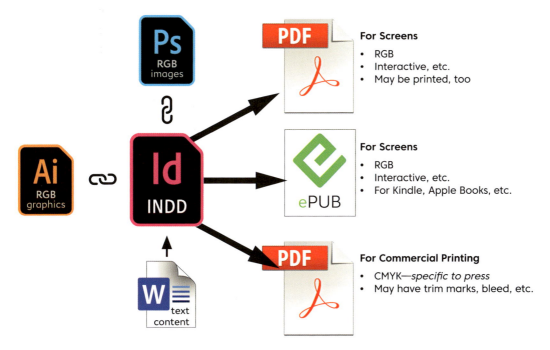

Color Settings

One way in which we can ensure that documents we create in our Adobe software treat color in the same way is to synchronize their color settings. If you have access to Photoshop as well as InDesign, it's best to configure settings there first, then use Adobe Bridge to sync them. If you have only InDesign, then configure your "InDesign Color Settings" (page 185).

Setting Working Space Profiles

Adobe software can be considered devices—the virtual devices we work in. Since they're software, we can *decide* how large a color space it uses (how broad a range of color we can access). This also means that we are deciding the colors our color numbers refer to.

Go to **Edit > Color Settings...** to see and configure your settings. If little of your work is commercially printed, I recommend one of the presets with "General Purpose" in the name. These will use sRGB as the "Working Space" for native RGB content. Since we can choose any CMYK space when exporting to PDF and I advise having few (if any) native CMYK elements, it doesn't really matter what the working CMYK space is.

I configured mine by choosing a preset called "Europe General Purpose 3." Although this book is professionally printed, I wanted sRGB to make the ebook version better match the printed book. Many would argue that AdobeRGB is the best choice for print, and they'd be right if print was my only concern. But I decided sRGB was adequate and its flexibility desirable.

Swatches &
Color Settings

Type &
Text Styles

Frames, Shapes
& Object Styles

Pages &
Spreads

Find/
Change

Long or
Complex Docs

Package
& Publish

3 Type & Text Styles

Text and table formatting can be stored and rapidly applied with styles. No matter how intricate or complex the formatting, it is usually no more difficult than a single click to apply it—provided you've created a paragraph, character, or table style for it. This chapter gets into the how (and why) of styles. Frankly, not using styles is not using InDesign.

Working with Type

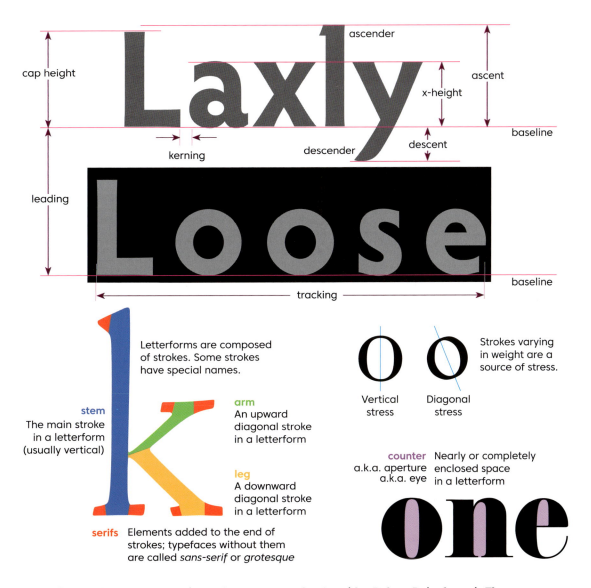

Type &
Text Styles

Frames, Shapes
& Object Styles

Pages &
Spreads

Find/
Change

Long or
Complex Docs

Package
& Publish

Many fine books have been written about typography. Consider Robert Bringhurst's *Elements of Typographic Style, Fourth Edition* (Hartley and Marks, 2013) and Ellen Lupton's *Thinking with Type, 3rd Revised and Expanded Edition* (Princeton Architectural Press, 2024). There are many websites on the topic as well. However, I wanted to illustrate a few terms here since you will encounter most of them in InDesign's interface and will have to make decisions about those and others when choosing type, what my friend Jason Hoppe calls "type casting."

When choosing fonts, you must decide between serif and sans-serif and wade through terms like "x-height" or "stress," and less measurable things like a typeface's personality. The resources mentioned above will help there. Adjusting type in InDesign is covered below.

Workspaces &
Preferences

Swatches &
Color Settings

Type &
Text Styles

Font Technologies

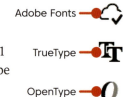

Adobe Fonts

TrueType

OpenType

When purchasing fonts or activating them with the Adobe Fonts service, you may find different formats and capabilities available. Although Type 1 were considered the most reliable, they are no longer supported. TrueType fonts are still reliable, but only some TrueType fonts are cross-platform.

So, Adobe and Microsoft developed OpenType to offer all the advantages of Type 1 and TrueType, avoid their problems, and support more glyphs—a lot more: up to 65,536. They often have special features and multiple alternates for many characters.

Adobe Fonts and Other Font Services

Adobe Creative Cloud subscriptions come with the Adobe Fonts service. Through it, you can "activate" many fonts for use in Adobe applications. In the Creative Cloud app, they are referred to as "Added." There, you may "install" those fonts to make them available to any program on your computer.

When opening a document with missing fonts, InDesign checks to see if they're available in Adobe Fonts and offers to activate them for you. Almost all fonts available for activation are OpenType fonts, and many come with diverse OpenType features. Of course, there are many services unaffiliated with Adobe who sell/license fonts, too. The Extensis Connect products work like the Adobe fonts service and integrate with Adobe apps (and others).

When you purchase or activate dozens or hundreds of fonts, you may crave a font manager more capable than, say, Apple's Font Book app. Extensis products include Suitcase Fusion, which allows a user to enable or disable fonts from any source (to keep your system's resources less busy). It also allows you to see all your fonts from InDesign and it activates fonts when a file is opened that requires them. Suitcase isn't the only font manager. FontAgent has been around for a while in various forms and does many of the things Suitcase does. FontBase is a free and popular app. There are many more that are for either Mac or Windows only.

Missing Fonts

If a font is missing, its text is highlighted in pink. **Choose Type > Find Font**, then highlight the noted font and choose a substitute in **Replace With**. I usually check **Redefine Style** then **Change All**. If you've enabled the preference to "Auto-activate Adobe Fonts" (page 176), you merely have to wait for those fonts to become available.

Adjusting Type in InDesign

Kerning & Tracking

Each glyph in a font has a width, which often includes a little bit of space on each side of it. We might naively picture a box or block for each glyph, with words formed by a row of abutting blocks:

Zero kerning (no letterspacing) is not what some expect.

Although that might seem like the right thing to do, it looks wrong, graceless—the "T" and the following "y" look too far apart. Luckily, font designers build kerning data into the metrics of fonts for many anticipated pairs of glyphs, adjusting how they should fit together. This default setting called **Metrics** is set in the **kerning** menu (labeled with V/A) found in the **Control panel**, **Character panel**, **Properties panel**, or anywhere basic text formatting is controlled.

At sizes like this caption, **Metrics** kerning setting usually provides good legibility. However, when text is large, even the kerning built into a font can be too spacious or just odd-looking.

While **Metrics** often suffices at body copy sizes (like this paragraph), at larger display sizes (like the questionable word "Typingly" above), we may want to choose **Optical** from the kerning menu:

InDesign's **Optical** kerning can be a quick and effective way to achieve pleasing letterspacing in larger text, like headers.

If even **Optical** kerning is insufficient, we manually kern by putting the text cursor between two glyphs, then holding down **option/alt** and tapping the left or right arrow keys (← or →).

For especially important, larger text, like titles, manual kerning often produces the best results.

Type &
Text Styles

Frames, Shapes
& Object Styles

Pages &
Spreads

Find/
Change

Long or
Complex Docs

Package
& Publish

Workspaces &
Preferences

Swatches &
Color Settings

Type &
Text Styles

If you like the relative spacing between each pair of glyphs, but wish for more or less letter-spacing proportionally applied over a whole range of glyphs (an entire word, paragraph, or more), highlight that range of text and use the same shortcuts as for kerning (**option/alt** plus ← or →). Instead of adjusting the kerning value or method, this changes the **tracking** value, labeled with **VA**.

When kerning, the space between each glyph can (and usually should) be different. However, tracking is a uniform adjustment performed to help text fit or for creative effect. Both are measured in thousandths of an "em," the current point size.

Leading

There are many reasons why you would want to adjust **leading**. If you make text larger and its leading had been fixed at a small value for the smaller type, it's likely that the leading will not change. That could yield a situation like the one below. Another reason could be the use of small-caps or all-caps, which have no descenders and may withstand a smaller leading value. Importantly, wide columns of text make it hard for the eye to track from line to line unless the space between each line is greater.

To adjust leading, the text needs to be selected. By default, that means highlighting every bit of text in the range where the leading needs adjusting. However, if you changed your preferences to "Apply Leading to Entire Paragraphs" (page 167), your selection just has to touch the paragraphs that need the fix. If it's only one paragraph, the cursor just has to be blinking somewhere in that paragraph.

yesterday's
klaxon

yesterday's
klaxon

We can change the leading to **Auto** or a numeric value (in points) via the leading menu (look for the ⚟ icon) in the **Control panel**, the **Properties panel**, the **Character panel**, or anywhere basic text formatting is done. Auto is usually 120% of the point size of the text, but even that can be redefined when making paragraph styles. To adjust leading visually for selected text, hold down **option/alt** then tap the up or down arrow keys (↑ or ↓).

Scaling

When you resize a text frame, the text's point size field in the **Control panel** or the **Character panel** can show two values (a recording of before and after values). To avoid this, set your **General Preference** "When Scaling: Apply to Content/Adjust Scaling Percentage" (page 164).

Proper Italic & Bold

Complete typefaces (font families) come with a number of fonts, most commonly italic and bold as well as regular. Faking these is discouraged as this just makes the text harder to read.

regular   italic   bold

Percipience   real: *Percipience*   **Percipience**

                       faux: *Percipience*   **Percipience**

The faux version for italic is made using the **Skew (False Italic)** field in the **Control panel**, and the faux bold is made by adding a .5 point stroke to the regular version. Note in the fake bold example how the counter in the "e" is nearly filled in.

Alignment

There are five alignments that yield ragged type, including the familiar Left, Right, and Center alignments. The last two, Towards or Away from spine, can be useful to keep text symmetrical across a spread. For example, the frames that hold page numbers benefit from these.

Ati ullabo. Nihilib erchitio exero magnatur aut provitatis sita parionest omnis ius. Te dolores aut vernatet dolute duluptatios sit aut evenimus aut qui consequunt, ut fuga.

Left

Ati ullabo. Nihilib erchitio exero magnatur aut provitatis sita parionest omnis ius. Te dolores aut vernatet dolute duluptatios sit aut evenimus aut qui consequunt, ut fuga.

Center

Ati ullabo. Nihilib erchitio exero magnatur aut provitatis sita parionest omnis ius. Te dolores aut vernatet dolute duluptatios sit aut evenimus aut qui consequunt, ut fuga.

Right

Ati ullabo. Nihilib erchitio exero magnatur aut provitatis sita parionest omnis ius. Te dolores aut vernatet dolute duluptatios sit aut evenimus aut qui consequunt, fuga.

Left justify

Ati ullabo. Nihilib erchitio exero magnatur aut provitatis sita parionest omnis ius. Te dolores aut vernatet dolute duluptatios sit aut evenimus aut qui consequunt, fuga.

Center justify

Ati ullabo. Nihilib erchitio exero magnatur aut provitatis sita parionest omnis ius. Te dolores aut vernatet dolute duluptatios sit aut evenimus aut qui consequunt, fuga.

Right justify

Ati ullabo. Nihilib erchitio exero magnatur aut provitatis sita parionest omnis ius. Te dolores aut vernatet dolute duluptatios sitenimus aut qui conse, fuga molore omnia.

Full justify

16

17

Ati ullabo. Nihilib erchitio exero magnatur provitatis sita parionest omnis ius. vernatet duluptatios sit

Ati ullabo. Nihilib erchitio exero magnatur provitatis sita parionest omnis ius. vernatet duluptatios sit

Away from spine

Ati ullabo. Nihilib erchitio exero magnatur provitatis sita parionest omnis ius. vernatet duluptatios sit aut evenimus

Ati ullabo. Nihilib erchitio exero magnatur provitatis sita parionest omnis ius. vernatet duluptatios sit aut evenimus

Towards spine

Solo beria pa volorpore, quia voloren ihicili antiat fugiatq adis dolum fuga. Itasimendae. Itatem nis nulloriant fugitaspitat quisimet qui autas adit verestrunt et issitat emollestia, nihil id milique sa que que est.

A **Forced Line Break** in justified text. Below, with a **Right Indent Tab**.

Solo beria pa volorpore, quia voloren ihicili antiat fugiatq adis dolum fuga. Itasimendae. Itatem nis nulloriant fugitaspitat quisimet qui autas adit verestrunt et issitat emollestia, nihil id milique sa que que est.

There are four Justify alignments, which differ only in how the last line of a paragraph is treated (left, right, or center aligned, or spread from left to right frame-edge). Narrow columns with these alignments can have uncomfortable word spacing and/or lots of hyphens. Inserting a **Forced Line Break** (**shift-return/ shift-enter**) can make word spacing even worse. I put a **Right Indent Tab** (**shift-tab**) just before the Forced Line Break to remedy the terrible spacing that the break incurs.

Type & Text Styles

Frames, Shapes & Object Styles

Pages & Spreads

Find/ Change

Long or Complex Docs

Package & Publish

Workspaces &
Preferences

Swatches &
Color Settings

Type &
Text Styles

Indents & Spacing

Adding simple Left and Right indents, especially when combined with Space Before and After, is an effective way to visually separate a paragraph from those around it. Consider an extended quote or excerpt, for example. For consistency, it's best to set these as part of a paragraph style. To do so in an ad hoc way, you can use the **Control panel** or the **Paragraph panel** (see figure).

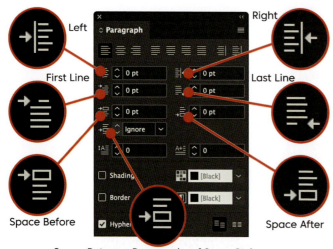

Space Between Paragraphs of Same Style

To create a hanging indent, first set a positive Left Indent (perhaps 12 points). Then set an equal but negative First Line Left Indent (as in -12 points). To remove the hanging indent, reverse those steps: Remove the First Line Left Indent first, then set the Left Indent to zero. You can do the analogous thing on the right-hand side with the last line of a paragraph: Set the Right Indent to a positive value, then set the Last Line Right Indent to a negative one. If you need more than a couple of paragraphs with hanging indents, it's best to make a paragraph style.

If you need only one hanging indent, or if you don't require consistency in them, there's a quick way to make one. In the first line of a paragraph, position the cursor to where you'd like the other lines left indented. Then insert the Indent to Here character by typing ⌘-\ (that's a backslash) on Mac or **Ctrl-** on Windows. When showing hidden characters, it resembles a dagger (†) character (see the example that follows). Unfortunately, there's no way to "record" this in a paragraph style.

Net·alibus†·velendam·venim·que·
endes·moluptaectur·si·
ipsanimus·aut·qui·ut·
ommolup·tiaeper

Indent to Here marker

Paragraph Styles

Professional layout is identified by its consistency, which is exactly what styles offer us. When last-minute format changes are needed across large documents, styles allow us to make those changes *very* rapidly.

Creating a Paragraph Style

InDesign makes it easy to create styles and offers several methods for doing so. The most reliable process involves first formatting some example text so that it exhibits most of the attributes we'd like to capture with a style. Then we create, name, and fine-tune the style. All three of those tasks can be done in a single step via the **Control panel** or the **Paragraph Styles panel**. There is a procedure using the **Properties panel**, but as it makes any fine-tuning more difficult, I avoid it.

via the **Control panel**

via the **Paragraph Styles panel** menu

or **option/Alt**-click on the New Style button

1   Create a text frame with some placeholder text (either your own jottings or using the **Type > Fill with Placeholder Text**). I try to have example paragraphs for common types like header, subhead, or body copy. Highlight a paragraph and format it much as you'd like it recorded (choosing the font, size, alignment, etc.) from the **Control panel** or the **Character** and **Paragraph panels**.

2   With the cursor still in the paragraph, use one of these methods to create the style:

- In the **Paragraph Styles panel** menu, choose **New Paragraph Style....**
- While holding down **option/Alt**, click on the New Style button (⊞) at the bottom of the **Paragraph Styles panel**.
- In the **Control panel**, use the Paragraph Styles menu (¶.) and choose **New Paragraph Style....**
- Click the Create Style button in the **Properties panel** and then type a name.

3   All but the last method will open the useful **New Paragraph Style** dialog box with a generic name highlighted. Take advantage of the moment to give the style an intuitive name (caption, heading, subhead, etc.).

Type & Text Styles

Frames, Shapes & Object Styles

Pages & Spreads

Find/ Change

Long or Complex Docs

Package & Publish

4 Check the important checkboxes: **Apply Style to Selection** and **Preview**. You may wish to opt out of (uncheck) the option to store this style in a Creative Cloud Library unless you know you'll want to access this style from another device. Thanks to a kind and empathetic product manager, InDesign will leave those boxes checked.

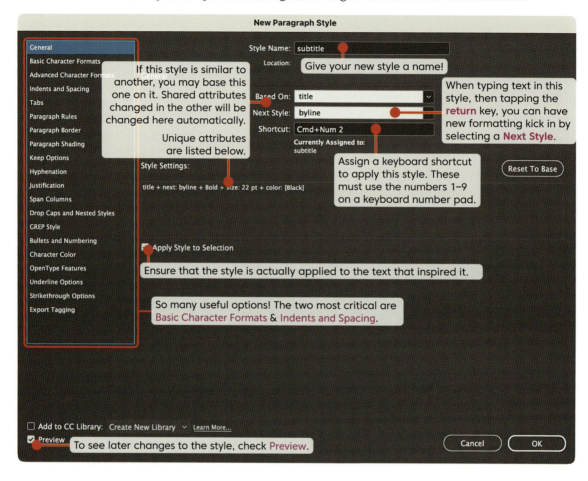

There are other options to consider as well. Some styles will be very similar to others. A subtitle may be just like a title except smaller and/or in a different color, for example. If you base the subtitle style on the title using the **Based On** menu, the shared attributes (perhaps font family) will be controlled by the title style's definition. To reset all attributes of your new style to those of the one on which it's based, click the **Reset To Base** button.

You may also designate a style to format paragraphs that follow those using the style you just created. In the figure, I chose the style *byline* as the **Next Style**. So, as I complete typing a subtitle paragraph and press **return**, the next paragraph will automatically use the byline style.

The **Style Settings** field shows the **Based On** style, the **Next Style**, then attributes unique to this style. While in this dialog box, you may also wish to make adjustments to the style's definition via the categories on the left. I describe them in the following pages. The most important (and least avoidable) are **Basic Character Formats** and **Indents and Spacing**.

Clicking **OK** or pressing **Enter** will commit your style.

Applying and Editing Paragraph Styles

Apply the style to a single paragraph by positioning your text cursor within it, and then clicking on the name of the style in the **Paragraph Styles panel**. If you've highlighted text that is within several paragraphs, each of those paragraphs, in their entirety, will be formatted with the style when its name is clicked. If a standalone (not threaded) text frame is selected and a style name clicked, all the paragraphs in it will change (even in overset text). This is handy for items like captions and sidebars.

Beware of clicking a style with nothing selected. If nothing is selected when you click a paragraph style's name, you've set that style as a default and it will be used to format the next text you create until you choose another default. It will also be the formatting that placed text files will inherit, depending on settings chosen when placing them.

If you've selected multiple paragraphs, and the first has a designated **Next Style**, you can right-click on it and choose **Apply "Stylename" then Next Style**. If that next style itself has a next, you can apply an entire sequence of styles!

To *safely* but quickly edit a paragraph style without either applying it or setting it as a default, do not left-click, but right-click its name in the **Paragraph Styles panel** and choose **Edit "Stylename"…**. Other methods may reformat text unintentionally.

Basic Character Formats

These include the most obvious and necessary attributes of your type: font family and style, size, etc. As discussed previously, these options may be set in the **Control panel** or the **Character panel**, but for paragraph formatting that recurs, these settings are best set in a paragraph style. Some potentially less obvious options are discussed below. For more about the characteristics they're controlling (leading, kerning, tracking), review the first pages of this chapter.

Leading

You may, of course, choose a set value for this baseline-to-baseline distance. If you choose **Auto**, then the leading will be some multiple of the size of your type. The default is 120%, but you can choose another value—see "Justification" (page 210).

Kerning

Most type designers have considered at least some value for the space between given pairs of characters. However, the number of possible combinations is likely far higher than any font's designer will have included in that font. Thus, we often find ourselves manually kerning display type like headers and titles.

For the majority of styles applied to those headers and titles, we can also choose to use **Optical** kerning, whereby InDesign attempts to calculate how to fit characters together. This is a quick option when we have different fonts next to each other and/or when the font designer hasn't built adequate kerning pairs into a font. If you find optically kerned text to be consistently a little too tight, you may use tracking to loosen it up.

Type & Text Styles

Frames, Shapes & Object Styles

Pages & Spreads

Find/ Change

Long or Complex Docs

Package & Publish

Workspaces & Preferences

Swatches & Color Settings

Type & Text Styles

Tracking

Tracking is, like kerning, space between letters, but it's applied to a range of text rather than individual pairs of characters. And, like kerning, it's measured as a fraction of the current point size, which we refer to as 1 em. So choosing a tracking value of 5 means that an extra $\frac{5}{1000}$ (five thousandths) of the point size is added between characters that use the paragraph style you're defining.

Case

Small Caps will leave full caps alone, but will convert lowercase characters to small caps (using the font's specifically designed small caps, if present, or by shrinking full caps by the percentage chosen in the **Advanced Type** preferences).

    All Caps will convert all lowercase characters to full caps, whereas **All Small Caps** will convert both uppercase and lowercase characters to small caps. **Lowercase** yields all lowercase, as expected.

Ligatures

This checkbox allows the use of special glyphs (characters) that replace an unfortunate collision of two or more others. Here, the f-i ligature: fit   fit

No Break

This checkbox prevents a paragraph from having line breaks. Generally, this is an option I almost always reserve for character styles, as I do for underline and strikethrough.

Advanced Character Formats

It is usually frowned upon to squish or squash text, especially disproportionately. When I do need to **Scale** text, it's usually by a very small amount done via "Justification" (page 210).

    When text needs to be lifted or lowered relative to the baseline, **Baseline Shift** can be employed. **Skew** is present so we can fake italics. But we don't do that, do we? Finally, **Language** is for choosing which dictionary is used for spell-checking paragraphs that use this style and for determining hyphenation. It does not translate!

Indents and Spacing

This is another key category of settings, as this is where we set **Alignment** (and other useful things). Besides setting these options in a paragraph style, you can find these in the **Control panel** or the **Paragraph panel**.

Alignment

If you've edited type in any other application, you are already familiar with **Left** and **Right** alignment, which leaves the other side ragged. **Center** allows both the left and right side to be ragged. See "Alignment" (page 199) for a full rundown.

Indents

How far from the frame edges should our text be? **Left** and **Right Indent** control that. You can have a different left indent for the paragraph's first line (**First Line Left Indent**) or a different right indent for the last line (**Last Line Right Indent**). Use **First Line Left Indent** rather than a tab: It's much easier to establish and maintain. You may create a "hanging" indent, where the first line is farther to the left than the other lines. To do this, you have to set the **Left Indent** *first*, then set the **First Line Left Indent** to a negative number numerically no larger than the left indent.

What a product. Nihilib a chi-tio exero magnatur aut provitatis sita pario nest. natet dolute dolupta sit aut evenimus aut qui consequunt. $7.95

Indents used above:
Left and Right Indents = .375"
First and Last Line Indents = -.375"

Align to Grid

This forces each baseline to align to the baseline grid set in your **Grid** preferences. One does this to ensure that baselines align across columns. There are other ways, but most find this method easier than using the same leading for all elements. However, I find that using **Align to Grid** sometimes creates larger than desired gaps between some elements.

Space Before and Space After

The space above the headers on this page is not created with an extra paragraph return. The style for that subhead has 14 points of **Space Before** assigned to it (above its leading, which is greater than the height of its characters). The larger headers have more. Now note any headers at the top of a page. Since it's the first line of a text frame, InDesign intelligently doesn't add that space, whereas extra paragraph returns would cause an unsightly gap.

Space Between Paragraphs Using Same Style

Consider a long list, before and after which you need space. **Space Before** and **Space After** will accommodate that, but often produce too much space between *each item in the list*. We can specify the space between consecutive paragraphs that use the same style.

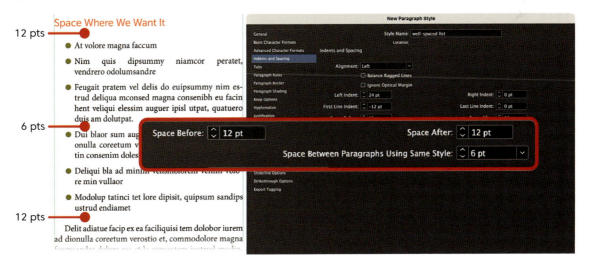

Type & Text Styles

Frames, Shapes & Object Styles

Pages & Spreads

Find/ Change

Long or Complex Docs

Package & Publish

Ignore Optical Margin

The **Story panel** has an option—its only one, in fact—to enable **Optical Margin Alignment** for an entire story. This attempts to make text margins look straighter (from a distance) by offsetting glyphs based on their relative density. Thus, a capital "T" may be slightly outdented and a quotation mark much more. Styles with **Ignore Optical Margin** checked are "opted out" of this.

Without Optical Margin:
Thus, a capital "quote" much more.

With Optical Margin:
Thus, a capital "quote" much more.

Tabs

When we press the **Tab** key, a tab character is produced in the text. To show it (and other normally hidden characters), choose **Type > Show Hidden Characters** or use the shortcut **⌘-option-I/Ctrl-Alt-I**. Unlike a space, which is relative to the current point size, tabs throw text to a fixed position. The default positions (every half-inch) are only marginally useful, so we set our own positions by setting tab "stops" with the **Tabs panel**. In principle, we could also do this in the **Paragraph Style Options** dialog. However, it is remarkably difficult to use the latter, so we'll focus on the **Tabs panel**. A paragraph style needing those tab stops can then be redefined so its definition will include them.

In this figure, I've shown hidden characters (**⌘-option-I/Ctrl-Alt-I**) to reveal the tab character, created when I tap the **Tab** key.

Text after the tab character resumes at the left-justified tab stop at the 2" mark.

The "hanging" indent was created by shift-dragging the **Left Indent** marker inward.

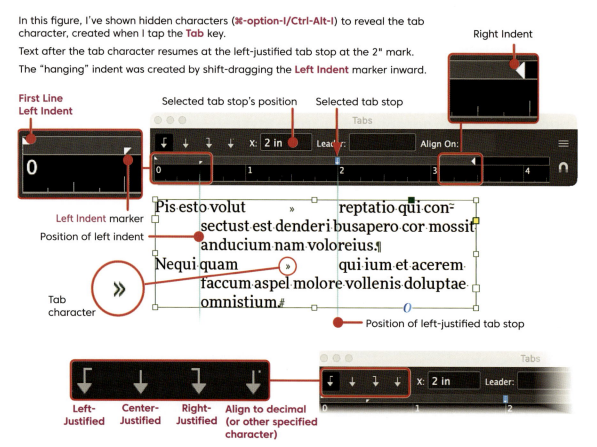

Right Indent

**First Line
Left Indent**

Selected tab stop's position   Selected tab stop

Left Indent marker

Position of left indent

Tab
character

Position of left-justified tab stop

Left-
Justified

Center-
Justified

Right-
Justified

Align to decimal
(or other specified
character)

Note: The **Tabs panel** is the only panel not accessible from the **Window** menu! You'll find it in the **Type** menu.

A solid rule of thumb is to have one custom tab stop for each tab character you intend to have. While our cursor is still in a text frame, summoning the **Tabs panel** will cause it to be positioned nicely along the top of the active frame. If the panel is elsewhere on-screen when you insert your cursor into some text, click the small magnet icon on the right side of the **Tabs panel** to get it to jump atop that text frame. In the previous figure, a tab was typed after a short phrase. Then, in the small gap over the **Tabs panel** ruler, I clicked just above the two-inch mark. That position was fine-tuned with the field labeled **X:** (the tab-stop position field). Immediately, any of InDesign's default (and always invisible) stops to the left of mine were eliminated and the text after the tab character aligned on my custom tab stop.

The first time you ever do this, it's likely that the text will left align on that stop because the default is a **Left-Justified tab** stop. However, you may wish for the following text to center around that position, or perhaps right-align to it. With a stop highlighted, click on an icon for a different type of tab stop, or hold down **option/Alt** and click the stop itself to cycle through. Use the **Tabs panel** menu to create evenly spaced repeats of a selected tab.

Below, the text between two tab characters is centered around the first tab stop. The last bit of text in each paragraph has a decimal, so I used the last type of tab stop called **Align to decimal (or other specified character) tab**. What a mouthful! If there were another character on which I wanted the text to align, I would have entered it in the **Align On:** field, which becomes available when this type of tab stop is chosen.

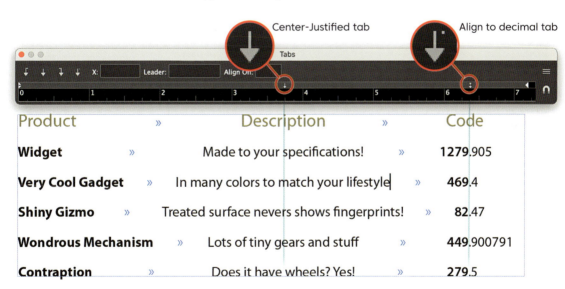

Note: If a paragraph style is controlling the formatting of a paragraph to which you've added tab stops, you should redefine the style so it has this new tab information. Right-click on the style's name and choose **Redefine Style**. Creating a style from text containing tabs will record their tab-stop position and kind.

Workspaces & Preferences

Swatches & Color Settings

Type & Text Styles

Paragraph Rules

A rule is a line, generally a thin one. **Paragraph Rules** are lines that appear near the top and/or bottom of a paragraph. I emphasize "near" because although they are called **Rule Above** and **Rule Below**, they actually appear not very far after and not at all above the paragraph they're applied to, without a bit of adjustment.

Although you can set these in an ad hoc way for any paragraph via the **Control panel** menu, I almost always set these in the context of a paragraph style. To enable a **Rule Above** or **Rule Below**, choose which one you want from the menu in the **Paragraph Rules** section of the **Paragraph Style Options** dialog box, then click the **Rule On** checkbox. With **Preview** enabled, you should see a line along either the first or last baseline of the paragraph. Choose how thick you want the rule to be with the **Weight** menu. Like any stroke, you may also choose a **Type** (**Dashed**, **Dotted**, etc.) and **Color**, which defaults to match the color of the text. Also similar to any other stroke, if the **Type** has gaps, you may choose a **Gap Color** to fill them.

The **Width** of the rule can be that of the column in which the paragraph appears or just as wide as the top or bottom line of text (for rule above or below, respectively). From there, you can adjust **Left Indent** or **Right Indent**, with negative values widening the rule. I have sometimes used this for creative effects that extend beyond the edge of the frame. But if you need to "stay within the lines," check the box **Keep In Frame**.

Finally (although you may wish to do this step early), the **Offset**. This adjusts the position of the rule, with positive values pushing the line in the promised direction. That is, if it's **Rule Above**, positive offset moves it higher; if it's **Rule Below,** positive offset moves it lower.

In the past, I would use a thick rule to act as shading on one-line paragraphs like headers. Now, however, we have a dedicated feature for that. Keep reading!

Paragraph Border & Paragraph Shading

Sometimes one or more paragraphs really need to stand out. In the past, we might put them in a frame to which we apply a stroke, a fill, and some inset. We would then have to anchor that frame inside another so it moved with the flow. But that anchored frame wouldn't necessarily respect the column structure of the text around it.

Paragraph Borders and **Paragraph Shading** act like virtual frames with strokes and/or fills, respectively, with greater flexibility than real, anchored frames. Each can take its own **Color**. Each can have a specified **Corner Size** and **Shape** (and each can be different from the others!)—see "Live Corners Widget and Corner Options Dialog Box" (page 248) for more.

Then came the night of the first falling star. It was seen early in the morning, rushing over Winchester eastward, a line of flame high in the atmosphere. Hundreds must have seen it, and taken it for an ordinary falling star. Denning, our greatest authority on meteorites, stated that the height of its first appearance was about ninety or one hundred miles. It seemed to him that it fell to earth about one hundred miles east of him.

A paragraph with both shading and a border, set with different offsets and corner effects.

The controls for the size of each are a bit intricate. Before deciding on how much the **Offsets** should be (positive is larger, negative smaller), determine from where each is measured.

The **Top Edge** can start at the top of the first line's **Ascent** (top of a lowercase "d" or "k," for example), or its **Baseline** (so the shading or border won't include the first line at all!), or its leading (its entire line-height). I usually choose **Ascent**.

Likewise, for the **Bottom Edge** of the shading or border, I most often choose **Descent** (like the very bottom of a lowercase "y" or "p") rather than **Baseline**, which would miss those dangling parts.

The **Width** starting point can be either that of the **Text** only (excluding left or right indents) or that of the **Column** (including all indents). To be consistent with my usual vertical choices, I most often choose **Text**.

From there, I add what small **Offsets** I require to give an even amount of space all the way around.

Paragraph Border has the unique option to have different stroke weights on each side. This means you can have a line running down just one side of your text, or on both sides, almost like vertical paragraph rules.

If a paragraph splits across frames or columns, should a line be drawn across the bottom of the first portion and top of the next? If so, check the box **Display Border if Paragraph Splits Across Frames/Columns**. With this, any side borders will reach the bottom of the first frame or column and start at the top of the next with no horizontal border between them.

Oddly, there's a control for both borders and shading in the **Paragraph Border** settings: **Merge Consecutive Borders and Shading with same Settings**. So, if you have multiple consecutive paragraphs that should be shaded and/or bordered without a break in between, you need to check this box. But what if you don't want a border? Set the stroke weights to zero!

Finally, unique to **Paragraph Shading**, you may ensure that shading doesn't slip beyond the edges of the frame by checking **Clip To Frame**. And to implement an interesting use-case suggestion, **Do not Print or Export** prevents the shading from being seen anywhere but in InDesign. This could make it easy to designate paragraphs as ones that need attention or should be left alone. For example, you may use shading in a template to literally highlight the paragraphs a user should edit or avoid, but a PDF exported from that document would have no shading.

Keep Options

These options help us to avoid finding the last line of a paragraph at the top of a column or page (known as a widow), or the first line alone at the bottom of a page (called an orphan). If you've learned those terms reversed, you're not alone, but these are the more widely held definitions. Using the **Keep Lines Together** checkbox, even the default to keep the first two and last two lines together does wonders. The cost? You may end up with a space at the end of a page. Most consider that a fair trade to avoid those bereaved typographic elements.

If the paragraph we're configuring is a header, we likely will want to keep **All Lines In Paragraph together**. Also, to prevent the even more perverse situation of a header at the bottom of a column with the text it "heads" in the next, we'd set **Keep with Next** to 1 (or 2) lines.

Type &
Text Styles

Frames, Shapes
& Object Styles

Pages &
Spreads

Find/
Change

Long or
Complex Docs

Package
& Publish

Workspaces &
Preferences

Swatches &
Color Settings

Type &
Text Styles

Finally, you might think you need to break up one long, threaded story into several stories to always have chapter titles at the top of a page. However, you could set the chapter title style's **Start Paragraph** option to **On Next Page** (or **In Next Column**, **In Next Frame**, **On Next Odd Page**, or **On Next Even Page**), depending on your layout.

Hyphenation

This helps us set the whither and whether of hyphenating, and otherwise attempt to make our type look even and professional. Text that is justified often needs help to keep the space between words from becoming awkward. Hyphens help. When text is ragged on one side (as in left, center, or right aligned), many designers will forego hyphens altogether. To have hyphenation, we check the **Hyphenate** checkbox. Once enabled,

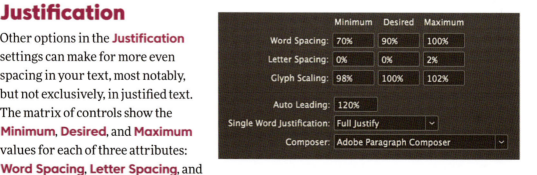

we can set rules and have engaging arguments about which options we should choose. There are at least two boxes I'd suggest unchecking: **Hyphenate Last Word** and **Hyphenate Across Column**. I'm never pleased to have to turn a page to find the second half of a word I started on the previous page.

When columns are narrow, the slider that gives more favor to either **Fewer Hyphens** or **Better Spacing** may help (or frustrate). The set of rules above may also make hyphens less of a plague, but they are really just guidelines that InDesign takes into account with other calculations. The **Hyphen Limit** is the number of consecutive hyphens you are willing to tolerate. The **Hyphenation Zone** will never come into play unless you have ragged text *and* disable the fabulous **Paragraph Composer** in the **Justification** settings, which I strongly discourage.

Justification

Other options in the **Justification** settings can make for more even spacing in your text, most notably, but not exclusively, in justified text. The matrix of controls show the **Minimum**, **Desired**, and **Maximum** values for each of three attributes: **Word Spacing**, **Letter Spacing**, and **Glyph Scaling**. For ragged text, only the central (**Desired**) values play a part. The percentages are calculated from the font's designed settings. So, if you wish to decrease the space between letters by 8% of the space already present in the font data, you'd change the desired **Letter Spacing** to -8%. To increase the space between words by 10% of the designed value, you'd enter

110% for **Word Spacing**. The minimum and maximum set the range of variation allowed in justified text.

Glyph Scaling is controversial. However, modest changes (~1%) should be very difficult to detect.

The only one of the last controls in **Justification** that one might alter is **Auto Leading**. If you would prefer it to be more (or less) than 120% of the size of the type, this is where you change it on a per paragraph style basis. However, since leading is so important to my documents' grids, I almost always set it to an absolute value rather than auto. If you have narrow columns of justified text with words long enough to get a line to themselves, you can decide what to do when that typographical unicorn confronts you with **Single Word Justification**. We should leave the **Composer** set to the fine **Paragraph Composer**, which gives us better spacing throughout a paragraph and therefore our documents.

Span (& Split) Columns

Those who do newspaper layout, or at least lay out articles in a way reminiscent of newspapers, like to have as much of an article as possible in a single frame: the headline, maybe a subhead, the byline, and, of course, the copy. Several columns may be desired for the article copy, but the headline likely needs the full width of the frame or, in the past, a separate frame.

We can use a paragraph style option called **Span Columns** for the headline (and the subhead and byline in the figure below), but allow the copy to be divided by the frame's columns. There are few options for spanning: over how many columns should a paragraph be allowed to span (choices are 2–5 or all) and the space above and below the spanned text.

At right, a list of strangely familiar names occupy four virtual sub-columns in this single-column frame.

Below, the first three paragraphs span the three columns that the body copy obeys.

Type & Text Styles

Frames, Shapes & Object Styles

Pages & Spreads

Find/ Change

Long or Complex Docs

Package & Publish

Workspaces &
Preferences

Swatches &
Color Settings

Type &
Text Styles

Split Columns—A Hidden Feature

Another challenge is the opposite concern. For example, when confronted with a narrow list and a wide column into which to flow it, you may wish to use more of the available space. So we go to the **Span Columns** feature (weird, right?), but choose **Split Column** from its **Paragraph Layout** menu. There are more choices because we have more gaps to define. First, choose how many **Sub-columns** we want. As with spanning, we choose some space both before and after. We also get to decide how much space is on the sides of our sub-columns: between them with **Inside Gutter**, and to the left of the first and to the right of the last sub-column with **Outside Gutter**.

Span Columns

Paragraph Layout:	Split Column ⌄
Sub-columns:	4
Space Before Split:	12 pt
Space After Split:	12 pt
Inside Gutter:	0.1667 in
Outside Gutter:	0 in

If there's an unsplit paragraph after the ones that use a style that includes splitting, the split paragraphs will attempt to balance (divide instances evenly). If the list I used had just two more names, it would have balanced perfectly.

Drop Caps and Nested Styles (and Line Styles)

Paragraph styles control entire paragraphs. That makes them so easy to apply: With the cursor merely blinking in a paragraph, without the need to highlight even a single word, one click on a paragraph style's name applies it to the paragraph, from the first letter through the (hidden) end-of-paragraph marker.

Words or phrases that should look different (bold, italic, different font or color, etc.) are controlled by "Character Styles" (page 221). Sometimes, there are consistent patterns of formatting that we need: The first letter may need to be larger, or certain phrases must be italicized or bold in a certain order. Here are a couple of examples:

Marvelous **Quick Apply**. Use **⌘-return/Ctrl-enter**
then start typing the name of a style, menu item, or
script. Hit **return/enter** to apply **esc** to change
your mind. E
mossinctur?
volor auditio

Drop Caps

Lines	Characters	Character Style
6	1	Giant Drop Cap
☑ Align Left Edge		☐ Scale for Descenders

Drop Caps

The text above has a 6-line **Drop Cap** with a character style applied to it that sets a different font and color. **Align Left Edge** aligns the cap to the left edge of the column or frame (or inset if there is any). **Scale for Descenders** will include the descender of the letter, if present, in the calculation of the height. Thus, if your drop cap is actually a lowercase letter (a "y" or "p," for example), you're still covered. Finally, you can drop as many **Characters** as you like or need. I hope you've noticed that the example paragraph with the drop cap is actually an InDesign tip.

Nested Styles

This cozy-sounding feature automatically "nests" character style–formatted text within a paragraph. In the following example, a caption paragraph contains data in a certain order with—and this is important—specific glyphs/markers in reliable places. More plainly, I'm using a **Forced Line Break**

A **Forced Line Break** typed by holding the **shift** key when hitting **return**.

This creates a line break within a single paragraph, and a landmark for a **Nested Style** to use. In this example, commas are the other style-triggering landmarks.

(a.k.a. "soft return") and commas to separate some of the data. If I used this caption paragraph style throughout a document, I'd be careful to use those characters consistently in each one.

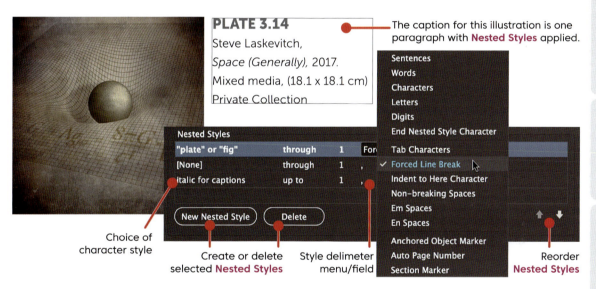

The caption for this illustration is one paragraph with **Nested Styles** applied.

Choice of character style

Create or delete selected **Nested Styles**

Style delimiter menu/field

Reorder **Nested Styles**

I first created the two character styles I wanted to nest. Character styles are the subject of the next section of this chapter. One of those styles, called "'plate' or 'fig,'" changes the case to all caps, the color to gray, and increases the size by about 15%. That's the formatting I wanted for the plate number. The second, for the title of the work, is called "italic for captions" and italicizes text. For the text between the two (the artist's name), I wanted no character style applied.

To create these **Nested Styles**, I created the paragraph style for the caption, setting the **Basic Character Formats** first, then clicked on the **Drop Caps and Nested Styles** category. A click on the button **New Nested Style** begins our walk through the paragraph, starting at its beginning. From the first menu, which at first reads **[None]**, I chose "plate" or "fig", the style I made for that first bit of text. Next I chose how far it should go. From the second menu I chose **through** (rather than **up to**); I left the **1** in the field that follows; and finally, from the last menu (which can also be an entry field!), I chose **Forced Line Break**.

Type & Text Styles

Frames, Shapes & Object Styles

Pages & Spreads

Find/ Change

Long or Complex Docs

Package & Publish

Workspaces &
Preferences

Swatches &
Color Settings

Type &
Text Styles

Note: Even with the **Preview** enabled, your choices will not display until you either proceed to the next item or click elsewhere in the dialog box.

Upon creating the first nested style, I picture myself standing at the point in the paragraph immediately after its effect. In the example above, that would be just after one **Forced Line Break**. From that point all the way through the comma following the artist's name, I want no character style applied. I have to tell InDesign that so I can format what follows that comma. So, I'll create another **New Nested Style**, choosing **[None]** as the style, **through**, **1**, and, since the last menu has no comma, I'll type one into the hybrid menu/field. Previewing this is not thrilling since we're asking that nothing change here.

But the last nested style will show us something. The previous has moved us along to the title of the piece, where I chose the style "italic for captions." How far to apply this one? I didn't want to italicize the comma after the title, so I chose **up to** this time, quantity **1**, and, again, I typed a comma in the field.

One can apply as many nested styles as a paragraph can accommodate. I suppose I could have applied more here, but I showed restraint.

GREP Style

The find/change feature usually replaces content, and with GREP, it can find what to replace with abstract text patterns. See the "Find/Change" chapter of this Compendium to read about the magic of "GREP" (page 305). A GREP *style* is more like find/decorate. We don't change the content beyond formatting it. Nonetheless, it's a powerful feature that almost all of the text in this book is experiencing. In this book, when I type "the **Layers panel**," a character style is automatically applied to the key phrase to color and format it.

Most paragraph style formatting is defined by the **Basic Character Formats**, and often by **Nested Styles**. But we can apply character styles automatically to certain text patterns. How?

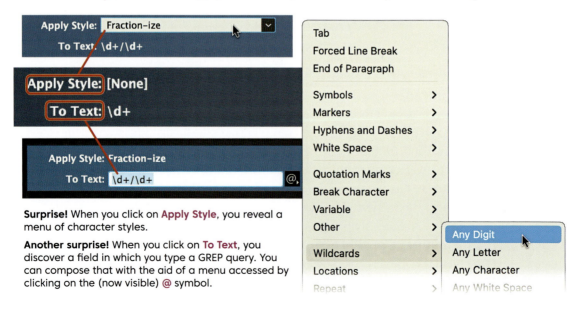

Surprise! When you click on **Apply Style**, you reveal a menu of character styles.

Another surprise! When you click on **To Text**, you discover a field in which you type a GREP query. You can compose that with the aid of a menu accessed by clicking on the (now visible) @ symbol.

In the **Paragraph Style Options** dialog, click **GREP Styles**. Click **New GREP Style** to expose the terrible interface that controls this lovely feature. Why "terrible?" Because it doesn't appear interactive until you interact with it! Click on the words **Apply Style** to discover that you can choose the character style that will be applied.

Click below that on the words **To Text** to enter text and/or the code for the ongoing GREP query InDesign will execute. When a match is found, the style you chose gets applied to it. The query could be as simple as the name of your company or product, and the style may render it in an appropriate font and color. In the case of this book, we look for something more abstract: a capitalized word preceded by "the" and a space and followed by a space and the word "panel."

After reading the "Find/Change" chapter of this book, the query for this will make far more sense. But here's a quick breakdown:

My first attempt was to style a word beginning with an uppercase letter, preceded by "the," then followed by a space and the word "panel."

```
(?<=[tT]he )\u\w+ panel
```

The **Positive Lookahead** contains text that should precede the text we're styling, but should not be styled itself. Here, that's the word "the" (with either an uppercase or lowercase "T") followed by a space. Sadly, the rest of the code fails to style longer panel names:

Now speak we of the **Layers panel** and the Character Styles panel and the Type tool.

So, I added the provision for *zero or more* capitalized words before "panel." Since I style tool names the same way, I added the option for the last word to be either "panel" *or* "tool."

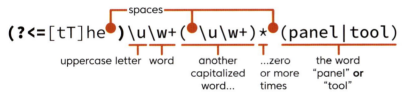

Now speak we of the **Layers panel** and the **Character Styles panel** and the **Type tool**.

Bullets and Numbering

InDesign paragraph styles can maintain the appearance of lists, sub-lists, and all the way to sub-sub-sub-sub-sub-sub-sub-sub-lists! (That's nine levels deep, if you're counting.) These paragraphs can begin with bullets (which can be *any* glyph, not just traditional bullets: "•") or with "numbers" (which can be letters or Roman numerals, and can contain some arbitrary text, too). Numbered paragraphs can be interrupted by pages of non-numbered ones and can resume smoothly where they left off.

To create a bulleted list style, create a new paragraph style and go to its **Bullets and Numbering** section. For **List Type**, choose **Bullets**. For the **Bullet Character**, choose one that is listed or, to choose another, click the **Add...** button to the right. You will then be presented with every glyph in the current font, but you can choose from any font installed in your system (be sure to check the box for **Remember Font with Bullet** when choosing a glyph).

Set the **Text After**. This is usually a tab so its position can be set absolutely (independent of

Type & Text Styles

Frames, Shapes & Object Styles

Pages & Spreads

Find/Change

Long or Complex Docs

Package & Publish

Workspaces &
Preferences

Swatches &
Color Settings

Type &
Text Styles

the text's point size). You cannot type tabs and many other special characters into the available field, but the small menu to its right presents a list of any character you may want here. What appears in the field is a *metacharacter*: "^t" is a tab, for example. These codes for special characters are also used in text **Find/Change**, but not GREP.

Just below **Text After**, you can designate a **Character Style** to be applied to the bullet and the text you chose to have after it.

Last, and very conveniently, there are settings for **Bullet or Number Position**, where you can set **Left** and **First Line Indent** as well as the position of the tab you likely used above. If you have a **Left Indent** wider than the bullet and its text after, the **Alignment** setting becomes effective. Choosing **Right Alignment** right-aligns the bullet (or number) to that position. This is more reliable and useful with numbers, as it keeps a consistent space between number and the text that follows (right).

8 Il·illant·et,·quibea·q
um·et·mo·odipid·qu

9 Volupta·cum·eria·ne
ni·ssitatatene·num·l
nimilit·exerem·non

10 Archita·ereped·mod
em·quatum·reperna
ut·elenti·sam,·nonse

11 Vid·eum·es·et·volor

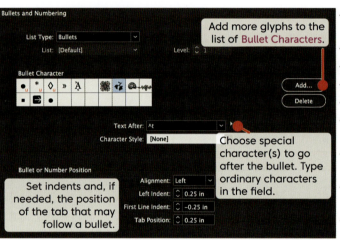

Kingdom of Mycenae (c. 2110–c. 1100 BC)

Kingdom of Epirus (330 BC–167 BC)

Kingdom of Macedon (808–146 BC)

Alexandrian Empire (334–323 BC)

Kingdom of Cyrene (632–30 BC)

Thessalian League (?–170s BC): confederation of Greek city states

Chrysaorian League (?–203 BC): confederation of Greek city states

Aetolian League (370–189 BC): confederation of Greek city states

Achaean League (256–146 BC):

If you choose **Numbers** for the **List Type**, many more choices appear. You can have multiple, independent numbered lists in the same document if you *name* each one. For example, numbered section headers and numbered figures or captions can happily coexist (and not interfere in each other's numbering) as long as each has its own paragraph style and the list itself is given a name. To name a list, choose **Numbers** as the **List Type**. Just below that menu will be one called **List**, from which you choose **New List....** In the dialog box that appears, enter a name that you can access later from other styles (perhaps sub-lists that should get number hints from this one).

Note: It is by naming a list that it can be numbered sequentially even in different stories and frames. For captions that should be numbered, like the ones in the following example, this is critical. To achieve this, check the box in the dialog labeled **Continue Numbers across Stories**.

The **Level** indicates whether the list is top level (1), a sub-list (2), etc. Be sure to choose the same name for a sub-list as you might have for the more primary one with which it should be associated. That is, the name designated for a level one list should be chosen for level two, three, and so on if they are related. InDesign refers to more primary lists as "Previous" ones. So, the **Restart Numbers at This Level After:** checkbox (in the **Numbering Style** section) activates when you choose level two or greater. Notice in the example below that the paragraphs that begin with a letter (level 2 lists) restart "numbering" after each header, which are level one.

Figure 1. Kyme, Aeolis, 165-140 BC. Silver Tetradrachm (31mm, 16.46 g). Kallias, magistrate. Head of the Amazon Kyme; horse standing with one-handled cup below raised foreleg.

I. **THE FIRST HEADER**
   a. Fictem es repres mi, as estiis aborum qui nossint hicil ius, omnimol orenimped ut cimuscillut volupta tquias net quatiatus.
   b. Perias explabo rupiduc ienetur? Omniscia debis tem eum est ab ium labore eos parcium.

II. **THE SECOND HEADER**
   a. Volupta volorio bere con ea veriore ilitatet faccae sinctis cimuscillut ex evelende nes illoriae.
   b. Ostrum rem saperi doluptat modipsam, utem non eatur? Lorum endiore.

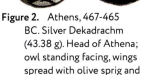

Figure 2. Athens, 467-465 BC. Silver Dekadrachm (43.38 g). Head of Athena; owl standing facing, wings spread with olive sprig and crescent to upper left.

III. **THE THIRD HEADER**
   a. Second level list item (sub-list). Lorati ullabor epudis is sum cum aris aliqui quodit omnis co ipsam nonsequam labore eos parcium ex evelende nes illoriae. Et prendisqua si ne quae perspit ipiditius andunt quatis con cum iliquas perovid ullore.

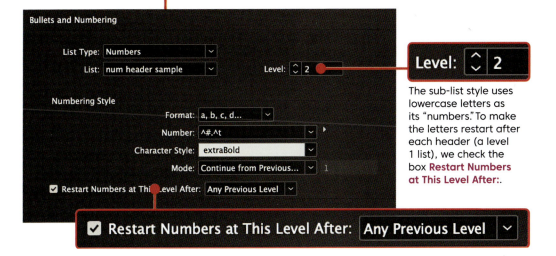

The sub-list style uses lowercase letters as its "numbers." To make the letters restart after each header (a level 1 list), we check the box **Restart Numbers at This Level After:**.

Configure the appearance of your list. In the **Numbering Style** section, choose a **Format:** letters (uppercase or lowercase), Roman numerals (uppercase or lowercase), or Arabic numerals, with or without leading zeros.

Just below the format we configure the **Number** itself. This can be an entire phrase and

Type & Text Styles

Frames, Shapes & Object Styles

Pages & Spreads

Find/ Change

Long or Complex Docs

Package & Publish

Workspaces &
Preferences

Swatches &
Color Settings

Type &
Text Styles

doesn't even need to include a number! You may type words in this field and add special characters via the small menu icon just to the right of it. "^#" is the "number" itself, whether it's a letter or a number. As with a bullet, you may apply a character style to the number string, too.

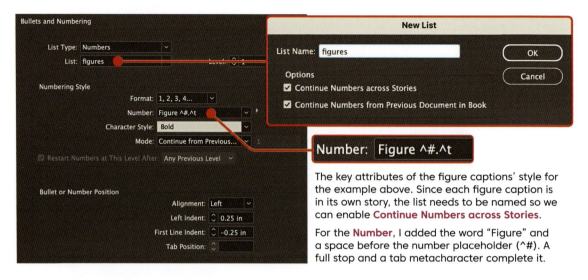

Number: Figure ^#.^t

The key attributes of the figure captions' style for the example above. Since each figure caption is in its own story, the list needs to be named so we can enable **Continue Numbers across Stories**.

For the **Number**, I added the word "Figure" and a space before the number placeholder (^#). A full stop and a tab metacharacter complete it.

Right-clicking when your cursor is within a numbered paragraph shows a menu that will include **Restart Numbering** and **Convert Numbering to Text**. The latter will allow you to edit a bullet or number as you would any other text. Unless it is converted to text, it will remain an entity that you cannot directly select or edit. If it is converted to text, it will no longer automatically number itself when numbered paragraphs are added above it or deleted.

Numbering order within a story is automatic and intuitive. The numbering of standalone frames, like captions, is usually intuitive. However, when these are on the same page, the numbering is tied to the order in which the frames were created. This can make it difficult to add a new numbered caption between two existing ones. There is a loophole: If these frames are anchored to another story, the numbering is tied to the order in which the anchor markers occur.

Character Color

When editing a paragraph style, this is where you choose the color of the text. If a swatch doesn't currently exist in the color you desire, double-click on the **Fill Color** box and you can create a swatch on the fly. Oddly, after creating this swatch, it doesn't always appear in the list. However, if I visit another part of the same dialog box, like **Basic Character Formats**, then return to **Character Color**, that swatch is now available.

It's generally best to apply no stroke to text unless it's really large and of a heavy weight.

OpenType Features

OpenType fonts can offer fabulous features. To unlock those features in either paragraph or character styles, we use the options in the **OpenType Features** section.

So Very Flourishy *So Very Flourishy*

Without (above) and with **Swash Alternates**.

A **Slashed Zero** is clearly distinguished from the letter O.

Ø O

With most fonts, applying **Fractions** to an entire paragraph does terrible things to non-fractions.

7 ⅛ in· (18.1 cm)

Some new fonts intelligently apply the feature only where appropriate. You can use a character style to apply only where needed.

7 ⅛ in. (18.1 cm)

Figure Styles

The way numbers (figures) are displayed. Some fonts offer the full set of variants:

1123581321
1234567890

Tabular Lining
Full-height figures of equal width

1123581321
1234567890

Proportional Lining
Full-height figures with varying widths

1123581321
1234567890

Tabular Oldstyle
Varying-height figures with fixed, equal widths

1123581321
1234567890

Proportional Oldstyle
Figures with varying height and varying widths

Stylistic Sets

Some type designers provide entire sets of alternate glyphs. You can enable one or more by selecting them from this menu. Brackets indicate a nonexistent set.

Underline & Strikethrough Options

Underlines and strikesthrough (strikethroughs?) are much more common to character styles (in the next section of this chapter) than paragraph styles. Like with **Paragraph Rules** and **Paragraph Borders**, one can choose weight, color, and offset. At first, it looks like an underline and a strikethrough are the same feature with different starting points: underline along the baseline, strikethrough higher. With offset, they can be at the same altitude. The difference? **Strikethrough** prints above the text, **Underline** below.

Type & Text Styles

Frames, Shapes & Object Styles

Pages & Spreads

Find/ Change

Long or Complex Docs

Package & Publish

Workspaces &
Preferences

Swatches &
Color Settings

Type &
Text Styles

Output Tagging

When exporting as HTML, whether on its own or embedded inside and ePub, or as a PDF, each paragraph can be tagged in a way familiar to anyone who does web design. In HTML, larger bits of text are usually tagged as a paragraph (p) or as a header (h1–h6). You can indicate which tag is most appropriate for a given type of paragraph through its paragraph style option called **Output Tagging**.

Style information (anything decorative) is usually contained in an accompanying CSS file. Upon export, InDesign writes the style information as a CSS class, the name of which matches the paragraph style.

So a paragraph governed by a style named "body" might export HTML like:

```
<p class="body">Some text.</p>
```

And CSS like:

```
p.body {
        font-family: "Kepler Std", serif;
        font-size: 11px; …
        }
```

A subhead might be more appropriately marked up (tagged) with a class or without, like this:

```
<h2>A Subtopic Here</h2>
```

If HTML and CSS are unfamiliar to you, that's okay. This is the last you'll see of either, unless and until you read the last chapter, "Packaging & Output."

Character Styles

Paragraph styles control entire paragraphs. We rely on character styles to format exceptions within paragraphs. A good, fair, and recurring question my students ask is, "why bother?" We can simply highlight text, reach up to the **Control panel** and choose some different formatting. True, but there are several consequences.

Consistency

Even with something as seemingly trivial as setting text to italic, consistency can be a challenge. In just one font family—Garamond Premiere Pro, for example—I have 17 variations of italic! If we initially chose Light Italic Display as our standard italic, it would be so easy to miss it later on and accidentally choose one of the others. Inconsistency like this is a hallmark of amateur layout.

However, if we create a character style named "Our Italic," we can apply it with just one click and with perfect consistency. As the formatting needs of an exceptional word or phrase become more elaborate, maybe including a different font, color, tracking, and/or size, the likelihood of getting the formatting consistent diminishes and the speed advantage of a character style becomes more obvious.

Most large organizations have (or probably should have) style guides to maintain their brand. Paragraph and character styles go a long way to ensure that we are working within those guidelines. When we highlight a paragraph to which a paragraph style has been applied, that style's name is highlighted in the **Paragraph Styles panel**. If there is no plus sign (+), all is well. When there is a plus sign, it means some "override" (formatting that deviates from the paragraph style's definition) is present.

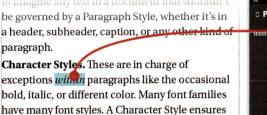

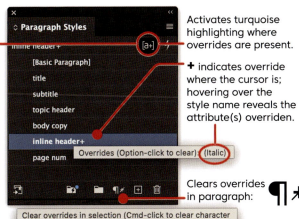

Activates turquoise highlighting where overrides are present.

+ indicates override where the cursor is; hovering over the style name reveals the attribute(s) overriden.

Overrides (Option-click to clear): (Italic)

Clears overrides in paragraph: ¶ ✳

Clear overrides in selection (Cmd-click to clear character overrides only, or Cmd-Shift-click to clear paragraph-level overrides only)

A process to clear all overrides is to select all text and then click the **Clear Overrides** button (see above). To preserve desired deviations, we create character styles. Read on.

Type & Text Styles

Frames, Shapes & Object Styles

Pages & Spreads

Find/ Change

Long or Complex Docs

Package & Publish

Workspaces &
Preferences

Swatches &
Color Settings

Type &
Text Styles

Protection

When confronted with overrides, especially where style guides are enforced, the temptation is to simply clear them all. Many folks do, especially if their inner enforcer is lively that day. But what if the override was perfectly within spec, using approved fonts, colors, etc.? It wouldn't matter. That override, along with any others that may have violated our style guide would be eradicated if we merely highlighted all the text and clicked the **Clear Overrides** button at the bottom of the **Paragraph Styles panel**.

However, if that text had been formatted with a character style, no override would have been indicated, and the formatting would have been protected when other overrides were cleared. Since clearing overrides is often a step in the cleanup of a document before publication, character styles protect "authorized" formatting at that stage.

Overrides can occur even if we don't introduce them. Depending on the procedure we follow, placing Word documents can introduce many overrides, some quite strange. When that happens, I apply character styles to protect the "overrides" I wish to keep, and then I clear the rest.

Creating a Character Style

To create a character style I usually use selected text as an example. As we edit a document, we may discover the need for a new character style—text that should be bold, orange, a different font, etc. We select and apply that formatting to some text, then, leaving it highlighted, we create a new character style via the **Character Styles panel** menu or the [A] button in the **Control panel**, choosing **New Character Style…**. You can also **option-click/Alt-click** the **Create New Style** button at the bottom of the **Character Styles panel**.

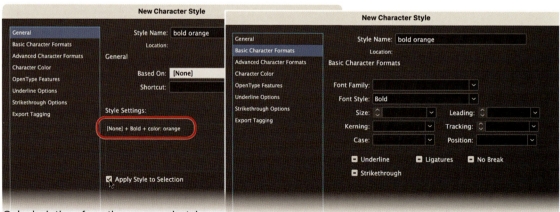

Only deviations from the paragraph style definition are recorded! Brilliant!

Be sure to check the **Apply Style to Selection** box.

Blank is beautiful! The empty fields and checkboxes set to ignore are further confirmation that this character style applies only the formatting we want and nothing else.

An alternate approach, especially for simple formatting, is to create the style with nothing selected and choose the attributes it should control. We can usually anticipate the need for italic, bold, and a few other simple variations within our paragraphs. I will typically create these early so they're ready to go. Remember, only the attributes you choose are included.

The character style formatting choices are similar to but more limited than those we find in paragraph styles. Review those starting with "Basic Character Formats" (page 203).

In the **Character Style Options** dialog box (called **New Character Style** when first created), checkboxes have three states: checked (attribute is applied), unchecked (attribute removed), and with a hyphen (Mac) or a square (Windows), indicating the attribute is ignored.

Applying a Character Style

With text highlighted, a click on the name of the character style applies it to that text. You may also use the **Character Styles** menu in the **Control panel**.

A method that becomes convenient with practice is **Quick Apply**. If you are writing or editing in InDesign, it's likely that your hands are on the keyboard. The shortcut **⌘-return/ Ctrl-enter** summons the **Quick Apply panel** with your cursor in its text field. Simply start typing the name of the character style you want to apply, and the list of styles below (which includes menu items and scripts as well) shortens, perhaps even highlighting the style you want. The arrow keys navigate the list, too. Press **return/enter** to apply the style and dismiss **Quick Apply**. It feels slow at first, but after a couple of uses, it lives up to its name.

Create a character style here

Character style list

The **Control panel**

Editing a Character Style

To edit any style, I recommend right-clicking its name and choosing **Edit "stylename"**. And that's a right-click with *no* left-click first! Why?

Because we apply styles by left-clicking their names and you may not want to apply the style to whatever is currently selected. Or worse, you may unintentionally set that style as a default if you have nothing selected. This happens somewhat regularly since nothing on the page will change if a style is chosen with no text highlighted. Only later when new text is made is the default setting discovered. You may find it mysterious that text you create is bold when the paragraph style applied doesn't include bold.

Tip: Occasionally deselect everything, **⌘-shift-A/Ctrl-shift-A**, then inspect your styles panels. Anything that's highlighted is a default. Be sure the default character style is **[None]**.

You can use **Quick Apply** to edit a style, too. Summon the panel with **⌘-return/Ctrl-enter**, highlight the style to be edited as described above, then use **⌘-return/Ctrl-enter** *again*. This opens the **Style Options** dialog box. Who needs a mouse?!

Output Tagging

As with paragraph styles, character styles can help tag text that is exported as ePub or HTML. The only difference is that the tags are applied inline (to a few words, perhaps, using the span tag) rather than to blocks (like the p tag for paragraphs).

Frames, Shapes
& Object Styles

Pages &
Spreads

Find/
Change

Long or
Complex Docs

Package
& Publish

Workspaces &
Preferences

Swatches &
Color Settings

Type &
Text Styles

Table & Cell Styles

To give visual structure to text, we can use tab characters and tab stops, as discussed in "Tabs" (page 206). But for longer runs of structured text, especially if the source is Microsoft Excel, tables are more suitable.

InDesign's default table style is not attractive: Each cell has a black stroke. To apply more attractive formatting easily and consistently requires making a custom table style and its attendant cell styles. Cell styles can apply paragraph styles to their content automatically, too.

Creating all those styles can take time. If the source of the table is a spreadsheet built and thoroughly formatted in its source application, it may be counterproductive to recreate that formatting in InDesign. In that other app, I'd likely export the table as a PDF and place it into InDesign as a graphic. If the formatting is disposable, then I'd place into my document only the data as an InDesign table with the original formatting removed, as described below.

Placing a Table

A table must be in a text frame. InDesign can create a text frame if you forget to insert your cursor into one before placing a table. However, we usually have a target story in mind: for example, the part in an annual report just after "Our fabulous earnings last year."

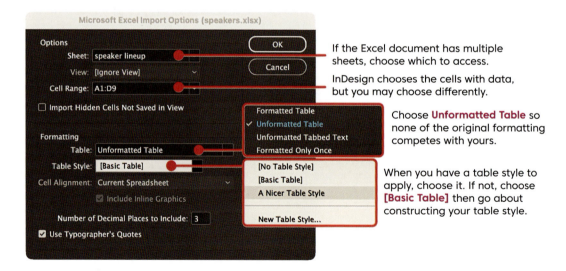

If the Excel document has multiple sheets, choose which to access.

InDesign chooses the cells with data, but you may choose differently.

Choose **Unformatted Table** so none of the original formatting competes with yours.

When you have a table style to apply, choose it. If not, choose **[Basic Table]** then go about constructing your table style.

I typically create an otherwise empty paragraph, usually not indented, with my cursor blinking in it. Getting the table's data into that text is as easy as using **File > Place** (be sure to **Show Import Options**) and choosing a Microsoft Excel file or a text file, with either CSV (Comma Separated Values) or tab delimited text. When placing an Excel sheet, you can specify the **Sheet**, the **Cell Range**, and whether the data comes in as a table at all or as **Unformatted Tabbed Text**. Placed as a table, you may either preserve Excel's formatting (**Formatted Table**) or strip it (**Unformatted Table**), and you can choose to apply an InDesign table style if you have one. Interestingly, when choosing a table style, you should also choose **Unformatted**

Table to avoid a collision of Excel and InDesign formatting. Numeric data can be rounded to a more modest **Number of Decimal Places to Include**, too.

Note: The only tool used when editing a table is the **Type tool**! A table may look like an inline object, and in a way it is, but we interact with it using only the **Type tool**.

If a table imports with an extra row, simply click in a cell in that row, then use **⌘-delete/ Ctrl-Backspace**. An unwanted column? Use **shift-delete/shift-Backspace**. If you take the time to select (highlight) a row or column, you can right-click and choose **Delete > Row**.

An issue that arises fairly often with data-rich tables is overset cells. These show a red dot rather than all the data that should be in a cell. You usually just need to make that row or column larger. Sometimes you need to dig a bit deeper and adjust the cell's inset. To select an individual cell to edit its attributes, use the **Type tool** with the cursor within the cell and drag slightly upward or downward. Don't drag far. If you keep going, you will highlight multiple cells. Once the cell is selected, you can adjust many of its attributes in the **Control panel**.

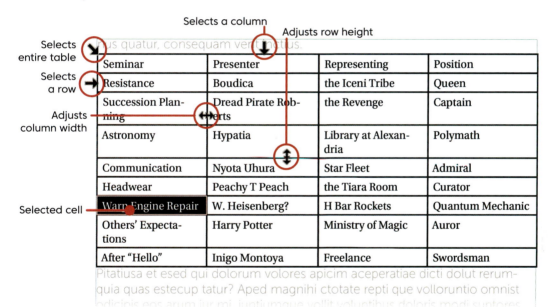

Seminar	Presenter	Representing	Position
Resistance	Boudica	the Iceni Tribe	Queen
Succession Planning	Dread Pirate Roberts	the Revenge	Captain
Astronomy	Hypatia	Library at Alexandria	Polymath
Communication	Nyota Uhura	Star Fleet	Admiral
Headwear	Peachy T Peach	the Tiara Room	Curator
Warp Engine Repair	W. Heisenberg?	H Bar Rockets	Quantum Mechanic
Others' Expectations	Harry Potter	Ministry of Magic	Auror
After "Hello"	Inigo Montoya	Freelance	Swordsman

To select an entire row quickly, move your cursor to its left edge. When it becomes a right-pointing arrow, click to highlight the row. A down arrow appears when you have the cursor at the top of a column, allowing you to select it. Clicking at the upper-left corner of a table selects it all.

You have to get the cursor in the right place to adjust row or column sizes with the **Type tool**. When you hover the cursor over a column boundary, it becomes a two-headed arrow. Click and drag, and all the columns to the right of that line move to allow the one to its left to become larger or smaller. If you'd prefer to move only the dividing line, borrowing room from one column to give to another, hold the **shift** key as you drag. It's the same for rows. If you **shift**-drag the table's right edge, however, *all* the columns grow or shrink proportionately. **Shift**-drag the bottom edge of the table to adjust the row heights proportionately.

Type & Text Styles

Frames, Shapes & Object Styles

Pages & Spreads

Find/ Change

Long or Complex Docs

Package & Publish

Table and Cell Formatting

With one or more cells selected, the **Control panel** offers options for formatting them. If you have only small tables and very, very few of them, this is perhaps sufficient. But having a table style will serve you better, as it can more readily be copied to other projects and edited. I suggest that, despite knowing it's a time-consuming task to create a table style.

With a table cell selected, the Control panel fills with options, here separated into 3 sections, enlarged below

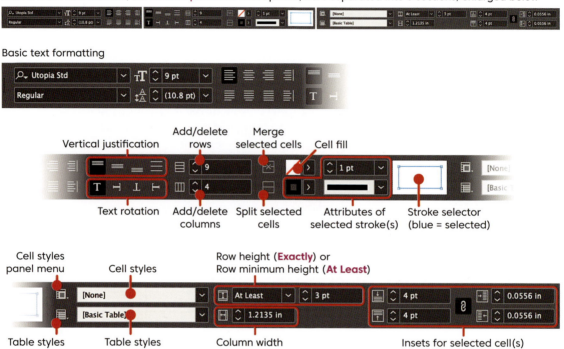

Basic text formatting

Vertical justification — Add/delete rows — Merge selected cells — Cell fill

Text rotation — Add/delete columns — Split selected cells — Attributes of selected stroke(s) — Stroke selector (blue = selected)

Cell styles panel menu — Cell styles — Row height (**Exactly**) or Row minimum height (**At Least**)

[None] — [Basic Table] — At Least — 3 pt — 1.2135 in — 4 pt — 0.0556 in — 4 pt — 0.0556 in

Table styles panel menu — Table styles — Column width — Insets for selected cell(s)

I often start the process with experimentation, using the formatting options in the **Control panel**. Some of the options are similar to text frame options, like "Inset Spacing" (page 253) and "Vertical Justification" (page 253). One option is unique and a bit tricky: the ability to alter stroke attributes differently for each edge of a cell. That is, the top, bottom, left, and right strokes around a cell can have different colors, weights, or types! But beware: The right edge of one cell could be the left edge of a cell next to it.

The **Stroke Selector** in the **Control panel** shows selected strokes as highlighted in blue. Clicking an edge deselects it, shown in gray. It takes getting used to clicking something to *de*select it! Double-clicking selects or deselects all four sides.

Table Style To-Do List

SEMINAR	PRESENTER	REPRESENTING	POSITION
Resistance	Boudica	the Iceni Tribe	Queen
Succession Planning	Dread Pirate Roberts	the Revenge	Captain
Astronomy	Hypatia	Library at Alexandria	Polymath
Communication	Nyota Uhura	Star Fleet	Admiral
Headwear	Peachy T Peach	the Tiara Room	Curator
Warp Engine Repair	W. Heisenberg?	H Bar Rockets	Quantum Mechanic
Others' Expectations	Harry Potter	Ministry of Magic	Auror
After "Hello"	Inigo Montoya	Freelance	Swordsman

The figure above shows the same table as the one in the section "Placing a Table" (page 225). However, this is how it looks after a table style was applied. That table style is doing a number of things: It's applying that alternating pattern of fills and it's calling upon cell styles to decorate the three kinds of cells present here (header cells, left column cells, and the remaining "body" cells). A table style can actually identify *five* types of cells and auto-apply styles to them. In this table, I opted not to use cell styles for right column cells or footers.

The cell styles are applying paragraph styles to format the text within them. The cell styles also remove the strokes around each kind of cell.

So, creating a table style involves creating cell and paragraph styles, too. If any of those paragraphs needed GREP or nested styles, I would also have had to create character styles. It can be a bit of work, but the reward is that later, when I have another table that should look similar, it will require only one click to make it that way.

The first row of most tables, like the one above, is a header. Since I had a cell style for the header row's cells, the table style applied it to those cells for me. To designate one or more rows as a header, highlight the top row(s), right-click, and choose **Convert to Header Rows**. Bonus: If a table is long enough to traverse more than one text frame or column, headers automatically repeat at the top of each.

Let's start with the text and paragraph styles, the base of the style cascade, then move up to cell and table styles.

Type & Text Styles

Frames, Shapes & Object Styles

Pages & Spreads

Find/ Change

Long or Complex Docs

Package & Publish

The Paragraph Styles

Either by sketching out ideas or experimenting with the **Control panel** to format your table, you'll develop a sense of how many different kinds of cells you'll need, and from there, how many paragraph styles you'll need to decorate them. Most of the cells in this table are what I'd call body cells, showing the bulk of the data. For the text formatting, I opted for center alignment and a condensed and lightweight sans serif font.

For the left column, to which the others are subordinate, I chose a heavier weight. Finally, I chose all caps and center alignment for the header text. Later, when I chose a dark blue for the header cells' fill, I changed its paragraph style to use **Paper** (a.k.a. white) as the **Character Color**.

The Cell Styles

I almost always create these with the **Cell Styles panel** (**Window > Styles > Cell Styles**). It is also possible to use the small version of the **Cell Styles panel** menu that appears in the **Control panel** when a cell is selected. It's accessed via the small icon to the left of the list of cell styles. Yes, it is hard to find!

So, use the **Cell Styles panel** menu and choose **New Cell Style…**, which brings us to that dialog box's **General** page. Below are options in each page of the dialog box.

General

I start with the style that will govern my body cells and name it appropriately. Also, here I can choose the paragraph style for text in this kind of cell. For subsequent cell styles, I often use **Based On** and choose my body cells' style.

Text

To give breathing room within a cell, even without strokes, I use a bit of **Cell Inset** on each side. In case a row gets taller, I choose **Vertical Justification** to determine where the text should be in the cell vertically (just like with a text fame). When squeezing a longish phrase into a narrow column, some use **Text Rotation** to turn the text in a cell sideways (**90°**). Note that any field you leave blank will not override a setting. That is, if you leave insets blank, it'll be on you to apply insets to each cell manually.

Graphic

If all that's in a cell is a graphic frame, you may control how it is inset and whether it's clipped in favor of keeping a constant cell size.

Strokes and Fills

To remove strokes, I usually set the **Weight** to **0**. Of course, choose whatever you want for weight, color, and stroke type. In the example, I chose a blue **Cell Fill** color for my header cell style. However, for the body and left column cells, I anticipated that the table style will apply the alternating row colors, so I left their fills blank.

Diagonal Lines

If you want them, you can have them: Choose stroke weight, color, and type, as well as whether the diagonals are in front of or behind other content.

The Table Style

Where it all comes together! From the **Table Styles panel** menu (**Window > Styles > Table Styles**) choose **New Table Style….** The list of options is similar to cell styles.

General

Here, the big task is to choose the cell styles you've built for the major kinds of cells in your table. You may have extra cell styles to apply to special cells. You can have styles automatically applied for the **Left Column**, **Right Column**, **Header**, **Footer**, or general **Body** cells. The UI says "Body Rows," but what do they know?

Table Setup

If my cell styles haven't already dealt with the strokes surrounding a table, I can set it with the **Table Border** settings. Since a table occurs in the flow of a story, it also usually needs a little **Space Before** and **Space After**.

Row Strokes and Column Strokes

When cell styles have not been configured to deal with strokes, you can set them here in a limited way. Especially nice is the ability to have **Alternating Patterns**: every other stroke dashed, for example, or a different color. For the table in the example, I chose no pattern at all.

Fills

I very often choose an **Alternating Pattern** here. The zebra-striping can make it easier for the eye to follow a row, especially in a very wide table.

Type &
Text Styles

Frames, Shapes
& Object Styles

Pages &
Spreads

Find/
Change

Long or
Complex Docs

Package
& Publish

Loading Styles from Other Docs

Each styles panel menu has at least one Load Styles command. You can choose to load only the kind of styles that panel controls (**Character**, **Paragraph**, **Object**, **Table**, **Cell**), and all but the **Object Styles panel** menu offer something more broad. The **Paragraph** and **Character Styles panels** offer **Load All Text Styles...** and the **Table** and **Cell Styles panels** offer **Load Table and Cell Styles...** (surprise!).

An actual surprise is that the last of those (**Load Table and Cell Styles...**) also loads paragraph and character styles! These commands trigger two dialog boxes. The first asks which document you'd like to steal, eh, load your styles from. Then you are shown a list of all the styles requested. You have the option to check or uncheck as many as you wish.

Sometimes it's faster and more targeted to open the document from which you would like load styles. **Edit > Copy** items that use the styles you'd like to use in another document.

In your target document (the one that needs the styles), **Edit > Paste** deposits the copied material and adds its styles. I follow that with a simple **delete** or **Backspace** to remove the pasted item, but the styles will remain. I think of the item I paste as a courier—the person who delivers the pizza rarely stays for dinner.

You can drag assets into the **Creative Cloud Library panel**, and then drag them out into any other document to place them (and their styles) into that document. In each of your style options dialog boxes, there is a checkbox to add that style to the CC Library, from which it can then be applied in any document (and added to the styles panels for the document in which it was applied).

Finally, you can save individual frames or groups as InDesign snippets. These are lightweight documents that can be placed into a document and bring their assets (styles, swatches, etc) with them. To create a snippet:

1   Select items you'd like to share.
2   Go to **File > Export** and choose **InDesign Snippet** as the format (file type).
3   Choose a name and location, then commit.

Even faster: Simply drag and drop the content out of InDesign and onto your computer's desktop, for example. The name will be generic, however. Either way, the file will have the extension "idms" and will have a very small file size if it contains no images. You can use **File > Place** or drag and drop to add a snippet to a document. Deleting the snippet's contents will leave any styles behind.

4 Frames, Shapes & Object Styles

Absolutely everything in InDesign is either a frame or in one. This chapter covers how to manage those frames and the content they hold, and how to take control of frames' positions and sizes.

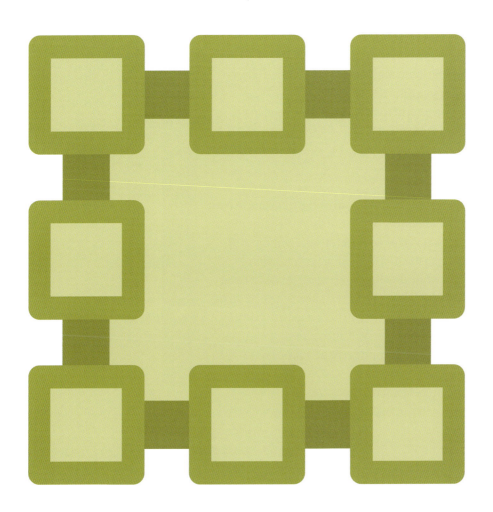

Creating Frames and Shapes

The shapes we create in InDesign serve to either be decorative or hold images or text. Interestingly, InDesign offers two sets of nearly identical tools to do this: **Shape tools** and so-called **Frame tools**. I write "so-called" because the shapes we make with either set of tools can be used as frames and/or be decorated with fills, strokes, effects, etc. The difference? Shapes we draw with the **Frame tools** are born with no fill and no stroke, as they're usually intended as placeholders, but we may add color to them later. The **Shape tools** have whatever appearance we've set as our default—that is, any fill, stroke, effect, or setting that we choose when nothing is selected.

The only other and surprising difference is that "frames" can be selected more easily. "Shapes" without a fill need to be selected or dragged by their edges, whereas a "frame" can be dragged easily without a fill.

Regardless of which set of tools you use, the mechanics, discussed below, are the same.

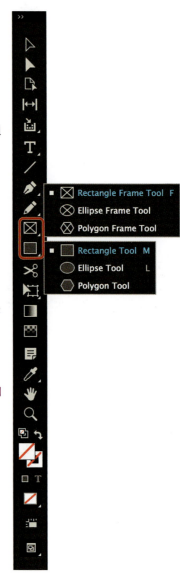

Rectangle

With either the **Rectangle Frame tool** or the **Rectangle tool** chosen, you drag diagonally to create the shape (whether up or down, left or right, it makes no difference). Holding **shift**, especially as you finish the shape, yields a perfect square. Holding **option/Alt** while drawing a rectangle grows it from the center outward. Holding down the **spacebar** *while still in the act of creating the shape* allows you to change its position. Keeping the mouse button depressed and releasing the **spacebar** allows you to resize and reshape as you continue to draw the shape.

Releasing the mouse completes the shape.

One click with this tool brings up a dialog box in which you can enter the height and width of the rectangle.

Ellipse

Just as with the rectangles, you drag diagonally to create ellipses. **Shift** yields circles, and **option/Alt** grows them outward as you drag. And again, holding the **spacebar** periodically while still drawing the ellipse allows you to fine-tune its position on the fly.

A click on the page opens a dialog for entering the dimensions of an ellipse.

Workspaces & Preferences

Swatches & Color Settings

Type & Text Styles

Frames, Shapes & Object Styles

Gridify

This is another modification that is engaged while you are drawing a shape (*not* after it's drawn). This is useful if, for example, you want twelve identical ellipses to cover half a page. Start as if you're drawing a single ellipse that covers half the page, but before you release the mouse, tap the **up** and/or **right arrow** keys. ↑ creates and adds rows of the shape you're drawing; → creates columns. ↓ and ← remove rows and columns, respectively. This also works while drawing text frames (they'll be threaded) and when placing images.

Pressing ⌘ + **arrow**/Ctrl + **arrow** while creating the grid will change the distance between rows or columns (**up** and **down** for row spacing, **left** and **right** for column spacing). Some users think they need very large hands for this because they've forgotten that there's a ⌘/Ctrl key on both sides of the keyboard. When you finally release the mouse, you'll have a grid of shapes, text frames, or images.

The Gap Tool

After you've created a grid, you may still adjust the gaps between columns or rows with the **Gap tool**: ⟷ . When you hover the **Gap tool** cursor over the space between rows or columns (a gap), it highlights in gray the gap that you're about to affect. Dragging with no keys held down, it moves the gap by resizing the shapes to either side of it. The objects to one side are made smaller, while those on the other side are enlarged. So, in the case of a four-by-four grid, you'd be resizing eight objects simultaneously!

By holding down modifier keys, you open up more possibilities. Holding down the ⌘/Ctrl key resizes the gap. The **option/Alt** key moves the objects on either side of the highlighted gap, resizing neither gaps nor objects. The **shift** key moves only the gap between the two objects on either side of the cursor. **Shift** can be combined with the other modifiers to limit gap resizing (**shift** with **option/Alt**) or object movement (**shift** with ⌘/Ctrl) to only the gap or objects immediately adjacent to the cursor.

It's best to practice this with a grid as you mash keys to build muscle memory.

Polygon

The gridify feature can make many polygons, too. Sadly, the arrow key trick conflicts with the way you change the number of sides on the polygon you are drawing. As you're drawing a polygon, *keeping the mouse button down*, a quick tap of the **spacebar** tells the arrow keys to do something other than make rows and columns of shapes. After that tap, the **up arrow** adds sides and **down** reduces. The **right arrow** increasingly pushes in the middle of each side to make a star. The **left arrow** reduces this "star inset."

Alternatively, one click with this tool brings up a dialog box in which you can enter the height, width, number of sides, and amount of star inset. That number of sides and amount of star inset will be the default when drawing a polygon until you change it again.

7 sides

7 sides with
20% star inset

Frames, Shapes & Object Styles

Pages & Spreads

Find/ Change

Long or Complex Docs

Package & Publish

Workspaces &
Preferences

Swatches &
Color Settings

Type &
Text Styles

Frames, Shapes
& Object Styles

The Stroke Panel

The **Control panel** offers a few stroke options: the **Weight**, color, and **Type** (solid, dashed, dotted, etc.). The **Stroke panel** (**Window > Stroke**) offers considerably more. With an object selected, you can also access the **Stroke panel** from the **Properties panel** by clicking the underlined word **Stroke**. Subtle but pleasant options are **Cap** and **Join**. A **Round Join** slightly softens sharp corners and a **Round Cap** can round the ends of dashes, underlines, paragraph rules, or, indeed, any line.

Stroke Type

Some stroke options sound pretty obscure (until you need them), others are really cool. Among the latter is **Type**, of which there are three categories: **Stripe** (**Solid**, **Thick-Thin**, **Wavy**, etc.), **Dash** (**Dashed** and various **Hash** options), and **Dotted** (regular and **Japanese Dots**). Most impressively, you can make your own!

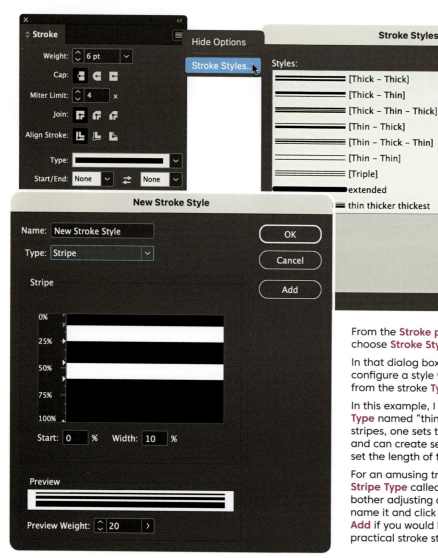

From the **Stroke panel** menu, choose **Stroke Styles....**

In that dialog box, click **New...** to configure a style you can choose from the stroke **Type** menu later.

In this example, I configured a **Stripe Type** named "thin thicker thickest." For stripes, one sets the width of each stripe and can create several. For dashes, we set the length of the dashes and gaps.

For an amusing treat, create a **Stripe Type** called "Rainbow." Don't bother adjusting any settings, just name it and click **OK** to commit, or **Add** if you would like to create more practical stroke styles as well.

Align Stroke

By default, a stroke straddles the edge of a shape. However, when an object really needs to maintain its size, I may set the stroke to **Align to Inside**. However, if I cannot allow a stroke to obscure the frame's content, perhaps an image, I'll set it to **Align to Outside**.

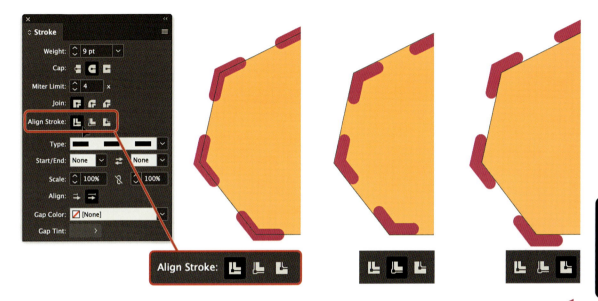

Gap Color

All the stroke types (except **Solid**) have gaps. You can choose a color to fill those gaps in the **Stroke panel** (near the bottom: **Gap Color**). For a dotted stroke, the dots themselves will be the main stroke color, but the space around and between those dots is the **Gap Color**.

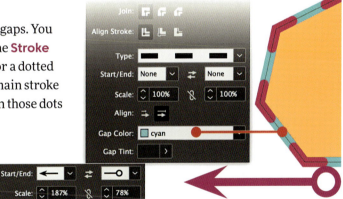

Start/End

This is simply a way to attach decorative ends to an open line. Note that each end can be scaled.

Miter Limit

An obscure setting, but many are dismayed by truncated corners, so I should mention it. As the angle of a corner diminishes, the extent of its corner (**d** in the figure) increases. When that length exceeds a certain multiple of the stroke weight (**w**), the point gets truncated. Luckily, we can adjust that multiple: the **Miter Limit**. By increasing it, a corner is allowed to get longer and pointier.

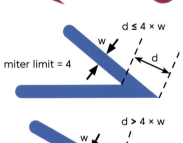

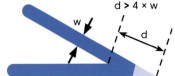

Frames, Shapes & Object Styles

Pages & Spreads

Find/ Change

Long or Complex Docs

Package & Publish

Workspaces &
Preferences

Swatches &
Color Settings

Type &
Text Styles

Frames, Shapes
& Object Styles

Groups and Their Content

We group multiple objects to better ensure that one doesn't get moved or transformed without the other(s). Examples: images and captions, callouts and arrows, or a logomark and logotype.

It is not uncommon to group groups together, too. You might group several image-caption pairs, for example, to maintain their spacing or proximity to each other. First, let's look at a bunch of ungrouped objects. The **Layers panel** is included below because it provides a way to see all the objects on a spread and whether they are grouped. Learn about "Layers" (page 314).

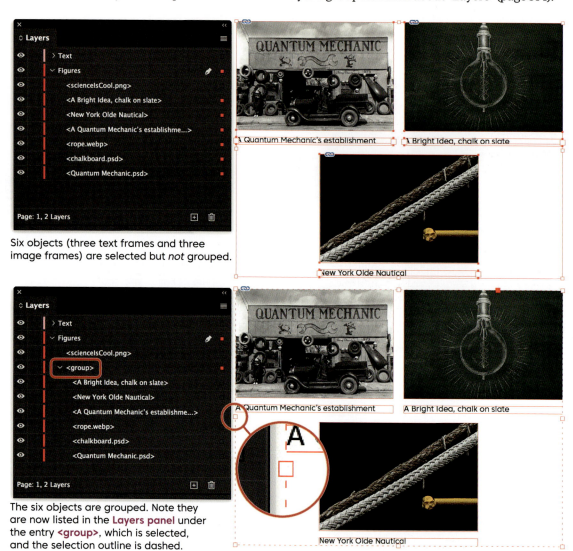

Six objects (three text frames and three image frames) are selected but *not* grouped.

The six objects are grouped. Note they are now listed in the **Layers panel** under the entry **<group>**, which is selected, and the selection outline is dashed.

If we group the objects above by using ⌘-G/Ctrl-G (or **Object > Group**, or by right-clicking and choosing **Group**), they are now outlined by a dashed line and the **Layers panel** shows that we now have a group. If we click the arrow **>** icon to the left of a layer's name, then the one to the left of a **<group>**, each of those icons will now be a **v** and you will see the group's contents.

Accessing a Group's Contents

Double-click to get in, **escape** to get out. This is a wonderfully consistent and powerful rule in InDesign. Sadly, there are quirks with groups, but they are few and can be overcome.

For example, let's say we wish to move our three captions up or down a little bit. If we double-click on one of them with the **Selection tool**, it's selected! We can hold down the **shift** key and click to select a second caption. But try for a third one, and the whole group gets selected. This is a decades-old bug.

However, we can use the **Layers panel** instead to select the third one (and so on). To the right of every entry in the **Layers panel** is a small square that serves as that entry's proxy. If an object is selected, the proxy lights up in the color associated with that layer. It works in the other direction, too. You may also click a proxy to select its object, then **shift-click** other proxies to add their objects to your selection.

Double-click the first object in a group that you'd like to select, and it will be selected. If you turn to the **Layers panel**, you can **shift-click** on the "proxy" squares for other objects to select them.

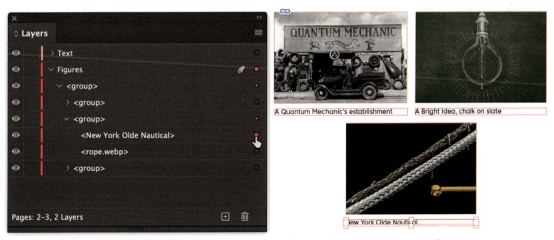

Double-click repeatedly to tunnel your way into a nested group of groups. Use the **esc** key to extricate yourself one level at a time. But use the **Layers panel** to select several objects.

Frames, Shapes & Object Styles

Pages & Spreads

Find/ Change

Long or Complex Docs

Package & Publish

Workspaces &
Preferences

Swatches &
Color Settings

Type &
Text Styles

Frames, Shapes
& Object Styles

Alignment & Distribution

Layout isn't simply about getting a bunch of text and image frames on a page or spread. Hopefully, we create a nice arrangement of them. To help us achieve that, a number of features exist.

Guides

As you may know from other applications you have used, guides are nonprinting lines to which you can snap objects. As you move an object around on a page, when the object's edge gets close to a guide, it gently attaches itself. I say "gently" because you can easily move the object past this point without noticing.

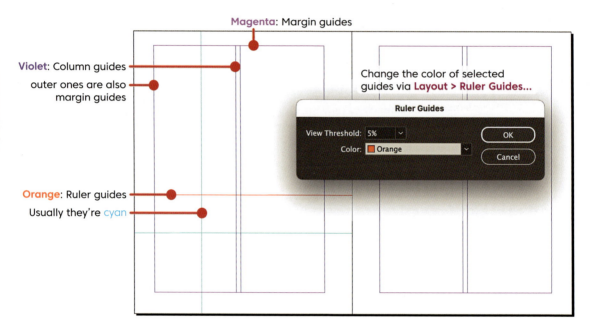

Magenta: Margin guides

Violet: Column guides
outer ones are also margin guides

Change the color of selected guides via **Layout > Ruler Guides...**

Ruler Guides
View Threshold: 5%
Color: ▮ Orange
OK
Cancel

Orange: Ruler guides
Usually they're cyan

When you create a new document, you specify its margins and the number of columns on each page. Actually, you're specifying where margin and column guides should be. If you desire more structure for your spreads, you may add ruler guides as well. Arbitrary ruler guides can be drawn by dragging them from the rulers at the top or left edge of the document window.

Freshly created ruler guides are selected when you first draw them (unless something else was selected when you created the guide). You may select a guide with the **Selection tool**. When a guide is selected, you can precisely position it via the **Control panel** or the **Properties panel**: **X** position for vertical guides, **Y** for horizontal. Change the color of selected guides by choosing **Layout > Ruler Guides...**, where you may also choose a magnification level below which those guides aren't shown. Note that selected guides appear dark and don't reveal their color until deselected.

A method for creating many guides at once as a custom grid is to choose **Layout > Create Guides....**

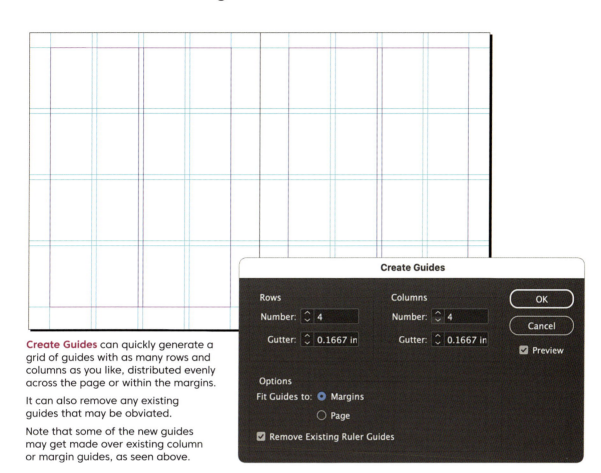

Create Guides can quickly generate a grid of guides with as many rows and columns as you like, distributed evenly across the page or within the margins.

It can also remove any existing guides that may be obviated.

Note that some of the new guides may get made over existing column or margin guides, as seen above.

I delete any generated guides that overlap existing margin or column guides (as above). You may have those rows or columns of guides divide up the page or the margins (**Fit Guides to:**), and you can remove previous experiments with the **Remove Existing Ruler Guides** checkbox.

Smart Guides

Even if your layout doesn't require a strict grid, you likely will still want objects aligned to each other or to parts of the page. **Smart Guides** (and the **Align panel**) make that easy.

As you move an object slowly, green lines will indicate when it's aligned (or spaced evenly) with others. Violet lines show when it's aligned to the page, and magenta lines show when it's aligned to the margins. When you have few shapes, **Smart Guides** are super-helpful.

Below: Simulated **Smart Guides** indicating...

The space between the three shapes is evenly distributed as the polygon is dragged to make that so.

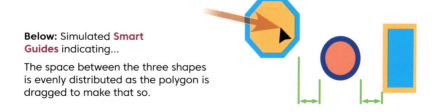

Frames, Shapes & Object Styles

Pages & Spreads

Find/ Change

Long or Complex Docs

Package & Publish

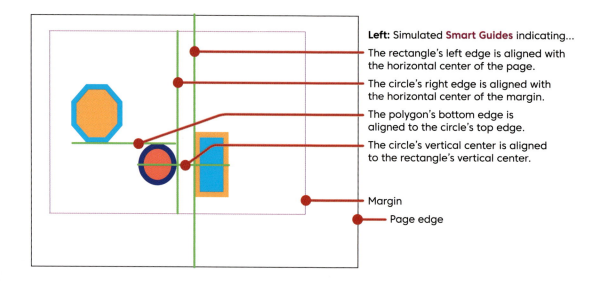

Left: Simulated **Smart Guides** indicating...

The rectangle's left edge is aligned with the horizontal center of the page.

The circle's right edge is aligned with the horizontal center of the margin.

The polygon's bottom edge is aligned to the circle's top edge.

The circle's vertical center is aligned to the rectangle's vertical center.

Margin

Page edge

Align Panel

I adore the **Align panel**! The icons are easily recognizable for what they do and their names clearly state their function (are you listening, Illustrator?).

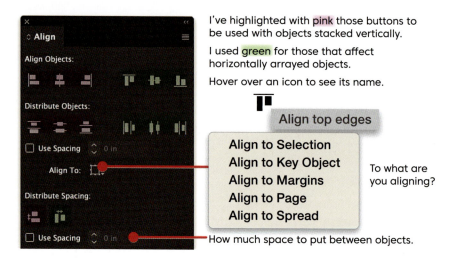

I've highlighted with pink those buttons to be used with objects stacked vertically.

I used green for those that affect horizontally arrayed objects.

Hover over an icon to see its name.

Align top edges

Align to Selection
Align to Key Object
Align to Margins
Align to Page
Align to Spread

To what are you aligning?

How much space to put between objects.

Many of these icons also appear in other panels, but all options are always available via the **Align panel**: **Window > Object & Layout > Align**.

Imagine several objects (which could be any combination of text, image, or unassigned frames). When distributed according to their horizontal centers (the midpoint between the left and right edges), they won't look evenly distributed if they're different sizes.

What gives the best impression of even distribution is equalizing the space between them. When we choose **Align To: Align to Selection** in the **Align panel**, the outermost objects maintain their position and objects between them are moved. But if you select more than one object, then give one of them a single extra click with the **Selection tool**, it will exhibit a blue highlight on its edges:

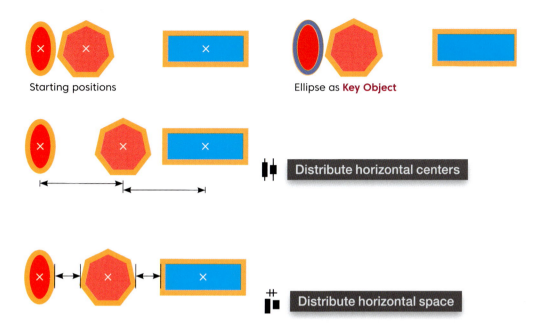

The ellipse above right is a **Key Object** and the **Align To:** menu now will show a small key icon. This object will keep its position as you engage alignment settings. You can set one object to be the key before aligning top edges, then another when you distribute right edges, for example. Also, when aligning to a **Key Object**, the **Use Spacing** checkbox under **Distribute Spacing** becomes active (with a default value of 0). You may enter any distance you wish, then use a distribute space button. The selected objects will now be that far apart.

You can enable the **Use Spacing** feature at any time, but InDesign will keep the topmost or leftmost object in place and move the other selected objects to achieve the specified distribution. **Align to Margins** treats the margins much like key objects. If you choose **Align top edges**, for example, the tops of all selected objects will align to the top margin. Distribution will attempt to lay out objects evenly within the margins. **Align to Page** and **Align to Spread** behave analogously: The page or spread are the items to which objects align.

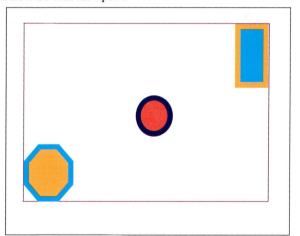

With **Align to Margins** chosen, and both **Distribute vertical space** and **Distribute horizontal space** applied.

Frames, Shapes & Object Styles

Pages & Spreads

Find/ Change

Long or Complex Docs

Package & Publish

Transforms

There are so many ways to get objects where and how we want them! Let's have a look at most of them, from the free-form to the highly precise.

Reference Point
This part of an object should remain in place if the object is scaled or rotated.

Rotate or flip around the reference point.

Flip indicator

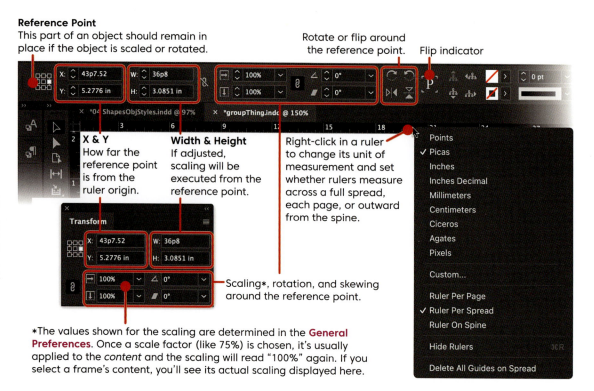

X & Y
How far the reference point is from the ruler origin.

Width & Height
If adjusted, scaling will be executed from the reference point.

Right-click in a ruler to change its unit of measurement and set whether rulers measure across a full spread, each page, or outward from the spine.

Scaling*, rotation, and skewing around the reference point.

*The values shown for the scaling are determined in the **General Preferences**. Once a scale factor (like 75%) is chosen, it's usually applied to the *content* and the scaling will read "100%" again. If you select a frame's content, you'll see its actual scaling displayed here.

Both the **Control panel** and the **Transform panel** (**Window > Object & Layout > Transform**) offer fields that allow us to specify position and/or size to at least four decimal places!

Note: With almost all transforms done by mouse, button, or keyboard shortcut, holding down the **option/Alt** key yields a transformed *copy* of your object rather than transforming the original.

Size and position can also be recorded and applied swiftly with object styles. See "Size and Position Options" (page 279).

Position: X Location & Y Location Fields

Sometimes you want a thing where you want it. Both the **Control panel** and the **Transform panel** have various fields where we can enter values by which to move an object. Note that the ruler measurements can be per spread or per page, or start at the spine. Thus, the value in those fields will change. They also change based on the chosen reference point.

Movement

Sometimes you want a thing somewhere else. Of course, you can drag objects around with the **Selection tool**, dropping them anywhere. Or you can select an object and use the arrow keys to nudge it. Holding down the **shift** key as you press the arrow keys accelerates nudging by ten times, whereas **⌘-shift/Ctrl-Shift** with the arrow keys nudges only one-tenth the usual distance. That distance can be set in the **Preferences:** See "Cursor Key" (page 169). But for precise positioning, we have the options above, some of which are also in the **Properties panel**.

With the Selection Tool—Two Ways

This will not be a surprise: If you drag an object with the **Selection tool**, you move it (avoiding the **Content Grabber** if it's an image frame, unless you wish to move the image within its frame). Holding down the **option/Alt** key as you drag creates a copy of the object at the location where you release the mouse.

A second, easily missed method is to select one or more objects then double-click on the **Selection tool** in the **Tools panel**. This summons a dialog box where you can enter a precise movement. You can also choose to move either the original (by clicking **OK**) or a copy (by clicking **Copy**). Be sure to activate the **Preview** to see what's going on.

Scaling

When scaling, be aware of how the **When Scaling** preferences are set. See "When Scaling: Apply to Content/Adjust Scaling Percentage" (page 164).

With the Selection Tool & Bounding Box

Simply dragging the corner of a frame's bounding box will resize it. Holding **shift** will preserve its proportions. To resize a frame and its content, hold down the **⌘/Ctrl** key. Use **⌘-shift/Ctrl-shift** to resize the frame and its content without distorting either.

Scale Tool

Found in the same part of the **Tools panel** as the **Rotate tool**, the **Scale tool** shares something important with its cousin: an axis around which the transformation takes place. You click on the object to set the axis, move the cursor a distance away from that axis, and prepare to drag. To make this a little more intuitive, I suggest that after setting the axis, you position the cursor at about a 45° angle from the axis before dragging. Then, as you drag toward the axis, the object (and any content within it) will scale roughly proportionally. The **shift** key will make it exactly proportional. Phrased differently, dragging at a 45° angle scales both the width and the height, whereas dragging up and down with the **Scale tool** scales only the height, and dragging left and right scales only the width. Tricky. Practice is recommended (remember you have

Frames, Shapes & Object Styles

Pages & Spreads

Find/ Change

Long or Complex Docs

Package & Publish

Workspaces & Preferences

Swatches & Color Settings

Type & Text Styles

Frames, Shapes & Object Styles

unlimited undo).

Warning: If you drag too far, you may flip the image. If you scale an image, I suggest clicking on the **Content Grabber** (the donut at the center of the image), then consulting the **Scale X Percentage** and **Scale Y Percentage** fields to see if they are the same. If not, you've distorted the image. If one or both are negative, you have flipped the image in that dimension. The **Flip indicator** will also show this: The "P" will be flipped. Correct the issue, if needed, then tap the **esc** key to select the frame again.

Width & Height Fields

In either the **Control panel** or the **Transform panel**, you can directly enter a width and/or height. If they're linked (the chain to their right is active), both values will change to keep the object the same shape (also called its *aspect ratio*). If you resize an image frame this way, you may have to follow up with fitting commands; see "Frame Fitting Options" (page 261).

Regardless of the units showing in those fields, you may use others (and arithmetic) as long as you include an abbreviation of the units of measurement with the value(s). For example, two inches can be entered "2i", "2in", ".5i + 6p6", "8/4i", etc.

Scale X Percentage & Scale Y Percentage Fields

Depending on your **When Scaling** preferences, these fields will likely show "100%" almost always. If you choose, say, 75% from the small menus to the right of either of these fields, the frame and its content will shrink to three-quarters of their former size. The **Scale** fields will then immediately read 100% again—your new starting point.

If you are curious about the scaling of an image *inside* its frame, you will have to select it (click the **Content Grabber** or double-click off-center).

Rotation

With the Selection Tool & Bounding Box

If you've selected an object and then move the **Selection tool** cursor just beyond any corner of that object, you'll see a curled arrow inviting you to rotate the object. If you approach an angle of rotation to which another object on the same spread has been rotated, a **Smart Guide** will gently snap

this object to the same angle. Holding the **shift** key will snap the rotation to 45° angles (45, 90, 135, etc.).

Rotate Tool

Just below the halfway point of the **Tools panel** are the **Transform tools**, including the **Rotate tool**. The default (the one shown if you haven't changed it) is the **Free Transform tool**. Right-click it (or whichever tool is showing) to choose any of the other three. Note the letter to the right that you may press to access each tool (at least two of them make sense).

The **Rotate tool** offers one benefit over using the **Selection tool** for rotation: You may choose the point on the page around which something rotates (the axis of rotation). The usual procedure to use the **Rotate tool** is to first select an object (here, an image), then with the **Rotate tool**, click at the point around which you wish the rotation to occur (it can be anywhere at all, on the object or not). In this example, I clicked about halfway down the left-hand side of the image, in the middle of one of the lamps.

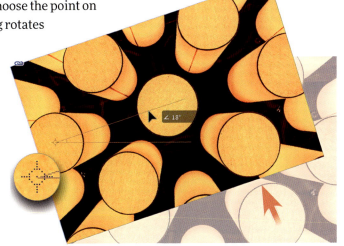

Then you drag. From where is not critical, though I'd recommend it not be very close to the axis of rotation. I chose the middle of the image in this case, but I could have dragged from anywhere. You don't get much finesse if you drag too close to the axis, much like one doesn't get much leverage pushing a door open near its hinges.

As you drag, InDesign shows you the angle of rotation so far and a growing wedge. Holding the **shift** key would snap the rotation every 45°, and holding the **option/Alt key** would rotate a copy rather than the original.

Rather than dragging, you may double-click on the **Rotate tool** in the **Tools panel**. You can then enter an exact angle the object should rotate around the axis of rotation you've set.

Rotation Buttons & Angle Field

For a quick 90° rotation, you can use the **Control panel**. First set the **Reference Point** (looks like the figure at right), then click either the **Rotate 90° Clockwise** or **Rotate 90° Counter-Clockwise** button.

Near those buttons is a field where you can enter an angle. The object will then be rotated that much around its reference point. Review the figure on page 242.

Frames, Shapes & Object Styles

Pages & Spreads

Find/ Change

Long or Complex Docs

Package & Publish

Workspaces &
Preferences

Swatches &
Color Settings

Type &
Text Styles

Frames, Shapes
& Object Styles

Reflection

With the Selection Tool & Bounding Box

If you drag the edge of a frame past the opposite edge (via one of the handles on its bounding box), the image will be flipped. An interesting method, but the **Flip** buttons are faster and more reliable.

Flip Buttons

When either (or both) of these are deployed, an object flips around its reference point. The **Scale Percentage** fields, **Rotation Angle** field, and **Flip** indicator will all remind you of that.

If you rotate or flip an object, the **Flip** indicator will help you identify the transformation:

No transform   Rotated 90° clockwise   Flipped vertically   Flipped horizontally and
rotated 90° clockwise

Shearing

Shear Tool

Like the **Scale tool**, it can transform an object either vertically or horizontally if you drag in that direction.

Shear X Angle Field

The **Shear angle** tells you how "out of plumb" the vertical lines are in the object you sheared. In this image, that's about 20°.

Free Transform Tool

The greatest advantage of the **Free Transform tool** over the **Selection tool** is that it will scale both frame and content by default. You still need the **shift** key to prevent distortion to content if you free-transform an image or text frame.

After starting to drag a corner of a frame with this tool, you may shear the shape by holding down ⌘**/Ctrl**.

Pathfinder

To assemble a shape or frame from multiple pieces, the first four commands in the menu **Object > Pathfinder** are just the thing you need. To fuse two or more shapes together, choose **Add** from that menu. **Subtract** punches holes: The top object becomes a hole in what's behind. To move an object fore or aft of another, select it and right-click, then choose **Arrange > Send** to Back or Bring to Front (don't bother with Backward or Forward, as you may have to do that too many times).

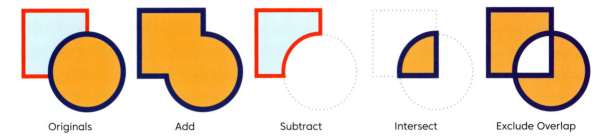

Originals   Add   Subtract   Intersect   Exclude Overlap

Compound Path

A fly's eye is actually composed of many very tiny eyes. Thus, we say it has compound eyes—one made from many. If you want what looks like, say, 35 circles to act as a single frame, you can have that.

You'd select all of those circles, and then choose Object > Paths > Make Compound Path. With that path selected (I so want to say "those paths," but it's now a single entity), you can place an image in it and see the scene as though you're looking through 35 portholes.

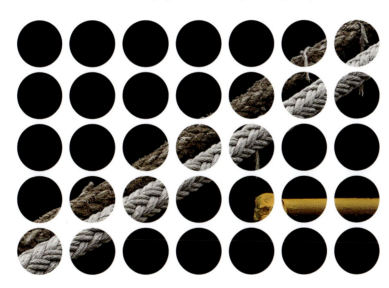

Frames, Shapes & Object Styles

Pages & Spreads

Find/ Change

Long or Complex Docs

Package & Publish

Workspaces & Preferences

Swatches & Color Settings

Type & Text Styles

Frames, Shapes & Object Styles

Live Corners Widget and Corner Options Dialog Box

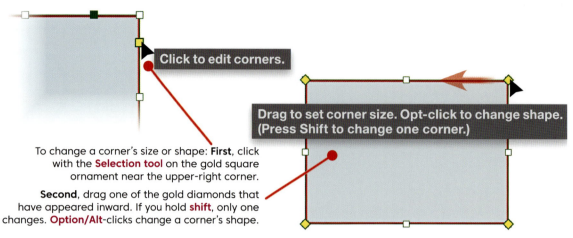

Click to edit corners.

Drag to set corner size. Opt-click to change shape. (Press Shift to change one corner.)

To change a corner's size or shape: **First**, click with the **Selection tool** on the gold square ornament near the upper-right corner.

Second, drag one of the gold diamonds that have appeared inward. If you hold **shift**, only one changes. **Option/Alt**-clicks change a corner's shape.

Every rectangle (any rectangular frame) exhibits a square gold **Live Corners widget** near its upper-right corner. Clicking it engages the corner-editing feature. Drag a diamond to increase a corner's size. Once the corners have some size, **option/Alt**-clicking on a diamond cycles through various shapes. Note that holding down the **shift** key while adjusting the size or shape of a corner changes only that corner.

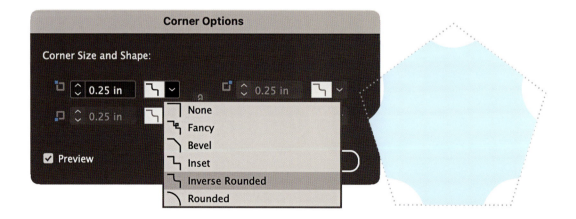

Rounded   Fancy   Bevel   Inset   Inverse Rounded

Corner Options

Corner Size and Shape:

0.25 in   0.25 in

0.25 in

- None
- Fancy
- Bevel
- Inset
- Inverse Rounded
- Rounded

☑ Preview

Any shape with corners can be decorated like this. Go to **Object > Corner Options...** and choose shape and size. For non-rectangular shapes, all corners get the same treatment.

Direct Selection Tool

Instead of selecting an entire object with the **Selection tool**, you can use the **Direct Selection tool** to select one the object's *anchor points*, the very tiny dots along the perimeter of any shape or frame in InDesign. Even **Text Wrap** paths can be edited with this tool. It's easiest if the shape is not selected at all as you approach one of its anchor points with this tool; otherwise you're editing the entire shape rather than a single point.

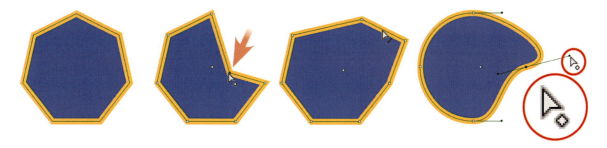

You can drag a point to create a wholly custom shape. You might also drag a path segment (the line between points) to move an entire edge. Anchor points on curved shapes have handles that control the trajectory of a path from one point to the next. You can edit these with the **Direct Selection tool** as well.

Both the standard **Selection tool** and the **Direct Selection tool** are derived from very similar tools in Adobe Illustrator, where they are a bit easier to use. Other tools borrowed from Illustrator include the **Pen tool**, the **Pencil tool**, and the ones lurking behind them in the **Tools panel** (accessed by a right-click on either the **Pen** or **Pencil tool**).

Although the ability to sculpt basic shapes with the **Direct Selection tool** means you may not need Illustrator often, more complex vector shapes are much easier to make there, if you have access to it. Then, simply copying in Illustrator and pasting in InDesign will gain you a fancy frame in the latter.

Frames, Shapes & Object Styles

Pages & Spreads

Find/ Change

Long or Complex Docs

Package & Publish

Text Frames & Text Frame Options

We can exercise a great deal of control over how our content looks even before we adjust any typographic options (leading, kerning, and such). For more on typographic features, see Compendium chapter 3, "Type & Text Styles" (page 194).

The options under discussion here are adjusted without having to use the **Type tool** at all. To judge some of these features, you may wish to have some content to play with. Draw a text frame with the **Type tool**, then right-click and choose **Fill with Placeholder Text**. Don't like it? Undo, then do it again. It'll be randomly different each time.

Frame to Content & Content to Frame

A reliable, if slow, method for switching between a frame and its content is to simply switch between the **Type tool** and the **Selection tool** in the **Tools panel**. It is far quicker, however, to double-click in a text frame with the **Selection tool**—the tool will change automatically and the text cursor will blink at the point of the double-click.

To return to editing the container, or as I prefer to phrase it, to "get out" again, tap the **esc** key. Get it? "Get out" = "escape!" In fact, we'll see this is a general rule in many contexts.

Double-click with the **Selection tool** where you'd like to edit text to quickly summon the **Type tool**.

When editing text with the **Type tool**, press the **esc** key to select the text frame and choose the **Selection tool**.

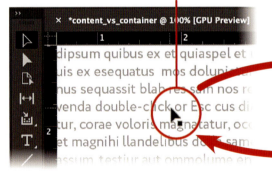
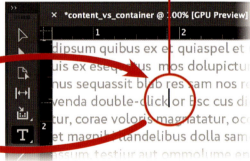

Linking Text Frames

One continuous flow of text is called a *story*. Often, that story flows from one frame to another. When it does, we say that the story is *threaded* among linked text frames. When you have (or expect) more text than can fit

Ucit dem debis dollictus quaectuscit hit es persper iatemo denduci neturepudi arborpor emoluptae nullestotate offic to torro magnat aut rerchil imporum eaque officia sequo qui

Overset text is indicted by the red plus sign in the **out port**.

into one text frame, InDesign offers many ways to thread that story. If you already have more content than fits (called *overset text*), its frame's **out port** turns red and shows a plus sign. The method you choose for threading a story will depend on whether you already have frames into which to flow the text. It also matters if you need more pages to accommodate all the content. Most methods start with clicking on the **out port** of an existing text frame with the

Selection tool. Clicking an **out port** "loads" the cursor. Depending on where you move that cursor, you may see its appearance change to indicate its behavior. Holding down modifier keys also changes its look and behavior. Here are some of your choices:

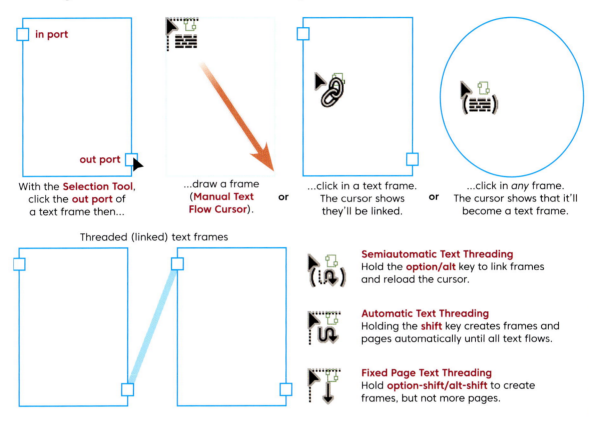

With the **Selection Tool**, click the **out port** of a text frame then...

or

...draw a frame (**Manual Text Flow Cursor**).

or

...click in a text frame. The cursor shows they'll be linked.

...click in *any* frame. The cursor shows that it'll become a text frame.

Threaded (linked) text frames

Semiautomatic Text Threading
Hold the **option/alt** key to link frames and reload the cursor.

Automatic Text Threading
Holding the **shift** key creates frames and pages automatically until all text flows.

Fixed Page Text Threading
Hold **option-shift/alt-shift** to create frames, but not more pages.

Manual Text Flow

When the loaded cursor is not over an existing frame, it exhibits a squared-off corner. Simply drag diagonally to create a new text frame; it will link to the first one automatically. You should also see a line that connects the **in port** of the new frame to the **out port** of the first one. If you do not, be sure that you are not in **Preview Mode**. You may also need to go to **View > Extras > Show Text Threads**.

If you hover the loaded cursor over another existing text frame, the cursor will show a link icon (a chain). Clicking within that text frame will link the two frames together. If you hover over an unassigned frame or shape, the cursor will show an icon that looks somewhat like text enclosed in parentheses. Clicking will convert that shape or frame into a text frame and link it to the first one.

Semiautomatic Text Threading

If you need to thread multiple frames together, it becomes tedious to repeatedly click on **out ports** to reload the cursor. Instead, if you hold down the **option/Alt** key when you make or click in a frame, that frame will be linked to the previous one *and* your cursor will be reloaded so you can continue onto the next one.

Frames, Shapes
& Object Styles

Pages &
Spreads

Find/
Change

Long or
Complex Docs

Package
& Publish

Automatic Text Threading

A common scenario: In an InDesign document with only one or very few pages, your cursor is loaded with potentially dozens of pages of text (maybe you are placing a text file). Clicking in the upper-left margin of an empty page creates a text frame as big as the margins. Rather than manually create more pages, click **out ports**, and flow text from page to page, you need only hold the **shift** key when clicking on that first page's upper-left margin. **Shift**-clicking will create not only the first frame, but more pages as well, each with a frame as large as its margins, until all the text has flowed!

There is an even more powerful way to automatically generate pages and flow text from page to page. It leverages a parent page feature known as a **Primary Text Frame**. Read about those in the next chapter: See "Primary Text Frames & Smart Text Reflow" (page 291).

Fixed Page Text Threading

This method is similar to automatic text threading, but is better in situations where you have a fixed page limit. Holding down **option-shift/alt-shift** will create frames on the pages that already exist, but will not add more pages.

Scaled Text Preferences

As mentioned in the discussion of preferences, there's a way to know the original size of type after it has been scaled with its frame. This setting, called **Adjust Scaling Percentage**, is found in the **General Preferences** (⌘-K/Ctrl-K). If enabled, a text frame scaled to 150%, for example, will show that scaling in the **Control panel** ever after, making it easy to set it back to 100%. If the text size had started at 10 points, it will read **10pt(15)**, which can be confusing. Worse, this actual change of size doesn't trigger a style override that can be cleared. If you liked the new frame size, but wanted the text to be 10 points again, you might have to set it to 6 2/3 points (10 ÷ 1.5 = 6 2/3)! This is not worth the trouble. I set the preference to **Apply to Content**. For unique content like book titles, I often scale frame and text to a size that pleases visually and never look back. However, when a text frame gets accidentally resized, I can quickly get the correct type size again by clearing a style override or choosing the size I need.

Text Frame Options

A small number of text frame options can be adjusted via the **Control panel**. The rest require the **Text Frame Options** dialog box, which is opened by choosing **Object > Text Frame Options...** or the shortcut **⌘-B/Ctrl-B**.

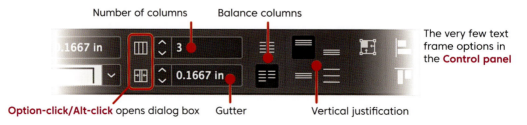

Number of columns   Balance columns

The very few text frame options in the **Control panel**

Option-click/Alt-click opens dialog box   Gutter   Vertical justification

Columns

Any text frame can have multiple columns. The number of columns can be set in a few places: the **Control panel**, the **Properties panel**, or via the **Text Frame Options** dialog box. You can also set column width parameters.

Fixed Number

Choose a number of columns and a gutter (space between columns), and InDesign will divide the frame evenly and calculate a width for each column. If you enter a width, the frame's width will change to accommodate it. However, this column width value is a bit fugitive: Change the width of the frame, and InDesign will adjust the column widths again to divide the frame evenly. If you need a column with a fixed width, choose…

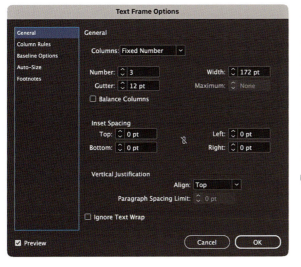

Unbalanced (left) and balanced columns (right)

Fixed Width

When set, if you manually adjust a text frame's width, it will snap to whole-column widths. For example, if you start with a three-column frame with two-inch wide columns and then attempt to widen the frame just a little, it will suddenly grow a bit more than two full inches wider (the column width plus a new gutter).

Inset Spacing

Inset pushes the text inward, away from the frame's edges. Note the chain in the center of these fields. When intact, it ensures all the values remain equal. If disabled, each value can be unique. Use inset when you add a stroke or fill color to your text frame. I also use inset for captions that abut an image to yield a predictable amount of space between the image and the words.

Vertical Justification

When the text doesn't cover the full depth (height) of a frame, you can choose where the text is positioned vertically within the frame. The sensible default is **Top**. The other choices can be useful, too. When you change this to **Bottom**, the last baseline will fall along the bottom edge of the frame (assuming there is no inset).

Frames, Shapes
& Object Styles

Pages &
Spreads

Find/
Change

Long or
Complex Docs

Package
& Publish

Center will attempt to give as much space above the text as below it.

Justify will put the top line at the top of the frame, and the last baseline at the bottom. Leading throughout will be adjusted to evenly divide the space between lines. If you choose **Justify**, you may also enter a value for **Paragraph Spacing Limit**. This will force InDesign to first add space after each paragraph in the frame (up to the specified limit). Once that limit is reached, leading is added to each line to justify the text top to bottom. If the **Paragraph Spacing Limit** is very large, InDesign will create only space between paragraphs and not affect leading.

Baseline Options

First Baseline Offset

You can choose where the first baseline of your text is relative to the top of the frame. Doing so can make it easier to have content align pleasantly across columns or pages.

Ascent is the default. The first baseline is as far down from the top of the frame as an ascender is tall. That is, any ascenders in the first line just kiss the top of the frame. However, since capital (uppercase) letters are typically shorter than ascenders, alignment between such a frame and another may not look correct. Thus, a caption frame next to an image may appear better aligned with its image if we choose…

Ascent—for ascenders
Ascenders touch frame-top.

Cap Height
Caps touch frame-top.

Leading
Leading controls first baseline's position.

x-height—GOOD FOR SMALL CAPS
Good for small caps and vertical centering.

fixed (min = x)
Where x = any absolute value. The other offsets are affected by type attributes. Sometimes, you just want what you want.

Cap Height, in which the caps perfectly touch the top edge of the frame. I usually reserve this for standalone frames.

Leading is the setting used for the text frame you're reading right now. When combined with well-calculated leading, we can best ensure that text aligns with an underlying baseline grid (below). If it's difficult to guarantee that the first line will have a leading value consistent with the baseline grid (odd-sized headers, perhaps), then **Fixed** may be appropriate.

x-Height, like **Cap Height**, is best used with standalone frames. Lowercase letters and small caps touch the top. Vertically centered text *appears* more centered with this setting.

Fixed, combined with a **Min** value equal to your baseline grid setting, helps keep text flowing along that grid, since it is independent of font attributes.

Baseline Grid

The **Text Frame Options** dialog box offers you a chance to apply a **Custom Baseline Grid** to specific text frames. Although I seldom do so, this affords a good opportunity to discuss how to use baseline grids generally.

The **Baseline Grid** preference settings are document-specific and create virtual lines along which your text's baselines can run. Choose **InDesign CC > Preferences > Grids** (on a Mac)/ **Edit > Preferences > Grids** (on Windows) to set these. You can use paragraph styles to force your text to "Align to Grid" (page 205), or the baselines may be aspirational—that is, it's on you to ensure the leading you apply to your text lands the text on this grid if you want it to.

These are the settings for the illustrated spread below:

Color:	**Light Blue**	Because I was too lazy to change it.
Start:	**57.87 pt**	That's how far from the top of the page my primary text frame is.
Relative To:	**Top of Page**	Other choice is **Top Margin**, but these text frames are located a bit higher than the top margin.
Increment Every:	**14 pt**	This is my fundamental leading. Headers may have twice this value, and/or use **Space Before** or **Space After** equaling a multiple of this value.
View Threshold:	**75%**	If I zoom out sufficiently (below 75% in this document), the grid lines disappear. This is good, as they'd be overwhelmingly dense at that point.

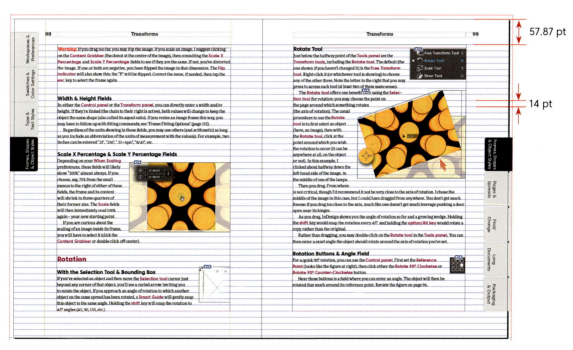

Auto-Size

This is an option for standalone text frames (not threaded to others). The setting I use most frequently is illustrated here: allowing only the height to change (to maintain column width), keeping the top edge fixed.

Workspaces & Preferences

Swatches & Color Settings

Type & Text Styles

Frames, Shapes & Object Styles

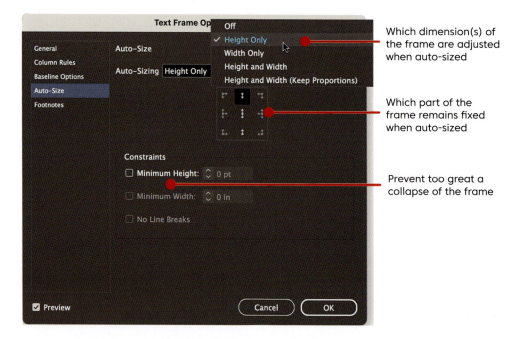

Which dimension(s) of the frame are adjusted when auto-sized

Which part of the frame remains fixed when auto-sized

Prevent too great a collapse of the frame

For frames that contain a very short phrase (such as a headline or title), allowing both dimensions to change may work well, especially if you disallow line breaks (the last checkbox).

The nicest thing about this feature is that it prevents text from becoming overset. It's disturbing to find the last words of a caption missing when something's gone to press!

I also appreciate a frame's shrinking to prevent extraneous parts of it from dangling where it might get selected accidentally with other items.

Footnotes

This allows footnotes of a particular text frame to span across the frame's columns. Also, you may specify some space that appears around those footnotes.

If this is a behavior you would like to make document-wide, you should do so by choosing **Type > Document Footnote Options…** then going to the **Layout** tab. There are many options here for configuring the look and feel of footnotes.

Image Frames & Linked Images

Image frames are created in several ways: when we place an image either freely on a spread or into an awaiting "unassigned" frame, or when we simply paste an image in InDesign, embedding it. Pasting images is not advised—read on.

Linking vs. Embedding

An InDesign best practice is to keep image documents separate from our layout document. In so doing, the images that appear on our layouts do not bloat the InDesign document's file size or compromise its performance. This also allows us to more easily edit those graphics files and see those edits in InDesign.

Embedding gives us the one small advantage of having most of our assets in one document, making it more portable. A small document with very few images may work fine this way, but we usually create PDFs as our deliverable, which better ensures preserving text formatting, too. In my work, it is a rare graphic that is embedded.

When we place images and graphics, a link is established between our layout and the image file. To keep that link healthy, there are dos and don'ts that we'll need to discuss. But first, how do we place a file, and thus establish that link?

Placing Images

The most reliable way to place an image or graphic file is to use **File > Place...** then navigate to the image file you'd like to include in your layout. You may also drag images into InDesign. The native file formats of Adobe Illustrator and Adobe Photoshop (.ai and .psd, respectively) may offer extra options. To enjoy these, use **File > Place...** then check the box labeled **Show Import Options**. These will consist mostly of choosing which layers in those documents should be visible when they are placed in InDesign. You can place an image multiple times, with different layers visible each time.

You may also choose more than one image or graphic at one time. For example, if there are several images in the same folder, it would be easy to click one, then **shift-click** on an image down the list to select those two and all the images in between; or click one, then **⌘-click/Ctrl-click** to highlight discontiguous images. Then click the **Open** button.

That creates a loaded **Place Gun,** a cursor bearing the likeness of the image (or one of the images if you chose multiple). If you chose multiple images, the cursor will also show you a number indicating how many images have been loaded.

Place Gun with one image

Place Gun with three images

Workspaces &
Preferences

Swatches &
Color Settings

Type &
Text Styles

Frames, Shapes
& Object Styles

With your **Place Gun** loaded, you have several ways to, eh, discharge it. If you simply click where there's nothing, InDesign will create a frame as big as the image or graphic (the size designated in the originating application) and fill the frame with the image. There is a high probability that an image will be much too large this way. Many cameras capture images with many millions of pixels. They deliver these pixels spread out over a large area with a low density—often 72 pixels per inch (ppi). An image that is 3,000 pixels across at 72 ppi will be placed 42 *inches* wide! Luckily, we don't need to go to Photoshop to deal with that. If you do click to place the image and find it to be huge, undo (**⌘-Z/Ctrl-Z**) to reload the cursor.

Instead of clicking, drag. As you drag across the page, you'll notice that the shape of the box being formed is the same shape as the image. When you release the mouse, the frame will be as large as you drew it and the image will fill that frame exactly. A image that is 3,000 pixels across squeezed into a frame that is 8 inches wide will have a pixel density (*resolution*) of 375 ppi. In InDesign, we call that the image's *effective resolution*, since its actual resolution was only 72 ppi.

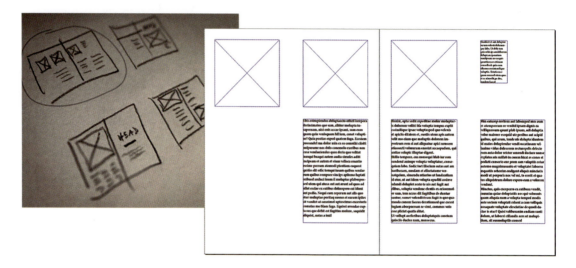

If we're using a template, it's likely the designer included empty frames to hold images. Graphic designers learn early to use pencil and paper to draw many quick sketches of a layout, called thumbnails. I claim that these get the worst ideas out of your system and provide a few good ones. Later, the more promising sketches can be migrated into InDesign in the form of placeholder text and empty frames most likely drawn with the **Rectangle Frame tool**.

If you do have empty frames awaiting images to fill them, you can click on each with a loaded **Place Gun**. You may have to adjust how the images fit each frame, but we'll get to that shortly.

If a frame is selected when you place an image using **File > Place…**, another checkbox in that dialog box comes into play: **Replace Selected Item**. Thus, if you select a frame, empty or not, then place an image, the image will automatically take over that frame, removing any content that was there. I sometimes fail to notice that I have a text frame selected when I place, then I find that the text is gone, and there's an image in its place. Here, some joke about a picture being worth a thousand words would be appropriate, but I'll leave that to you. Luckily, a quick undo gives you a loaded cursor with which you can place the image elsewhere.

Placing a Grid of Images

It is possible to place many images simultaneously. To do so, we need a **Place Gun** with multiple images in it. So go to **File > Place…**, as usual, and choose multiple images, or drag multiple image files directly from a folder in the operating system. Either way, you have a cursor with a number in it. Note the number; is it conducive to making an even grid? Odd numbers can be tricky. If it's seven images, you could create a two-by-four grid with an empty slot. That's allowed, of course, but unfortunate. Nine images, however, make a lovely three-by-three grid.

With the loaded cursor in hand, start dragging and keep that mouse button down! Once you've started dragging, use the arrow keys to create more (↑ or →) or fewer (↓ or ←) columns and rows. Review "Gridify" (page 233) for more—*much* more.

When you have enough areas to accommodate your images, you can release the mouse. You will now have a grid of identically sized frames with images fit proportionally within each one. This means there's some extraneous frame, which may not trouble you. But if the images vary much in size or shape, you may consider using "Frame Fitting Options" (page 261).

 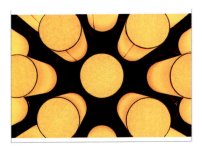 

Frame to Content & Content to Frame

Editing the size or shape of images and their frames is often one of the tougher challenges for a new InDesign user. If one resizes the frame with the **Selection tool**, the frame alone is resized, either cropping the image in it or leaving a gap between the edge of the image and that of the frame. But several methods can be used to select the image within its frame so it, too, can be resized or repositioned.

Frames, Shapes & Object Styles

Pages & Spreads

Find/ Change

Long or Complex Docs

Package & Publish

The **Control panel** buttons **Select content** and, above it, **Select container**.

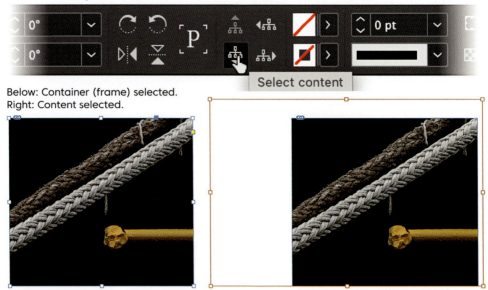

Below: Container (frame) selected.
Right: Content selected.

One method involves two buttons that can be found in the **Control panel**: **Select Content** and **Select Container**.

You may also use the speedy method suggested for text frames: double-clicking "to get in," and pressing the **esc** key "to get out" again. There's a twist with image frames: You can double-click to get in (content editing) *and* to get out (frame editing)!

Content Grabber

The last good method is to use the **Content Grabber**, the concentric circles in the middle of an image frame (also known as "the donut"). Using nothing but the **Selection tool**, *drag* the donut to reposition an image within its frame. When finished, the frame is still selected. If we *click* on the donut (**Content Grabber**) without dragging, then the content is selected. Double-clicking or pressing the **esc** key will select the frame.

When you hover your **Selection tool** over the **Content Grabber**, it becomes a hand. Drag it to recompose the image within its frame. Click this "donut" to select the content (to resize it, perhaps).

A bonus with the **Content Grabber**: If content has been rotated, a line will appear in the donut's center, tilted at the same angle that the content has been rotated!

Image and **Content Grabber** rotated 17°

The one danger that's presented by the **Content Grabber** is that it may be dragged accidentally. When you're rearranging frames on a page quickly, it's easy to inadvertently grab the grabber and pull an image completely out of its frame! Of course, you can undo (**⌘-Z/Ctrl-Z**), but that will leave the content selected, so you would also have to hit the **esc** key to have the frame selected. For this reason, a friend and colleague of mine despises the donut! He simply disables it and uses the double-click method instead. To disable the **Content Grabber**, go to **View > Extras > Hide Content Grabber**. While in that menu, notice the other things that can be hidden or shown. There are lots of "extras."

The least efficient way to reposition or resize an image is to switch to the **Direct Selection tool** then click on the image. When the cursor is over the image, it will be shown as a hand inviting you to reposition the image, but not the frame. Or you can grab a corner and resize (holding down the **shift** key to prevent distortion). You can then choose the **Selection tool** and click on the edge of the frame to select it again.

Frame Fitting Options

When an image's size doesn't match the size of its frame, we may wish to do something about that. Again, InDesign lavishes choices upon us. With one or more image frames selected, these choices can be reached in several places: buttons in the **Control panel**, by right-clicking, or in the **Object** menu. For the last two options, a **Fitting** submenu is shown.

The most commonly needed (and safer) commands are **Fill Frame Proportionally** and **Fit Content Proportionally**. The "proportionally" part means "without distortion."

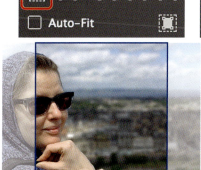
Fill frame proportionately

Fit content proportionately

Fit content to frame

Fill Frame Proportionally will resize the image so it completely fills the frame with the least amount of crop. A tall image in a square frame will have its top and/or bottom cropped, but not its sides. If there's an area of the page that you want filled with an image, to set a mood

Frames, Shapes & Object Styles

Pages & Spreads

Find/ Change

Long or Complex Docs

Package & Publish

Workspaces &
Preferences

Swatches &
Color Settings

Type &
Text Styles

Frames, Shapes
& Object Styles

perhaps, this is the command you need. You may adjust the image's position with the **Content Grabber** for a better composition. In the previous figure, hidden (cropped) parts are shown as translucent.

Fit Content Proportionally will show the entire image (no cropping), and may leave some empty areas in the frame. To get the frame to fit the image snugly, use…

The most dangerous choice: **Fit Content to Frame**. If the frame is square and the photo in it is not, the result can be disturbing. To confirm that something bad has occurred, select the image inside its frame. I'd just click on the "Content Grabber" (page 260). A look at the scaling in the **Control panel** for the portrait on the previous page reveals that the horizontal and vertical scaling are different (56% and 85%, respectively).

 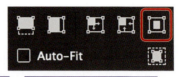 

Fit Frame to Content   Center Content   Content-Aware Fit

Fit Frame to Content aligns each edge of the frame with the image within. No crop, no extraneous frame. A fast way to achieve this is to double-click on a frame's corner handle. Double-clicking a side handle resizes only that dimension. For example, double-clicking the handle at the center of the top edge resizes the frame only vertically.

Center Content does exactly what it says: If the content is off-center, whether it's larger or smaller than the frame, it will be centered. I reduced the example image's size for clarity.

Content-Aware Fit attempts to detect the subject of the image and make it fit within the frame in a pleasing way. This may be a handy default for product shots in a catalog…or not. It may yield images of various magnifications when consistency is required. If you find that this setting works well, you may set it as the default behavior in **General Preferences**.

Object > Fitting > Frame Fitting Options… opens a dialog box that allows you to apply settings to a frame so it might automatically fit its content as desired! Choose one of the first three fitting options and **Auto Fit**. If you then resize the frame, the image will maintain the fitting options you chose. You can set these options on an empty frame so that when an image is placed into it, the image will do what it's supposed to. Further, you can specify that a small amount of the image is cropped on any side. So if your images have a rough edge or unwanted border, you can get rid of that automatically, too. If you don't need the crop function, you can set **Auto Fit** from the **Control panel**. These options are available only on image frames.

Generative Fill and Generative Expand

When you create an empty frame, the **Contextual Task Bar** offers a **Text to Image** button. Clicking it provides a text field into which you enter a prompt and a button to **Generate** three variations on that theme. The **Generate** button also opens the **Text to Image panel**, in which those variations can be seen and other options accessed.

Alternatively, you can open the **Text to Image panel** (from the **Window** menu), then the **Content Type** (either **Photo** or **Art**) and the **Aspect Ratio** of the image, which, as of this writing, defaults to **Square** rather than the **Frame dimensions**. When choosing **Art** as the result, clarify the medium with your prompt. In the example below, I wrote "watercolor painting."

When using either the task bar or the panel, each time you click **Generate**, three variations are generated from which to choose.

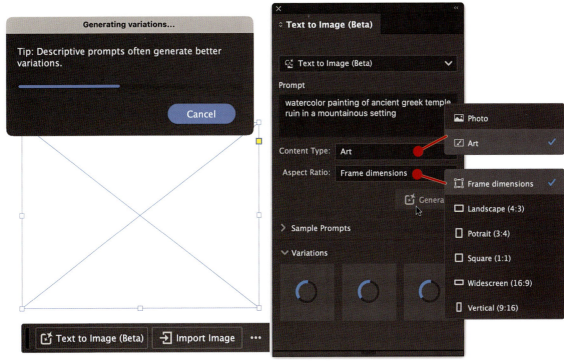

After clicking the **Generate** button, you'll see a progress bar accompanied by a tip and suspence-building animations where the resulting variations will appear. I like to choose **Content Type** and **Aspect Ratio** before I generate anything so I don't impinge uselessly on my generative AI quota.

Look over the results and generate more if necessary. The entire field of generative AI is in rapid development. So, I have to qualify that *as of this writing*, the resolution of the result is limited to about four million pixels.

Frames, Shapes & Object Styles

Pages & Spreads

Find/ Change

Long or Complex Docs

Package & Publish

Be sure to look at each variation in case the first one isn't to your liking. In this case, I advanced from one to the next via arrow buttons in the **Contextual Task Bar**.

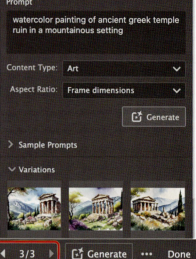

Generative Expand uses the same technology to add to an existing image. Enlarge an image frame, then choose **Generative Expand** from the **Text to Image panel**. A prompt is optional.

I expanded the frame containing this image, then chose **Generative Expand** in the **Text to Image panel**.

Below, one of the three results achieved using no prompt to guide the process. The color shift apparent here may be resolved by the time you read this—or it may remain something to watch for.

Edit Original

One of the more useful benefits of linking to an image or graphic is that it can be edited easily in its original application (usually Photoshop or Illustrator). The most straightforward way to do this is to select the image in InDesign, then right-click and choose **Edit Original**. Soon, another application launches with that document open. Complete your edits and save your changes, and when you return to InDesign, you'll see the image in its new state.

The **Links panel** also affords a way to edit placed images, graphics, and, under certain circumstances, linked text. You can manually highlight an image name in the **Links panel**, or select it in the layout, then click the **Edit Original** button (resembles a pencil).

Modified Links

A funny thing can happen if you edit and save that linked graphic without using InDesign's **Edit Original**. The image's appearance in InDesign won't update automatically and there will be warnings issued: a dialog box upon opening the document containing the link and an icon in both the **Links panel** and the upper-left corner of the image. This warning icon indicates that the link's status is "modified." To update modified links, do one of the following:

- Click **Update Modified Links** in the dialog box.
- *Double-click* on the error icon in the **Links panel**.
- *Single-click* on the icon in the upper-left corner of the image frame.
- Choose **Update Link** or **Update All Links** from the **Links panel** menu.

Notifications that a link has been modified: as the document containing the link is opened (left), on the image frame (center), and in the **Links panel** (right).

Missing Links & Relinking

Sometimes, the message you see when opening a document says that there are **Missing Link(s)**. This requires more effort to correct than updating modified links: You have to locate the missing file, if it actually still exists. When you place an image, InDesign notes not only the filename, but also the entire path to the image; every folder, subfolder, etc. If any part of that path changes—say you move an image to another folder or rename the image or one of the folders along that path—InDesign can no longer find that image!

Notifications that a link has is missing: as the document missing the link is opened (below), on the image frame and in the **Links panel** (right).

Missing link status icon

Relink button

Path to last known location of graphic

So when you see that dialog box warning of **Missing Link(s)** and you click **OK**, you are faced with the task of finding where that missing image is now. Note that the likeness you see in the document is a proxy that InDesign creates so you can better recognize the image you're seeking. The proxy does not have sufficient data for high-quality output. If it's truly lost (deleted, for example), you will have to find a substitute or delete the image from your document.

To deal with a missing link via the **Links panel**, there are clues. When an image is selected (or its name is highlighted in the **Links panel**) you can reveal more information by using the disclosure button (**>**) in the lower-left corner of the **Links panel**. In the **Link Info** that appears will be the last known path to the image. To tell InDesign where the image is, double-click on the missing link status indicator icon, then navigate to the file's location.

If you'd prefer to link to a substitute image (and not just for missing ones), use the chain-like **Relink** button. Again, you navigate to and choose an image file.

When relinking, you may have to fuss with the frame fitting options.

Note: The **Link Info** contains a lot of potentially useful information—for example, **Scale** values and the **Effective PPI**. Recall that "effective resolution" (page 258) is the pixel density of an image that has been resized.

To see more information in either **Link Info** or as a column in the **Links panel** list above it, use the **Links panel** menu and choose **Panel Options...**. Check the box for each item about which you may be curious.

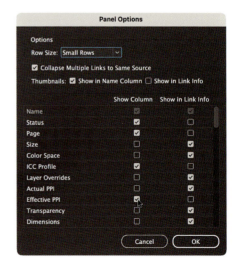

Effects

InDesign offers many ways to nondestructively alter the appearance of objects. We can use **Corner Options** to alter the shape of corners on any object (that has corners), and we can use **Effects** to do things like create **Drop Shadows** or have an image fade out (**Feather**).

Effects Panel & Dialog Box

There are many effects available via the **Effects panel** (or the *fx* section of the **Control panel**). Some of the more frequently used are illustrated below.

All attributes (and the text) are opaque except the fill, which is 85% opaque.

Dark green drop shadow down and left.

Tracks as planters along the Highline in New York City, 2012

Let's start with the text frame over the image above. Although the text within it is fully opaque, the fill of the frame is only 85% opaque. In the **Effects panel** I highlighted **Fill** then adjusted the **Opacity** slider. For the image frame's shadow, I used the *fx* menu and chose **Drop Shadow...**:

Frames, Shapes & Object Styles

Pages & Spreads

Find/ Change

Long or Complex Docs

Package & Publish

Even a simple shadow has many controls. Most are shared with other effects and are listed below. So, while exploring the **Effects** dialog box, keep these in mind.

Mode   Blend modes are used to make shadows darken what they are cast upon (**Multiply**) and to make glows lighten whatever might be behind them (**Screen**), for example.

Angle   For a shadow, this is the direction from which the virtual light must be shining. For other effects, like feathers, this is an adjustment to the specified side to which the effect is applied.

Distance   And also the **Offsets**, in concert with **Angle**, control the position of a shadow.

Size   For shadows and glows, their full, fuzzy extent. For example, with a size of 0 (zero), a shadow will be sharp-edged and exactly as big as the object casting it.

Choke or Spread   This controls the abruptness of a transition. **Choke** makes a directional feather more abrupt, for example, and **Spread** makes a shadow less fuzzy.

Noise   This is applied to shadows and feathers to make them more grainy. This can help them hold up when output to certain kinds of printers. Note that a little goes a long way! Use sparingly, if at all.

Shape   Only in the **Direction Feather**, **Shape** takes a few values. **Leading Edges** and **All Edges** make it appear that an irregularly shaped object is being eroded from one direction, whereas a half-inch feather to **First Edge Only** means that the first half-inch of the object experiences the fade. This setting is used for figures throughout this book wherever you see a fade-in.

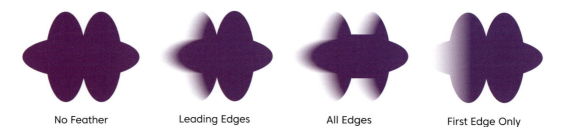

No Feather   Leading Edges   All Edges   First Edge Only

Text Wrap & Anchored Objects

These are features used throughout this book. Wherever you see an image, figure, or illustration, it has been *anchored* to nearby text that refers to it. Wherever you see text offset by an image, figure, or illustration, the offset is created by **Text Wrap**, a kind of force field applied to the graphic that pushes text a specified distance away from that graphic. **Text Wrap** and **Anchored Objects** are powerful and useful features, but they have quirks, too.

Text Wrap: Force Fields on Frames

Text Wrap is applied to objects that should move text out of their way, not to the text that is moved. Although there are a few text wrap buttons in the **Control panel**, the best way to control this feature is with the **Text Wrap panel**.

There are several forms of wrap for different circumstances and different kinds of objects that are being wrapped. Let's look at each kind, but not in order: We'll save the trickiest one for last.

Wrap Around Bounding Box

This is the simplest form of **Text Wrap**. By keeping the offsets locked with one another, you can specify, in one place, the distance between the text and the image. If you disable the lock, each side can be specified independently.

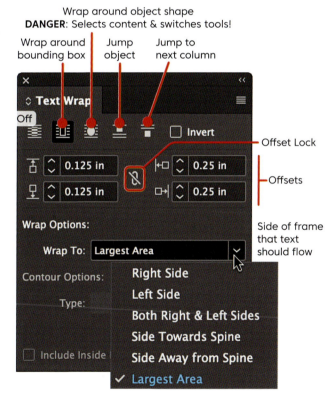

If the object with text wrap doesn't straddle two text columns, you will have to specify which side to **Wrap To**. For ease, I usually choose **Largest Area** (to flow text where there's more room for it).

Frames, Shapes & Object Styles

Pages & Spreads

Find/ Change

Long or Complex Docs

Package & Publish

Workspaces & Preferences

Swatches & Color Settings

Type & Text Styles

Frames, Shapes & Object Styles

Jump Object & Jump to Next Column

In some situations, there may not be a comfortable amount of room on either side of the image, so it's best if the text just skips right over the image.

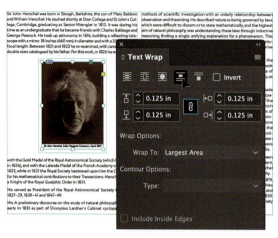

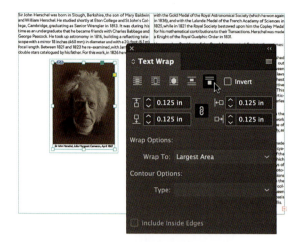

Jump object causes the text to skip over the image.

Jump to next column is best if the object is close to the bottom of a column and would leave just a small amount of text below.

Wrap Around Object Shape—It's Tricky!

Especially because of the odd side effects that accompany this option (discussed below), there are few situations in which to use this type of text wrap. In those situations, when we want a non-rectangular force field, it's awesome.

When would that be? When you have:

- A non-rectangular InDesign shape or frame (ellipse, polygon, or a custom shape).
- A placed Illustrator graphic.
- A placed photo with its subject surrounded by either transparency or relatively nondescript pixels over which text is still legible. *This will require that the image be behind the text.*

In the first of those examples, simply choose the **Wrap around object shape** text wrap and set the **Offset**. You may not need to do more. However, I almost always choose **Wrap To: Largest Area** under **Wrap Options** in this and the other scenarios listed.

In the **Type** menu under **Contour Options**, choose **Graphic Frame** or **Same as Clipping** to follow the shape of the frame.

When a placed graphic has a subject surrounded by white or transparency, **Detect Edges** works best.

Warning: When you first choose **Wrap around object shape** text wrap, InDesign selects the image or graphic within its frame (as if you had clicked on the **Content Grabber**). If you attempt to drag the image, it will move without its frame! InDesign also switches tools from the **Selection tool** to the **Direct Selection tool**. So be sure to hit the **esc** key (so the frame is selected once again), then choose the **Selection tool** again.

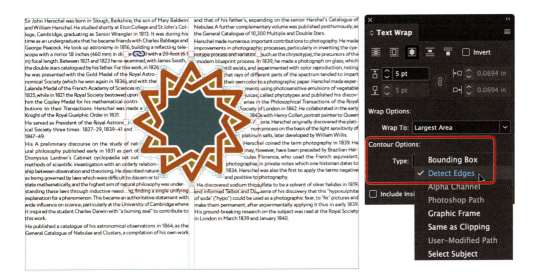

In the **Contour Options Type** menu is an algorithm borrowed from Photoshop: **Select Subject.** The name says it all. To prevent text from running inside any holes or concavities in the subject's shape, I choose **Wrap To: Largest Area** as well.

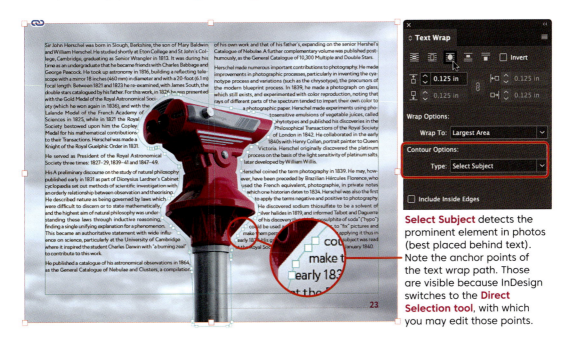

Select Subject detects the prominent element in photos (best placed behind text). Note the anchor points of the text wrap path. Those are visible because InDesign switches to the **Direct Selection tool**, with which you may edit those points.

The least-used options are **Alpha Channel** (the contour of a selection saved in Photoshop) and **Photoshop Path** (a vector shape saved to Photoshop's **Paths panel**). If you are facile with Photoshop and familiar with those features, enjoy!

User Modified Path becomes selected when you edit the perimeter of the text wrap path. InDesign switches to the **Direct Selection tool** to invite this risky possibility.

Anchored Objects

When I write phrases like "The image below demonstrates…" or "This figure…," I'm depending on that image or figure being near to what I'm writing. To ensure that is the case, I anchor my figure or illustration to a paragraph, so that if the paragraph is shifted up or down, the illustration moves with it. When working with anchored objects, I recommend viewing hidden characters (**Type > Show Hidden Characters**) and ensuring that text threads are shown (**View > Extras > Show Text Threads**). If either of these say **Hide** instead of **Show**, don't choose them!

Inline Objects—In the Flow

Small frames can be pasted right into the flow of text as if they were just another character. In a sentence with, "…next to the *size* field: [iT ⌄ 12 pt]," that small figure is an **Inline Object**, the simplest kind of anchored object.

Above Line & Custom

Anchor a frame (or group) either **Above Line** or with **Custom** settings by dragging the ornament just left of the upper-right corner of the frame (or group) to somewhere in a text frame. The color of that square ornament will match the frame edges and is set with "Layer Options" (page 314).

Above: To create an **Above Line** or **Custom** anchored object, we drag the anchor ornament to the position in the text to which we want it anchored.

Right: We now have symbols indicating success:

A yen symbol (¥) is the **Anchor Marker**, a dimensionless glyph in the text.

The anchor ornament is now an anchor, indicating that that frame is anchored.

At that point, the anchored frame is custom anchored with incomplete settings. To fine-tune those settings or to make the frame or group an **Above Line** object, select the object then choose **Object > Anchored Object > Options…** or **option-click/Alt-click** on the anchor symbol (the ⚓ where the square ornament was). The settings displayed in the following figure are for the figure above. I anchored that figure to an empty paragraph above this one. I wanted that figure to be centered in my margins and have a space between it and the paragraphs above and below.

Be sure you can see special characters in your text: Use **Type > Show Hidden Characters**. The now visible yen sign (¥) in the text is the *anchor marker*. It is a proxy for the object: Cutting, copying, or pasting it is cutting, copying, or pasting the anchored object itself. That can be tricky because that character has zero width in the layout. I find it easier to do if my cursor is blinking near that marker and then I access the **Story Editor** (⌘-Y/Ctrl-Y or **Edit > Edit in Story Editor**). In that window, the anchor marker resembles an anchor rather than a yen symbol and is easy to select. It can even be dragged and dropped elsewhere in the story as well as copied and pasted.

Custom Anchored Objects—Anchored Frames on a Short Leash

Custom anchored objects are easy to make but *much* more difficult to fine-tune. Select the object then choose **Object > Anchored Object > Options...** or **option-click/Alt-click** on the anchor symbol (the ⚓). In the **Anchored Object Options** dialog box, choose **Custom** from the **Position** menu.

Since you may need the same settings for many objects, you will likely create an object style that captures these settings so they can be applied consistently. The following instructions assume this and try to steer you away from pitfalls. Refer to the figure showing the **Anchored Object Options** dialog box (page 275) as you read these instructions. Learn about object styles in the next section of this chapter.

1 Relative to Spine The object you're currently editing may be on the left page or right page of a spread. To have your settings reflect across the spine for objects that may fall on the other side of it—for example, to keep anchored objects on the inside or outside of facing pages, rather than to the left or right—check this box.

Workspaces & Preferences

Swatches & Color Settings

Type & Text Styles

Frames, Shapes & Object Styles

2 Keep within Top/Bottom Column Boundaries   If an object is anchored to text low on a page, this prevents the object from dangling too low, possibly off the page. That's why I check this box. This means that some objects may not obey the position settings discussed next.

When you drag the anchor ornament to a position in a story, InDesign configures a few of the following settings. I almost always have to tinker with them to get them where I want them.

3 Anchored Object Reference Point   When positioning anchored objects, we can refer to different parts of it. In the figure that follows on the opposite page, I was most concerned with where the top edge of the object is, so I chose a point along that edge in the dialog box (enlarged at right). The object I was editing was on a page to the right 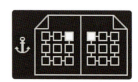 of the spine, so the reference point I chose corresponds to its upper-left corner. With **Relative to Spine** checked, this is reflected on a facing page. So I should refer to this as the object's top-inner corner, I suppose.

4 Anchored Position   This is the section where you can sense the minds of the engineers who made this. Although you may have dragged the object to a specific position inside a text frame, you may base the position of the object on the frame's edge, the edge of the page it's on, or the page margins. Basing an object's horizontal position on the anchor marker's, it will move left and right as I edit text—generally not desirable. Thus, I usually choose **Text Frame** in the **X Relative To** menu.

However, I often base the vertical position on the line in which the anchor marker is placed. Since I'm concerning myself with the object's top edge in this example (see 3 above), I would choose **Line (Cap Height)** in the **Y Relative Menu** because that looks more aligned to my eye.

The vertical position is now unambiguous. But since I chose to base my horizontal (X) position on the text frame, I have to specify which *part* of the text frame. So, for the **Anchored Position Reference Point**, I chose the outer edge.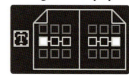

Finally, how far from the text frame should that top-inner corner of the object be? And how far above or below should it be from the cap heights of the line to which it's anchored? For the latter, I chose 0 (zero) for the **Y Offset** to maintain the nice visual alignment.

If the **X Offset** were also set to zero, the object would abut the text frame. A positive value would move them farther apart. I wanted them to overlap, so I chose a negative value. To prevent the object from obscuring text, I also applied "Text Wrap" (page 269).

Look carefully at the following figure. I made the object (an image frame in this case) less opaque so you might see the hazard.

Anchored Objects with Text Wrap

An anchor marker, which represents the anchored object, is part of the line that it's in. **Rule:** If that object has text wrap applied, it will only push lines that come *after* the one to which it is anchored. After all, if it were able to push the text to which it was anchored, it would push itself, which would push the text again, pushing itself again, in an endless loop. Thus, the rule.

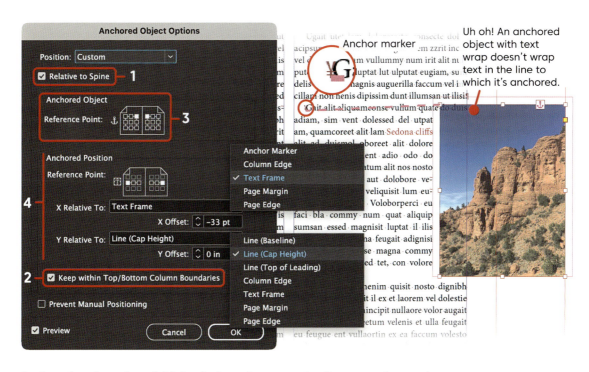

Anchor marker

Uh oh! An anchored object with text wrap doesn't wrap text in the line to which it's anchored.

In the printed version of this book, the reference point figures on the previous page are anchored to empty paragraphs above the paragraphs that refer to them. Those empty paragraphs are set to have zero leading, thus no height. In fact, all figures in this book that appear to the side of text are anchored to empty paragraphs with no height!

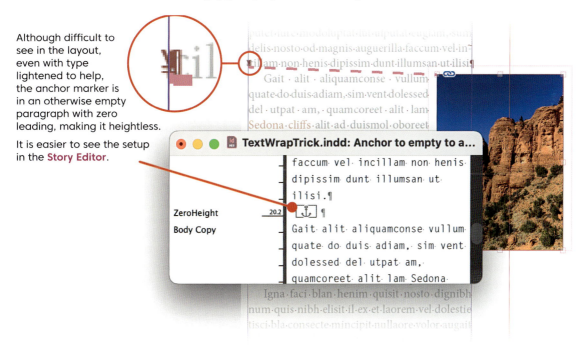

Although difficult to see in the layout, even with type lightened to help, the anchor marker is in an otherwise empty paragraph with zero leading, making it heightless.

It is easier to see the setup in the Story Editor.

Frames, Shapes & Object Styles

Pages & Spreads

Find/ Change

Long or Complex Docs

Package & Publish

Workspaces &
Preferences

Swatches &
Color Settings

Type &
Text Styles

Frames, Shapes
& Object Styles

Object Styles

Object styles can control any attribute of any object you can create in InDesign! That is, everything discussed in this chapter. However, like a character style, object styles can have a light touch, affecting only those attributes you want them to. Maybe you wish to change a fill color without affecting the stroke weight, or you desire a style that applies some text frame options but nothing else. Of course, an object style can be made to affect *every* attribute, too, including an object's size and/or position on the page.

Creating an Object Style

To create an object style, start by selecting an object that possesses attributes you would like to record (so they can be applied to other objects). Then use one of the following methods:

- Click on the **Object Style** button in the **Control panel**; or
- Open the **Object Styles panel** menu and choose **New Object Style...**; or
- Click the **Create new style** button at the bottom of the **Object Styles panel** while holding **option/Alt**.

Create style via the **Control panel** (right),

or create style via the **Object Styles panel** menu,

or create style via an **option/Alt**-click
on the **Create new style** button.

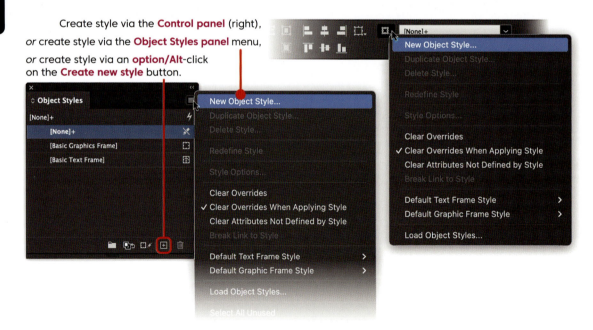

Any of these will present you with a powerful (and a bit intimidating) dialog box. At the top of it, give the style a descriptive name. At the bottom of the dialog box, be sure to check **Apply Style to Selection** and **Preview** so that this object, the model for the style, is actually governed by the style. Also, with **General** highlighted on the left, you will see a list of the **Style Settings** on the right. This pretends to be a synopsis—your style at a glance, as it were–but, like for everything else in this dialog box, there's a scrollbar!

On the left are all of the attributes that we can control within an object style. The checkboxes for **Basic Attributes** and **Export Options** can either be checked or set to ignore. If the attribute is ignored, the object's current settings for that attribute won't change when the style is applied. The checkboxes for the **Effects** have three states: checked, unchecked, and ignored. For example, an object with a drop shadow will lose it if **Drop Shadow** is unchecked, retain it if set to ignore, or perhaps have its settings changed if the box is checked.

Speaking of settings, you will not see them by merely clicking the checkbox; you must highlight the name of the attribute to see its settings. Even more hidden are the effects for fill, stroke, and text. To see those, you must first choose from the menu called **Effects for**. With so much to find, it's no surprise that the list of **Style Settings** (in **General**) is so long.

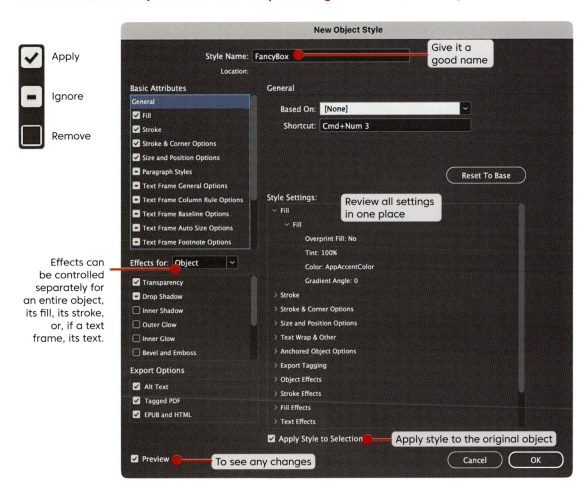

Apply

Ignore

Remove

Effects can be controlled separately for an entire object, its fill, its stroke, or, if a text frame, its text.

This dialog box offers a way to create a keyboard **Shortcut** for applying the style. The shortcut must use one or more modifier keys (⌘/**Ctrl** at least, but may also use **option/Alt** and/or **shift**) and a number.

If another style had been applied to the object when the new style was created, the new one will be **Based On** the old. Any attributes they share will be controlled by the old style, and only differences between the two will be controlled by the new style.

Workspaces &
Preferences

Swatches &
Color Settings

Type &
Text Styles

Frames, Shapes
& Object Styles

Applying an Object Style

It's as easy to apply an object style as it is the other styles: Select then click. Specifically, select what you want to change—in this case, a frame or group—then click on the style's name in the **Object Styles panel**. You may also choose the style from the object style menu in the **Control panel**, or use **Quick Apply** (**⌘-return/Ctrl-Enter**). You cannot apply an object style while editing text. If you want to apply an object style to the frame whose text you're editing, hit the **esc** key first (to access the **Selection tool** and select the frame in one step). Then you can apply the style.

Object Styles and Groups

I've mentioned several times that an object style can be applied to a group. But there is a peril in doing so.

Warning: Applying an object style to a group applies it to *every individual object* in the group! If styles had been applied to those objects previously, they are no longer applied and the appearance of those object may change in unexpected ways.

Workaround: Don't apply styles to groups. The following steps preserve each object's styles and allows their container its own styling. With practice and by using the shortcuts mentioned, the whole process can be done in seconds.

1 Cut the group with **Edit > Cut** or **⌘-X/Ctrl-X** so it's in memory to be pasted later.
2 Draw an empty frame with the **Rectangle Frame tool**. I just hold down the **F** key to access that tool long enough to draw a randomly sized frame.
3 With that empty frame selected, paste into it with either **option-⌘-V/Alt-Ctrl-V** or **Edit > Paste Into**.
4 Follow up with **option-⌘-C/Alt-Ctrl-C** or **Object > Fitting > Fit Frame To Content**. Note how the modifier keys of these last two shortcuts are the same and that "V" and "C" are next to each other on the keyboard. This allows both shortcuts to be applied very rapidly.
5 Apply an object style to that frame and it won't contaminate its contents.

Overrides and Clearing Them

When a selected object's attributes have been altered in a way that deviates from a style's definition, those deviations are know as overrides and a plus sign appears next to the style's name.

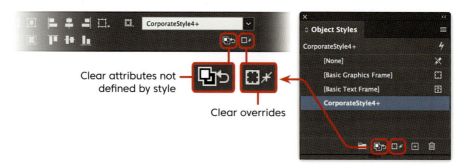

Clear attributes not
defined by style

Clear overrides

To force the object's attributes back into compliance with the style's definition, you can usually just click the **Clear overrides** button in the **Object Styles panel** or the **Control panel**: ⊡✳.

If the object style has been set to ignore certain attributes, they can be changed without InDesign issuing an override warning. For example, you may have set the **Stroke & Corner Options** section to be ignored.

If the corners of that object are later made rounded, no plus sign will show up because changes to ignored attributes are not considered overrides. However, there's another button that will set ignored attributes to None (their default), the **Clear attributes not defined by style** button: ⊡. Sometimes, when I have a mysteriously persistent plus sign that is not cleared with the **Clear overrides** button, this button succeeds.

⊡ Stroke & Corner Options

Checkbox indicates this category is set to "ignore"

Editing an Object Style

The greatest reward for using a style comes when the inevitable request is made to change it. Sure, it's easy enough to change, say, the fill color of a few objects manually. But if you have hundreds of them....

Just as with paragraph and character styles, the safest way to edit an object style is to right-click its name and choose **Edit "stylename"....** And that's a right-click with *no* left-click first! Why? Because we apply styles by left-clicking their names and you may not want to apply the style to what's currently selected. Or worse, you may unintentionally set that style as a default if you have nothing selected. It would be disconcerting to create new objects and find them using your most garish object style.

Tip: To avoid trouble, occasionally deselect everything, **⌘-shift-A/Ctrl-shift-A**, then inspect your styles panels. Anything that's highlighted is a default. Be sure to set the default in the **Character Styles panel** to **[None]** and choose relatively generic object and paragraph styles.

The Attributes Controlled by Object Styles

Object styles record all the attributes of a frame, whether a text frame, image frame, or a shape you've created in InDesign. This entire chapter essentially has been a preamble, a discussion of what an object style can record. Below, I'll provide references to the relevant sections for how to configure those attributes. But first, let's look at how object styles can control the size and/or position of objects.

Size and Position Options

Just as we may want appearance attributes like fill or stroke to be consistent for similar objects, we often want consistent size and placement. Since these options were introduced in 2018, position could be recorded relative to margins and page edges, but not the spine of a spread (unlike anchored objects). Despite this obvious and persistent deficit, this feature is still powerful and very welcome.

Frames, Shapes & Object Styles

Pages & Spreads

Find/ Change

Long or Complex Docs

Package & Publish

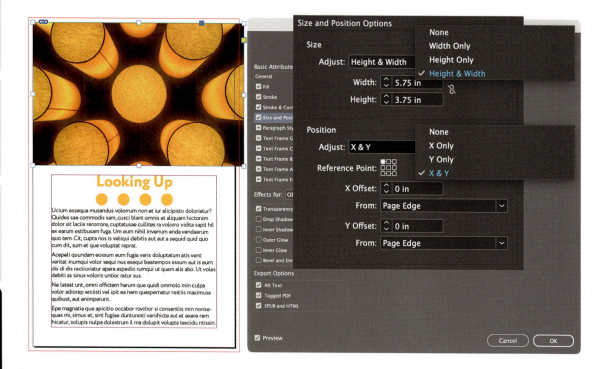

Above is an example. I placed an image then manually sized and positioned it to serve as the model for the object style I was about to make. The page is 5.5" wide and the bleed is set to 0.125", and so the width of the image is 5.75" to cover that span. I used the **Object Styles panel** to choose **New Object Style...** and highlighted **Size and Position**.

Since I wanted to record the full dimensions of the image, I chose **Height & Width** from the **Size Adjust** menu. Those dimensions, 3.75" and 5.75" (respectively), were duly noted.

To record both the horizontal (X) and vertical (Y) position, I chose **X & Y** from the **Position Adjust** menu. My image *moved*! Why? Look at the figure above. Note that the **X Offset** and **Y Offset** are both 0 (zero) and measured **From** the **Page Edge**. As indicated by the **Reference Point**, the part of the frame that is zero inches from the page edge is the upper-left corner.

Unfortunately, as of this writing, the offsets cannot be set to negative values as they'd need to be to position the frame's edge at the bleed (the red line beyond the page edge).

So we need to choose a **Reference Point** whose position is a non-negative number horizontally and vertically. I chose the center (see the following figure). In this case, I set the **X Offset** to half the page width, which is 2.75".

The vertical center's position is slightly trickier. It needs to go down from the top edge of the page a distance equal to half the image's height, then back up 0.125" for the bleed. So, in the **Y Offset** field, I typed "3.75/2-.125" letting InDesign do the arithmetic for me. The answer is 1.75, by the way.

You should know that I and many others have submitted requests for those fields to take negative values and for the position to be based on distance from the spine as well as the top-left corner of a page. With luck, they will fix this deficit soon.

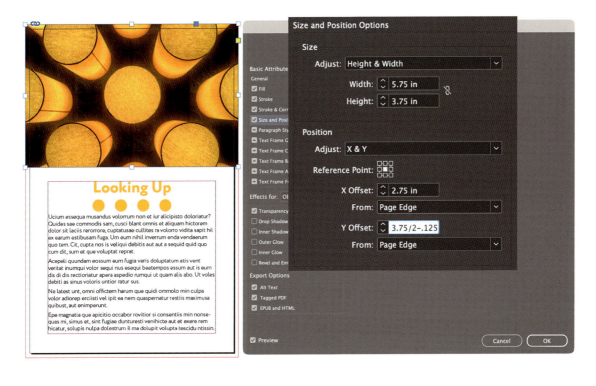

Everything Else

All the other attributes an object style records are elsewhere, most in this chapter:

Fill and Stroke   Read about choosing colors for fills and strokes on page 178

Stroke & Corner Options   See "The Stroke Panel" (page 234) and "Live Corners Widget and Corner Options Dialog Box" (page 248).

Paragraph Styles   See "Paragraph Styles" (page 201) and "Next Style" (page 202).

Text Frame Options   See "Text Frames & Text Frame Options" (page 250).

Story Options   See "Ignore Optical Margin" (page 206).

Text Wrap & Other   See "Text Wrap: Force Fields on Frames" (page 269). "Other" is simply whether the object with the style is nonprinting or not. Makes me wonder why this isn't called "Text Wrap & Nonprinting."

Anchored Object Options   See "Anchored Objects" (page 272).

Frame Fitting Options   See "Frame Fitting Options" (page 261).

Export Tagging   See "Export Tagging" (page 348).

Object, Stroke, Fill, and Text Effects   See "Effects" (page 267).

Export Options (Alt Text, Tagged PDF, ePub and HTML)   See "Object and Conversion Settings" (page 355).

Frames, Shapes & Object Styles

Pages & Spreads

Find/ Change

Long or Complex Docs

Package & Publish

5 Pages & Spreads

The page is a stage on which your documents' actors—type and graphics—perform. The narrative comes to life with images worth at least a thousand words and expressive, well-cast (type-cast?) fonts.

Anatomy of a Spread

Most of the settings discussed below (like page margins, columns, etc.) are set when creating a document, changed globally via **File > Document Setup...**, or edited on a page-by-page basis via **Layout > Margins and Columns....** The last of these is best done with "Parent Pages" (page 287).

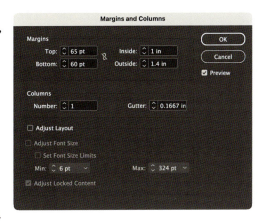

Margins, Columns & Bleed

Whether in print, in an ePub, or online, the content we read is hopefully displayed in a friendly, usable context. White space helps us see hierarchy and draws our eyes to the words that matter. So we should try to give our content a context that is easy on the eyes.

When we create a document with **Facing Pages**, InDesign creates *spreads*: two or more pages that face each other, like the ones you're reading now (although e-readers may present individual pages instead). Below are elements we adjust to make those spreads user-friendly.

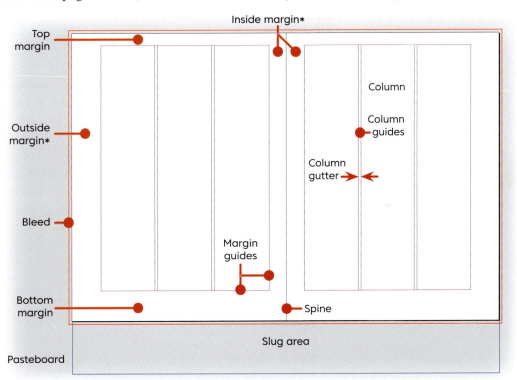

Margins   The spaces between our main content and the page edge. In a document without facing pages, side margins are identified as "left" and "right." With spreads, we often leverage page symmetry, so it's convenient that side margins are then identified as "inside" (near the spine) and "outside."

Pages & Spreads

Find/ Change

Long or Complex Docs

Package & Publish

Workspaces & Preferences

Swatches & Color Settings

Type & Text Styles

Frames, Shapes & Object Styles

Pages & Spreads

Pasteboard　　The area in InDesign beyond the pages. Many InDesign users put assets here that they *might* need, or assets that they *suspect* they don't need, but aren't sure enough to delete. Logos, text frames, photos we hope we'll have room for, etc., all find themselves "out there." Unless content is in the bleed or slug areas and we choose to include those, nothing on the pasteboard prints, exports, or gets *packaged* (see "Package" on page 346).

Bleed　　When images or other graphic elements need to print to the very edge of the page (like the tabs on these pages), we actually position them a little over the edge. Since printers can't print edge-to-edge, we print on larger paper and trim to our desired size. In case of trim error, we provide extra image over that line. You should ask your commercial printer how much bleed they require.

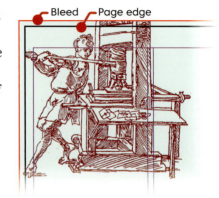

Bleed　Page edge

Slug　　A slug is a label or note to yourself or others. The slug area is some space you've allotted on the pasteboard for that note. In the print and PDF export dialog boxes, you can choose to include that area if you wish. Data that finds its way there can include modification dates, client names, print instructions, and reminders of where one has left off the day before.

Columns & Column Guides　　Of course, if you want to have multiple columns of text, column guides show you where they should be (consistently) and even help you create them. As you create text frames, they will snap to column guides in handy ways. But you may simply wish to divide your pages for the sake of consistent composition of other elements besides text. With the addition of horizontal ruler guides, you can create a complete grid to which you can snap frames of all sorts.

Use **Layout > Create Guides…** to generate rows and columns of ruler guides much faster than you can make them manually. To create an arbitrary vertical guide, drag from the ruler on the left side of the document window. Drag down from the ruler at the top to create horizontal guides. Hold down **⌘/Ctrl** to make the guide span a spread. Holding **shift** snaps to ruler ticks.

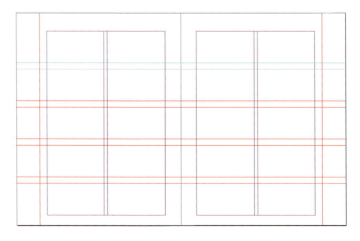

Navigating Pages

Getting from page to page is pretty important and useful. So, there are lots of ways to do it.

The Pages Panel

One way to get around your document is via the **Pages panel**.

A parent spread with a color label applied

The **Pages panel** menu

Selected page

Parent pages

Page size menu

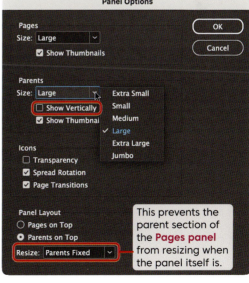

First, make the panel more useful and efficient by using the **Pages panel** menu to choose **View Pages > Horizontally**. To do something similar for the top section (parent pages, to be discussed shortly), use the **Pages panel** menu and choose **Panel Options....**

In the **Parents** section of that dialog box, I uncheck **Show Vertically** to save space at the top in the panel, even if I choose to make the parent page thumbnails larger.

At the bottom of the dialog box, I like to fix the size of the **Pages panel's** parent section since I rarely need it to vary.

This prevents the parent section of the **Pages panel** from resizing when the panel itself is.

Pages & Spreads

Find/ Change

Long or Complex Docs

Package & Publish

Now, to navigate from spread to spread, double-click on page *numbers* in the **Pages panel**. To view a single page, double-click on a page *icon* (oddly, you may have to do that twice the first time). A possibly precarious situation arises if you single-click!

Single-clicking a page's number or a parent page's name highlights its icons. But you are really still editing the pages whose *numbers* are highlighted!

In both the situations shown at right, the page 2–3 spread is what you'll see in the document window.

In a new document without content to guide you, you'd be hard-pressed to know that!

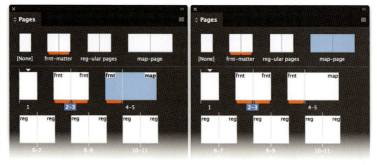

To avoid the mistake illustrated above, double-check that you've successfully double-clicked by looking at the **Pages panel** and noting if the page icons *and* corresponding numbers are both highlighted. Fortunately, there are two other ways to navigate that are worth mentioning and avoid the hazard outlined above.

At the bottom-left of the document window is a small field displaying the current page number so you may confirm you are where you thought. To its right is a menu from which you can choose a page to edit (including parent pages). On either side of that field and menu, there are buttons for going to the **Next** or **Previous Page**, or the **Next** or **Previous Spread** if you've chosen **Fit Spread in Window** from the **View** menu.

And there are shortcuts! **Shift-Page Down** advances one page forward, **Shift-Page Up** goes back one page.

To go forward or back one *spread*, use **option-Page Down/Alt-Page Down** and **option-Page Up/Alt-Page Up**, respectively.

The page menu at bottom-left of the document window.

Go to page

Page: 13

OK

Cancel

The shortcut ⌘-J/Ctrl-J opens a dialog box with its one and only field highlighted and ready for you to type the number (or parent prefix) of the page to which you want to get.

If you know the number (or parent page prefix) of the page you want, use the shortcut **⌘-J/Ctrl-J** (or, less quick, **Layout > Go To Page...**). A dialog box opens with its lone field highlighted so you can type a number (or parent page prefix) then hit **return/Enter**. That field is also a menu from which you can choose a page. This is my favorite method as it's very fast and reliable.

Don't remember the page where you were but need to get back to it? Use **⌘-Page Up/Ctrl-Page Up**. This won't work if your cursor is in a text frame, so hit the **esc** key first.

Workspaces & Preferences

Swatches & Color Settings

Type & Text Styles

Frames, Shapes & Object Styles

Pages & Spreads

Parent Pages

Documents ranging in size from brochures to books (like this one) may have several different kinds of pages: pages tailored for front matter, tables of contents, the beginnings of chapters or sections, etc. To serve as a form of template for those kinds of pages, InDesign offers parent pages. Other software offer similar features like master slides in Microsoft PowerPoint or Apple Keynote. InDesign's parent pages were formerly called "master pages," so you may find many users still referring to them as such.

Content placed on a parent page will appear on all the pages that use that parent. Much of my time preparing a document is spent on the parent pages of that document. The items that are best put on parent pages include one or more **Current Page Number Markers**, running headers, placeholder frames for images and/or text, and guides. When we create a system of guides on a parent with the **Layout > Create Guides...** command, those guides will appear on every page to which the parent has been applied, allowing consistent positioning of elements aligned to those guides throughout.

Creating a new parent is easy: Either use the **Pages panel** menu or right-click in the top section of the **Pages panel** (where the parents are) and choose **New Parent...**.

[Re]naming Parents

The default names for parent pages are simply a single-letter prefix plus the word "Parent": *A-Parent*, *B-Parent*, etc. Keeping in mind that a prefix can be up to four letters, I name my parent pages to reflect their function. I use practical prefixes and names like *frnt-matter*, *TOC-pages*, and *reg-ular pages*. To rename a parent, right-click on a parent's current name (for example, A-Parent) then choose **Parent Options for "A-Parent"...**. Give it a **Prefix** and a **Name**.

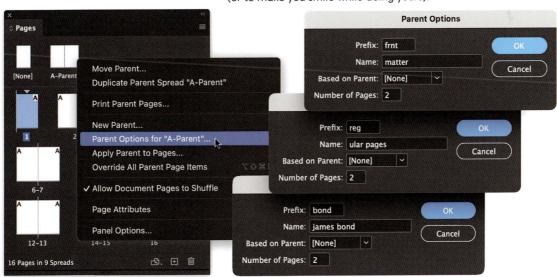

Renaming **Parent Pages** to better know their job
(or to make you smile while doing yours).

Pages &
Spreads

Find/
Change

Long or
Complex Docs

Package
& Publish

Workspaces &
Preferences

Swatches &
Color Settings

Type &
Text Styles

Frames, Shapes
& Object Styles

Pages &
Spreads

Current Page Number Marker

By far, the most common object placed on a parent page is the **Current Page Number Marker**. As the name implies, this very special character reveals the page number of the page currently under examination. On a parent page, it displays that parent's prefix. On every page to which that parent is applied, this marker shows a page number with the formatting chosen in the **Numbering and Section Options** dialog box, as discussed in "Sections & Numbering" (page 292). So that page "number" may actually be a letter or a Roman numeral, perhaps.

The simplest way to place this character is to create a small text frame on a parent page, then with the text insertion cursor blinking, right-click and choose **Insert Special Character > Markers > Current Page Number**. There's also an engaging keyboard shortcut: **⌘-option-shift-N/Ctrl-Alt-shift-N**. At first glance, few think they will memorize this, but the frequency with which we add page numbers increases the likelihood that you will if you try.

Applying Parent Pages

A robust way to apply a parent to one or more document pages is to right-click on a parent's name and choose **Apply Parent to Pages….** You may then specify a range of pages, or even list discontiguous ones by separating each number with a comma. The prefix of the parent will be shown in a top corner of the page icons to which the parent was applied.

In the **Pages panel**, you may drag a parent's name onto a page icon to apply it to that one page. To apply a parent to a spread, drag the parent's name below the page icons and just left or right of the numbers, watching for both icons to highlight. Yes, it's as tricky as it sounds.

Applying Parent Pages to Parent Pages

When you create a new parent, you may "base" it on another. A parent based on another has that other parent applied to it. You can apply parents to parents as you would to other pages, too.

A realistic scenario is having one parent responsible for only page numbers and two others, each with different margin or column structure but also requiring page numbers. We would apply the page number parent to the others, then those others would be applied to our document pages. Then, if you need to edit the page numbers, there's only one place you need to go.

The [None] Parent

Very commonly, we decorate a number of parents and apply them to a variety of document pages. But then we note a document page that needs *none* of those decorations (page numbers, logos, etc.). If we drag the **[None]** parent to a page icon, the prefix of the parent formerly applied vanishes, as do all the elements that parent has on it. Later, you can simply look at a page icon and see which, if any, parent is applied.

An alternative is to highlight one or more page icons, then use the **Pages panel** menu **> Parent Pages > Hide Parent Items**. I strongly dislike this method as it leaves no trace in the **Pages panel**.

Overrides

I often refer to the parent page content that we see on the document pages to which the parent is applied (like the text frames holding the **Current Page Number Markers**, for example) as echoes of that content. On those document pages (not parents), that content is inaccessible, since it's not really on those pages. However, if you *really* need to select that content on a document page, it can be selected if it's made a *local override*. We do this so that we might change something about that object only for that page.

Sometimes, overriding a parent page object is easy (indeed, sometimes it's automatic), as in the case of using **File > Place...** to load the cursor with an image or text, then clicking on a placeholder frame "echoed" from the parent. Otherwise, overriding a parent object requires holding down **⌘-shift/Ctrl-shift** while clicking on it with the **Selection tool**.

Warning: Even when overridden, the original object on the parent page often still controls many attributes of the overridden one!

This was hugely confusing for me for some time, so let's consider an example. Say we have a yellow circle drawn in the middle of a parent page. On every page to which the parent is applied, there's a yellow circle in its center. If we move that circle on the parent, it moves on every page. If we change its color or geometry (size or shape), we see those edits on the other pages too. Keep those three things in mind: **position**, **geometry**, and **appearance**.

Initially, if we try to move or even select the circle on a document page (not on the parent), we cannot. But if we use the keys **⌘-shift/Ctrl-shift** with the **Selection tool**, the object can be selected! If we stop there, it's almost as if we did nothing: Edits made to that circle on the parent still show on every page, including the page where we overrode it! That's weird enough, but it gets stranger.

Moving that overridden circle on the document page breaks *part* of its relationship with the circle on the parent—the location relationship—but its geometry and appearance (e.g., colors, stroke weight, etc.) are still governed by the parent circle. So changing the parent circle's color to red changes all of the circles, even the one we moved. But as you do more to that override, you will break all three of its ties to the parent. Changing its color, position, *and* geometry severs all connections, unless we reapply the parent to the page where our override is. Then our override will vanish and the inaccessible parent object reappears.

To keep our override even if we apply the parent again, we can select it and then go to the **Pages panel** menu **> Parent Pages > Detach Selection from Parent**. Now it's as if that object was never a parent page item (on that one page, anyway). Reapplying the parent will reintroduce the parent object and our detached object will remain, too.

If you've overridden several items and wish only one be removed in favor of its original on the parent, select it then use the **Pages panel** menu **> Parent Pages > Remove Selected Local Override**.

This interesting and confusing relationship between parent objects and their overrides exists so that we can have unique content in frames on document pages, but the frames' position, geometry, and appearance can still be controlled from a parent. Read on for more!

Pages & Spreads

Find/ Change

Long or Complex Docs

Package & Publish

Parent Text and Image Placeholder Frames

Consider the possibility of using a parent to "template" the look and feel of the opening spreads of a book's chapters or a magazine's sections. Another parent controls the appearance of the more ordinary pages that follow until the next chapter or section.

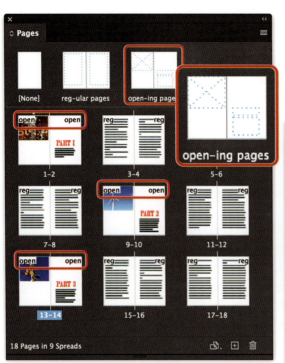

Left: The parent called "open-ing pages" is applied to three spreads. Its structure is apparent on those spreads with content placed into the echoed placeholder frames.

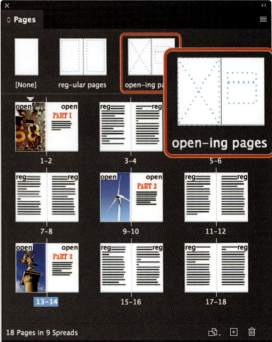

Right: After enlarging the placeholder frame on the left page of the parent spread and moving the text frames on the right page, content on the document spreads automatically follows suit.

Frame fitting options had been applied to the placeholder image frame set to **Fill Frame Proportionally**. Thus, the images resize, too.

In this example, an initial design called for the left page of an opening spread to have an image covering its upper half, and the right page to have text in its lower half. So a placeholder frame was drawn with the **Rectangle Frame tool** on the left, and **Frame Fitting Options** were applied and set to **Fill Frame Proportionally**. Two text frames were drawn on the right side.

That parent spread was applied to three document spreads, and then content was placed in the placeholder frames. Since I used **File > Place** to load the cursor with the content I wanted, clicking on those frames made them *local overrides* and inserted the content.

Later, upon resizing and repositioning the parent frames, the content on every page that uses that parent also adjusted immediately. In the example, the image frame was made to fill the entire left page, and the text frames on the right were moved upward on the page.

This awesome capability is why we tolerate the complex relationship between parent frames and their local overrides.

Workspaces & Preferences

Swatches & Color Settings

Type & Text Styles

Frames, Shapes & Object Styles

Pages & Spreads

Primary Text Frames & Smart Text Reflow

In the chapter about frames and content, we discussed "Automatic Text Threading" (page 252). Clicking the **out port** of an overset text frame loads the cursor, then **shift-clicking** at the top-left margin of another page will create a frame and flow text into it. If text remains unflowed, more pages will get made until all the text is visible. Although this is very cool, there's something cooler and more controllable: **Smart Text Reflow**. This function is especially helpful when it's combined with a special kind of parent text frame called a primary text frame.

Like other powerful features, this one works best if we plan ahead. Indeed, the best way to create primary text frames is when creating a new document. The options here create a document with parent spreads (**Facing Pages**), but only one document page to start. On the parent spread, there will be a text frame on each page, fit to the margins on each page. Although the text frames are on a parent spread, they are automatically accessible as overrides on the document pages so users like us can immediately start typing, pasting, or placing text into them.

Note: This is different than *any* other text frame on a parent. To be accessible on a document page, other parent text frames have to be overridden by either placing text into them or by **⌘-shift/Ctrl-shift**-clicking on them.

But just like other overridden parent frames, if we adjust the primary text frames on the parent, the ones on the document pages change, too.

To differentiate a primary text frame from another type of text frame, it has a special icon near its upper-left corner when selected. When combined with the **Type** preference "Smart Text Reflow" (page 167), primary text frames really begin to shine. Simply put, when you place what should be many pages of text into a document with too few pages (or even just one), **Smart Text Reflow** adds more pages (using the same parent as the one you placed the text on) and flows the text into the primary text frames on each page until there is no more text.

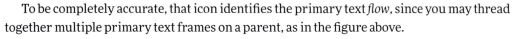

To be completely accurate, that icon identifies the primary text *flow*, since you may thread together multiple primary text frames on a parent, as in the figure above.

Checking the box **Delete Empty Pages** in the **Smart Text Reflow** preference does exactly what it says when primary frames find themselves emptied, as would happen if the type in a story were made smaller or tracked more tightly.

Pages & Spreads

Find/ Change

Long or Complex Docs

Package & Publish

Sections & Numbering

Very long publications are broken up into multiple InDesign documents using "The Book Feature" (page 334). But publications of a more modest size can have **Sections**, each of which can be numbered differently (and in different styles) and automatically trigger changes in running headers/footers.

Starting and Editing Sections

Every document's first page is also the first of a **Section**. This is indicated by the small triangle above that page, and double-clicking that triangle is a way to access the **Numbering & Section Options** dialog box. To begin a new section, highlight a page icon, then right-click it and choose **Numbering & Section Options**, which will open the dialog box *and* start a section on that page.

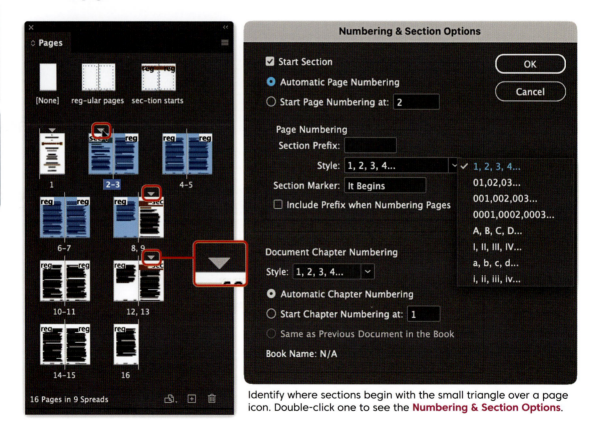

Identify where sections begin with the small triangle over a page icon. Double-click one to see the **Numbering & Section Options**.

Numbering Pages in a Section

In the **Numbering & Section Options** dialog, you can choose the numbering **Style**—for example, lowercase Roman numerals for front matter. In a following section, you can restart numbering with Arabic numerals. InDesign does not allow the confusing situation that would arise if two sections used the same style of page numbering and the count was restarted for each section. If two pages are given the Arabic numeral "2" or the letter "C," for example, you can imagine the chaos that would ensue when you tried to print or export a range of pages.

There are several ways to alleviate that confusion. One, as mentioned above, is using different style numbers: letters, Roman numerals, Arabic numerals, etc. Adding a unique **Section Prefix** can also make the page "number" unique; a prefix of "A-" would make a page number "A-3," perhaps. The prefix won't appear on the page itself unless you check the option **Include Prefix when Numbering Pages**. Whether the prefix appears on the page or not, its "name" will include it. So you could then print a page range of iii–C-7, for example, or A2–B2 without ambiguity.

Another option is in the **General Preferences**: Set **Page Numbering** to **Absolute**. Although the numbers displayed on the pages won't change, they will still restart or use a prefix as you've specified in the **Numbering & Section Options** dialog. But choosing a range of pages is easier and the **Pages panel** will show pages numbered 1 through the last in numerical sequence. So, if page *iii* is the third page of the document, and page *C-7* is the thirty-fifth, you'd print the range 3–35.

Without changing the preferences but knowing that you wanted to output the third through thirty-fifth page, you may add plus signs to what would be the absolute numbers: "+3-+35" would print that range.

My advice is to keep it intuitive if you can. If your document requires numbering to restart when a new section begins, keep those numbers unique by changing style (e.g., Roman to Arabic) or adding a prefix.

The last section of that dialog, **Document Chapter Numbering**, is best controlled from InDesign's Book feature. We'll discuss it in the chapter "Long or Complex Docs" (page 313).

Section Markers

Another option in the **Numbering & Section Options** dialog box is **Section Marker**. This is text that can automatically appear in a running header or footer (or anywhere in text, if you like). The most common case is to put the **Section Marker** character on a parent in a footer or header frame. Do this by right-clicking in the text frame then choosing **Insert Special Character > Markers > Section Marker**—it will look like the word "Section." But on pages that use that parent, you will see the text you entered in the **Section Marker** field or it will be blank.

This is similar to the current page number marker. It looks like the parent's prefix on a parent, but displays the page number, styled as discussed above, on document pages.

reg#	A **Current Page Number Marker** (left) and a **Section Marker** (right) Bottom of a parent page prefixed "reg"	Section#
	Below: Bottom of a document page that uses that parent	
4#		The Red Planet#

Pages & Spreads

Find/ Change

Long or Complex Docs

Package & Publish

Workspaces & Preferences

Swatches & Color Settings

Type & Text Styles

Frames, Shapes & Object Styles

Pages & Spreads

Shuffling

When dragging pages or spreads in the **Pages panel**, InDesign will "shuffle" pages in order to keep two pages in each spread and to keep a cover or title page (the first, lone page in a facing-page document). To start a document with a spread or to build gatefold spreads, we disallow shuffling. From the **Pages panel** menu, uncheck **Allow Document Pages to Shuffle**. Now you can drag pages more freely, attaching them to the left or right of other pages or spines. But keep an eye on the cursor to know what the result will be when you release the mouse.

    In each of the following examples, the first page is dragged to a new location, the result displayed in the panel on the right.

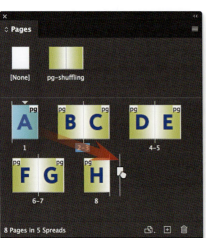
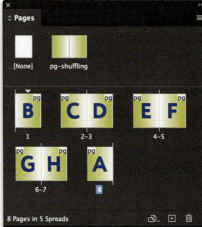

Left: While pages are allowed to shuffle, moving the first page to the end causes all the other pages to reassemble in new spreads, with the page that had been second now acting as a cover page.

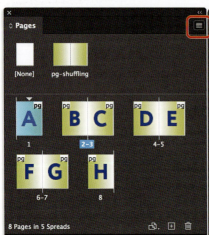
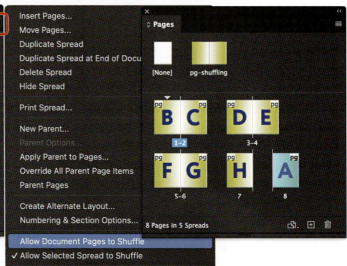

Use the **Pages panel** menu to disallow document page shuffling.

Once done, pages can be placed anywhere, even forming single-page spreads in a facing-page document.

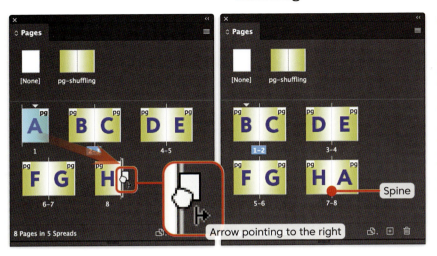

Left and Below: Once shuffling is *disallowed*, we can attach that page anywhere. Watch the cursor carefully for hints, particularly about which side of the spine the page will attach to!

A bracket indicates that the page being moved will attach to another. A tiny arrow will indicate whether the page will end up a left or right page.

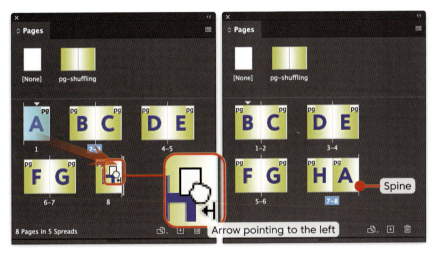

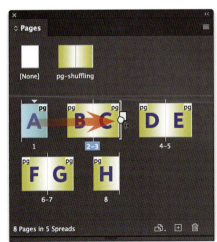

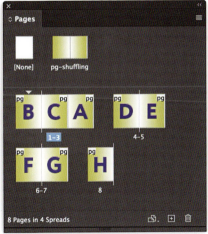

Pages & Spreads

Find/ Change

Long or Complex Docs

Package & Publish

Building Gatefolds

By attaching a page to the outer edge of another (the side away from the spine), you can create a gatefold. In the case illustrated below, the spread consisting of pages 5–8 has two pages on either side of the spine. That spread was created with the methods described above, with the expectation that the two outer pages (5 and 8) will fold outward to reveal more content.

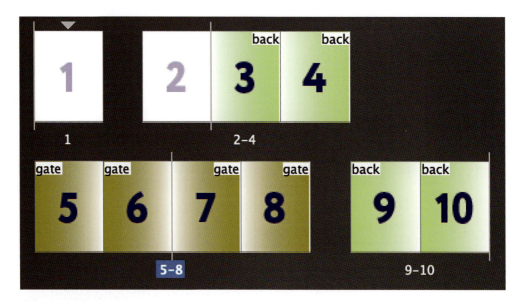

To prevent those outer pages from buckling while still folded inward, they should be narrower than the others. You can select each page with the **Page tool**, then use the **Control panel** or the **Properties panel** to set the precise width of each. Consult your printer, as they may have exact dimensions or may request another procedure entirely.

Also, the back sides of pages 5–8 in the figure above will need to be configured to have the same width as their front sides. In this example, the other sides of pages 5 and 6 would be pages 4 and 3, respectively. Pages 10 and 9 are the backsides of pages 7 and 8.

Page Size & Layout Adjustment

Sometimes, you need InDesign documents in different sizes. Creating gatefolds is just one excuse for doing so. Another is the **Alternate Layout** feature, in which two or more layouts exist in the same document for the same content—a print layout and a mobile device layout for an e-book version, for example.

Page size and accompanying margin dimensions, etc., are first set when a document is created. Subsequently, the size of selected pages can be altered with the **Page tool**. The page size used by an entire document can be set via **File > Document Setup...** or by creating an alternate layout (**Layout > Create Alternate Layout...**).

There have been various methods for adjusting the position and size of content in documents whose page size had to change. In the **Margins and Columns** dialog box is the **Enable Layout Adjustment** checkbox. This feature uses page margins, columns, and guides to adjust the size and position of objects snapped to them (or very nearly so) when we change page size, page orientation, or margin or column dimensions. For very simple layouts, this has done marginally well (pardon the pun).

In my experience the newest method, **Adjust Layout** (discussed below), offers the best results with a reasonable number of controls, whether you're adjusting just the margins of a page, an entire page's geometry, or the geometry of all the pages of a document.

Adjust Layout

Access this feature from **File > Adjust Layout**—in which you can set parameters for the automatic adjustment of existing page content to accommodate the new dimensions. You can also access this feature from the **Properties panel** and via **Layout > Margins and Columns....** The last location does not offer all the options accessible from the others, however.

The way you access this feature, and what you choose within it, depends on your reasons for the adjustment. If it's a matter of making a small adjustment to margins at the request of your printer, use **Layout > Margins and Columns....** For a poster, postcard, or one sheet, you may need to change more. For example, if you originally designed a poster to be printed on super B-sized paper (330 mm x 483 mm, about 13" x 19"), but find you need it on Tabloid (11" x 17"), the **Adjust Layout** dialog box can resize everything, even the type, in one go. With this, a small postcard's content can be upsized to a much larger size coherently. In the example in the following figures, roughly square pages have been resized to letter page size.

If you choose to **Adjust Font Size**, you can set a minimum and maximum size. When a page is resized, items in the margin or pasteboard areas will remain in those areas, and graphics of

Pages & Spreads

Find/ Change

Long or Complex Docs

Package & Publish

Workspaces & Preferences

Swatches & Color Settings

Type & Text Styles

Frames, Shapes & Object Styles

Pages & Spreads

various kinds will keep their proportions, and their frame dimensions (crop) will be guided by content-awareness (to attempt to keep their subject in view).

Original document had 9.5" square pages. I used **Adjust Layout** to change those to letter size. I did not use **Adjust Font Size**.

With no subsequent adjustment, this is the result of **Adjust Layout** with **Auto-adjust margins**. Impressive!

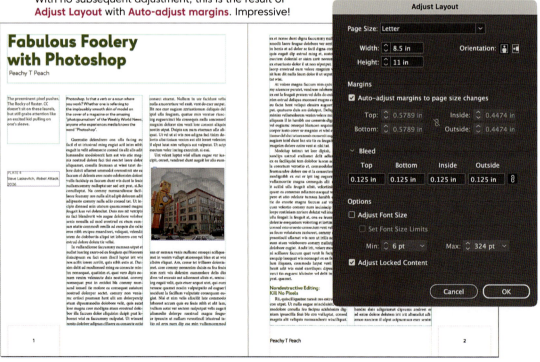

6 Find/Change

InDesign's Find/Change feature is about significantly more than replacing one word with another. In many documents, it's the primary way I apply formatting! The more you learn about what can be found and how it can be changed, the more likely it is that you'll love this feature as much as I do.

The Basics

Before getting to the fancy bits, let's be sure we know what options we have for straightforward searches. Many of the buttons in **Find/Change** are small and cryptic, but useful. There are also well-intentioned but risky features, too. To access it, either go to **Edit > Find/Change…** or use the shortcut **⌘-F/Ctrl-F**. For simple text queries, be sure to be in the **Text** tab.

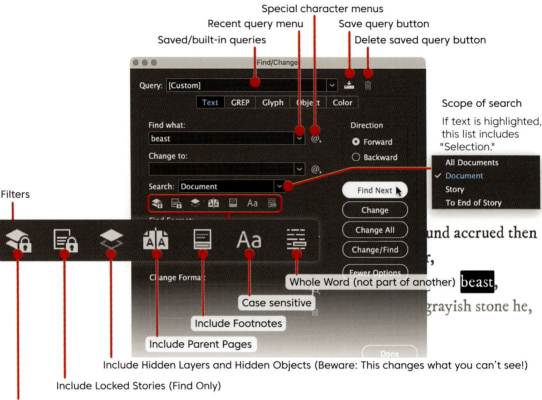

To find a word (or phrase) anywhere it occurs in a document, type that text in the **Find what** field. To simply find instances of that text without necessarily changing it, click the **Find Next** button. If **Backward** were chosen under **Direction**, this button reads **Find Previous** and searches backward from your cursor's location. In the figure above, I searched for the word "beast." Since the **Case Sensitive** filter wasn't enabled, this search would also have found "Beast" or "BEAST."

When finding and changing a word that appears both capitalized and lowercase without enabling case sensitivity, InDesign will make sure that the replacement matches the case of the found text!

There are many ways to limit or expand your search with those filters. Another that is very good to know about is **Whole Word**. It ensures that what you've put in the **Find what** field is not part of some other word.

Let's look at a cautionary example.

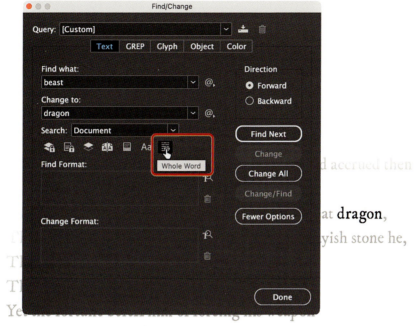

Above, I added "dragon" to the **Change to** field then clicked **Change All**. I hadn't specified that "beast" should be sought only if it is a whole word, so "beastly" became "dragonly." A quick undo (**⌘-Z/Ctrl-Z**) fixes that, even if 500 changes had been made. Enabling the **Whole Word** button ensures a less silly result on the next try.

As you can see, that small, easily missed button is pretty useful when you need it. Since **Find/Change** retains settings somewhat tenaciously, I sometimes fail to notice that I've left this function (or others) active when I search for something hours later.

Setting Scope

Similarly useful, and treacherous, is the **Search** menu, where we specify how broadly **Find/Change** should search. It defaults to **Document** if nothing is selected, **Story** if a text frame is selected or your text cursor is blinking within one, and **Selection** if text is highlighted. Think about that: Just by changing what's selected, you automatically change the scope of a search. I sometimes highlight a word, copy it, then paste it into the **Find what** field to be sure I haven't misspelled it. I hit **Change All** and InDesign reports that one change was made, which is puzzling when I know that word is used many times throughout a document. But when I highlighted the word, it became the only part of the document InDesign was searching! So...

Tip: Before clicking **Change All**, cut your eyes over to the **Search** menu and buttons.

Find/
Change

Long or
Complex Docs

Package
& Publish

Workspaces &
Preferences

Swatches &
Color Settings

Type &
Text Styles

Frames, Shapes
& Object Styles

Pages &
Spreads

Find/
Change

Find/Change Formatting

A quick way to *remove* content is to enter it in **Find what**, and leave both **Change to** and **Change Format** blank, then clicking **Change All**.

If you wish to *format* some content, leave **Change to** blank, but click on the **Change Format** box to configure its numerous settings. In the example below, I set **Find what** to "dragon," and when I clicked on the **Change Format** box, I chose a **Font Style** of **Bold** (in **Basic Character Formats**), a **Character Color** of red, and **Title Case** (in the **Change Case** section).

Actually, it would have been better if there had been a character style that did most of that. I would then have been able to choose it in the **Style Options** section which appears when the dialog opens. Unfortunately, character styles cannot change case like Find/Change does.

Clicking the box under **Change Format** opens a dialog in which you configure the formatting you want to apply to found text.

Once those settings are specified, click **OK** in that dialog. Always check the scope in the **Search** menu (above, it's set to **Story**). Then click **Change All**. Because settings tend to be sticky here, it's important to clear them when you're done. Those icons that look like cupcakes are actually trash cans that clear settings. Using them prevents later searches from changing more than words.

Despite a student's once mistaking them for cupcakes, the trash cans clear find/change format settings.

I often leave both **Find what** *and* **Change to** blank, and use only the formatting boxes. In a recent document, I used a format-only find/change to replace all text that was manually formatted as bold with a character style that made the text red but kept it in a normal weight. Specifically, I clicked in the **Find Format** box, went to **Basic Character Formats** in the resulting **Find Format Settings** dialog, and chose **Bold** in the **Font Style** menu. When I clicked the **Change Format** box, I remained in the **Style Options** section so I could choose a character style made previously called "just red." I was fortunate that nothing else was bold except what I wanted to change, so I clicked **Change All** and it was done!

If I had to be more careful about where the search was done, I could have highlighted the text to search and set the scope of the search to **Selection**, or specified a paragraph style in **Find Format Settings**.

There is a somewhat common practice for workflows in which writers just write, and the styling and layout is in other hands. The writer will add a unique code or symbol at the beginning of some paragraphs to signal that they are different than standard body copy. This keeps their fingers on the keyboard and minds on the words. For example, in front of an unformatted header, a writer may add "# " (that's a hash mark plus a space, a common way to mark up a top-level header using syntax called *markdown*). That is what to put into the **Find what** field. Then you can click on **Change Format** and select a paragraph style that decorates that kind of header. This would have to be followed up with a second find/change with the formatting cleared so that each use of "# " is removed (replaced with nothing).

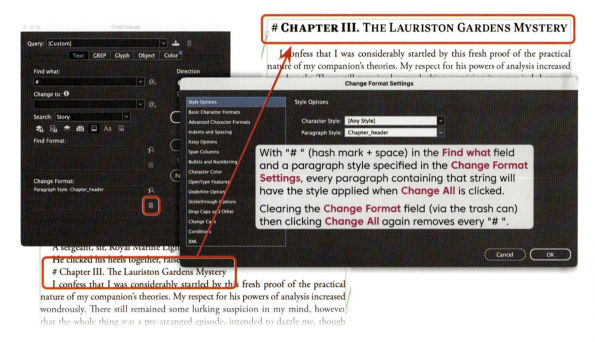

Tip: Setting both **Find Format** and **Change Format** to the same style (e.g., a paragraph style for a text search, or an object style for an object search) is a fast way to globally clear overrides to those styles.

Special Characters and Metacharacters

Sometimes we need to search for (and/or change to) a character we don't know how to type, like a trademark symbol, for example, or a character that literally cannot be typed in the **Find what** or **Change to** fields (like a tab character). To the right of those fields is a menu that looks like an **@**. In it is a list of symbols, typographic spaces and characters, InDesign markers, and

Workspaces & Preferences

Swatches & Color Settings

Type & Text Styles

Frames, Shapes & Object Styles

Pages & Spreads

Find/ Change

more. With this, you can replace tabs with em spaces, for example. However, what appears in the **Find what** or **Change to** fields won't look like the entity you chose; instead, InDesign uses *metacharacters*. So a tab is rendered as **^t** (caret + "t") and a copyright symbol as **^2**. The caret character itself is rendered as **^^**. Once you know the metacharacter for a symbol, you may type it in those fields yourself, too, if you know where the symbol is. A caret can be typed with **shift-6**, for instance.

Wildcards are also useful. For example, the wildcard for *any letter* (**^$**) followed by "hat" would find "chat," "phat," "that," and "what" (and maybe something else), but not " hat," since a space isn't a letter. But using the wildcard for *any character* (**^?**) would find " hat." When it comes to more abstract searches that involve things like wildcards, there's an entire section of **Find/Change** that is awesomely powerful, if a little geeky: **GREP** (coming up shortly).

Another clever feature is the ability to use the contents of the clipboard for **Change to**. So anything that can be in a flow of text and that you can copy or cut, including graphics, can be used. In the example below, I copied a graphic to my clipboard. In **Find what**, I inserted a bullet, and in **Change to** I chose (from the special character menu) **Other > Clipboard Contents, Unformatted**. If the graphic had been inline and formatted (with baseline shift, for example), I could have preserved that formatting with **Clipboard Contents, Formatted**.

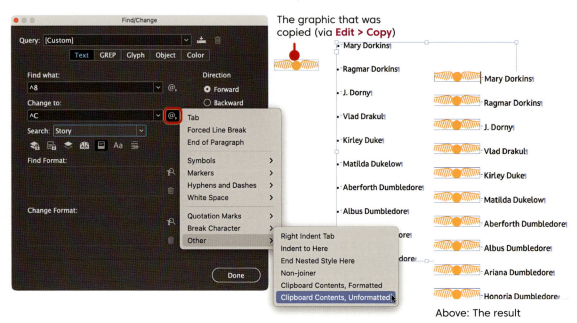

Tip: To save queries that you may need again, click the **Save Query** button at the top-right of the **Find/Change** dialog. You'll be prompted for a name you'll find later in the **Query** menu.

GREP

Literal strings are easy to look for, but more abstract patterns require thought and some code. In the **Text** tab, metacharacters may have looked and acted a bit like code, but they aren't GREP, whose syntax is different and far more powerful. Since everyone asks, **g/re/p** ("**g**lobally find **r**egular **e**xpression and **p**rint") was an early Unix command that found a text pattern (*regular expression*) and printed its occurrences. It has a long and colorful history.

InDesign comes with a bit of GREP code built into the special character menu in the **GREP** tab of **Find/Change**, including wildcards that represent letters, digits, upper- and lowercase characters, and locations in text (the end or beginning of paragraphs, for example).

There are many resources on this topic. My favorite is the book *GREP in InDesign, Third Edition* by Peter Kahrel (https://amzn.to/4f2fPky). I recommend it enthusiastically.

A Bit Geeky & Very Helpful

Let's revisit an example from earlier. We need to find all paragraphs that open a chapter and apply a chapter header paragraph style to them. Earlier, we benefited from a writer who put something unique at the beginning of every such paragraph. But what if they didn't?

Such a paragraph may start with the word "Chapter" (capitalized), followed by a space, then either a number or a word. Odds are slim that any other paragraph opens with that word, so we can use that starting position to find chapter header paragraphs and apply the correct style.

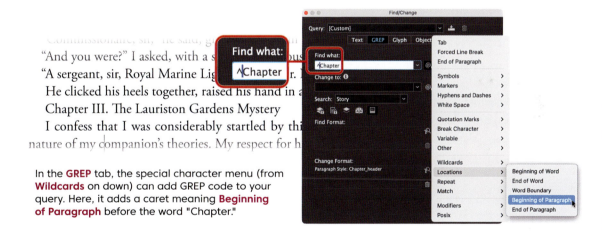

In the **GREP** tab, the special character menu (from **Wildcards** on down) can add GREP code to your query. Here, it adds a caret meaning **Beginning of Paragraph** before the word "Chapter."

So in the **GREP** tab of **Find/Change**, we type "Chapter" in the **Find what** field. Beware: GREP is case-sensitive. In front of that word, we need a special character. From the **Special characters** menu, we choose **Locations > Beginning of Paragraph**. This inserts a caret (**^**), which indicates the start of a paragraph. A dollar sign (**$**) means "end of paragraph." In **Change Format**, we choose our *Chapter_header* paragraph style. When we click **Change All**, every paragraph with our pattern is formatted. Any occurrence of the word "Chapter," even capitalized, won't be styled unless it's the opening word of its paragraph.

Find/
Change

Long or
Complex Docs

Package
& Publish

Building a Query

My first experience with grep was with a list of 800 names, the members of the Seattle InDesign User Group that I ran at the time. Unfortunately, the list was not made surname first. It was like the list shown here, though I doubt the folks in this list were members.

Mary Dorkins
Ragmar Dorkins
J. Dorny
Vlad Drakul
Kirley Duke
Matilda Dukelow
Aberforth Dumbledore
Albus Percival Wulfric Brian Dumbledore
Ariana Dumbledore
Honoria Dumbledore
Kendra Dumbledore
Percival Dumbledore
B. Dunstan
Dudley Dursley
Marjorie Dursley
Petunia Dursley

Let's consider a simple case of the data that confronted me: **Givenname Surname**. Almost all were like that. What I needed was **Surname, Givenname**. That is, I had a chunk of characters, a space, then another chunk of characters; but I needed the second chunk of characters to come first, followed by a comma and a space, then the first chunk of characters.

The **Find what** query could be built like this: choosing the **GREP Special characters menu > Wildcards > Any Character** enters a period (**.**). That's right, a simple dot in GREP means "any character." (I suggest *acceptance* is the right attitude here, rather than *comprehension*.) But I wanted a chunk of characters, so I chose **Special characters menu > Repeat > One or More Times**, which inserted a plus sign. Thus, "**.+**" means "one or more characters." That could be the given name, but since "any character" can include spaces and more, it could also be the entire name! So I needed to be more specific.

So I added a space and another "**.+**" to mean two chunks of characters separated by a space. My **Find what** now read like this: **.+ .+**

Now, I often use code even for spaces since they're hard to see in that small field. The code for "horizontal space" (which includes various size spaces and tabs) is **\h**. So my query could have been **.+\h.+** but I didn't know that back then.

In the **Change to** field, I needed a way to refer to the chunks on either side of that space so I could transpose them. It took some time to figure out that meant I needed a "Marking Subexpression," which in practical terms means surrounding each chunk with parentheses. This "marks" them so they can be referenced in the **Change to** field. So my final **Find what** reads: **(.+) (.+)**

To refer to the second chunk (the surname) we use **$2,** and the first is **$1**. Since we want a comma and space between them, that made my **Change to $2, $1**. How did I get lucky with the middle names? Grep used the *longest* match for the first chunk, then a space, then the surname.

More Grep Queries

If you look at the list in the **Query** menu at the top of **Find/Change**, many of the options use grep. Consider the one for **Phone Number Conversion (dot format)**.

Find what: **\(?(\d\d\d)\)?[-.]?(\d\d\d)[-.]?(\d\d\d\d)**

Change to: **$1.$2.$3**

This finds any North American phone number and returns one like this: 206.555.5555.

In the **Change to** field, the only special characters (beyond the metacharacters of a plain Text search) are the Founds (**$1** = **Found 1**, etc.). So the periods there do *not* mean "any character," as they do in the **Find what** field above.

Sometimes, when configuring a query in grep, we need to include a character that means something in GREP code, like a period or parenthesis. To search for a literal period, we use a backslash in front of it **\.** to "escape" the period.

So in the phone number search above, we are looking for the *possible* use of literal parentheses: **\(?**, where the question mark means zero or one of them (or as I prefer to phrase it, "maybe it's there, maybe it ain't"). We're also using parentheses to group the digits into groups we can refer to in the **Change to** field. Each **\d** means "any digit," and we can scan across that query and pick out three, three more, then four of them, as in a North American phone number. Another way to look for exactly three digits is **\d{3}**, which could make that whole query a little shorter: **\(?(\d{3})\)?[-.]?(\d{3})[-.]?(\d{4})**

The square brackets contain literal characters between which we're to read "or." So between each chunk of digits, there could be a hyphen, a dot, or a space. Or there could be none of those things, so the question mark is added after the bracket to mean zero or one of those.

It's a wonderfully thought-out query that we didn't have to come up with! If you don't like the dot format, just change the **Change to**. **($1) $2-$3** would give (206) 555-5555.

Another approach to searching for a choice of characters if there are multiple options is to use the pipe character (**|**). Since I live fairly close to Canada, I see two spellings for center: center or centre. To search for both, I can use **cent(er|re)**.

In a case where a letter may or may not be in a word, the **?** (zero or one) comes in handy: **harbou?r** finds "harbor" and "harbour." I can replace either with my preferred version. Might it be capitalized? Then look for **[Hh]arbou?r**. If we're looking for a capitalized word, we can specify an uppercase letter (**\u**) that's followed by one or more lowercase letters (**\l+**). Thus **\u\l+** will match "Photoshop" but not "InDesign."

We often need to find characters that appear before or after others, but don't wish to include those others when we use **Change to**. For example, we could want to change the ordinal after a number ("st," "nd," "rd," or "th") to a superscript, but not the number. But each of those letter combinations appear in words, too. To specify that the entity behind (before) the text we're interested in changing is a number, we use a *positive lookbehind*. It looks like this: **(?<=)**, with the character that's just before the text we want to match inserted after the equal sign. For a digit ("**\d**"), it would be **(?<=\d)**. The whole query (the lookbehind and the text we want to match) looks like this: **(?<=\d)(st|nd|rd|th)**

There's also a positive lookahead for something that comes after the text we're matching. The **Negative** versions means the entity does *not* precede or follow the text we're seeking.

I sometimes wish to find any paragraphs that begin with a lowercase letter. We know now that the caret (**^**) means beginning of paragraph, and **\l** is a lowercase character, thus we'd use: **^\l**. Unfortunately, this also finds lowercase letters after a forced line break. To exclude lowercase letters that follow those, we use a negative lookbehind: **(?<!)**, putting the code for a forced line break (**\n**) after the exclamation mark.

So, to find a lowercase letter that starts a paragraph but *doesn't* follow a forced line break, the query is: **(?<!\n)^\l**

Find/ Change

Long or Complex Docs

Package & Publish

Finding & Changing Glyphs

Sometimes you just need the right character. In InDesign, we can highlight a single glyph, and we'll be shown alternates underneath it (if any exist). Of course, we may wish to substitute a glyph with one that is completely different.

What is a glyph, anyway? A glyph a visual way to represent a character. There may be several (or many!) glyphs for a single character. In InDesign, go to **Type > Glyphs**. In the **Glyphs panel**, each little box holds a glyph in the font chosen at the bottom of the panel. Some fonts may have *thousands* of glyphs!

In the font Bickham Script Pro Bold, these are glyphs for the lowercase **e**

Using Glyphs You Can't Type

I frequently need glyphs that I know a font has but cannot be accessed with the keyboard. An example seen throughout this book has been the symbol for the macOS command key: ⌘. When I need it, I *could* open the **Glyphs panel**, choose the font at its lower-left corner, then scroll through the glyphs it contains until I find this one. With my cursor inserted where that glyph is needed, I can then double-click it in the **Glyphs panel** and it will be inserted. That's fine for occasional use, but not for the high frequency I require for this specific glyph.

A more efficient workflow is using a relatively unique glyph that is easily typed and later using Find/Change to replace it with the desired one. In the example below, I chose the copyright symbol as the stand-in glyph.

You highlight whatever it is then right-click choosing **Load Selected Glyph in Find**. This opens Find/Change in its **Glyph** tab with the selected glyph visible in the **Find Glyph** window.

After the document has been populated with the stand-in glyph, open the **Glyphs panel**. If necessary, choose which font contains the pretty glyph you'd prefer to use from the font menu at the bottom of the panel. The **Show** menu near the top has groupings to help make the number of glyphs shown less intimidating and hopefully helps you find the one you're looking for. Once you do find it, right-click on it choosing **Load Glyph in Change**.

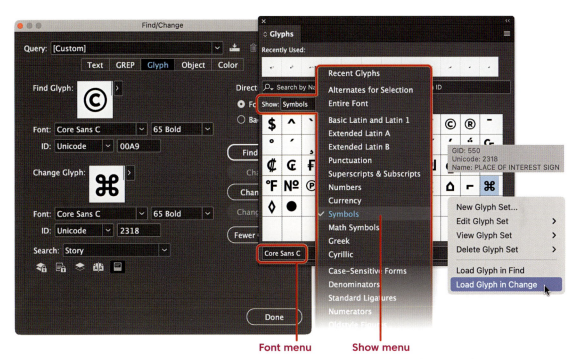

Font menu   Show menu
limits which glyphs are shown

Each glyph is now shown in its appropriate field in Find/Change. Set the scope in the Find/Change **Search** menu, then click **Change All**. Each stand-in is replaced with your desired glyph.

⌘-option-J¶

⌘-S¶

shift-⌘-whatever#

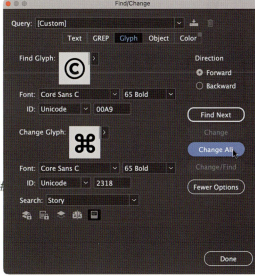

Find/Change

Long or Complex Docs

Package & Publish

Workspaces &
Preferences

Swatches &
Color Settings

Type &
Text Styles

Frames, Shapes
& Object Styles

Pages &
Spreads

Find/
Change

Finding & Changing Objects

The last section of **Find/Change** is **Object**. When you click on either **Find Object Format** or **Change Object Format**, you are shown a dialog box with all the descriptive power of the **Object Style Options** dialog. Any attribute that any object can possess (including an object style!) can be chosen here.

The Powers of Description

You can "describe" an object by as few or as many attributes as you like. Of course, as you set more attributes, your search becomes more restrictive and specific. Below, I set **Find Object Format** by clicking its box, choosing **Stroke**, and setting the weight to 5 pt. Thus, when I hit **Find Next**, an object with a 5 pt stroke was selected. I set **Change Object Format** to both a new stroke weight and a specific fill color. When I clicked **Change All**, anything with a 5 pt stroke now had a 10pt stroke and a purple fill. Just as with the other types of searches, watch out for the scope (the **Search** menu) to be sure it's set broadly or specifically enough.

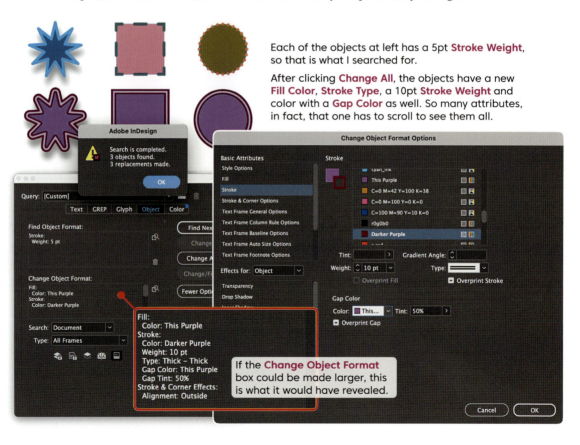

Each of the objects at left has a 5pt **Stroke Weight**, so that is what I searched for.

After clicking **Change All**, the objects have a new **Fill Color**, **Stroke Type**, a 10pt **Stroke Weight** and color with a **Gap Color** as well. So many attributes, in fact, that one has to scroll to see them all.

If the **Change Object Format** box could be made larger, this is what it would have revealed.

Finding & Changing Color

This is as easy and obvious as it sounds. Choose from the lists of colors used in a document for both finding and changing. A color for which there is no swatch will be referred to as "(Unnamed Color)."

You can specify a range of tints to be sought and a tint to apply when the change color is applied.

Since this tab allows changing color of both text and objects at once, it can save us the time of doing separate text and object queries if color was all we wished to change.

Warning: If the color of a changed object or bit of text was defined by a style, that style will now indicate an override.

Find/ Change

Long or Complex Docs

Package & Publish

Workspaces & Preferences

Swatches & Color Settings

Type & Text Styles

Frames, Shapes & Object Styles

Pages & Spreads

Find/ Change

Find/Replace Font

Although *not* part of the Find/Change feature, this function has some things in common with it and is a fundamental troubleshooting aid. This feature is usually first discovered when opening a document with missing fonts. If the missing font is not available from Adobe Fonts or we want to choose a substitute, we can click the **Replace Fonts...** button in the **Missing Fonts** dialog box.

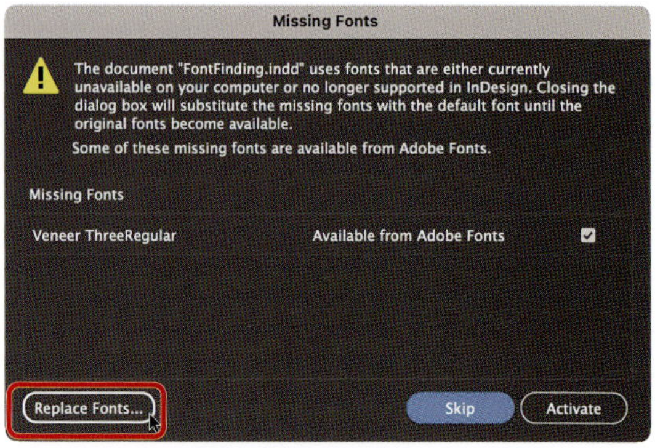

At any time, whether or not fonts are missing, access **Find/Replace Font** by choosing **Type > Find/Replace Font....** In it, you'll see an alphabetized list of all the fonts used in the document. Any missing fonts will be shown at the top of the list with a warning symbol.

If you wish to choose a substitute for a missing font, click the **Replace Fonts...** button when you see the Missing Fonts warning.

If you've enabled automatic font activation of Adobe fonts, you might not see this window. If you would still like to choose a substitute, read on.

Click to highlight any font in the list. If it's missing but available from the Adobe Fonts service, it will show a checkbox to the right and you may click the **Activate** button. To choose a substitute for that or any font, highlight it, then choose a replacement from the **Font Family** menu below the list. There are no previews, so it's best if you already know what you want.

When ready, click **Change All**. Repeat for each font that needs a replacement.

Bonus: When replacing one font with another, any style specifying the original font can be redefined automatically to use the new font! Be sure to check the box for **Redefine Style When Changing All**.

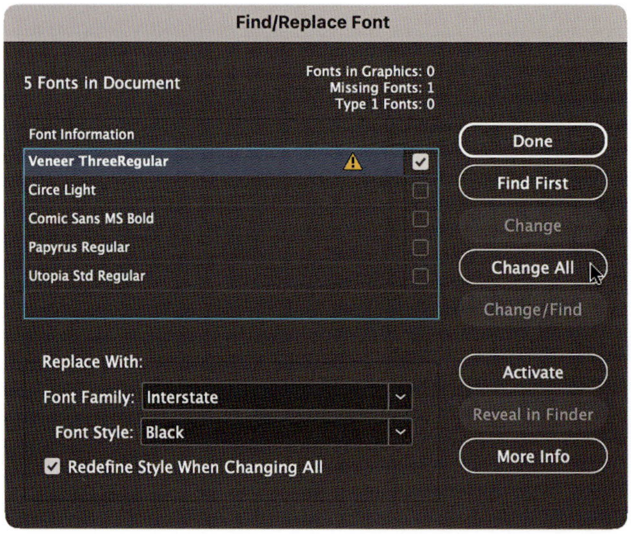

7 Long or Complex Docs

Whether we're concerned about a reader finding her way through a great deal of content, or about ourselves as we assemble a large or complex publication, there are features to help.

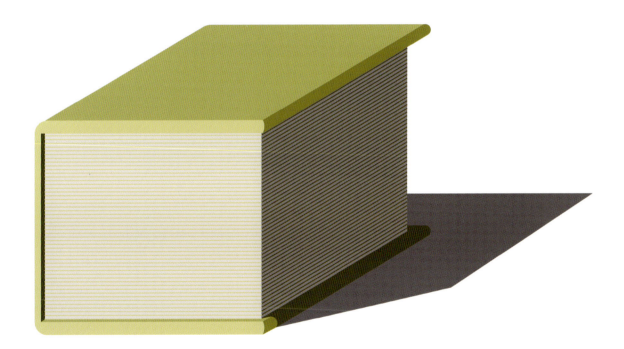

Workspaces &
Preferences

Swatches &
Color Settings

Type &
Text Styles

Frames, Shapes
& Object Styles

Pages &
Spreads

Find/
Change

Long or
Complex Docs

Layers

Unlike in Photoshop, where it is common to have dozens of layers, InDesign documents typically have few layers and often only one, the default layer with the inspired name "Layer 1." They can do so because each item on a spread is merely content in a layer, rather than a layer itself, as it would be in Photoshop. Commands like **Object > Arrange > Send to Back** give us a way to control stacking order and position items visually below (behind) others. But as a document becomes more complex, layers give us greater control, and not just for stacking, although that's a fine place to start.

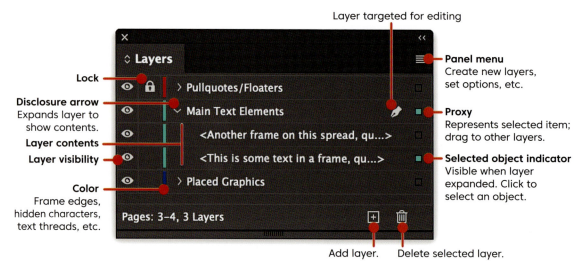

Layer targeted for editing

Lock

Disclosure arrow
Expands layer to
show contents.

Layer contents

Layer visibility

Color
Frame edges,
hidden characters,
text threads, etc.

Panel menu
Create new layers,
set options, etc.

Proxy
Represents selected item;
drag to other layers.

Selected object indicator
Visible when layer
expanded. Click to
select an object.

Add layer.   Delete selected layer.

Creating & Using Layers

The first item in the **Layers panel** menu is **New Layer....** I like to use this method for creating layers because it encourages me to both name the layer and choose a color for its content's edges. An existing layer's name can be changed by either double-clicking the current one or right-clicking it and choosing **Layer Options**.

Layers are available across all pages, and hiding a layer hides its content on all pages. If that layer is above all the others, its content, even parent page content, will be above all the rest. When I have multiple layers, I tend to color the topmost one red and the bottommost one blue. A third layer in between those, I color it green. From the top, that's red, green, and blue.

The small arrow to the left of a layer's name in the **Layers panel** can be clicked to disclose the items populating that layer on the current spread. If the listed items overlap on the spread, the topmost object is topmost in the **Layers panel**, too. Dragging an item's name below another's will set that object's **Z order** (stacking order) to be below the other object's.

To the left of the disclosure arrow is a bar in the color associated with objects on that layer. Frame edges and several other nonprinting attributes will be displayed in this color so you can know what layer the object inhabits.

If a layer is expanded so you can see its contents, a square will be filled with that color next to any selected object. Conversely, clicking an uncolored small square selects the object it's next to. This is wonderful if one object is difficult to click in the layout or is part of a group (whose content can also be "disclosed" with a small arrow to the left of the group). I sometimes right-click an object's name in the **Layers panel** and choose **Select and Fit Item** to both select and center the item on my screen. Note that when an object is selected, the small square to the right of its layer's name will also fill with that color. That square is then a proxy for the object and can be dragged to other layers (if you have any), even without expanding them.

Reordering Layers

Dragging a layer by its name above or below others puts its content above or below the content in the other layers. The example in the previous figure is not an arbitrary one; for esoteric output reasons, I often want images (especially those with transparent bits) to be below text. By having a layer for them, I'm encouraged to put them there.

You may also wish to ensure that some items, like page numbers or running headers, are never obscured, even by full-bleed images. Having those elements on a layer at the top of the stack could be a nice way to arrange that.

Segregating Types of Content

Segregating content into distinct layers allows us to do some pretty cool things. Layers can be set to be nonprinting (double-click a layer's name to see that option). Why would you do that (besides as a prank on colleagues)? You may wish to leave notes or instructions in a template, for example, without the risk of their being output.

Another example: You may wish to protect some content from accidental edits. To accomplish that, click to the right of the small eye icon (eye-con?) to lock the layer. If a layer is expanded to show its content, you can lock individual items instead.

Speaking of that eye-con, it controls a layer's visibility. Consider a multilingual document in which only one language at a time is to be output. You may have one InDesign file that you can export as a PDF, but with only some layers visible each time. Another example would be a textbook; the teacher's edition would have content not visible in the student edition.

The shortcut **⌘-;/Ctrl-;** (semicolon) toggles the visibility of *all* guides. I sometimes put my ruler guides on a layer of their own so I can hide them without hiding my margin or column guides. To easily select all ruler guides, use the shortcut **⌘-option-G/Ctrl-Alt-G**. You can then drag the proxy to another layer, which can be either locked (locking the guides) or hidden (hiding them).

Deleting Layers

The safest command for deleting layers is found in the **Layers panel** menu: **Delete Unused Layers**. This is something I do when a project is finished. If you highlight a layer and click the little trash can at the bottom of the **Layers panel**, you'll be warned if there's content on it—a good thing, as that content will get deleted with the layer. If you feel that you have too many layers, a better solution is to merge them. Highlight two or more and then choose **Merge Layers** from the **Layers panel** menu.

Long or Complex Docs

Package & Publish

Workspaces &
Preferences

Swatches &
Color Settings

Type &
Text Styles

Frames, Shapes
& Object Styles

Pages &
Spreads

Find/
Change

Long or
Complex Docs

Tables of Contents (TOCs)

Manually building a table of contents for a large document is one of the punishments awaiting those who fail to use paragraph styles for headers and subheaders. InDesign's ability to scour long or complex documents (including Book documents composed of many individual files) to automatically create a table of contents is one of the great rewards for using paragraph styles.

Preparation

Consider this document: Each chapter header has a paragraph style called *Chapter title* applied to it. Major topics (like the one at the top of this page) have their own style, as do the headers under them (like "Preparation" just above). In this book's table of contents, I chose to include the first three heading levels as its entries.

I *strongly* recommend making a mock-up table of contents with its own paragraph styles to decorate the entries. Those entries will be generated from text using styles you'll choose (usually, those for headers). In my case, I made styles with names like *TOC chap header*, *TOC topic header*, and *TOC header*. I wanted names that clearly showed that these would be used only in my table of contents (TOC). When InDesign is configured to look for text that uses certain styles, you are offered the unlikely option of using the same styles to decorate the TOC entries. I've never wanted this. So it's best to have other styles at the ready.

You'll also need a paragraph style for the TOC's title (usually the word "Contents," but that's up to you). And you'll be offered the chance to choose a character style for the page numbers that appear in the generated entries. In the case of this book, I made a character style that gives a consistent size and weight to the page numbers, no matter what the rest of the entry is like.

InDesign offers to create styles for you when the TOC is generated. You'll see InDesign's proposed style names in the list of styles where you also find your own. The styles on offer become real if you choose them. However, their settings are very generic and you'll have to redefine them anyway. Again, it's best to make your own styles of your TOC's entries.

Creating the TOC

The **Table of Contents** dialog box generates a loaded text cursor when you click **OK**, with which you can create a text frame or place the newly generated TOC in existing frames, usually primary text frames. To get to that dialog box, choose **Layout > Table of Contents....**

There is a lot to configure in that dialog box (see the following figure), so I use my dummy TOC to guide me. To gain access to all of the available options, click the button labeled **More Options**, if you see it. On the other hand, if the button says **Fewer Options**, don't click it. Near the bottom of the dialog, check **Include Book Documents** if you need to trawl for styles in all the documents of a **Book** document. See "The Book Feature" (page 334) for more on that.

Near the top of the dialog, in the **Title** field, enter the text that should appear at the top of the TOC, and choose the **Style** to its right. In the following example, I'm building the TOC for a magazine, so I chose "articles" as my TOC's title. There are three more sections to this dialog.

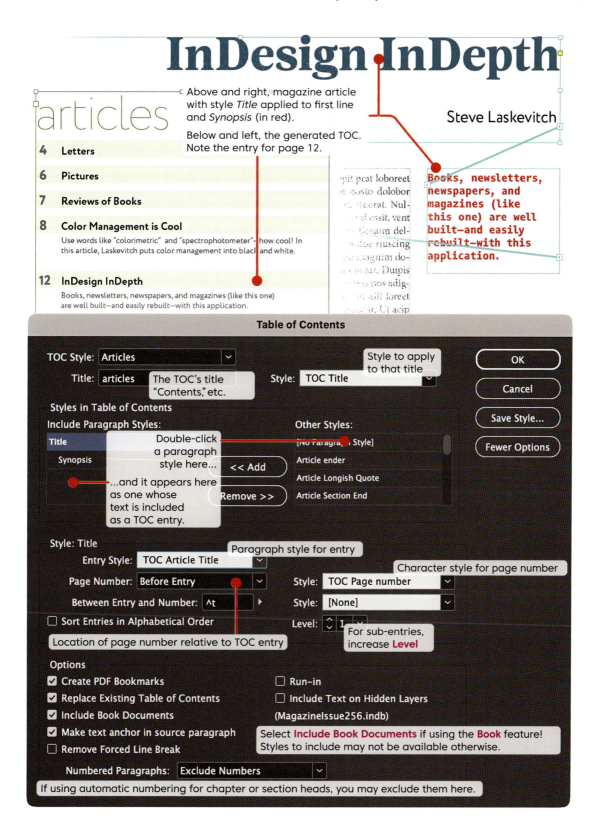

InDesign InDepth

Steve Laskevitch

Above and right, magazine article with style *Title* applied to first line and *Synopsis* (in red).

Below and left, the generated TOC. Note the entry for page 12.

articles

4 Letters

6 Pictures

7 Reviews of Books

8 Color Management is Cool
Use words like "colorimetric" and "spectrophotometer"—how cool! In this article, Laskevitch puts color management into black and white.

12 InDesign InDepth
Books, newsletters, newspapers, and magazines (like this one) are well built—and easily rebuilt—with this application.

Books, newsletters, newspapers, and magazines (like this one) are well built—and easily rebuilt—with this application.

Table of Contents

TOC Style: Articles

Title: articles — The TOC's title "Contents," etc.

Style: TOC Title — Style to apply to that title

OK | Cancel | Save Style... | Fewer Options

Styles in Table of Contents

Include Paragraph Styles:
- Title
- Synopsis

Double-click a paragraph style here...
...and it appears here as one whose text is included as a TOC entry.

<< Add | Remove >>

Other Styles:
- [No Paragraph Style]
- Article ender
- Article Longish Quote
- Article Section End

Style: Title

Entry Style: TOC Article Title — Paragraph style for entry

Page Number: Before Entry — **Style:** TOC Page number — Character style for page number

Between Entry and Number: ^t — **Style:** [None]

☐ Sort Entries in Alphabetical Order — **Level:** 1 — For sub-entries, increase **Level**

Location of page number relative to TOC entry

Options
☑ Create PDF Bookmarks
☑ Replace Existing Table of Contents
☑ Include Book Documents
☑ Make text anchor in source paragraph
☐ Remove Forced Line Break

☐ Run-in
☐ Include Text on Hidden Layers
(MagazineIssue256.indb)

Select **Include Book Documents** if using the **Book** feature! Styles to include may not be available otherwise.

Numbered Paragraphs: Exclude Numbers

If using automatic numbering for chapter or section heads, you may exclude them here.

Long or Complex Docs

Package & Publish

Workspaces &
Preferences

Swatches &
Color Settings

Type &
Text Styles

Frames, Shapes
& Object Styles

Pages &
Spreads

Find/
Change

Long or
Complex Docs

Styles in Table of Contents Section

Used in tandem with the **Style** section, this is where we choose the styles whose text will become entries in the table of contents. Double-clicking on a style listed in the **Other Styles** box on the right adds it to the **Include Paragraph Styles** list on the left. Simple TOCs, like those for a novel in which we want only the chapter headers noted, may have only one style chosen. For this magazine example, each article has a title with a style called *Title* applied to it and a short synopsis with a style surprisingly called *Synopsis*. So, in the **Other Styles** list, I double-clicked on each of those names (in that order).

Before proceeding, it's best to highlight the first style listed in the box under **Include Paragraph Styles**.

Style Section

With a style highlighted in **Include Paragraph Styles**, you configure how the entries derived from it are formatted and logically structured.

In the magazine example, each full entry consists of an article's title text as the primary entry (with a page number to its left) and that article's synopsis, the secondary entry. With *Title* highlighted above, the **Style** section is renamed **Style: Title**, for clarity. I then check that it's **Level** is set to **1**.

I usually highlight each chosen style and check its **Level** before adjusting other entry settings. Those consist of choosing a paragraph style to decorate each entry, whether a page number for it comes before or after (or at all), what kind of space (or bullet or line break) is between the entry and page number, and, finally, character styles to be applied to the number and/or the separator, if any.

So, to continue with magazine's TOC: Text using the style *Title* will form level one entries and have a style named *TOC Article Title* applied. The **Page Number** is set to **Before Entry** with a default tab (shown as "**^t**") chosen to be **Between Entry and Number**. To select anything else, use the special character menu `Between Entry and Number: ^t ▶` barely noticeable next to the current choice. I chose a character style for the numbers (*TOC Page Number*) to make them larger and bolder than the rest of the entry.

With *Synopsis* highlighted above, I set the **Level** to **2**, a style for that entry, and chose no page number since I already had one from the level one entry.

What if you need a TOC entry to help a reader find a specific page, but prefer to not have the text it uses to appear on that page? There are three common methods to do this:

- Set the frame that holds the text to be **Nonprinting** using the **Attributes panel**; or
- Put the text on a hidden layer, then check the box **Include Text on Hidden Layers** in the **Options** section of the **Table of Contents** dialog; or
- Place the text frame *mostly* on the **Pasteboard** but barely overlapping the page.

I prefer the first method because I can see the text when I zip through my pages in InDesign, but it disappears in **Preview** mode and won't output. I may forget the text exists if it's on a hidden layer or if I'm zoomed too close to see text that is mostly offstage.

Options Section

Okay, I'm including one setting from the previous section since I feel it's misplaced. Here they all are:

Sort Entries in Alphabetical Order   Sorts not by page number, as usual. Admission: The reason this is in the **Style** section is you can choose to do this for only your level two entries, for example.

Create PDF Bookmarks   Your entries will be in Acrobat's or Reader's bookmarks panel if you export later as a PDF.

Replace Existing Table of Contents   The first attempt rarely works the way we intend. You may wish to build a second TOC for different styles, however. Like a list of figures or contributors, for example. Thus, you would want to keep both.

Include Book Documents   Publications like magazines, annual reports, and, yes, books are usually built of multiple documents stitched together with the Book feature (discussed later in this chapter). To see and use the styles in all those files, you need this option.

Make text anchor in source paragraph   This makes the TOC interactive in a PDF or ePub as long as hyperlinks are included at export.

Remove Forced Line Break   You may have needed to break a header to read more nicely, but that break may well be unnecessary in the TOC entry.

Run-in   All the entries in one paragraph separated by semicolons.

Include Text on Hidden Layers   To use one of the methods discussed above (on the previous page) to create entries for text that is not apparent on the page.

Numbered Paragraphs   If the text being used for entries is being pulled from styles that use automatic numbering, as discussed in "Bullets and Numbering" (page 215), choose what part of those paragraphs to use: **Include Full Paragraph** (including numbers), **Include Numbers Only** (no text), or the default **Exclude Numbers**.

TOC Styles

You will likely generate a table of contents a few times before it's right, especially if it has several levels of entries. Sometimes you'll choose the wrong style to look for or to apply to the entry. When you finally dial it in, and you suspect you may need to use those settings again (the next issue of the magazine, for example), you can create a **Table of Contents Style**. I very much wish they called it a "preset" as the word "style" is used so much here.

When you're in the TOC dialog, and all the settings are correct, click the **Save Style...** button and give this preset a name. TOC styles are among the things that get synchronized in a **Book** file. They're also used to generate the electronic TOC in an e-book (like those read on an iPad or Kindle). You may generate an attractive TOC for e-books, but that is truly optional. However, having a TOC style is *not*; it's the way we describe the hierarchy in an e-book's code.

Long or Complex Docs

Package & Publish

We will discuss e-books in the "Packaging & Output" chapter of this book—see "ePub and Tagged File Formats" (page 348)—but the key part is creating an independent TOC style that excludes page numbers specifically for that medium. In a reflowable ePub, a reader can change the font or font size of the text, which makes the whole concept of a page rather fluid. TOC entries become hyperlinks that will take the reader to the correct page, so knowing the number of a page becomes irrelevant.

To load TOC styles from a different document (a previous project, perhaps), choose **Layout > Table of Contents Styles...** where you can click a **Load** button. You can also create new or edit existing TOC styles, but it's done a bit blindly, as this approach doesn't immediately generate a TOC afterward.

Updating a Table of Contents

What if there are changes to any of the text that the TOC references? Although tables of contents don't update automatically, it's easy to prompt them. Insert the **Type tool** cursor *anywhere* in the TOC. Then choose **Layout > Update Table of Contents**. That's it!

Workspaces & Preferences

Swatches & Color Settings

Type & Text Styles

Frames, Shapes & Object Styles

Pages & Spreads

Find/ Change

Long or Complex Docs

Text Variables

Tables of contents aren't the only InDesign feature to extract content based on the styles applied to it. Text variables can be a convenient way to repeat or reference text that uses a paragraph or character style. The text you see along the tops of pages in the print edition of this book uses text variables to remind you of which topic is under discussion.

Variables can also be a way to insert document data, like date and time of the most recent edit or output. And they can be used to extract and render metadata from placed images for captions. As in so much, there is good news and bad with this feature.

Chapter Numbers

When using the **Book** feature (discussed at the end of this chapter), you can inform each document which chapter it is or to begin automatic chapter numbering. To display the number, we insert a text variable: Right-click and choose **Insert Variable > Chapter Number**. The chapter number will display in the same style as the text around it. Here is this chapter's number: 7. (Yes, that "7" is a variable. I used the **Book** feature to set the first chapter of the Compendium section as "1." This is the seventh.)

Another way to insert variables and, better, to define your own, is by going to **Type > Text Variables** and choosing either **Insert Variable** or **Define….** So I don't redefine a default variable that I could be using, I choose **Define…** and click **New….** The settings below produce this:

Compendium chapter 7

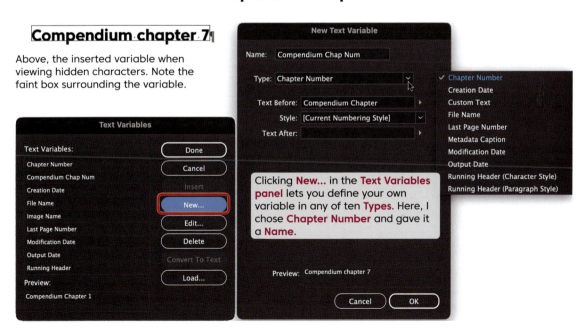

Above, the inserted variable when viewing hidden characters. Note the faint box surrounding the variable.

Clicking **New…** in the **Text Variables panel** lets you define your own variable in any of ten **Types**. Here, I chose **Chapter Number** and gave it a **Name**.

If I put that in a narrow text frame, however, it will look like this:

Compendiumchapter7

Warning: Text variables don't break across lines. I bet you wondered when I'd get to the bad news. If the space available is too narrow, the variable text will get crushed. After nearly 550 users requested that variable text wrap, a member of the InDesign team assured us in 2017 that "We have added this feature in our backlog for future release." After this many years, my hope has diminished.

If we redefine the variable to be less verbose, it will change everywhere and may fit in narrower quarters. Or we can select the variable, right-click, and choose **Convert Variable to Text**, and the following will result: It will wrap, but it will no longer update if the chapter number changes.

Compendium chapter 7

Captions

We can type our own captions, but if our images have metadata, we can generate captions that utilize it. Although we use a different procedure for automatic captions, they are text variables.

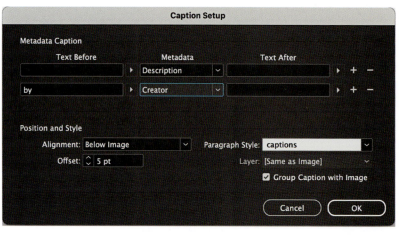

Choosing **Object > Captions > Caption Setup...** yields this dialog. In it, we can choose which embedded *metadata* to include in a caption. But beware of bugs. Although there was data in the **Creator** metadata field, InDesign doesn't read it. If you choose **Author** instead, it will actually read the **Creator** data.

Metadata can be added to images in many places, including the macOS and Windows operating systems, Photoshop, Adobe Bridge, Lightroom, and others. For the image below, I added data to the **Description** and **Creator** fields in Lightroom's Metadata panel. In InDesign, **Object > Captions > Caption Setup...** allows us to choose which metadata to include (and any text around it) in captions we later generate.

To make the caption, I right-clicked a selected image and at first chose **Captions > Generate Live Caption**. The first problem was that InDesign didn't read the **Creator** metadata.

To force it to do so, I had to choose **Author** in the **Caption Setup** dialog—an obvious (and long-lived) bug.

Then I saw the result: The description was crushed on one line. If all my captions are very short, this may not be an issue. If a linked image's metadata changes, the caption will automatically change as well. But few captions are short enough, and metadata like this doesn't often change. So I used **Undo**, and this time right-clicked and chose **Captions > Generate Static Caption**. Since **Static Captions** are *not* variables, they are not linked to their source nor do they get crushed when the space is too narrow. Once these are generated, they're just text.

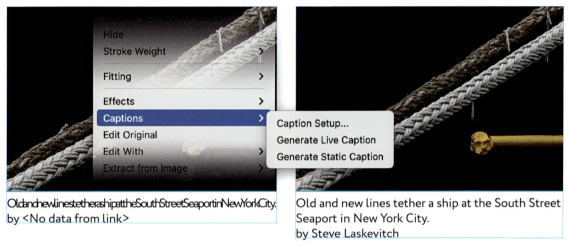

Left, a **Live Caption** with the correct Creator metadata field chosen, but not read due to a bug in InDesign.

Right, a **Static Caption** made after changing **Creator** to **Author** metadata in **Caption Setup**.

In both cases, the **Description** metadata was correctly read, but only the **Static Caption** wraps multiple lines.

Running Headers

These text variables are among the most useful. If you're reading this in print, you'll see a running header at the top of each page of this spread reading "Text Variables." The variable at work there "sees" the last (most recent) use of the paragraph style applied to the header introducing this topic two pages back.

Use **Type > Text Variables > Define…**, then click the **New** button. I usually name a variable after the style to which it refers. I chose "topic title" and selected **Running Header (Paragraph Style)** as the **Type**. Although I have very rarely used the character style variant, it is a handy way to use just part of a paragraph, excluding bullets or automatic numbering, for example.

For a running header, we are usually referring to a topic that is ongoing, and so we want the most recent use of it. Thus, it's usually best to choose **Last on Page** for **Use**. We can choose a wide variety of special characters to automatically be added before or after the text we're grabbing, or we may type into the **Text Before** or **Text After** fields. InDesign even supplies a thoughtful way to remove punctuation or change the case of the text.

To insert the variable, we locate our cursor in a text frame (for running headers, this is usually on a parent page, and often near the **Current Page Number** marker), right-click, and choose **Insert Variable > [name of variable]**.

On a parent page, the variable will be shown as the variable's name in angle brackets, like this: **\<topic title\>**. On document pages, they will display the text of the most recent use of the paragraph style you designated, but in the style you applied to the variable.

So, this header...

A Big Header

...may have this variable   **A big header**

How I'd set up a variable for the example above. Unlike the actual running headers at the tops of this book's pages, I chose to change the case to **Sentence Case**.

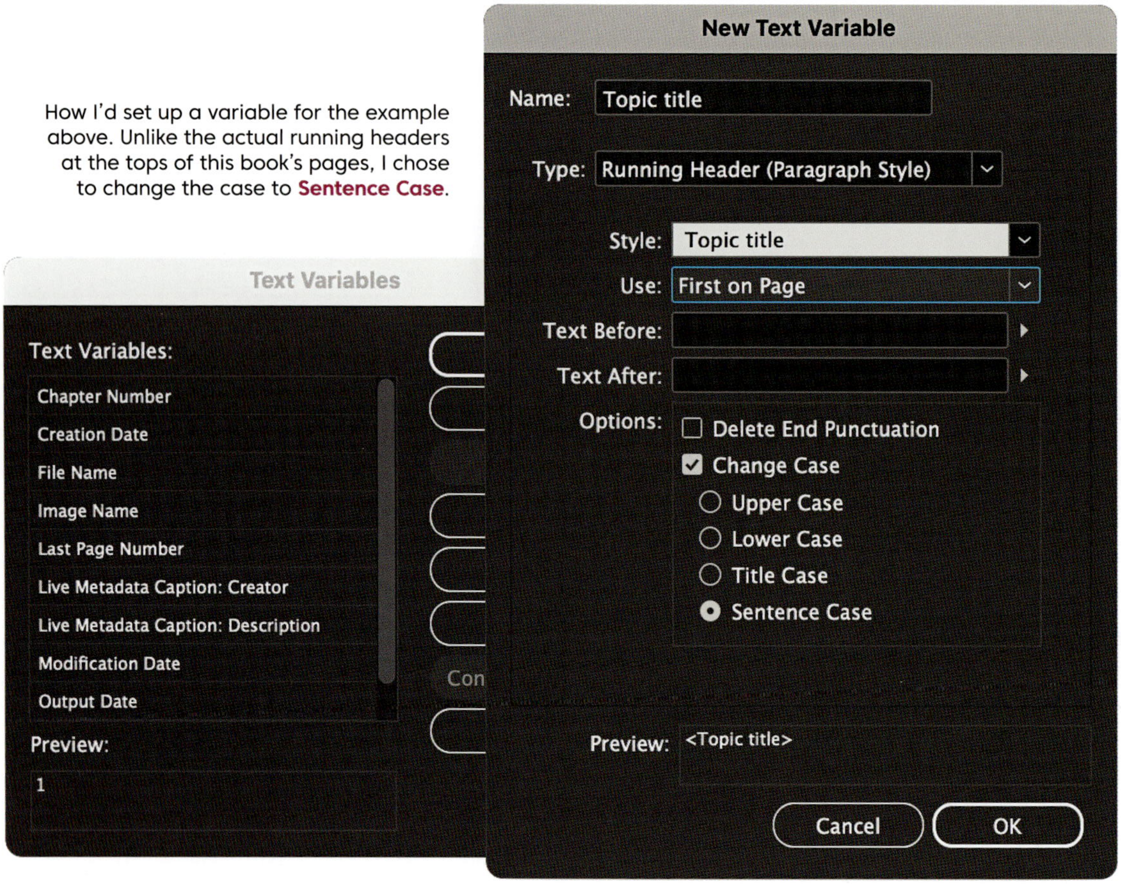

Text Variables

Text Variables:

Chapter Number
Creation Date
File Name
Image Name
Last Page Number
Live Metadata Caption: Creator
Live Metadata Caption: Description
Modification Date
Output Date

Preview:

1

New Text Variable

Name: Topic title

Type: Running Header (Paragraph Style)

Style: Topic title

Use: First on Page

Text Before:

Text After:

Options: ☐ Delete End Punctuation
      ☑ Change Case
        ○ Upper Case
        ○ Lower Case
        ○ Title Case
        ● Sentence Case

Preview: \<Topic title\>

Cancel   OK

Warning: Yes, another bug! When you change the text to which a variable refers, you'll have to force the page to redraw to confirm that the variable has noted the edit. Simply zooming out and in again will do it. Otherwise, it *appears* that the variable is not updating, although it is.

Workspaces & Preferences

Swatches & Color Settings

Type & Text Styles

Frames, Shapes & Object Styles

Pages & Spreads

Find/ Change

Long or Complex Docs

Cross-References

Cross-references are a hybrid of text variables and TOC entries. Like both of those features, cross-references ("x-refs") refer to and can echo text that uses a style. Like TOCs, they most often cite the page on which to find that text—e.g., "see *Calca 2: Hemn (Configuration) Space* on page 917." Since cross-references are usually hyperlinks in electronic documents like ePub, I often suppress the appearance of page numbers in that medium. Access the **Cross-References panel** via **Window > Type & Tables > Cross-references**.

Building a Cross-reference

There are several steps to create a cross-reference:

1. **Know what it's referencing**. Look at the text you're about to reference and, since you can create a cross-reference to another document, be sure InDesign has access to it (open that other doc, for instance). A cross-reference can cite an entire paragraph, a paragraph number, a partial paragraph up to some character you can specify (like a tab), or a named text anchor to reference a word or phrase.
2. **Insert the text cursor where you want the reference to appear**. Unlike a table of contents, while you build the cross-reference, it will preview in real time.
3. **Begin the process**. Use the **Cross-References panel** menu to choose **Insert Cross-Reference...** or use the **Create New Cross-Reference** button at the bottom of the panel. You'll then be looking at the **New Cross-Reference** dialog box.
4. **In the New Cross-Reference dialog box, choose to what the reference is linking**. Since you did step 1, you know whether to choose **Paragraph** or **Text Anchor** from the **Link To:** menu.
5. **In the New Cross-Reference dialog box, choose the document that contains that destination**. This is especially important and powerful when working within a **Book** file, since it is composed of multiple InDesign documents.
6. **Consider how the reference will actually be phrased**. The cross-reference feature has many built-in "formats," essentially templates, each of which can be edited, and you can make your own. There are many options available for that.

The Destination

Usually, I create cross-references that link to entire paragraphs—short ones like headers. Sometimes, I link to parts of paragraphs, like paragraph numbers (when the text referenced uses the **Bullets and Numbering** feature, a common scenario for figure or table captions). If you need to refer to a key word or phrase, you can make it a *named text anchor* to which a cross-reference can link.

To create a text anchor, highlight the text to which you anticipate making a reference later. Go to the **Cross-References panel** menu and choose **New Hyperlink Destination....** For **Type**, choose **Text Anchor**. The **Name** is important, as it will be the text cited in the cross-reference.

Long or Complex Docs

Package & Publish

When hidden characters are visible, the anchor will resemble a colon. The TOC feature also has the option to create text anchors, so you may already see some in your text.

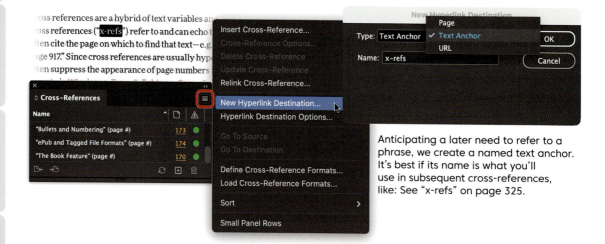

Anticipating a later need to refer to a phrase, we create a named text anchor. It's best if its name is what you'll use in subsequent cross-references, like: See "x-refs" on page 325.

By using the supplied building blocks when editing the reference's format, you may also include a **Chapter Number** and a **File Name**, and you can even apply a character style to portions of the reference. With so many options, you won't have to build many text anchors in your documents.

The Cross-Reference

First, insert the text cursor where you want the reference inserted. If you're to make reference to text in another document in a **Book**, make sure that other document is open!

See the following figure for reference. Choose what to **Link To**: a paragraph or text anchor. Then choose the **Document** that contains the reference's destination. If you're linking to a text anchor, you simply choose its name, then for **Cross-Reference Format**, choose **Text Anchor Name & Page Number**. If you're linking to a paragraph, it's a little trickier. On the left, choose the **Paragraph Style** that your destination text is using. Despite the search feature included in the dialog box, it's easier if you already know the style. Once the style is highlighted, each occurrence of it in the destination document is listed on the right. If you highlight one of those occurrences and look where your cursor was blinking, you'll see a preview of the developing cross-reference.

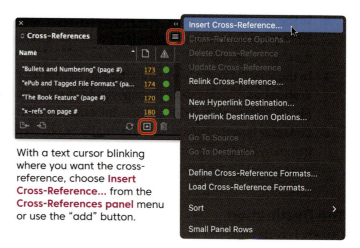

With a text cursor blinking where you want the cross-reference, choose **Insert Cross-Reference...** from the **Cross-References panel** menu or use the "add" button.

The formatting of the cross-reference may not be what you want just yet. The built-in list in **Format** is sufficient for most needs. If you simply want to cite the **Page Number**, choose that. You may choose **Full Paragraph & Page Number** for short paragraphs like headers. In the classroom, I often get asked the difference between **Full Paragraph** and **Paragraph Text** because few see any difference. There is *no* difference unless the paragraph uses automatic numbering. If it does, **Full Paragraph** includes the generated number text and **Paragraph Text** does not. The example illustrated below is a reference to a numbered paragraph in which the paragraph "number" is "Figure 1." It shows a caption that reads, "**Figure 1.**   Portrait in bronze of the emperor Marcus Aurelius, c. AD 161." The text "Figure 1." and the em space after it is all part of the paragraph "number" as defined in its paragraph style. So **Paragraph Number & Page Number** yields "Figure 1 on page 4."

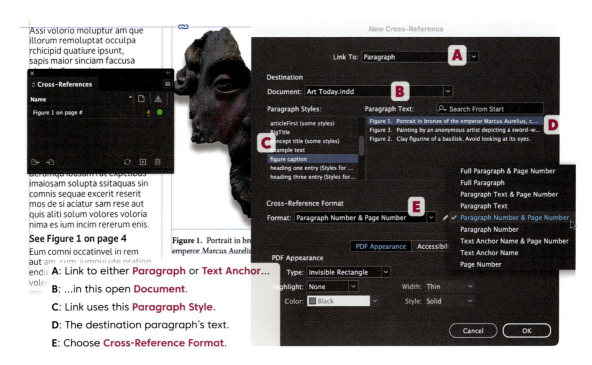

A: Link to either **Paragraph** or **Text Anchor**…

B: …in this open **Document**.

C: Link uses this **Paragraph Style**.

D: The destination paragraph's text.

E: Choose **Cross-Reference Format**.

That's good but I wanted a little bit more. So I created a custom format based on **Paragraph Text & Page Number**. I chose that preset, then clicked the pencil icon to its right, opening the **Cross-Reference Formats** dialog box (which disables the preview, sadly).

Since I wanted a new custom format, I added it to the list by clicking the plus sign (**+**) at the lower left of the **Cross-Reference Formats** dialog box (not the one on the right). I input a name that mimics the format I'm building so I can readily identify it. The **Definition** field is where we construct our format by a combination of typing and choosing from the **Building Block** **+** or **Special Character** **@** menus. Building blocks look like HTML or XML tags using "<" and ">" to form placeholders. Some are easy to figure out. `<paraText />` is paragraph text, `<paraNum />` is paragraph number, and `<pageNum />` is page number. So, **Paragraph Number & Page Number** looks like this:

```
<paraNum /> on page <pageNum />
```

Long or Complex Docs

Package & Publish

The **Cross-Reference Formats** dialog has a checkbox to apply a **Character Style for Cross-Reference**, but it applies to the entire thing. I had a character style that I wanted applied to just the paragraph number. So, from the building block menu, I chose **Character Style**. This added a pair of tags to the end of the format, because that's where my cursor was:

```
<paraNum /> on page <pageNum /><cs name=" "></cs>
```

The first of those is the "opening tag" and requires the name of the character style ("cs") to be inserted between the quote marks. In my case, the style's name was "red," since it colors text red. I wanted this applied to the paragraph number alone, so I copied the opening tag and pasted it in front of **<paraNum />** and the closing tag just after **<paraNum />**:

```
<cs name="red"><paraNum /></cs> on page <pageNum />
```

I changed the **Name** of the custom format, clicked the **Save** button, then clicked **OK**.

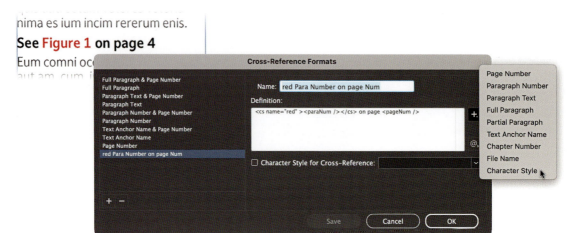

Footnotes and Endnotes

Both of these features insert a reference into the text flow (usually a number) and create a note either at the bottom of the page on which the reference occurs (a footnote) or later in the document (endnote). Both have a number of options that require more time and decision-making than deep insight. Nonetheless, there are a few important things to note (pardon the pun).

It's useful to create a paragraph style for the kind of note you use. It certainly doesn't have to be perfect because, like all paragraph styles, it can be edited later. But when you adjust the **Footnote** or **Endnote Options**, you'll be asked to choose a style for the note. You can also choose a character style for the reference. For clarity, I've created styles that make the reference and note text purple in the examples that follow.

Add Footnotes

Right-click and choose **Insert Footnote**, which inserts a reference number and allows you to enter the note text. To format both, choose **Type > Document Footnote Options….** The **Footnote Options** dialog has two tabs, the first of which is **Numbering and Formatting**.

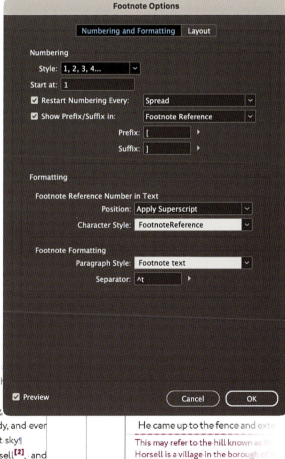

Numbering Style can be asterisks, letters, or other glyphs.

"Numbering" can be restarted on each page, spread, or section.

A **Prefix** or **Suffix** can be added to the reference and/or the note itself. Here, brackets are added to the reference only.

The reference can be super- or subscripted or "normal," that is, as large as and inline with the story in which it occurs.

We choose a character style for the reference and a paragraph style for the note. **Separator** is what's between the number and text in the note—here, a tab.

 flowed as it had flowed for immemorial years. The fever of war presently clog vein and artery, deaden nerve and destroy brain, develop.

All night long the Martians[1] were hammering and stirring, indefatigable, at work upon the machines they were making ready, and ever and again a puff of greenish-white smoke whirled up to the starlit sky.

About eleven a company of soldiers came through Horsell[2], and

1 » Those awful beings from Mars‡

2 » Horsell was first documented in the 13th century, although the parish church of St Mary the Virgin is believed to date from the middle of the 12th century. The name probably comes from the Anglo-Saxon *horig scylf*, meaning "muddy slope".

He came up to the fence and exte

This may refer to the hill known as H Horsell is a village in the borough of north-west of Woking town centre. The sand pits of Horsell Common a Common has since been designated

3 » This fruit is widely appreciated for it texture, and sweetness. Rich in vitam

Workspaces & Preferences

Swatches & Color Settings

Type & Text Styles

Frames, Shapes & Object Styles

Pages & Spreads

Find/ Change

Long or Complex Docs

As mentioned above, I often create the styles requested by those **Footnote Options** before I open the dialog box to configure them. In the example, I added brackets to the reference as both **Prefix** and **Suffix** (but not to the number in the footnote text) and chose a character style to make the reference number bolder and purple.

Much under the **Layout** tab is dedicated to the space around and between footnotes. The lower section is dedicated to a **Rule Above** (a line) that can be drawn between the story text and the footnote(s). In this example, it's a solid, purple, .75 point rule.

As a footnote grows more verbose, it gets taller. It is possible that it may even reach up to the line that contains its reference (as it does in the illustration). For this reason, I suggest leaving the **Allow Split Footnotes** checkbox enabled. This allows the footnote to continue into the next page. You'll see an indicator that a footnote has split: ▶. When a footnote continues on another page, the **Continued Footnotes Rule Above** will be used. **Span Footnotes Across Columns** lessens the chance that a note will split to another page.

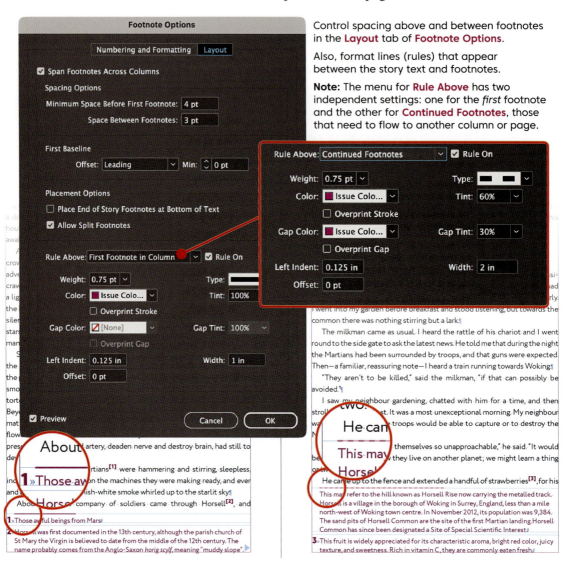

Control spacing above and between footnotes in the **Layout** tab of **Footnote Options**.

Also, format lines (rules) that appear between the story text and footnotes.

Note: The menu for **Rule Above** has two independent settings: one for the *first* footnote and the other for **Continued Footnotes**, those that need to flow to another column or page.

Endnotes

The **Endnotes** feature is very similar to the **Footnotes** feature. When we right-click to **Insert Endnote**, a reference is inserted at that point and our text cursor is now blinking in the note awaiting its content. However, with an endnote, we're likely looking at another page, possibly one that's far from where we inserted the reference. Choose **Type > Document Endnote Options...** to get options similar to those for footnotes. You can convert all or some footnotes to endnotes (and the other way around): **Type > Convert Footnote and Endnote**.

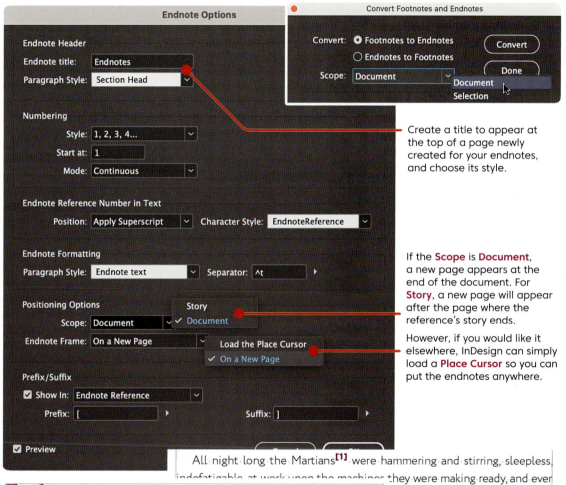

Create a title to appear at the top of a page newly created for your endnotes, and choose its style.

If the **Scope** is **Document**, a new page appears at the end of the document. For **Story**, a new page will appear after the page where the reference's story ends.

However, if you would like it elsewhere, InDesign can simply load a **Place Cursor** so you can put the endnotes anywhere.

Note: With the text cursor within an endnote, right-click and choose **Go to Endnote Reference**. When right-clicking with the cursor at the reference point, the choice is **Go to Endnote Text**.

Indexes

An index is something very, very few of us should contemplate making ourselves. There are professional indexers for the same reason there are professional electricians: We *might* be able to do the work ourselves, but the pros have the minds and skills to do it better than we ever could. The American Society for Indexing website (asindexing.org) has an indexer finder. Hiring a professional is money well spent.

Nonetheless, here are some of the basics for those who wish to try. For more details on making your own index, see https://helpx.adobe.com/indesign/using/creating-index.html. Keep in mind that you're building a list of concepts, not words. Each concept will be an index **Topic**, and each occurrence of that concept is a **Reference**.

Create a Topic List

Although an optional first step, creating a topic list is strongly recommended. It ensures that you are consistent and are less likely to be redundant. Later, you'll be able to add references to each more easily as well. Set the **Index panel** to **Topic** mode, then use the **Add** button or panel menu to add as many topics (or subtopics) as you like.

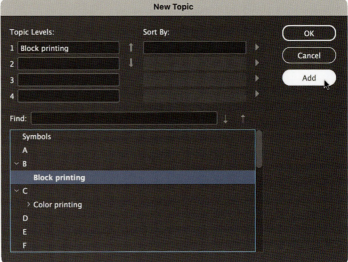

With the **Index panel** in **Topic** mode, use the **Add** button or panel menu to add a **New Topic**. Create a hierarchy of topics, subtopics, etc., then click **Add** to continue with new topics or **OK** when done.

Create References and Index Markers

At each occurrence of a reference to a topic, you create a marker. Highlight the text that references one of your topics. Set the **Index panel** to **Reference** mode. Highlight a word or phrase, then use the **Add** button or panel menu to create a reference. InDesign will create a marker there to note the location of that reference.

When creating a reference, you can specify how long a range of pages are referenced.

For example, if the highlighted text is a header, its topic may continue until there's another occurrence of the style used by that header, or until another document section begins. These and more are options in the dialog's **Type** menu (see figure below).

To create a reference for an existing topic, highlight the topic in the lower part of the dialog box. If you didn't create a topic for the reference you're making, you can create it at the top. I recommend creating references after the text is complete and edited. Otherwise, markers may get deleted accidentally.

When creating a reference, you can specify how long a range of pages are referenced.

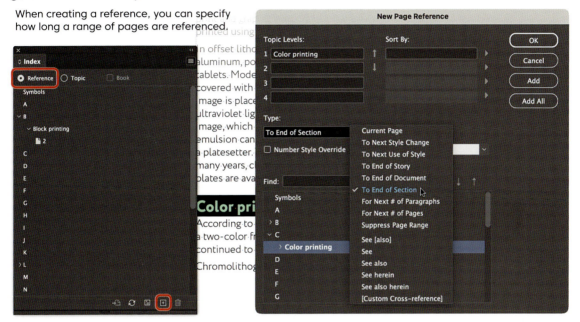

Generate the Index

This action creates an InDesign story that you can flow onto a page or into a document of its own as part of a **Book**.

For the title of the index and for its various entries, you may choose styles you've made or allow InDesign to generate ones you can later edit. Be sure to choose **More Options** to do so. The button will then read "Fewer Options."

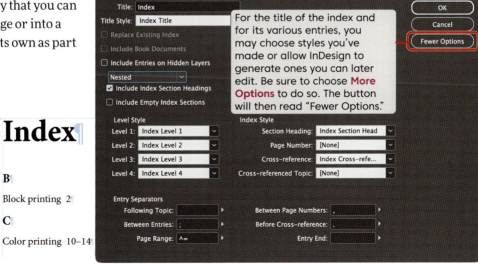

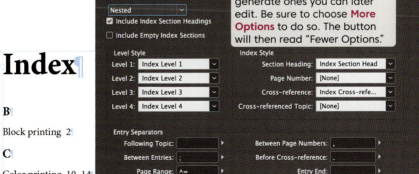

The Book Feature

First, let's throw a pair of giant quotes around the word "book." In InDesign, a **Book** is a database document that we use to assemble multiple documents into a single publication. So whether you're making a magazine, an annual report, a proposal for an engineering project, or a book, you may wish or need to break down the project into discrete pieces. Sometimes each member of a team works on an individual document. Later, someone, maybe you, gets to collect those into one big entity.

Some aspects of making a **Book** document are easy, especially if you know at the outset that you're going to use the feature. It can be more difficult to break up a single document into many, depending on how it's built. A novel with few or no illustrations can easily be done in a single document of several hundred pages. But if you suspect that the publication is going to have many graphics populating a hundred pages or more, you can be sure InDesign will start to bog down unless you break it up into logical units like chapters.

To ensure consistency between documents in a **Book**, we can sync many settings across them: styles, swatches, numbered lists, and even parent pages. Page numbering can continue smoothly from one document to the next, if we choose. And if we arrange to have one document per chapter, the chapter numbering can be somewhat automated as well.

When saving documents, a certain order of operations needs to be followed. But let's discuss the making of **Books** before we discuss their quirks and bugs.

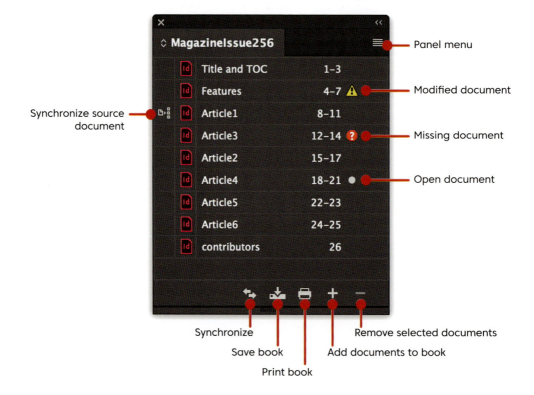

- Panel menu
- Modified document
- Synchronize source document
- Missing document
- Open document
- Synchronize
- Save book
- Print book
- Add documents to book
- Remove selected documents

Workspaces & Preferences

Swatches & Color Settings

Type & Text Styles

Frames, Shapes & Object Styles

Pages & Spreads

Find/ Change

Long or Complex Docs

Creating and Populating a Book

Since a **Book** is a kind of document, we simply use InDesign's **File > New > Book...** command. We'll be prompted for a name and location to save it. The **Book** document presents as yet another panel on screen! But it's a database that manages documents we add to it. Once added, you should open those documents only by double-clicking their names in the **Book's** panel, not through the computer's operating system.

To add documents to this little database, we click the plus sign (+) at the bottom of the panel. We can then choose as many documents as we wish (easier if they're in the same folder).

Warning: By default, each document's page numbers will change when added to a **Book** file. To prevent this until you've put them in the right order, go to the **Book panel** menu and select **Book Page Numbering Options....** There, you can *temporarily* disable **Automatically Update Page & Section Numbers**. When all the documents are added

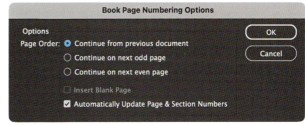

and in the right order, I often look them over to see if, when page numbering resumes, pages should be added to keep opening pages as odd numbered, for example, or if I'm willing to let some start on the left and some on the right. Some publishers insist that a chapter start on a right (odd-numbered) page. If you need to do this, check **Continue on Next Odd Page** and **Insert Blank Page** to bridge any gaps.

When all or none of the documents are highlighted (far left), some **Book panel** menu items read differently than they do when fewer than all are highlighted (above).

Long or Complex Docs

Package & Publish

The **Book panel** menu has many important options, but please note that some change depending on whether documents are highlighted in the panel or not. If so, then many options are specific to the highlighted document(s) *only*. If all the documents (or none of them!) are highlighted, we see those menu options that pertain to the book as a whole. Also note the **Save Book** option in the panel menu. When you make changes in this panel, be sure to choose that option or use the **Save** button. Remember, a **Book** is a file! So when you're done working on it, save it and then choose **Close Book** to reliably close it before quitting InDesign.

Remember "Sections & Numbering" (page 292)? If you want a specific document to begin a new section with a restart of numbering, you can access its **Numbering and Section Options** (and open the document) by double-clicking that document's *page numbers* in the **Book panel** rather than the name as usual. In the same dialog, you can also specify which chapter that document should be. Display that chapter number with a **Text Variable** that shows "Chapter Numbers" (page 321).

Document Syncing and Status

The documents that compose the **Book** may have seen changes to style or swatch definitions that differ from other documents.

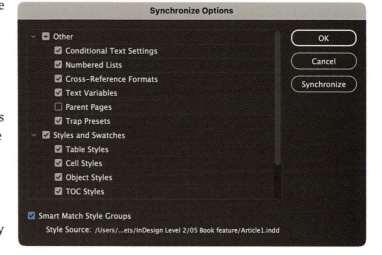

Ensure that one document has the definitive styles and/or swatches. Click to the left of the source document in the **Book panel** to choose it as the source when synchronizing.

Control what is synced by using the **Book panel** menu and choosing **Synchronize Options….** Perhaps one doc has the right swatches and another has the right styles. Each can serve as the source for a round of syncing, with all the options unchecked except for the feature(s) you want synced that time. Then, making sure no documents are highlighted, or only those that should be synced, then click the **Synchronize** button. Each document is opened invisibly and its assets you chose are set to match your source document's. When the process completes, a message notifies you that documents "may have changed." Well, I sure hope so.

The full list of things that can be synchronized is quite long: conditional text settings, numbered lists, cross-reference formats, text variables, parent pages, trap presets, table styles, cell styles, object styles, TOC styles, character styles, paragraph styles, and swatches. Syncing parent pages can be a disaster, so it's unchecked by default. **Smart Match Style Groups** cleverly notes whether uniquely named styles are in groups or not in any given document. If they're in a group in the style source, they'll be put into groups in the other documents.

Workspaces & Preferences

Swatches & Color Settings

Type & Text Styles

Frames, Shapes & Object Styles

Pages & Spreads

Find/ Change

Long or Complex Docs

When you open a document in a **Book**, a circle appears to its right in the **Book panel**. The circle disappears once you successfully save and close the document. When there is no icon it means all is OK. A warning that the file was modified outside the **Book's** purview (yellow warning triangle) appears if you had edited the document when the **Book** file wasn't open, or even if the panel was collapsed to an icon! I approach it like this: If I can't see the file listed in the **Book panel**, the panel can't see me edit the file. I know, weird. But it's a way to deal with a bug that we've had for a long time.

If a file is moved, deleted, or renamed, it might have a "missing document" icon next to it. Finally, if the **Book** file is on a server where multiple people have access to both it and the files it manages, anyone can open the **Book**. However, if one user opens a document, it shows as locked and "in use" to the other users in their **Book panel**.

Long or
Complex Docs

Package
& Publish

Conditional Text

Not all content is for everyone. We have the ability to stipulate the conditions in which some text should be seen and output and when it shouldn't. The **Conditional Text panel** is where you create and apply conditions that are assigned to selected text.

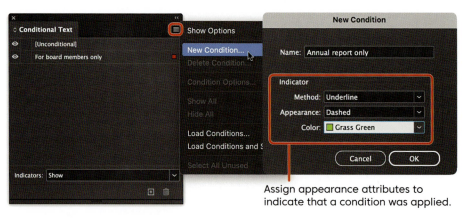

Assign appearance attributes to indicate that a condition was applied.

Once conditions are created, highlight text then click on the name of the condition to apply it. Now it's easy to hide all text with that condition applied:

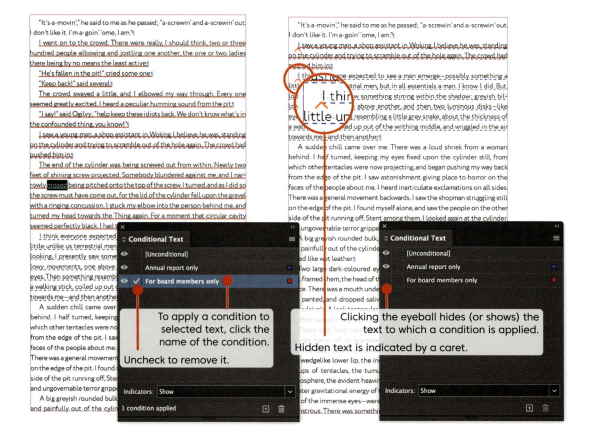

To apply a condition to selected text, click the name of the condition. Uncheck to remove it.

Clicking the eyeball hides (or shows) the text to which a condition is applied. Hidden text is indicated by a caret.

Workspaces & Preferences

Swatches & Color Settings

Type & Text Styles

Frames, Shapes & Object Styles

Pages & Spreads

Find/ Change

Long or Complex Docs

8 Package & Publish

The document is done and needs only to be delivered. Various recipients require different deliverables, each with its own quirks and concerns. Luckily, there is just a handful of likely suspects. We'll discuss those in the order in which they're most likely to be requested.

Workspaces &
Preferences

Swatches &
Color Settings

Type &
Text Styles

Frames, Shapes
& Object Styles

Pages &
Spreads

Find/
Change

Long or
Complex Docs

Package
& Publish

PDF

The Portable Document Format (PDF) is the most common way we share our finished layouts. Anyone with Adobe's free Acrobat Reader application can open a PDF and consume its content. And that's just about *everyone*. Those who want to edit PDFs or add extra functionality to them can use Adobe Acrobat Pro, the powerful sibling to Reader. Adobe has been very effective at making PDF and these apps nearly ubiquitous—maybe a little too effective: My training company often gets calls from prospective students who want to learn how to use "Adobe." With some gentle questioning we confirm they're trying to learn more about Adobe Acrobat.

The advantage of sharing a document as an Acrobat PDF rather than a Word or InDesign document is that PDFs retain the layout and text formatting of the authoring application without the recipient needing to have the author's applications or fonts. When I receive Word docs from clients, I moan because just opening them will change them. Adobe built PDF to retain a faithful likeness to the original at the cost of making it hard to edit. But even that has become easier with the right software.

PDFs can be configured for a variety of print output devices or can be set up for entirely electronic consumption. Their file sizes can be very small (at the cost of image quality, usually) or large. There is no one PDF to rule them all; different eventualities often demand a differently configured PDF. Luckily, our recipients can often guide us and Adobe provides many presets to achieve common configurations.

Presets

InDesign can export (**File > Export...**) to many different file types. But when it's PDF I need, I stop just short of that command and use **File > Adobe PDF Presets**, choosing the preset that most closely matches my needs. You'll be prompted for a name and location to which to save the PDF. Then you still need to interact with another dialog box with many options. If you cancel at either stage, no PDF is made.

Define...

[High Quality Print]...

[PDF/X-1a:2001]...

[PDF/X-3:2002]...

[PDF/X-4:2008]...

[Press Quality]...

[Smallest File Size]...

The **Presets** in square brackets ("[" and "]") are built-in and cannot be changed. But if you do customize the settings in the **Export Adobe PDF** dialog, you'll see the name of the preset with the word "modified" appended to it. You can save those customizations as your own preset to use later. And there are many things that you might choose to change! A private student once asked me to explain the pros and cons of *every* option. Twenty minutes later the student asked me to "stop, please." Luckily, I covered the crucial things in the first five minutes, and few people other than prepress professionals need to know much more. Speaking of those special folks...

Better printing companies will often suggest which preset to choose or supply a custom preset they have made to suit their workflow. I recently consulted the website of one such printer and found wonderfully detailed advice for preparing files for output, as well as a downloadable PDF preset. If your printer supplies such, you will need to "install" it. Some commercial printers will instead show images of the various pages of the **Export Adobe PDF** dialog box, hoping you will match what they're showing. Either way, you'll need to "define" a PDF preset.

Choose **File > Adobe PDF Presets > Define....** If you're trying to follow instructions and screenshots, you'll press the **New...** button. You will then navigate to a dialog box that is nearly identical to the one you use when actually exporting. We'll get there in a moment.

If you've downloaded a preset, you'll press the **Load...** button, then choose the file you downloaded (it will have an extension of ".joboptions").

We will look at many of the details of this preset and some others as we go through the **Export Adobe PDF** dialog box.

General Options

When you use **File > Adobe PDF Presets** or go to **File > Export...** and select **Adobe PDF (Print)**, you'll be faced with the **Export Adobe PDF** dialog.

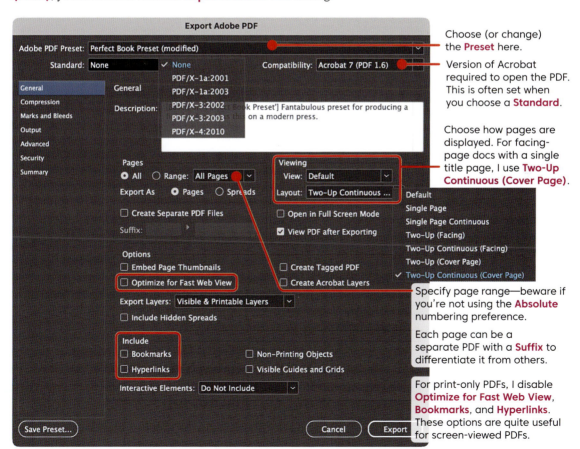

Choose (or change) the **Preset** here.

Version of Acrobat required to open the PDF. This is often set when you choose a **Standard**.

Choose how pages are displayed. For facing-page docs with a single title page, I use **Two-Up Continuous (Cover Page)**.

Specify page range—beware if you're not using the **Absolute** numbering preference.

Each page can be a separate PDF with a **Suffix** to differentiate it from others.

For print-only PDFs, I disable **Optimize for Fast Web View**, **Bookmarks**, and **Hyperlinks**. These options are quite useful for screen-viewed PDFs.

Workspaces &
Preferences

Swatches &
Color Settings

Type &
Text Styles

Frames, Shapes
& Object Styles

Pages &
Spreads

Find/
Change

Long or
Complex Docs

Package
& Publish

Although there are important options found here, I often leave **General** for last, since some of its settings get altered if you change the preset. This is where you specify the range of pages to be exported (much easier to do if you have chosen **Absolute** page numbering in your **General Preferences**). You may choose for each InDesign page to be a PDF page, or you can have each PDF page be a "reader spread" by choosing to **Export As Spreads**. However, that setting and a number of others are *not* recommended for most PDFs destined for print.

Viewing has a welcome set of options for whomever will open the PDF. For **View**, I invariably choose **Fit Page** so that no recipient is looking at only the top third of page 1 when they open the document. If my document is a series of single pages, I'll choose **Single Page** or **Single Page (Continuous)** for **Layout**. If I have spreads (a.k.a., "facing pages"), one of the **Two-Up** options is more appropriate. There's even provision for a single title page followed by spreads (the options with **Cover Page** in the name). Always choose to **View PDF after Exporting** to catch things you may have missed.

For PDFs destined for online viewing, there are many options to keep the file size low. One is the **Preset** called **Smallest File Size**, although you may find that the cost of "smallest" is too great, as image quality suffers greatly. More on that when we discuss **Compression**. Other options in **General** are the inclusion of modestly interactive elements, like any **Hyperlinks** you may have built. **Bookmarks** can be generated from an InDesign TOC, too. If you've built more elaborate interactivity involving buttons and transitions, then the export process should start with going to **File > Export...** and choosing **Adobe PDF (Interactive)** and its set of export options.

Create Tagged PDF is required to include tags for disabled accessibility. **Create Acrobat Layers** makes a PDF layer for each InDesign layer. You can choose which InDesign layers from the **Export Layers** menu. The **All Layers** choice means it, even including layers that have been made invisible or nonprinting!

Compression

If you choose the **Smallest File Size** preset, note that all color images will experience **Bicubic Downsampling to** 100 ppi if their *effective resolution* is more than 150 ppi. See "Placing Images" (page 257) for more on that term. Grayscale images will be made 150 ppi. Those resolutions *may* be appropriate for onscreen viewing. But the combination of **Compression** and **Image Quality** are **JPEG** and **Low**, respectively. After viewing the result, you'll likely increase the quality to **Medium** or higher, yielding a larger but more palatable file.

The print-friendly settings shown in the following figure use **ZIP** compression rather than **JPEG**, as file size is not so critical and **ZIP** is lossless compression, unlike **JPEG,** which literally discards data! Since the compatibility is set to Acrobat 7, I could use **JPEG 2000** (an option for Acrobat 6 and higher), which yields a better looking JPEG, but **ZIP** is quite literally the best.

The **Downsampling** is also different. For this print preset, it's set to 300 ppi for images whose effective resolution exceeds 450 ppi. At the bottom of the dialog are two checkboxes that will make a smaller file size while causing no harm: **Compress Text and Line Art** and **Crop Image Data to Frames**. Some users get apprehensive about the latter until they're reminded that this is only cropping the images in the PDF, not the InDesign document.

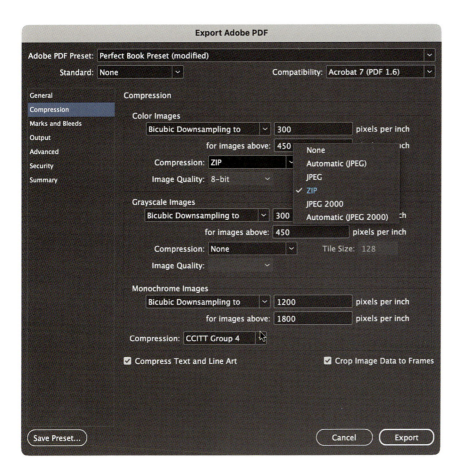

Marks and Bleeds

Now we step off the page to what surrounds it. Arrayed beyond the bleed are the **Crop Marks** that determine where the paper will be cut. Some printers may also want more information like filename or date (**Page Information**).

   Use the settings that your print shop asks for! If you've set your document's bleed to their specs, you can check **Use Document Bleed Settings**.

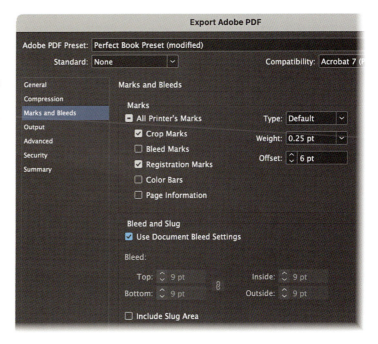

Output

This ties into the management of color as discussed in "Going Deeper: How Color Works" (page 186) . The key choice here is the **Destination**. If I'm creating a PDF to be viewed on-screen only, I'd likely choose sRGB, as that profile represents standard displays. For print, choose the profile indicated by your commercial printer—they may even supply one to install so you can choose it here. With a **Destination** profile chosen, specify the **Color Conversion: Convert to Destination (Preserve Numbers)**.

With a CMYK **Destination**, this choice ensures that all RGB content is converted to the printer's desired profile while maintaining any CMYK choices you may have made in InDesign.

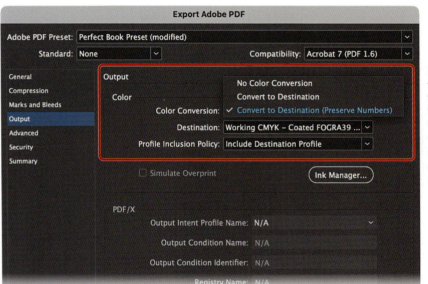

If your recipient wants you to convert RGB to CMYK, for example, you choose to do that here, as well as specify *which* CMYK.

The bulk of this Compendium's second chapter was written to explain these choices!

It is possible that you will be asked to do **No Color Conversion** so that your printers may do it themselves with the most up-to-date profile. Sadly, some ask for this because they have an early 1990s workflow. If they seem unaware of what a profile is, assume the latter. **Profile Inclusion** is also a decision of the print shop, as some of their software may not like to have that data embedded in the PDF.

The **Ink Manager** button is a great last-minute rescuer. The dialog box it opens is available at all times from the **Swatches panel** menu, too. Let's say you've built a brochure that includes logos from a dozen sponsors. Some of those logos use spot colors that require extra inks for which there is no budget. You don't have to rebuild each logo to use only CMYK (process color). You merely have to check a box in the **Ink Manager** as you export your PDF: **All Spots to Process**. Combined with **Use Standard Lab Values for Spots**, this will ensure increased color accuracy and consistency with other Adobe apps.

Another option is **Ink Alias**, which allows you to substitute one ink for another. One common use for that is swatches that use *nearly* the same color, but are actually different or for different surfaces. In the example, an uncoated paper version of a spot color is being "aliased" to the coated version. That one, in turn, could be aliased to a third, maybe a process ink.

The **Ink Manager** allows you to, among other things, convert any spot colors to the CMYK process. This is handy if you unknowingly added assets that use spots.

Here, one spot color, Pantone 305 U, has been "aliased" to another version of that color, so only one gets requested of your commercial printer.

If no spots should be used, check **All Spots to Process**.

Advanced

Only a few options are of interest here for those with reasonably modern workflows.

Under **Fonts**, you have the option to reduce file size by embedding only the font data of the characters you used in InDesign (a **Subset** of them). This could be troublesome if a recipient needs to make a small text change with a character you didn't embed. Thus, I choose 0% to force the full fonts to become part of PDFs, especially those for print.

Printers who have more current software to process PDFs can support transparency in the PDFs we send them. So if you're asked to supply Acrobat 5 or newer **Compatibility**, artwork in your document that includes transparent effects like drop shadows or blend modes will be passed along in the PDF. If the **Compatibility** is Acrobat 4, InDesign uses a bunch of processing tricks to maintain the look of your artwork, but without true transparency. This process is called flattening, and we choose a **Flattener Preset** that best fools the eye. We're lucky that this is becoming less necessary all the time.

Security

With **Document Open Password**, you can encrypt the PDF so it cannot be opened without a password that you choose. So if you're sharing a proprietary document, you can do so over less secure channels, comforted that an intercepted PDF can't be opened.

The **Permissions** portion is less secure, but it attempts to prevent certain actions (printing or extracting content) unless a password is provided. However, one can open the PDF in software that circumvents this.

Package

Most recipients are content with a PDF. But for our colleagues, the company archive, or our own, we need to supply our "native" files: the InDesign document(s), all the linked graphics, and fonts. In short, all the assets necessary to open and edit that project.

A Copy of Everything

When an InDesign project is complete and saved, we may wish or need to share it and its assets with others. However, those assets may be strewn over several hard drives and many folders. Luckily, if we don't have any missing links or fonts, we can make a package that leaves our assets in place and makes copies of them all consolidated in a folder. You may wish to review "Missing Links & Relinking" (page 265) and "Missing Fonts" (page 196).

To create the package folder, choose **File > Package....** You'll need to wade through a few dialog boxes, the first of which consists of a "preflight" check and summary. Unfortunately, you'll see a warning triangle that is wholly ignorable. The use of RGB images is apparently alarming to someone on the engineering team and no one else. I'm relieved when I see no missing fonts at the top, however.

If **Create Printing Instructions** is checked,

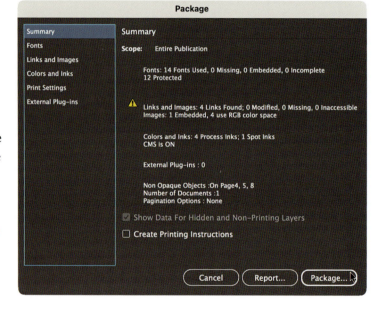

clicking **Package...** reveals a form, the content of which augments a text file that will be within the package. It informs the recipient how to get in touch with you and includes all the data you saw in the previous dialog box. Few read that doc, so we rarely check the box to create it.

The dialog that appears either after or instead of the printing instructions is the most significant. In it, you name the package, choose where to save it, and designate its contents. I almost always check the first five checkboxes. I want the package to have all the assets necessary to successfully open it. All the fonts, except Asian language (CJK) fonts and those from the Typekit service, will be copied to a subfolder called "Document fonts."

Copy Linked Graphics creates a folder called "Links" in which all placed images and graphics are copied. **Update Graphic Links in Package** ensures that those graphics know they're linked to the copy of your InDesign document.

Use Document Hyphenation Exceptions Only prevents the text from reflowing when

Workspaces & Preferences

Swatches & Color Settings

Type & Text Styles

Frames, Shapes & Object Styles

Pages & Spreads

Find/ Change

Long or Complex Docs

Package & Publish

opened on a computer with different hyphenation and dictionary settings.

Include Fonts and Links From Hidden and Non-Printing Content sounds useless, but is far from it. I often have nonprinting content that colleagues who open the InDesign document will need to see (instructions, for example). I may also have layers hidden with optional text or text in alternate languages.

Include IDML adds a file in *InDesign Markup Language*, a descriptive format that can be opened in now very old versions of InDesign. Some newer features (e.g., **Paragraph Shading**) may not be present, but the content will be intact.

Finally, **Include PDF (Print)** will include a PDF using the last settings used by your InDesign document, or you can choose any saved preset. I will sometimes include a PDF with a generic preset like **[High Quality Print]** for the sake of a recipient of the package who doesn't have InDesign.

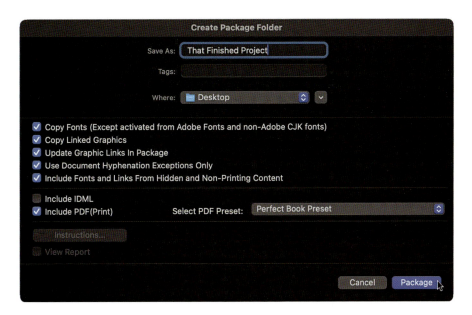

When you hit the **Package** button, you get to read the last dialog box: a message from Adobe's legal department warning that one cannot share fonts with those who do not have a license to use them. That dialog has a welcome checkbox labeled **Don't Show Again**. Committing that dialog finally allows the package to be generated. When this book is completed, I will make a package from the **Book panel** menu to give to my publisher.

Workspaces & Preferences

Swatches & Color Settings

Type & Text Styles

Frames, Shapes & Object Styles

Pages & Spreads

Find/ Change

Long or Complex Docs

Package & Publish

ePub and Tagged File Formats

HTML (*HyperText Markup Language*) is at the heart of a great many electronic document formats, especially on the web. With it, we "mark up" content with tags to tell each element what it is: like headers, subheaders, list items, and regular paragraphs. Software, like web browsers, benefit from the identification and hierarchy tags provide, and style each element based on its tag. For example, a top-level header, marked up with the `<h1>` tag, defaults to bold and quite large, whereas an item in a list (`<li>`, for "list item") would be indented and displayed with a bullet. Screen reader software for the visually impaired benefits from the hierarchies and the meaning given by markup tags. In markup, each of these tags appears at the beginning of an element, with a corresponding closing tag to mark its end: like `<h1>`Big Header`</h1>`.

Export Tagging

Each style we make (paragraph, character, or object) can have a tag associated with it via **Export Tagging**. Thus, when we export a document, its elements have the structure and meaning that tags bestow beyond their visual appearance. Entire books and courses exist created by folks far more fluent in the legal requirements and best practices around creating accessible, tagged PDFs. So, although I will focus primarily on ePub and HTML, there are important details in the following sections for all.

Tagging Text

I chose the `<h2>` tag for the chapter header paragraph style in this book. The topic header at the top of this page is tagged as `<h3>`. For spans of text to which a character style is applied, a tag called `<span>` is applied. To differentiate a `<span>` or `<h3>` that should look different than others, each can have its own "class" attribute.

Example for the HTML-curious:

```
<h3>Plain text to <span class="fancy">fancy</span> and back</h3>
```

might render as:

Plain text to *fancy* and back

In the **Export Tagging** pane of each style options dialog box, you can choose a tag (or type one that is not offered) and give a name for the class. Check out the following figure. The **Export Details** window in that pane shows both the tag and class name, as well as the styling code (CSS, *Cascading Style Sheet*) that will be written by InDesign to style each element as close to the print version as possible. Those two languages, HTML and CSS, work together; the first is the "what," and the second is how to decorate it. In each paragraph style for which I choose an **ePub and HTML Tag**, I also add a **PDF Tag**, so if I export a PDF, it will be more accessible.

Those who are familiar with CSS find themselves frustrated that they cannot customize the CSS they see in the **Export Details** window. However, during export to HTML or ePub, we can add a custom CSS file that we have authored that can fine-tune or override the one authored by InDesign.

When choosing a tag for a character style, I might choose **em** for a style that simply italicizes or **strong** for one that bolds, since that is the standard appearance for those tags. For the same reason, I'd also uncheck **Include Classes in HTML** and **Emit CSS**.

A paragraph style for a header will get one of the h tags (**h1**–**h6**), depending on its place in the hierarchy. An item in a list calls for a tag that isn't in the list, but you can type in "li" in the **Tag** field to have it more meaningfully marked up. For more ordinary paragraphs, **p**, the default, is a reasonable choice.

Most ePubs are reflowable; that is, readers may change font, text size, orientation, and more to suit their taste. When they do, the text reflows and the "page" count changes. Because of this, the concept of a page is somewhat meaningless in the world of e-readers. Page breaks in a print version will not match those in the ePub. However, there is a way to get a header to be at the top of a page. In the **Export Tagging** pane of the header style's **Paragraph Style Options** dialog, check **Split Document (EPUB only)**.

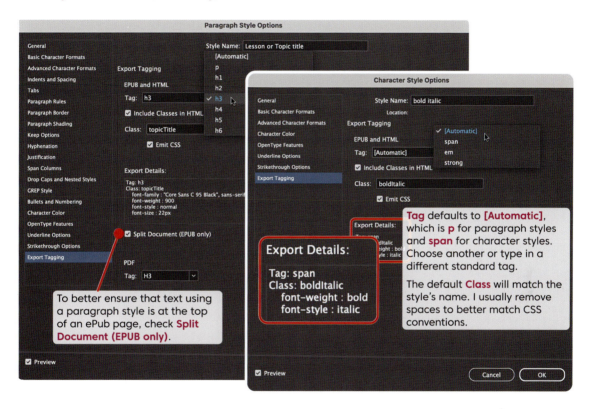

Since I'm comfortable writing CSS, I create a CSS file to finesse some of my styles. I know that printed page numbers will *not* correspond to whatever an e-reader device will display for "pages" in a reflowable ePub. So I use a character style to format cross-reference page numbers and my custom CSS to hide those referenced pages in a reflowable ePub. So a phrase like "see page 873" will simply not show up in the ePub because I will have applied a style to it called *hideFromEpub*, and CSS that says `.hideFromEpub { display: none; }`.

Workspaces & Preferences

Swatches & Color Settings

Type & Text Styles

Frames, Shapes & Object Styles

Pages & Spreads

Find/ Change

Long or Complex Docs

Package & Publish

Tagging Objects

Images and other frames can be tagged and have more elaborate export options applied with an object style or *ad hoc* with the **Object Export Options** dialog box.

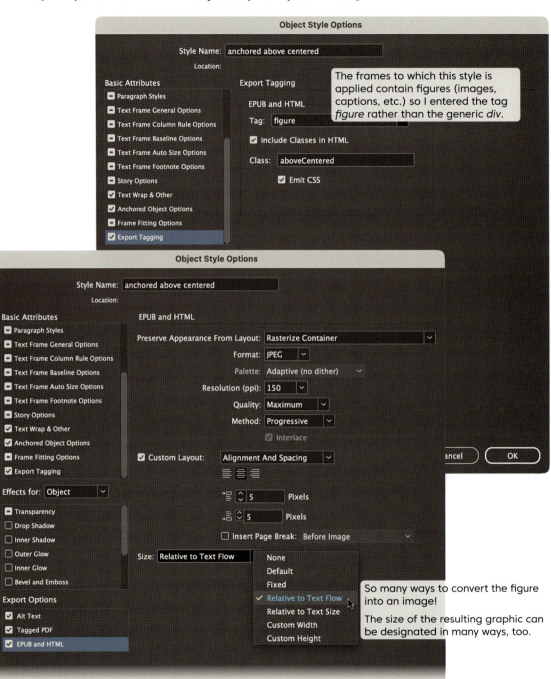

Frames using the style above will export with the *figure* tag, since that is the most meaningful for the content they'll contain: figures! Because of the side effects that surround "Object Styles and Groups" (page 278), this style is not applied to a group of image and text frames, but only to a frame into which that group is pasted. In an ePub or HTML document, that containing frame will be made a **Maximum Quality JPEG** of sufficient **Resolution (ppi)** for screen media. The **Size** of the exported JPEG is set to **Relative to Text Flow**. So if the frame is 65% as wide as the printed text frame, the JPEG will be 65% the width of the ePub text block.

In this book, there are figures *wider* than the text frame into which I'm typing, like the one above (on the previous page). For those, I chose a **Custom Width** of 100%. Besides percent, I could have used other CSS-compatible units like cm, mm, in, pt, px, vh, vw, vmin, or vmax. The aspect ratio of the frame will be maintained (there's no need to specify the height).

What Gets Exported and How

Note: To control the presentation order of content composed of both text and figures, the latter *must* be anchored to a text position. Review "Anchored Objects" (page 272). For example, each figure and image in this book is anchored to an otherwise empty paragraph so it "knows" where it is in that InDesign story.

The most reliable and intuitive way to choose what is included when exporting as ePub or HTML, and in what order it appears, is by adding those items (articles) to the **Articles panel**. The name of this panel has confused many. I suggest interpreting the word "article" as you would when discussing items like articles of clothing, not as written pieces.

Simply drag a frame into the **Articles panel** to add it. To add a story composed of multiple threaded text frames, drag the first of its frames into the panel, and the whole story is included as one entry. You'll be prompted for the name of the new article of which that story is a part. Subsequent items can be added to that existing article or added as new ones.

The **Articles panel** for the layout of the novel *A Study in Scarlet*. Two text frames are part of the *Front Matter* article (the first one is currently selected). The novel's entire narrative is one InDesign story (composed of many threaded text frames), so it's one entry in the **Articles panel**.

The **Articles panel** for this chapter. Surprised? Since *every* figure (including this one) is anchored to a paragraph in the chapter's story, they are part of that story and don't need to be added separately.

Package & Publish

Some publications, like novels, do perfectly well as reflowable ePubs. Others, like children's books, cookbooks, and others with precise layout do much better as *fixed-layout* ePubs.

With fixed layout, an attempt is made to maintain the position of *everything*. Thus, parent page items like page numbers make sense here. There is no need for the **Articles panel** to order content because all is included just as it is in the print version. However, as an electronic document, our cross-references can be tappable hyperlinks (just as we'd use in a reflowable ePub), so page numbers in those references are optional. Many of InDesign's interactive features are supported as well, subject to limitations of the physical reader and its software.

Left: A reflowable ePub in the Kindle Previewer app.

Below: A fixed layout ePub in the Apple Books app.

Both fixed and reflowable ePubs offer multiple means of navigation. Both can show a table of contents that you can navigate with a tap, generated by a **TOC Style** we create in our InDesign file before exporting.

Exporting an ePub

If I'm making a reflowable ePub, I will anchor images (whose **Object Export Options** are set) to where I want them relative to my text, and then drag content into the **Articles panel**. I need to drag only one text frame of a story to add the entire story. For a book, this usually means I add title page content, each independent bit of other front matter, the main text flow, and perhaps an index. I name all the articles and order them.

If I have designed a cover, I will note where it is located on my computer so I can designate it during export. One may also choose to rasterize the first page, which is useful if you have a particularly nice title page. I will also double-check that I have set **Export Tagging** correctly in my various styles.

As careful as I am, I will still miss *something*! But I'll find out after I use **File > Export... > ePub (Reflowable)** (in this example). Let's explore each part of that dialog.

General

Choosing a **Version EPUB 3** allows for better typography and interesting interactive features. Choose a **Cover** graphic from here, too. I create an image specifically for it. For **Navigation TOC**, it's best if you've created (and choose here) a **TOC Style**. The page numbers will not be included, so you can use the same one you might use for the print edition. But if you decide to include a table of contents in the body of the ePub as well, you'll likely have a

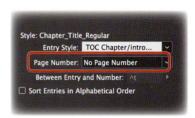

TOC Style without page numbers that can choose here. Review "TOC Styles" (page 319). **Page Navigation** supposedly yields consistent pagination across eReader devices, but I have not experienced that.

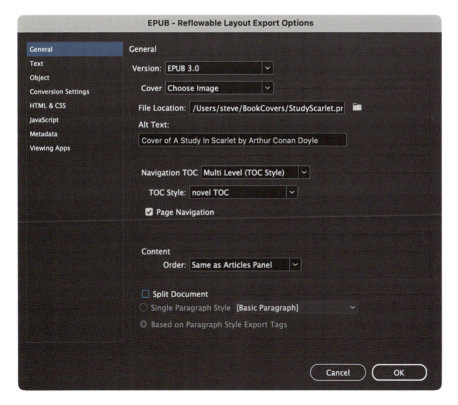

The **Content Order** will be **Same as Articles Panel**, since **Based on Page Layout** is very much *not* what it sounds like. That choice orders content leftmost first, then top down—usually a nightmare. So, we use the **Articles panel**!

Finally, the intent of **Split Document** is to ensure that content using certain styles, like chapter headers, is at the top of a page, even in this relatively pageless medium. If there is only one style that should behave this way, you can choose it here if you haven't also configured its **Paragraph Style Options** to do this. That is preferable, and necessary if there are several styles whose content should be first on a page. There are two ways to do this:

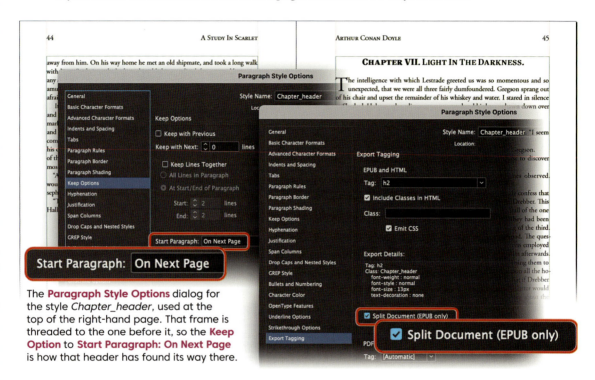

The **Paragraph Style Options** dialog for the style *Chapter_header*, used at the top of the right-hand page. That frame is threaded to the one before it, so the **Keep Option** to **Start Paragraph: On Next Page** is how that header has found its way there.

If you want the text to head a page *both* in print and in the ePub, use the style's **Keep Options** to specify that you wish to **Start Paragraph: On Next Page**. To have this behavior in the ePub only, go to the **Export Tagging** section and click the **Split Document (EPUB only)** checkbox.

Text

This section has far fewer options. One is **Remove Forced Line Breaks**. If you've used those *solely* to make better breaks for the print version, you will likely want to enable this option. However, this will remove *all* forced line breaks in the document, so be sure you want this.

In this medium with no real pages, where should footnotes be? Your choices are: **After Paragraph**, so footnotes will be below paragraphs containing the footnote reference; at the **End of the Section (Endnotes)**, essentially converting footnotes into endnotes; or, for ePub version 3, **Inside a Pop-up (EPUB 3)** when the reference is tapped.

Object and Conversion Settings

I strongly recommend using object styles' **EPUB and HTML Export Options** or at least the **Object Export Options** dialog box to ensure that each graphic in your publications is exported to the most appropriate format, resolution, and position. I use the settings on these parts of the export dialog as a last-ditch way to catch any image, probably small, that I might have missed. So I configure as follows:

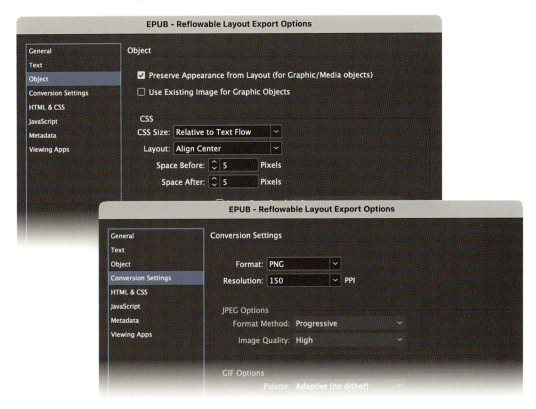

HTML & CSS

If you want to *completely remove* your InDesign text formatting to rely on the e-reader's settings only, choose **Don't include classes in HTML** and disable **Generate CSS**. If you wish to preserve as much of your print book's formatting as possible, you would leave the defaults, including classes and generating CSS for them.

I also **Include Embeddable Fonts** so those e-readers that support them will use the fonts I've chosen. Be warned, some devices will not. Learn to let go!

It is here you can choose **Additional CSS**; that is, your own custom CSS file(s) to refine or override InDesign's.

JavaScript

If you've programmed some behavior for elements using this scripting language, you can add JavaScript files, too.

Metadata

This data gets added in the deep recesses of the ePub and can be seen by e-readers and e-bookstores. However, when publishers submit books to Apple's iBookstore or to Amazon as a Kindle book, they will supply this information (and much more) that will overwrite the data in this form.

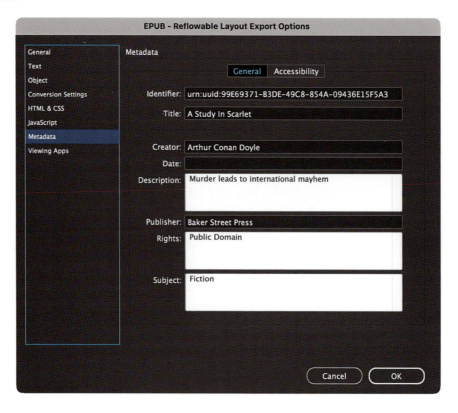

Viewing Apps

Here, you add the software applications with which you want to check your work. Adobe provides one called Adobe Digital Editions. It is, ironically, a notoriously poor e-reader. I primarily use Apple's *Books* app (on both my Mac and in iOS) and the *Kindle Previewer* app (available for Mac and Windows).

Last ePub Note

As mentioned throughout, some HTML and CSS knowledge is useful when working with ePub. With the right software, you can "crack open" an ePub and access the code inside to perfect the results. To edit an ePub's code, I use *BBEdit*, *calibre*, and *Sigil*. There are others, too. Sadly, that geeky fun goes beyond the scope of this book.

Workspaces & Preferences

Swatches & Color Settings

Type & Text Styles

Frames, Shapes & Object Styles

Pages & Spreads

Find/ Change

Long or Complex Docs

Package & Publish

Print

Outputting to a printer connected to your computer is remarkably similar to creating a PDF.

Print Dialog Box

If it's a subset of pages you wish to print, there are many ways to specify which ones. The easiest method is to highlight the pages you want to print in the **Pages panel**, then right-click on one of them and choose **Print Pages...** (or **Print Spreads...** if whole spreads are highlighted). To print an entire single document, choose **File > Print...**, or for a book, use the **Book panel** menu and choose **Print Book...**. The dialog box that appears will also allow you to specify a range of pages to print.

Be prepared to go between various sections of this dialog box to set all the options you need. You will especially have to balance the options in the **General** and **Setup** sections, but most of the dialog box will get visited before you're done. The more complex the printing system, the more experimentation you may need to do. The following guidelines will help with that.

First, and most importantly, choose the **Printer**. This allows InDesign to show you options specific to that device. I am embarrassed by how many times I've sent data to the wrong printer when more than one is available. When you choose, InDesign will interact with that printer's driver software, and if it's a Postscript printer (like many office laser printers), it will also read data from that printer's PPD (Postscript Printer Description). The **Setup** section of the dialog box will then show supported paper sizes, for example.

The buttons at lower left (**Page Setup...** and **Printer...** on a Mac, just **Setup...** on Windows) are means to access the printer driver software and are likely redundant if you take care elsewhere in this dialog box. In fact, if you choose things in the driver that contradict InDesign's settings, trouble could erupt. With inkjet printers, however, it may be necessary to tweak or disable the driver setting to complement settings in the **Color** section.

General

When specifying which pages to print, you may have to supply a lot of data (like a section prefix along with page number or letter), unless you're using **Absolute** page numbering. For example, if your document has two sections with prefixes "SecA" and "SecB" and they use different number styles, you may have to specify a range like "SecA:xii-SecB:27." With **Absolute** numbering, you may be able to use "12-45" if page SecB:27 is the 45th page, for example. Even with **Absolute** numbering, you can do fancy things. To print the first 8 pages, use "-8," or for page 15 to the last page, use "15-" with no need to specify the last page's number. Discontiguous ranges are allowed, too, separated by commas like this: "1-6, 13, 15-18, 20-."

Choosing to print **Spreads** rather than **Pages** is a nice way to make proofs of *reader spreads*. I may print a few spreads to get feedback on a document's design. When there are facing pages, *printer spreads* may be quite different; see "Print Booklet" (page 362). Also, if the first spread of the chosen page range is a single page (like a title page), the **Preview** in the lower left of the **Print** dialog may not show two pages. Temporarily exclude that first page to see if the spreads need to be printed smaller or turned 90° to fit the chosen paper (chosen in **Setup**).

Print

Choose how many **Copies** you desire. **Collating** them slows the process considerably. **Reverse Order** prints the last page first, useful if your printer spits out prints right-side up.

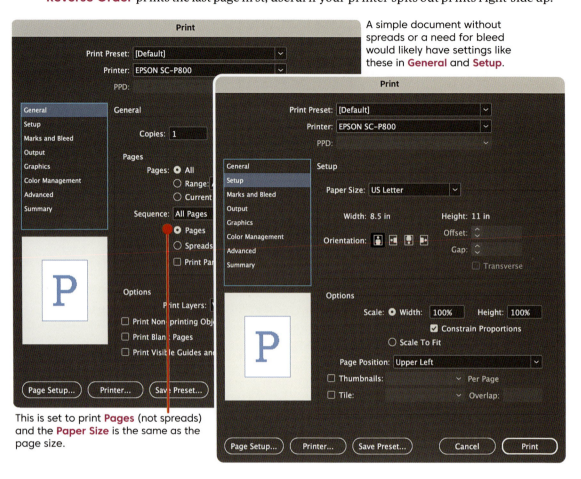

A simple document without spreads or a need for bleed would likely have settings like these in **General** and **Setup**.

This is set to print **Pages** (not spreads) and the **Paper Size** is the same as the page size.

Setup

Based on your printer choice, the choices for **Paper Size** will vary. If you need to squeeze a too-large page onto the paper in your printer, you can check **Scale To Fit**. Alternatively, you can **Tile** large pages onto multiple sheets of smaller paper (adhesive not included).

If you need to supply bleed, then you need to print on paper larger than your pages. When printing spreads, much more than that. Or shrink your pages or spreads to fit multiple on a single piece of paper.

Workspaces & Preferences

Swatches & Color Settings

Type & Text Styles

Frames, Shapes & Object Styles

Pages & Spreads

Find/ Change

Long or Complex Docs

Package & Publish

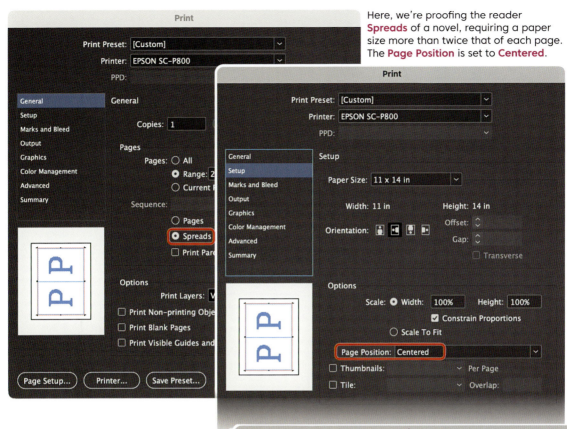

Here, we're proofing the reader **Spreads** of a novel, requiring a paper size more than twice that of each page. The **Page Position** is set to **Centered**.

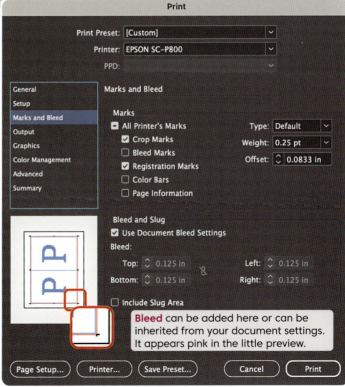

Marks and Bleed

If you're printing on paper larger than your pages (or spreads), you have room for **Crop Marks** and other informational ornamentation. You can set **Bleed** to match your document's, or choose some other value. If you've put notes in a **Slug** area, you can include that, too.

Output

Depending on whether the printer considers itself a CMYK or RGB device, your choices here will change. Inkjet printers and some laser printers want RGB data, which they separate into values for each of their inks or toners. To them, we send

Bleed can be added here or can be inherited from your document settings. It appears pink in the little preview.

Color data as **Composite RGB**. To devices that truly use cyan, magenta, yellow, and black ink or toner, we can send **Composite CMYK**. Often, for those devices, it's usually better to create a PDF and print that. A few of you (who work in print shops) may want to see **Separations**, and can then view the **Trapping**, **Flip**, and **Screening** controls.

Graphics

If you're printing drafts or other non-final versions, choosing **Optimized Subsampling** in the **Send Data** menu will yield decent-looking prints quickly. **Proxy** will be even faster, but graphics will have few legible features. To print no graphics at all, but boxes marked with an X, use **None**. This is useful for proofreading without the distraction of imagery. For your final work, choose **All**.

    The **Fonts** section is for Postscript printers only (not inkjets, for example), and the choices here can be tricky. Fonts can be stored at the printer (or drives attached to it). These are supposed to be listed in the PPD file. If you want to have a fast print, but have time to risk a choice that may fail, set **Download** to **Subset** and leave **Download PPD Fonts** unchecked. The first will send only those characters of a font that are used in the document. The second will not bother to send any font data for fonts listed in the PPD, as they're resident in the printer. If you get weird substitutions or characters go missing, you can choose to **Download PPD Fonts** and/or **Download Complete**. Either or both will slow the works, but will increase reliability.

Workspaces & Preferences

Swatches & Color Settings

Type & Text Styles

Frames, Shapes & Object Styles

Pages & Spreads

Find/ Change

Long or Complex Docs

Package & Publish

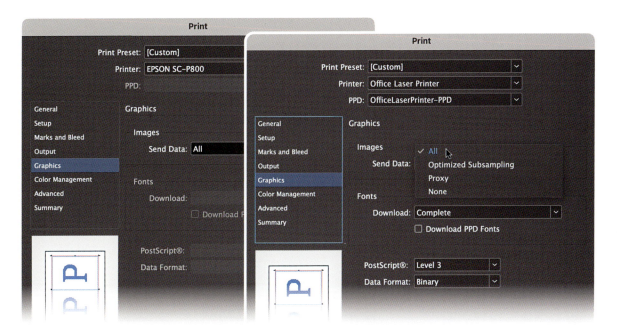

Color Management

In the **Output** section of the **Print** dialog, you usually choose one of the **Composite** settings (Gray, RGB, or CMYK). In the **Color Management** section, you pick specifically which gray, RGB, or CMYK profile should be used. This is what that whole color chapter is about! You thought you could skip it, but maybe not.

Most laser and inkjet printers should probably be sent **Composite RGB**. In the case of an office laser printer, I'd choose **sRGB** as the **Printer Profile** and let the driver take it from there. If I chose **Composite CMYK**, most printers around the office would expect **U.S. Web Coated (SWOP)**, so I'd choose that, checking the box **Preserve CMYK Numbers** for reasons explained elsewhere in this book—""CMYK-to-CMYK Conversion Can Be Dangerous" (page 192). For many inkjet printers, like the one a few feet from me, I'd choose a profile specific to it and the paper on which I'm printing.

Advanced

The key setting here is the **Transparency Flattener Preset**. For the best results (thus, when printing your finals) choose **[High Resolution]**. If your printer mistreats overlapping transparent objects or makes transparent effects (like shadows) look terrible, you can have InDesign rasterize the document by checking **Print as Bitmap** and choosing or typing whatever resolution you need. This essentially makes each page a big image that might be easier for the printer software to digest.

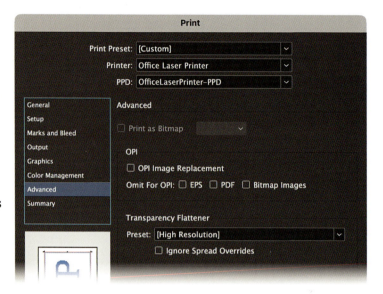

Print Booklet

Reader spreads are not printer spreads. Let's say you have a multi-page document with facing pages. In InDesign, when you look at pages 6 and 7, that's what the reader will see, too, once the document is printed and *assembled*. As an experiment, *carefully* remove the staples from the center of a thin weekly magazine. Go to some random page and examine what other pages are printed on the same piece of paper. You don't even have to remove the staples if it makes you feel bad. The process of getting pages on the correct sheets of paper is called *imposition*. If you need no more than one page per side of paper, **Print Booklet** can help you make printing your documents easier.

A four-page result from **Print Booklet**. Consider 8.5" x 11" pages on 11" x 17" paper folded in half.

Since this needs only one sheet of paper, this can use either **Saddle Stitch** or (a little silly) **Perfect Bound** with a four-page signature.

When you choose **File > Print Booklet…**, your primary choices for **Booklet Type** are **Saddle Stitch** (where every printed sheet will be folded in half and stacked, with staples "stitching" them together like the magazine described above) or **Perfect Bound** (in which groups of pages are bound together in *signatures* and the signatures are then bound together). I avoid the choices with **Consecutive** in the name because they do not perform as they should. With **Perfect Bound**, you must also specify the number of pages in each signature (in multiples of four, of course).

These eight pages could be printed **Perfect Bound** with one eight-page signature or, more simply, **Saddle Stitch**.

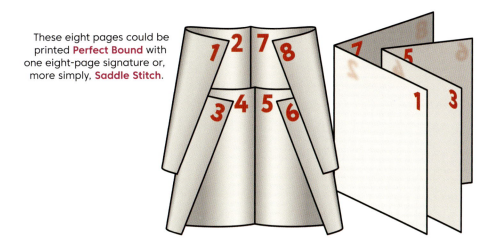

Keyboard Shortcuts

A great many InDesign commands and functions can be triggered via the keyboard. For example, simply tapping a letter can activate a tool. But most shortcuts involve one or more modifier keys, like those illustrated here. Note that these modifier keys are on *both sides of your keyboard*, allowing most shortcuts to be single-handed.

On the following pages are many of InDesign's default shortcuts. However, Adobe applications allow us to change or invent shortcuts for the commands we use most. Use **Edit > Keyboard Shortcuts...**, create a new **Set** based on the defaults, then make alterations.

I'm using this convention, as I have throughout the book:
Mac version/Windows version

Preferences		
Preferences > General...	⌘-K	Ctrl-K

File Menu		
Browse in Bridge...	option-⌘-O	Alt-Ctrl-O
Close	⌘-W	Ctrl-W
Document Setup...	option-⌘-P	Alt-Ctrl-P
Export...	⌘-E	Ctrl-E
File Info...	option-shift-⌘-I	Alt-Shift-Ctrl-I
New > Document...	⌘-N	Ctrl-N
Open...	⌘-O	Ctrl-O
Package...	option-shift-⌘-P	Alt-Shift-Ctrl-P
Place...	⌘-D	Ctrl-D
Print...	⌘-P	Ctrl-P
Save	⌘-S	Ctrl-S
Save As...	shift-⌘-S	Shift-Ctrl-S
Save a Copy...	option-⌘-S	Alt-Ctrl-S

Edit Menu		
Copy	⌘-C	Ctrl-C
Cut	⌘-X	Ctrl-X
Deselect All	shift-⌘-A	Shift-Ctrl-A
Duplicate	option-shift-⌘-D	Alt-Shift-Ctrl-D
Edit in Story Editor	⌘-Y	Ctrl-Y
Find Next	option-⌘-F	Alt-Ctrl-F
Find/Change...	⌘-F	Ctrl-F
Paste	⌘-V	Ctrl-V
Paste Into	option-⌘-V	Alt-Ctrl-V
Paste in Place	option-shift-⌘-V	Alt-Shift-Ctrl-V
Paste without Formatting	shift-⌘-V	Shift-Ctrl-V
Quick Apply...	⌘-return	Ctrl-Return
Redo	shift-⌘-Z	Shift-Ctrl-Z
Select All	⌘-A	Ctrl-A
Spelling > Check Spelling...	⌘-I	Ctrl-I
Step and Repeat...	option-⌘-U	Alt-Ctrl-U
Toggle search direction	option-⌘-return	Alt-Ctrl-Return
Undo	⌘-Z	Ctrl-Z

Workspaces &
Preferences

Swatches &
Color Settings

Type &
Text Styles

Frames, Shapes
& Object Styles

Pages &
Spreads

Find/
Change

Long or
Complex Docs

Package
& Publish

Layout Menu

First Page	shift-⌘-page up	Shift-Ctrl-Page Up
Go Back	⌘-page up	Ctrl-Page Up
Go Forward	⌘-page down	Ctrl-Page Down
Go to Page...	⌘-J	Ctrl-J
Last Page	shift-⌘-page down	Shift-Ctrl-Page Down
Next Page	shift-Page Down	
Next Spread	option-page down	Alt-Page Down
Pages > Add Page	shift-⌘-P	Shift-Ctrl-P
Previous Page	shift-Page Up	
Previous Spread	option-page up	Alt-Page Up

Type Menu

Create Outlines	shift-⌘-O	Shift-Ctrl-O
Create outlines without deleting text	option-shift-⌘-O	Alt-Shift-Ctrl-O
Go to Endnote Text	shift-⌘-E	Shift-Ctrl-E
Hide Hidden Characters	option-⌘-I	Alt-Ctrl-I
Insert Column Break	Enter	
Insert Forced Line Break	shift-Return	
Insert Frame Break	shift-Enter	
Insert Page Break	⌘-Enter	Ctrl-Enter
Discretionary Hyphen	shift-⌘--	Shift-Ctrl--
Nonbreaking Hyphen	option-⌘--	Alt-Ctrl--
Current Page Number Marker	option-shift-⌘-N	Alt-Shift-Ctrl-N
Indent to Here	⌘-\	Ctrl-\
Right Indent Tab	shift-Tab	
Straight Double Quote Marks	control+shift-'	Alt-Shift-'
Straight Single Quote (Apostrophe)	control+'	Alt-'
Insert Em Space	shift-⌘-M	Shift-Ctrl-M
Insert En Space	shift-⌘-N	Shift-Ctrl-N
Insert Nonbreaking Space	option-⌘-X	Alt-Ctrl-X
Insert Thin Space	option-shift-⌘-M	Alt-Shift-Ctrl-M
Tabs	shift-⌘-T	Shift-Ctrl-T
Track Changes > Next Change	⌘-page down	Ctrl-Page Down
Track Changes > Previous Change	⌘-page up	Ctrl-Page Up

Object Menu

Arrange > Bring Forward	⌘-]	Ctrl-]
Arrange > Bring to Front	shift-⌘-]	Shift-Ctrl-]
Arrange > Send Backward	⌘-[	Ctrl-[
Arrange > Send to Back	shift-⌘-[	Shift-Ctrl-[
Effects > Drop Shadow...	option-⌘-M	Alt-Ctrl-M
Fitting > Center Content	shift-⌘-E	Shift-Ctrl-E
Fitting > Fill Frame Proportionally	option-shift-⌘-C	Alt-Shift-Ctrl-C
Fitting > Fit Content Proportionally	option-shift-⌘-E	Alt-Shift-Ctrl-E
Fitting > Fit Content to Frame	option-⌘-E	Alt-Ctrl-E
Fitting > Fit Frame to Content	option-⌘-C	Alt-Ctrl-C
Group	⌘-G	Ctrl-G
Hide	⌘-3	Ctrl-3
Lock	⌘-L	Ctrl-L
Make Compound Path	⌘-8	Ctrl-8
Release Compound Path	option-shift-⌘-8	Alt-Shift-Ctrl-8
Select Container	Escape	
Select Content	shift-Escape	
Select First Object Above	option-shift-⌘-]	Alt-Shift-Ctrl-]
Select Last Object Below	option-shift-⌘-[	Alt-Shift-Ctrl-[
Select Next Object Above	option-⌘-]	Alt-Ctrl-]
Select Next Object Below	option-⌘-[	Alt-Ctrl-[
Show All on Spread	option-⌘-3	Alt-Ctrl-3
Text Frame Options...	⌘-B	Ctrl-B
Transform Sequence Again	option-⌘-4	Alt-Ctrl-4
Transform > Move...	shift-⌘-M	Shift-Ctrl-M
Ungroup	shift-⌘-G	Shift-Ctrl-G
Unlock All on Spread	option-⌘-L	Alt-Ctrl-L

Table Menu

Cell Options	option-⌘-B	Alt-Ctrl-B
Delete Column	shift-delete	Shift-Backspace
Delete Row	⌘-delete	Ctrl-Backspace
Insert Table...	option-shift-⌘-T	Alt-Shift-Ctrl-T
Insert Column...	option-⌘-9	Alt-Ctrl-9
Insert Row...	⌘-9	Ctrl-9

Workspaces & Preferences

Swatches & Color Settings

Type & Text Styles

Frames, Shapes & Object Styles

Pages & Spreads

Find/ Change

Long or Complex Docs

Package & Publish

Select Cell	⌘-/	Ctrl-/
Select Column	option-⌘-3	Alt-Ctrl-3
Select Row	⌘-3	Ctrl-3
Select Table	option-⌘-A	Alt-Ctrl-A
Table Setup...	option-shift-⌘-B	Alt-Shift-Ctrl-B

View Menu

Actual Size	⌘-1	Ctrl-1
Clear Object-Level Display Settings	shift-⌘-F2	Shift-Ctrl-F2
Fast Display Performance	option-shift-⌘-Z	Alt-Shift-Ctrl-Z
High Quality Display Performance	control+option-⌘-H	Alt-Ctrl-H
Typical Display Performance	option-⌘-Z	Alt-Ctrl-Z
Entire Pasteboard	option-shift-⌘-0	Alt-Shift-Ctrl-0
Hide Frame Edges	control+⌘-H	Ctrl-H
Hide Text Threads	option-⌘-Y	Alt-Ctrl-Y
Fit Page in Window	⌘-0	Ctrl-0
Fit Spread in Window	option-⌘-0	Alt-Ctrl-0
Show/Hide Guides	⌘-;	Ctrl-;
Lock/Unlock Guides	option-⌘-;	Alt-Ctrl-;
Show Baseline Grid	option-⌘-'	Alt-Ctrl-'
Show Document Grid	⌘-'	Ctrl-'
Show/Hide Smart Guides	⌘-U	Ctrl-U
Toggle Snap to Document Grid	shift-⌘-'	Shift-Ctrl-'
Toggle Snap to Guides	shift-⌘-;	Shift-Ctrl-;
Show/Hide Rulers	⌘-R	Ctrl-R
Toggle Overprint Preview	option-shift-⌘-Y	Alt-Shift-Ctrl-Y
Zoom In	⌘-=	Ctrl-=
Zoom Out	⌘--	Ctrl--

Window Menu

Color Panel	F6	
Swatches Panel	F5	
Control Panel	option-⌘-6	Alt-Ctrl-6
Effects Panel	shift-⌘-F10	Shift-Ctrl-F10
Info Panel	F8	
Layers Panel	F7	
Links Panel	shift-⌘-D	Shift-Ctrl-D

Align Panel	shift-F7	
Preflight Panel	option-shift-⌘-F	Alt-Shift-Ctrl-F
Separations Preview Panel	shift-F6	
Character Styles Panel	shift-⌘-F11	Shift-Ctrl-F11
Object Styles Panel	⌘-F7	Ctrl-F7
Paragraph Styles Panel	⌘-F11	Ctrl-F11
Text Wrap Panel	option-⌘-W	Alt-Ctrl-W
Character Panel	⌘-T	Ctrl-T
Glyphs Panel	option-shift-F11	Alt-Shift-F11
Index Panel	shift-F8	
Paragraph Panel	option-⌘-T	Alt-Ctrl-T
Table Panel	shift-F9	
Scripts Panel	option-⌘-F11	Alt-Ctrl-F11

Object Editing

Decrease scale by 1%	⌘-,	Ctrl-,
Decrease scale by 5%	option-⌘-,	Alt-Ctrl-,
End Path Drawing	Enter or Return	
Increase scale by 1%	⌘-.	Ctrl-.
Increase scale by 5%	option-⌘-.	Alt-Ctrl-.
Nudge down	↓	
Nudge down 1/10	shift-⌘-↓	Shift-Ctrl-↓
Nudge down 1/10 duplicate	option-shift-⌘-Down	Alt-Shift-Ctrl-↓
Nudge down duplicate	option-↓	Alt-↓
Nudge down x10	shift-↓	
Nudge down x10 duplicate	option-shift-↓	Alt-Shift-↓
Nudge left	←	
Nudge left 1/10	shift-⌘-←	Shift-Ctrl-←
Nudge left 1/10 duplicate	option-shift-⌘-Left	Alt-Shift-Ctrl-←
Nudge left duplicate	option-←	Alt-←
Nudge left x10	shift-←	
Nudge left x10 duplicate	option-shift-←	Alt-Shift-←
Nudge right	→	
Nudge right 1/10	shift-⌘-→	Shift-Ctrl-→
Nudge right 1/10 duplicate	option-shift-⌘-Right	Alt-Shift-Ctrl-→
Nudge right duplicate	option-→	Alt-→

Workspaces & Preferences

Swatches & Color Settings

Type & Text Styles

Frames, Shapes & Object Styles

Pages & Spreads

Find/ Change

Long or Complex Docs

Package & Publish

Nudge right x10	**shift-→**	
Nudge right x10 duplicate	**option-shift-→**	**Alt-Shift-→**
Nudge up	**↑**	
Nudge up 1/10	**shift-⌘-↑**	**Shift-Ctrl-↑**
Nudge up 1/10 duplicate	**option-shift-⌘-Up**	**Alt-Shift-Ctrl-↑**
Nudge up duplicate	**option-↑**	**Alt-↑**
Nudge up x10	**shift-↑**	
Nudge up x10 duplicate	**option-shift-↑**	**Alt-Shift-↑**
Pin Bottom Edge	**option-⌘-↓**	**Alt-Ctrl-↓**
Pin Left Edge	**option-⌘-←**	**Alt-Ctrl-←**
Pin Right Edge	**option-⌘-→**	**Alt-Ctrl-→**
Pin Top Edge	**option-⌘-↑**	**Alt-Ctrl-↑**
Resize Horizontally	**option-shift-H**	**Alt-Shift-H**
Resize Vertically	**option-shift-V**	**Alt-Shift-V**
Select all Guides	**option-⌘-G**	**Alt-Ctrl-G**

Panel Menus

Redefine Character Style	**option-shift-⌘-C**	**Alt-Shift-Ctrl-C**
Character > All Caps	**shift-⌘-K**	**Shift-Ctrl-K**
Character > Small Caps	**shift-⌘-H**	**Shift-Ctrl-H**
Character > Strikethrough	**shift-⌘-/**	**Shift-Ctrl-/**
Character > Subscript	**option-shift-⌘-=**	**Alt-Shift-Ctrl-=**
Character > Superscript	**shift-⌘-=**	**Shift-Ctrl-=**
Character > Underline	**shift-⌘-U**	**Shift-Ctrl-U**
Override All Master Page Items	**option-shift-⌘-L**	**Alt-Shift-Ctrl-L**
Redefine Paragraph Style	**option-shift-⌘-R**	**Alt-Shift-Ctrl-R**
Paragraph > Justification...	**option-shift-⌘-J**	**Alt-Shift-Ctrl-J**
Paragraph > Keep Options...	**option-⌘-K**	**Alt-Ctrl-K**
Paragraph > Paragraph Rules...	**option-⌘-J**	**Alt-Ctrl-J**
Tags > Autotag	**option-shift-⌘-F**	**Alt-Shift-Ctrl-F7**

Text and Tables

Align center	**shift-⌘-C**	**Shift-Ctrl-C**
Align force justify	**shift-⌘-F**	**Shift-Ctrl-F**
Align justify	**shift-⌘-J**	**Shift-Ctrl-J**
Align left	**shift-⌘-L**	**Shift-Ctrl-L**
Align right	**shift-⌘-R**	**Shift-Ctrl-R**

Align to baseline grid	option-shift-⌘-G	Alt-Shift-Ctrl-G
Apply bold	shift-⌘-B	Shift-Ctrl-B
Apply italic	shift-⌘-I	Shift-Ctrl-I
Apply normal	shift-⌘-Y	Shift-Ctrl-Y
Auto leading	option-shift-⌘-A	Alt-Shift-Ctrl-A
Auto-hyphenate on/off	option-shift-⌘-H	Alt-Shift-Ctrl-H
Decrease baseline shift	option-shift-↓	Alt-Shift-↓
Decrease baseline shift x5	option-shift-⌘-Down	Alt-Shift-Ctrl-↓
Decrease kerning/tracking	option-←	Alt-←
Decrease kerning/tracking x5	option-⌘-←	Alt-Ctrl-←
Decrease leading	option-↑	Alt-↑
Decrease leading x5	option-⌘-↑	Alt-Ctrl-↑
Decrease point size	shift-⌘-,	Shift-Ctrl-,
Decrease point size x5	option-shift-⌘-,	Alt-Shift-Ctrl-,
Decrease word space	option-⌘-delete	Alt-Ctrl-Backspace
Decrease word space x5	option-shift-⌘-delete	Alt-Shift-Ctrl-Backspace
Delete one word to the left	⌘-delete	Ctrl-Backspace
Delete one word to the right	⌘-del	Ctrl-Del
Find Next	shift-F2	
Increase baseline shift	option-shift-↑	Alt-Shift-↑
Increase baseline shift x5	option-shift-⌘-↑	Alt-Shift-Ctrl-↑
Increase kerning/tracking	option-shift-→	Alt-Shift-→
Increase kerning/tracking x5	option-⌘-→	Alt-Ctrl-→
Increase leading	option-↓	Alt-↓
Increase leading x5	option-⌘-↓	Alt-Ctrl-↓
Increase point size	shift-⌘-.	Shift-Ctrl-.
Increase point size x5	option-shift-⌘-.	Alt-Shift-Ctrl-.
Increase word space	option-⌘-\	Alt-Ctrl-\
Increase word space x5	option-shift-⌘-\	Alt-Shift-Ctrl-\
Load Find and Find Next instance	shift-F1	
Load Find with selected text	⌘-F1	Ctrl-F1
Load Replace with selected text	⌘-F2	Ctrl-F2
Move Down in Table	↓	
Move Left in Table	←	
Move Right in Table	→	

Move Up in Table	↑	
Move down one line	↓	
Move to First Cell in Table Column	**option-page up**	**Alt-Page Up**
Move to First Cell in Table Row	**option-home**	**Alt-Home**
Move to First Row in Table Frame	**Page Up**	
Move to Last Cell in Table Column	**option-page down**	**Alt-Page Down**
Move to Last Cell in Table Row	**option-end**	**Alt-End**
Move to Last Row in Table Frame	**Page Down**	
Move to Next Cell	**Tab**	
Move to Previous Cell	**shift-Tab**	
Move to beginning of story	**⌘-home**	**Ctrl-Home**
Move to end of story	**⌘-end**	**Ctrl-End**
Move to the end of the line	**End**	
Move to the left one character	←	
Move to the left one word	**⌘-←**	**Ctrl-←**
Move to the next paragraph	**⌘-↓**	**Ctrl-↓**
Move to the previous paragraph	**⌘-↑**	**Ctrl-↑**
Move to the right one character	→	
Move to the right one word	**⌘-→**	**Ctrl-→**
Move to the start of the line	**Home**	
Move up one line	↑	
Normal horizontal text scale	**shift-⌘-X**	**Shift-Ctrl-X**
Normal vertical text scale	**option-shift-⌘-X**	**Alt-Shift-Ctrl-X**
Table Object Down	↓	
Escape Table Object Context	**Escape**	
Table Object Left	←	
Object Move to Next Cell	**Tab**	
Object Move to Previous Cell	**shift-Tab**	
Table Object Right	→	
Table Object Up	↑	
Recompose all stories	**option-⌘-/**	**Alt-Ctrl-/**
Replace with Change To text	**⌘-F3**	**Ctrl-F3**
Replace with Change To text, Find Next	**shift-F3**	
Reset kerning and tracking	**option-⌘-Q**	**Alt-Ctrl-Q**
Select Table Cells Above	**shift-↑**	

Workspaces & Preferences

Swatches & Color Settings

Type & Text Styles

Frames, Shapes & Object Styles

Pages & Spreads

Find/ Change

Long or Complex Docs

Package & Publish

Select Table Cells Below		shift-↓
Select Table Cells to the Left		shift-←
Select Table Cells to the Right		shift-→
Select line	shift-⌘-\	Shift-Ctrl-\
Select one character to the left		shift-←
Select one character to the right		shift-→
Select one line above		shift-↑
Select one line below		shift-↓
Select one paragraph before	shift-⌘-↑	Shift-Ctrl-↑
Select one paragraph forward	shift-⌘-↓	Shift-Ctrl-↓
Select one word to the left	shift-⌘-←	Shift-Ctrl-←
Select one word to the right	shift-⌘-→	Shift-Ctrl-→
Select to beginning of story	shift-⌘-Home	Shift-Ctrl-Home
Select to end of story	shift-⌘-End	Shift-Ctrl-End
Select to the end of the line		shift-End
Select to the start of the line		shift-Home
Start Row on Next Column		Enter
Start Row on Next Frame		shift-Enter
Toggle Cell/Text Selection		Escape
Toggle Typographer's Quotes Pref	option-shift-⌘-'	Alt-Shift-Ctrl-'
Update missing font list	option-shift-⌘-/	Alt-Shift-Ctrl-/

Views, Navigation

100% size	⌘-1	Ctrl-1
200% size	⌘-2	Ctrl-2
400% size	⌘-4	Ctrl-4
50% size	⌘-5	Ctrl-5
Access zoom percentage box	option-⌘-5	Alt-Ctrl-5
Activate last-used field in panel	option-⌘-`	Alt-Ctrl-`
Close all	option-shift-⌘-W	Alt-Shift-Ctrl-W
Close document	shift-⌘-W	Shift-Ctrl-W
First Spread	Home or option-shift-page up	Alt-Shift-Page Up
Fit Selection in Window	option-⌘-=	Alt-Ctrl-=
Force redraw	shift-F5	
Go to first frame in thread	option-shift-⌘-Page Up	Alt-Shift-Ctrl-Page Up
Go to last frame in thread	option-shift-⌘-Page Down	Alt-Shift-Ctrl-Page Down

Go to next frame in thread	**option-⌘-page down**	**Alt-Ctrl-Page Down**
Go to previous frame in thread	**option-⌘-page up**	**Alt-Ctrl-Page Up**
Last Spread	**End or option-shift-page down**	**Alt-Shift-Page Down**
New default document	**option-⌘-N**	**Alt-Ctrl-N**
Open/Close all panels in side tabs	**option-⌘-Tab**	**Alt-Ctrl-Tab**
Save all	**option-shift-⌘-S**	**Alt-Shift-Ctrl-S**
Scroll down one screen	**Page Down**	
Scroll up one screen	**Page Up**	
Show/Hide all panels	**Tab**	
Show/Hide all panels except tools	**shift-Tab**	
Toggle Measurement System	**option-shift-⌘-U**	**Alt-Shift-Ctrl-U**
Toggle Character and Paragraph Modes in Control Panel	**option-⌘-7**	**Alt-Ctrl-7**

Tools

Add Anchor Point Tool	**=**		Page Tool	**shift-P**
Apply Color	**,**		Pen Tool	**P**
Apply Gradient	**.**		Pencil Tool	**N**
Apply None	**/**		Rectangle Frame Tool	**F**
Default fill and stroke colors	**D**		Rectangle Tool	**M**
Color Theme Tool	**shift-I**		Rotate Tool	**R**
Convert Direction Point Tool	**shift-C**		Scale Tool	**S**
Delete Anchor Point Tool	**-**		Scissors Tool	**C**
Direct Selection Tool	**A**		Selection Tool	**V**
Ellipse Tool	**L**		Shear Tool	**O**
Eyedropper Tool	**I**		Swap fill and stroke active	**X**
Free Transform Tool	**E**		Swap fill and stroke colors	**shift-X**
Gap Tool	**U**		Toggle Text and Object Control	**J**
Gradient Feather Tool	**shift-G**		Toggle preview	**W**
Gradient Swatch Tool	**G**		Type Tool	**T**
Hand Tool	**H**		Type on a Path Tool	**shift-T**
Line Tool	****		Zoom Tool	**Z**
Measure Tool	**K**			

Workspaces & Preferences

Swatches & Color Settings

Type & Text Styles

Frames, Shapes & Object Styles

Pages & Spreads

Find/ Change

Long or Complex Docs

Package & Publish

INDEX

+ (next to style name), 36

A

Absolute Numbering, 293

Adjust Scaling Percentage, 252

Adobe Fonts, 4
    auto-activate, 176

Adobe RGB, 191

Advanced Type preferences, 167

align objects, 240–241
    Align panel, 240–241
    key object, 241

align text, 199
    paragraph styles, and, 204

anchored objects, 97–102, 272–275
    custom, 272–274
    marker, 98, 272
    object styles for, 97–99
    text wrap, and, 100–101, 274–275

Animated Zoom, 12

Appearance of Black preferences, 174

Application Bar, 161

Apply to Content, 164

Articles panel, 351

Autocorrect preferences, 172

B

Baseline Grid
    paragraph styles, and, 205
    preferences, 170
    text frame options, 254–255

baseline shift, 169

black, appearance, 174

bleed, 283

Book document, 147–150, 334–337
    adding documents, 147, 334
    chapter numbering, 321–322
    closing, 150, 336
    creating, 335–336
    opening a document, 148, 335
    page numbers, 148, 335
    panel notifications, 334

reorder documents, 148
    saving, 150, 336
    sync documents, 336–337

booklet, print, 362–363

brochure project, 152–158

bullets, 114, 215–216

C

Calibre, 356

captions
    grouping with images, 236
    text variables and, 322–323

character styles, 37–47, 221–223
    applying, 42–47, 223
    clear overrides, 221–222
    copy and paste, 48
    creating, 40, 222–223
    editing, 223
    load, 49–50, 230
    output tagging, 223
    overrides, 221–222

choke (Effects), 268

clear overrides, 36, 221–222, 278–279

Clipboard Handling preferences, 176

CMYK, 180, 187–188
    conversion, 192

color
    CMYK, 180, 187–188
    conversion, 190–193
    find/change, 311
    HSB, 180
    Lab, 180, 188–190
    models, 186–188
    output, 344
    panel, 178
    process, 180
    profiles, 188–193
    ramp, 178
    RGB, 180, 186–187
    settings, 184–185, 193
    space, 188–193
    spot, 180
    swatch, *see* swatches

Color Mode, 180

Color Theme (interface), 11, 164